New Qing Imperial History

New Qing Imperial History uses the Manchu summer capital of Chengde and associated architecture, art, and ritual activity as the focus for an exploration of the importance of Inner Asia and Tibet to the Qing empire (1636–1911). The contributors argue that the Qing was not simply another Chinese dynasty, but was deeply engaged in Inner Asia not only militarily, but culturally, politically, and ideologically.

Emphasizing the diverse range of peoples in the Qing empire, this book analyzes the importance to Chinese history of Manchu relations with Tibetan prelates, Mongolian chieftains, and the Turkic elites of Xinjiang In offering a new appreciation of a culturally and politically complex period, the authors discuss the nature and representation of emperorship, especially under Qianlong (r. 1736–1795), and examine the role of ritual in relations with Inner Asia, including the vaunted (but overrated) tribute system.

By using a specific artifact or text as a starting point for analysis in each chapter, the contributors not only include material previously unavailable in English but allow the reader an intimate knowledge of life at Chengde and its significance to the Qing period as a whole.

James A. Millward is Associate Professor of History at Georgetown University, USA.

Ruth W. Dunnell is James Storer Associate Professor of History at Kenyon College, Ohio, USA.

Mark C. Elliott is Professor of Chinese and Inner Asian History, Harvard University, USA.

Philippe Forêt is a Research Fellow of the Swiss National Science Foundation and an Associate Researcher at both the Institute of Cartography of the Swiss Federal Institute of Technology at Zurich and the Space and Culture Laboratory of Paris IV Sorbonne University, France.

New Qing Imperial History

The making of Inner Asian empire at Qing Chengde

**Edited by
James A. Millward,
Ruth W. Dunnell,
Mark C. Elliott, and
Philippe Forêt**

RoutledgeCurzon
Taylor & Francis Group

LONDON AND NEW YORK

First published 2004
by RoutledgeCurzon
2 Park Square, Milton Park, Abingdon, Oxon, OX14 4RN

Simultaneously published in the USA and Canada
by RoutledgeCurzon
270 Madison Ave, New York NY 10016

RoutledgeCurzon is an imprint of the Taylor & Francis Group

Transferred to Digital Printing 2006

Typeset in Baskerville by
Florence Production Ltd, Stoodleigh, Devon

British Library Cataloguing in Publication Data
A catalogue record for this book is available from the British
Library

Library of Congress Cataloging in Publication Data
New Qing imperial history: the making of Inner Asian empire
at Qing Chengde/edited by James Millward . . . [et al.].
    p. cm.
    Includes bibliographical references and index.
    1. China – History – Qianlong, 1736–1795.   2. Qianlong, Emperor of
China, 1711–1799.   3. China – Ethnic relations – History – 18th century.
4. Chengde Diqu (China) – History – 18th century.   5. China – Capital
and capitol – History – 18th century.   6. China – History – Qianlong,
1736–1795 – Sources.   7. China – Ethnic relations – History – 18th
century – Sources.   8. Chengde Diqu (China) – History – 18th century
– Sources.   9. China – Capital and capitol – History – 18th century –
Sources.   I. Title: making of Inner Asian empire at Qing Chengde.
II. Millward, James A., 1961–
DS754.82.N49 2004
951'.032–dc22   2003021150

ISBN 0–415–32006–2

Printed and bound by Antony Rowe Ltd, Eastbourne

Contents

Illustrations

Figures

Tables

Contributors

Joseph A. Adler is Professor of East Asian Religions at Kenyon College. He is author of *Chinese Religious Traditions* (2002), co-author of *Sung Dynasty Uses of the I Ching* (1990), and translator of Chu Hsi's "Introduction to the Study of the Classic of Change" (1995).

Elisabeth Benard's most recent publication is the co-edited *Goddesses who Rule* (2000). She is a Professor on the Asian Studies Faculty at University of Puget Sound and Director of the Pacific Rim/Asia Study Travel Program.

Anne Chayet is Research Director at the "Languages and cultures of the Tibetan area" research unit of the CNRS (National Center for Scientific Research) in Paris. She has written or co-edited *Les temples de Jehol et leurs modèles Tibétains* (1985), *Le Yuanmingyuan, Jeux d'eau et palais européens du 18e siècle à la cour de Chine* (1987), *La femme au temps des dalais lamas* (1993), and *Art et archéologie du Tibet* (1994).

Ning Chia is Professor of History at Central College, Pella, Iowa and a current member of Board of Directors of ASIANetwork – a National Organization for Liberal Arts Institutions in Developing Asian Studies.

Ruth W. Dunnell is James P. Storer Associate Professor of Asian History at Kenyon College in Gambier, Ohio. She has published numerous articles and a book on the Tangut state, *The Great State of White and High: Buddhism and State Formation in Eleventh-century Xia* (1996).

Mark C. Elliott is Professor of Chinese and Inner Asian History at Harvard University. His extensive exploration of Manchu-language archives form the basis of his book, *The Manchu Way* (2001), a study of the Qing Eight Banner system.

Philippe Forêt is currently a Research Fellow of the Swiss National Science Foundation and an Associate Researcher at the Institute of Cartography of the Swiss Federal Institute of Technology in Zurich (ETHZ), where he is completing a project on the mapping history of Western China. His publications include *Mapping Chengde: the Qing*

Landscape Enterprise (2000), *La Haute-Asie telle qu'ils l'ont vue: explorateurs et scientifique de 1820 à 1940* (in collaboration, 2003), and *Une montagne plus haute que l'Himalaya: les résultats scientifiques inattendus d'un voyage au Tibet (1906–1908) et de la querelle du Transhimalaya* (2004).

Karen Gernant is editor and translator of *Imagining Women: Fujian Folktales* (1994). She is Emeritus Professor of History at Southern Oregon University.

James L. Hevia is Director, International Studies Program, the College of the University of Chicago. In addition to his interest in heritage in contemporary China, he has published extensively on Sino-British relations. He is author of *Cherishing Men from Afar* (1995) and most recently of *English Lessons: the Pedagogy of Imperialism in Nineteenth Century China* (2003).

Donald S. Lopez, Jr is the Carl W. Belser Professor of Buddhist and Tibetan Studies in the Department of Asian Languages and Cultures at the University of Michigan. In addition to his books *A Study of Svatantrika*; *Elaborations on Emptiness: Uses of the Heart Sutra*; *Prisoners of Shangri-La: Tibetan Buddhism and the West*; and *The Story of Buddhism*, he has edited many volumes on Buddhism. In 2000 he was elected to the American Academy of Arts and Sciences.

Scott Lowe is Professor and Chair of Philosophy and Religious Studies at the University of Wisconsin-Eau Claire, where he teaches on Asian religions. His publications include *Mo Tzu's Religious Blueprint for a Chinese Utopia: the Will and the Way* (1992) and recent scholarly articles on Chinese millennial movements, Falun Gong, and the *Mozi*.

James A. Millward is Associate Professor of Intersocietal History in the School of Foreign Service and Department of History at Georgetown University. He is author of *Beyond the Pass: Economy, Ethnicity and Empire in Qing Central Asia, 1759–1860* (1998) and *Xinjiang: a History of Chinese Turkistan* (forthcoming).

Nima Dorjee Ragnubs is co-author of *Treasures of Tibetan Art: Collections of the Jacques Marchais Museum of Tibetan Art* (1996). He is currently writing a history of his native state, Dagyab, in Kham, Tibet.

Evelyn S. Rawski is University Professor in the Department of History at University of Pittsburgh, and a former President of the Association for Asian Studies. Her books include *The Last Emperors: a Social History of Qing Imperial Institutions* (1998). She recently co-authored *Worshipping the Ancestors: Chinese Commemorative Portraits* (2001).

Deborah Sommer is Associate Professor in the Department of Religion at Gettysburg College. She is the editor of *Chinese Religion: an Anthology of Sources* (1995) and has most recently published "Ritual and Sacrifice in

Early Confucianism: Contacts with the Spirit World," in *Confucian Spirituality*, ed. Mary Evelyn Tucker and Tu Weiming (2003).

Van J. Symons, Professor of History at Augustana College, is the author of *Ch'ing Ginseng Management: Ch'ing Monopolies in Microcosm* (1981) and co-author with Sechin Jagchid of *Peace, War and Trade along the Great Wall* (1989).

Renqiu Yu is Associate Professor of History and Director of the Asian Studies Program at Purchase College, State University of New York. His book *To Save China, To Save Ourselves* (1992) was designated Outstanding Book in History by the Association for Asian American Studies in 1993.

Peter Zarrow, author of *Anarchism and Chinese Political Culture* (1990) and co-author of *Rethinking the 1898 Reform Period* (2002), is a fellow at the Institute of Modern History, Academica Sinica, Taiwan.

Note on transliteration

Wherever possible, we have used common English spellings of Inner Asian names and terms, and avoided use of terms and technical transliterations not readily pronounceable by the uninitiated. In places, however, we have deemed it helpful or necessary to employ transliterations from Manchu, Mongolian, Tibetan, Uyghur (Eastern or Central Asia Turkic), and Sanskrit in addition to those from Chinese. The following transcription systems are used, with the following abbreviations, wherever it is necessary to identify the source language:

Chinese (Ch.):   *Hanyu pinyin*
Manchu (Ma.):   Möllendorff
Mongolian (Mo.): Mostaert, as modified by Francis Cleaves, with these exceptions: č = ch; š = sh; γ = gh; q = kh and ǰ = j
Tibetan (T.):   Wylie (without hyphens)
Uyghur (U.):   There is no generally accepted system for transliterating Uyghur. For the few Uyghur names and terms in this volume, we have followed the system used in Henry G. Schwarz, *An Uyghur English Dictionary* (Bellingham, Wash.: Western Washington University, Center for East Asian Studies, 1992), with the following exceptions: ç = ch; x = kh; ş = sh; ñ = ng; g = gh

We have transliterated a few Sanskrit terms (S.) in italics with the standard diacritical marks used used in English. For the most part, however, Sanskrit terms have been Anglicized for convenience.

Where there are common English versions of names and terms, or where terms are frequently used in the text (as opposed to appearing once or twice in transcription) we have in some cases reproduced them in a manner deemed approachable to readers new to the material (for example, we use "lama," not *blama*). Primarily in the case of Tibetan, where technically correct transcriptions are unpronounceable to the uninitiated, we have in some cases substituted a version representing the Lhasa standard pronunciation of the term (thus, "Gelukpa" rather than Dge lugs pa).

Acknowledgments

This book has two points of origin that later serendipitously converged. In October 1990 Mark Elliott and James Millward accompanied Philippe Forêt on one of his field trips to Chengde and Mulan, where, thanks to their guide Zhao Hua and the Weichang Tourism Administration, they toured the palace complex and Mulan hunting ground, collected Manchu inscriptions from remotely situated steles, and dined memorably on game and "doufu brain." At the time, all three enjoyed dissertation funding from the Committee on Scholarly Communication with the People's Republic of China, and the Mulan trip informed each of their individual research projects.

Two years later, Ruth Dunnell and Evelyn Rawski began considering ways to help scholars grasp the Tibetan contribution to the social, political, and cultural history of late imperial China. From these efforts emerged a proposal for a workshop on the issue. Dunnell and Donald Lopez convened a planning meeting in December 1992 (funded by a project grant from the American Council of Learned Societies), where, with the assistance of Elliot Sperling, Robert Thorpe, Evelyn Rawski, James Hevia, and Griffith Foulk, they decided to focus the workshop on Chengde. In 1994, the National Endowment for the Humanities funded a Summer Institute entitled "Reading the Manchu Summer Palace at Chengde: Art, Ritual and Rulership in 18th Century China and Inner Asia." Elliott, Forêt, and Millward were fortunate to have been accepted as participants in this institute, held at the University of Michigan. Twenty-three participants, including the authors and editors of this book, together with institute leaders Hevia, Rawski, and Lopez and several outside lecturers, engaged in a month of discussion and research. The articles and translations in this book began as projects for this summer institute, though they have evolved considerably since then.

Besides the NEH, many other persons and organizations made possible the 1994 Summer Institute. Administrative assistant Marie Logan and her assistant, Karen Munson, of the University of Michigan Department of Asian Languages and Cultures steered the organization and implementation of the Summer Institute. Jennifer Eichman provided diverse preparatory services to the directors. The University generously made available a wide range of resources for the use of the summer institute participants, including access to library and computer facilities. The staff of the Harlan Hatcher Graduate Library at the University of Michigan was unfailingly gracious and helpful.

Following the institute, Ruth Dunnell together with Mark Elliott, Philippe Forêt, Karen Gernant, Jeanne Larsen, Donald Lopez, James Millward, and Evelyn Rawski undertook mutual editing of the curriculum guide materials and discussed plans for the production of a published volume. Deborah Sommer produced and distributed an excellent set of slides of Chengde and related topics which has been of great use to all of us in our teaching, lecturing, and research on Chengde and the Qing.

James Millward took over direction of the project from Ruth Dunnell in 1997, and with the help of a Small Grant from the China and Inner Asia Council of the Association for Asian Studies, a summer research grant (1998) and a junior sabbatical (1999–2000) from Georgetown University, Millward was able to revisit Chengde, write his chapter on the Torghuts, and conduct further editing of the manuscript. Irene Leung provided critical formatting and editing assistance, especially suggestions on images and ironing out problems that arose from the articles having been submitted in multiple software platforms.

Philippe Forêt managed image research, selection, preparation, and permissions for the final manuscript. The Sven Hedin Foundation in Stockholm has generously authorized us to reproduce photographs of the Chengde temples taken by Gösta Montell and previously published by Sven Hedin in *Jehol, Kejsarstaden* (Stockholm, Lars Hökerbergs bokförlag, 1931). Likewise, the Geography and Map Department of the Library of Congress has allowed us to reproduce details from two paintings at no cost.

We have been pleased to work with RoutledgeCurzon on this book. Asian division editors Rachel Saunders and Stephanie Rogers took on the project with great enthusiasm, contributing, among other things, the title. Sarah Moore at Florence Production copy-edited the manuscript, despite its many terms in Chinese, Tibetan, Manchu, and Mongolian, with patience and precision.

Over the years that we have been engaged in writing this book, the editors have been, among other things, also making additions of one sort or another to our families. Depending largely upon their age, these new family members have either helped this project along, or hindered it. Our love and gratitude to them all, in any case.

Abbreviations

The following abbreviations are used in the notes:

BSSZ beike	Yang Tianzai, "Bishu shanzhuang de beike jiqi lishi jiazhi"
BSSZ beiwen	Yang Tianzai, *Bishu shanzhuang beiwen shiyi*
CDDCS	Chengde diqu minyan fenhui (Research Group on the Folk Tales of the Chengde Region), *Chengde di chuanshuo*
CDFZ	Hai Zhong and Lin Congshang eds, *Chengde fuzhi* (Gazetteer of Chengde Prefecture)
DMJMBP	*Collected Works of Dkon-mchog-'jigs med dban-po II*
DQTL	*Da Qing tongli*
ECCP	Hummel, *Eminent Chinese of the Ch'ing Period*
LFYZL	*Qianlong chao neifu chaoben Lifanyuan zeli* (1756)
Macartney	Cranmer-Byng, *An Embassy to China: Being the Journal Kept by Lord Macartney*
QDRHZ	Hešen (He-shen), Qian Daxin *et al.* eds, *Qinding Rehe zhi* (Gazetteer of Rehe)
QLSL	*Da Qing lichao shilu, Gaozong (Qianlong) reign*

1 Introduction

Ruth W. Dunnell and James A. Millward

A certain early modern monarch, a man of towering ambition, undertook extensive renovations on the rural retreat first used by an earlier monarch as a hunting lodge. Armies of hydrologists, gardeners, carpenters, and masons transformed what had been a rather swampy piece of ground at the foot of a hill into a vast and meticulously planned garden and palace complex, its landscaping, plantings, and structures chosen to represent iconic scenes from across the continent. In time, the former modest villa was replaced by a glittering architectural showcase, studded with references to the monarch's military achievements and his cosmological position; artworks housed inside depicted the ruler as a god. The royal court took up residence in the complex, where courtiers and nobility from across the realm enjoyed rich feasts and spectacular entertainments. Not content to let guests enjoy the lovely setting on their own, however, the monarch personally wrote a guidebook instructing them in the proper viewing of its various vistas.

The above vignette might apply to Louis XIV and Versailles or, with a few modifications, to Fatepur Sikri, the Mughal emperor Akbar's recreation of an imperial camp in carved stone outside Agra.[1] It also describes the Qianlong emperor and Chengde, the subject of this book. All three sites were new capitals built at a rural remove from urban centers; all were attempts by absolutist monarchs to showcase, and by showcasing to consolidate, their imperial power.

The city of Chengde, in present day Hebei province, lies north of the Great Wall, 250 kilometers (*c.*155 miles) northeast of Beijing, roughly halfway between the Qing capital and the Manchus' favorite hunting grounds at Mulan (Ma. Muran; marked as Weichang on today's maps; see Figure 2). Western writings from the eighteenth century on refer to both the general area under the jurisdiction of Chengde, and the palace and temple complex itself as Rehe (or "Jehol" in French and German versions), after the "warm river" or hot spring that feeds the lakes at the center of the complex. Rehe also names the stream that flows from those lakes into the Wulie River which runs east of the villa and city of Chengde, flowing in turn into the Luanhe (Shangdu) River. In current Chinese practice, which we generally follow in this volume, both the region and the city are called Chengde.

Strategically situated on China's northern frontier, Chengde became a practical and symbolic command center from which the Manchu rulers coordinated relations between China, an expanding Russian empire, and Inner Asia (i.e. the Manchurian homelands, Mongolia and Mongol-inhabited areas, Tibet, and Xinjiang; Figure 1). The Chengde region had been home to non-Han peoples since early times, and functioned as an administrative center under the Liao, Jin, and Yuan empires. It lost this political role during the Ming dynasty (1368–1644), when the area was inhabited mainly by Mongol groups, but regained it under the rule of the Manchu emperors of the Qing (1644–1912). The Qing Kangxi emperor (r. 1661–1722) held yearly hunting parties there, sleeping in modest quarters; one of Chengde's early names was, in fact, "Upper Camp on the Rehe River" (*Rehe shangying*).² In 1703, Kangxi began construction at Chengde of the gardens and a more elaborate summer residence complex.

From 1703 to 1790, the Manchu rulers transformed the landscape at Chengde to reflect and celebrate the expansion of their empire into Central and Inner Asia. The Manchus, a people from the borderlands between Mongolia, Siberia, China, and Korea, had by the early seventeenth century begun to build an empire that would dissolve the old Great Wall barrier between China and Inner Asia and bring both into obedient service to their imperial vision. In Chengde, they established a new center for this empire. The gardens, palaces, and pavilions at the Bishu shanzhuang ("Mountain Villa to Escape the Heat") together with the Waiba miao ("Eight Outer Temples") replicated and brought together key cultural monuments of China, Tibet, and Central Asia, while the annual ceremonial gatherings and special audiences at Chengde likewise joined the peoples of those territories in submission to the Qing. The networks of personnel, urban enterprises, roads, waterways, farms, and lodges that came into existence to serve the summer capital at Chengde testified to the political efficacy of the imperial formula (some would say fiction) whereby the Qing resolved the conflict between agrarian China and largely nomadic Inner Asia.

Following the Jiaqing emperor's death in 1820, a combination of new geopolitical challenges led the Qing to neglect Chengde. Subsequently, the summer retreat fell into the hands of "abusive officials, helpless monks, and needy peasants" and rapacious warlords,³ its forests cut, its game over-hunted, its architecture ruined and raided for building materials. Today, after further depredations during the Cultural Revolution, Chengde has been revitalized as a popular tourist destination, an imperial theme park in service to the new Chinese state's vision of a multiethnic, multicultural polity.

New Qing imperial history

Recently, scholars have introduced the term "new Qing history" to refer to a wide-ranging revision of the history of the Manchu empire in China and Inner Asia carried out since the 1990s. The most prominent feature of this revision in Qing studies – it involves art historians, geographers, scholars of literature, and others besides historians – has been a new concern with the Manchus and their relationship to China and Chinese culture,[4] as well as that of other non-Han groups under Beijing's rule. This deconstruction of what had once been treated as a homogeneous Chinese population and culture has sometimes also been called the "ethnic turn in China studies"; it has questioned long-held assumptions about "sinicization" – the belief that conquerors and even neighbors of China were converted to Chinese ways by what was often depicted as a spontaneous and one-way process – and trained a skeptical eye on some of the more nationalistic and chauvinistic tenets of traditional Chinese historiography. Employing anthropological perspectives, scholars have re-examined the identity of the Manchus, Mongols, Chinese Muslims (Hui), Miao, and others in historical context.[5] While acceptance of these perspectives has not been universal,[6] many China specialists who might once have dismissed the Manchus simply as "barbarians who became Chinese" now appreciate the complex cultural, political, and ethnic questions posed by this northeastern confederation's conquest of Ming China. Moreover, more students of Qing history are studying the Manchu language.

Another concept re-examined by the new Qing history has been the notion that the Qing empire was, like its dynastic predecessors, "sino-centric," and that its conduct of foreign relations could likewise be said to follow a perduring pattern known to Western historians as "the tribute system." The notion that China, throughout history, adhered to a single, unchanging international outlook has been questioned and qualified from the first.[7] Nevertheless, this model's central image, of Chinese monarchs posturing as lord of all under heaven and insisting that foreigners conduct all diplomacy and commerce in the guise of offering tribute, has long influenced not only historians, but diplomats, politicians – even the Chinese themselves. John King Fairbank developed his concept of the tribute system based on research regarding nineteenth-century trade and diplomacy on the China coast, and expanded it into a general model of "traditional China's foreign relations." Closer consideration of the Qing period and the Qing empire as a whole, however, makes simple culturalist models of Qing foreign relations difficult to sustain; the Qing dealt with neighbors through a range of approaches, including political marriage, religious patronage, commerce, diplomacy and war, approaches that often had nothing to do with tribute or sinocentrism. Another problem with the notion that the Qing followed "traditional" patterns of Chinese foreign relations concerns what exactly "Chinese" and "foreign" mean in the Qing context. Fairbank considered Chinese culture to lie at the core of the Qing polity, but the

Manchu ruling elite often associated with their Inner Asian subjects (Mongols, Tibetans, and Turkic Muslims) more closely than they did with Han Chinese. This book focuses on these relationships with Inner Asia and their political and cultural foundations.

While challenging the concepts of sinicization, sinocentrism, and the tribute system model, the new Qing history has rediscovered the Qing as an Inner Asian, as well as a Chinese, empire. This aspect has, so far, received less sustained study than the issue of Manchu identity;[8] however, it is critical to our revised understanding of the significance of the Qing period. Moreover, given the persistent difficulties the Chinese Communist Party faces in extending its Chinese national vision to Tibet, Xinjiang, and even among Mongols in Inner Mongolia, the fact that the new, greater Chinese empire in Inner Asia is a Qing creation retains great significance today.[9]

As an extensive Eurasian polity, comparable not only to the Islamic "gunpowder empires" but also, in many respects, to the Muscovite and even Hapsburg and British empires, the Qing takes a new position in world history. The old view of the Qing (still sometimes voiced by non-China specialists)[10] as static, isolated and exceptional, cut off from currents of early modern history, no longer stands. Neither "Middle Kingdom," "Oriental despotism," nor "sick man of Asia" will serve to describe the expansive Manchu state which not only dispatched the weakened Ming, but restored order and prosperity in China proper and married the economic power of the Chinese heartland to its own military force to hold off Russia, crush the Zunghars, and add Mongolia, Xinjiang, and Tibet to the realm, thereby doubling the territory under Beijing's control. Hence, the above comparison between Chengde and Versailles: both were creations of powerful monarchs who complemented their military, economic, and political efforts by mustering cultural resources in pursuit of their centralizing projects.

The landscape and architecture of Chengde

The development of Chengde as a fulcrum of this dynamic Qing imperium owed much to its geographic site, which was favored both ecologically and geomantically. Although the climate of Chengde is actually little cooler in summer than Beijing (July average is 24.4 degrees Celsius, compared to 25.8 for Beijing), the man-made lakes and wooded hills of the villa compound may have generated cooling breezes for summer residents,[11] and these environs were certainly more comfortable than the expanses of walls and flagstones in Beijing's Forbidden City. The Mulan hunting ground to the north of Chengde is higher in elevation and much cooler. Chengde's river valleys, situated in the foothills of the Yanshan mountains to the west and the Xin'an mountains to the east (see Figure 2), receive abundant annual rainfall (570 millimeters at present). Resting in a basin ringed by hills, which provide natural fortification (Figure 6), Chengde also features unusual geological formations that have aroused the curiosity of religious pilgrims and tourists alike. The most famous of these uncanny rock formations is a club-shaped protrusion called Hammer Peak (Bangchui feng). Standing on a high bluff to the east of the Wulie River, this was a holy site for Tibetan pilgrims from the eleventh century on (Figure 11).[12]

The 560 hectare (227 acre) compound (Figure 3) encompasses palace, lake, mountain, and prairie landscapes. Construction began in 1703, in the latter part of Kangxi's reign, after his consolidation of control over China, the stabilization of the Qing border with an expanding Russian empire through the Treaty of Nerchinsk (1689), and the death of his western Mongol enemy Galdan (1697). In 1708 the Kangxi emperor named his growing summer residence "Bishu shanzhuang," Mountain Villa to Escape the Heat (it is, in fact, only a "villa" (*zhuang*) in the sense that mansions of Newport, RI are "cottages.") Three years later he installed the placard with this name inscribed in his calligraphy over the entrance to the Zhenggong palace, the main residential complex. Passing through this gate, one enters a series of courtyards separated by halls devoted to various formal and informal occasions, and the three other main wings of the palace complex. In 1754 the Qianlong emperor had the "Gate of Splendor and Propriety" (*Lizheng men*) erected south of the Zhenggong palace (Lizheng was also the name of the main gate to the imperial palace in Beijing (Dadu) under the Mongol Yuan dynasty). A signboard over this massive portal announces the name in Manchu, Mongol, Chinese, Uyghur, and Tibetan – all the scripts of the empire.[13]

The palace and its chambers are relatively modest constructions (Figure 7). According to Anne Chayet and Philippe Forêt, the "rural plainness" of the Zhenggong palace architecture, in contrast to the Forbidden City in Beijing, expresses not so much Confucian ideals of self-restraint as traditional Manchu virtues of "the simple life" that Chengde offered to the Kangxi, Qianlong, and Jiaqing emperors.[14] Such rustic simplicity, however, required forethought and effort.

The center of this contrived natural environment, the series of connecting lakes and islands constructed to the north and east of the palace, is the villa's chief attraction. The Kangxi and Qianlong emperors each designated thirty-six favorite views around the Bishu shanzhuang, with plaques and poems commemorating the charms of each. Most of these imperial vistas are in this lake district, where the waterways, dikes, bridges, rockeries, pavilions, and halls were designed to evoke the landscape of Jiangnan, the lower Yangzi region in south central China.[15] The emperors located 12 of their 72 vistas on centrally located Ruyi Island, where a cluster of buildings housed entertainment and official functions analogous to those of the Zhenggong palace complex. Here one could savor the refined delights of Jiangnan safe from its inconveniences or perils.[16]

Beyond these palaces and scenes reminiscent of China proper (*nei* or *neidi* in many Qing sources) lie other created landscapes that bespeak the outer territories of the Qing in Mongolia, Central Asia, and Tibet (*wai*). North of the lakes and northeast of the Zhenggong palace lies the prairie district, the Mongolian landscape of the "Garden of Ten Thousand Trees" (Wanshu yuan), a sparsely wooded area of elms, willows, and grassy clearings (Figure 8). Here, when needed, the Qing could erect yurts, tents, tables, a throne, acrobatic apparatus, and other furnishings for receptions, banquets, and entertainments. To the west of the Wanshu yuan was the Shimadai field, where the court sponsored horsemanship and archery competitions.

The large "mountain" district northwest of the Zhenggong palace has suffered deforestation and erosion, although recent government efforts have sought to reforest the hills and it has now become a favorite place for walkers, photographers, and mushroom-gatherers. Few traces remain of the original forty-four villas and temples, with their pavilions, kiosks, and gardens, but a small pavilion marks the highest point of the Bishu shanzhuang complex, where the emperors would be borne on the ninth day of the ninth lunar month (the Chongyang festival) to enjoy the "clouds and mountains on four sides" (Figure 10).[17]

Beyond the undulating stone wall that surrounds the Bishu shanzhuang – with ramparts and crenellations like sections of the Ming-era "Great Wall" north of Beijing – there were originally twelve Buddhist temples, of which nine survive today in part or whole. The eight main restored temples are known as the Eight Outer Temples (Waiba miao; Figure 4); two of the Eight Outer Temples were built in 1713 under Kangxi: the Temple of Pervading Benevolence (Puren si) in the southeast on the east bank of the Wulie River, dedicated to Amitayus, and the Temple of Pervading Excellence (Pushan si) just northeast of it. Both were built for the benefit of Mongol princes invited to Chengde for the celebration of the Kangxi emperor's sixtieth birthday. Both structures are architecturally Chinese, but were perhaps embellished to appeal to a Tibetan Buddhist clientele.[18]

The remaining six major temples were erected under Qianlong between 1755 and 1780. Qianlong wrote most of the dedicatory inscriptions himself, naming the occasion and model which inspired the construction of each temple.[19] The history of the construction of these temples is explored in the essay by Anne Chayet (Chapter 4). A brief introduction to the temples follows here.

The Temple of Universal Peace (Puning si; Figure 16), built in 1755, is modeled on the earliest Tibetan temple at Samye (Bsam yas), and commemorates the subjugation of the Zunghar Mongols (on which see Rawski (Chapter 2) and Millward (Chapter 8)). It sits near the west bank of the Wulie River five kilometers northeast of the Bishu shanzhuang wall. The Temple of Universal Blessing (Puyou si), erected just east of the Puning si in 1760, presumably also in conjunction with the pacification of Xinjiang, was largely destroyed in 1964. In 1764, the Temple of Pacifying Distant Lands (Anyuan miao; Figure 15) arose on the east bank of the Wulie River, on behalf of the 12,000 former Zunghars resettled by Qianlong at Chengde. It is modeled on the Ghulja (Kulja) Temple or Yili miao, which stood on the Yili River (in northern Xinjiang, also known as Zungharia or Yili) before it was destroyed by the Qing in 1756 during the Zunghar campaigns.[20]

South of the Anyuan miao and across the Wulie River from the Huidiji gate in the Bishu shanzhuang wall stands the Temple of Universal Joy (Pule si; Figure 18), constructed in 1766–67 for the Mongols who came to Chengde every year to pay homage to the Qing emperor. Qianlong's friend, counselor, Mongol lama, and Tibetan language tutor, the Jang gya (Lcang skya; Ch. Zhangjia) Khutukhtu, Rolpai Dorje (Rol-pa'i rdo-rje, 1717–86), guided the construction of this temple.[21] A key feature of its layout is the three-dimensional mandala of six-armed Chakrasamvara (Samvara) within a square enclosure in the anterior Xuguang Pavilion, a circular structure with a double cone-shaped roof supported by twelve pillars (Figure 17). The temple and statue of Samvara stand in perfect alignment with Hammer Peak to the northeast (Figure 18). Chakrasamvara is one of the three main tutelary deities (*yidam*) of the Gelukpa (Yellow Hat) sect of Tibetan Buddhism. Tibetans believed that Hammer Peak was a Shiva linga, or phallic symbol of the great Hindu god Shiva, whom Chakrasamvara bested in a spiritual contest. To counter and contain the Shiva potency believed to inhere in this chunk of rock, Jang gya recommended that Qianlong, himself a Chakrasamvara initiate, have a mandala to that tutelary deity enshrined in this temple.[22]

Surely the best known of the Eight Outer Temples is the Potala Temple (Putuozongcheng miao; Figure 12), Qianlong's homage to the Dalai Lama's Potala palace at Lhasa. Construction of this vast and ambitious complex west of the Wulie River and due north of the Mountain Villa wall began in 1767 and was completed in the fall of 1771. Completed to coincide with the Qianlong emperor's sixtieth (1770) and his mother's eightieth birthday (1771), it also celebrated the visits and gifts of various Mongol groups, including the recently submitted Zunghars and Torghuts who had just fled to Qing lands from west of the Volga (on which see Millward (Chapter 8)).

In the courtyard within the great red facade of the Potala Temple (the Dahongtai or "Great Red Terrace" which imitates the facade of the Lhasa Potala), stands the square Wanfaguiyi Hall (Hall of All Dharmas Returning to One; Figure 13) with a gilded copper two tiered stupa-style roof. It was in this hall that Qianlong received the leaders of the Torghuts in 1771 (see Chayet (Chapter 4) and Millward (Chapter 8)). In the summer of 1930, Swedish explorer Sven Hedin journeyed to Chengde to make replicas of this "Lama temple" and its furnishings for exhibition in Stockholm and Chicago. One complete replica appeared in the Chicago Century of Progress Exposition of 1933–34, and then in the New York World's Fair later in 1939.[23]

The last surviving structure of the Eight Outer Temples is the Temple of the Happiness and Longevity of Mt Sumeru (Xumifushou miao; Figure 14), constructed in 1780 in imitation of the Panchen Lama's residence at Tashilhunpo (Bkra shis lhun po) in Shigatse. The Xumifushou miao was built to accommodate the Third Panchen Lama (1737–80) during his 1780 visit to Chengde (see Zarrow's translation of the emperor's inscription for this temple, Chapter 15).[24] Destroyed in the nineteenth and twentieth centuries were the Temple of Vast Peace (Guang'an si), built in 1772 on Tibetan models, again to honor the empress dowager's eightieth birthday; the Arhat Temple (Luohan tang), a purely Chinese Buddhist structure modeled on a Zhejiang temple and built in 1774; and the Temple of the Statue of Manjushri (Shuxiang si), erected between 1774 and 1776 on the model of the temple by that name at Wutai shan.[25] The Arhat Temple was the only one of the original twelve Buddhist temples at Chengde that catered to Chinese (as opposed to Tibetan) Buddhist practitioners. Wutai shan, in Shanxi, was a Tibetan Buddhist pilgrimage site and "a religious center for the tribes of Inner Mongolia," hence the Shuxiang si was also a Tibetan Buddhist temple.[26]

Daoist and Confucian temples also dot the landscape at Chengde. Outside the south wall of the Bishu shanzhuang are the City God Temple (Chenghuang miao) and the Confucian temple (Wen miao). Joseph Adler examines the position of the Confucian "Temple of Culture" in the political-cultural landscape of Chengde.

Qing landscape efforts, in effect, transformed the topography of Chengde into a new, naturalized landscape that expressed the cultural ambitions and political accomplishments of the Manchu rulers. By recreating famous structures and scenery from Tibet to south China, the emperors and their architects produced a microcosm of the Manchu empire: a south China landscape in the southern sector of Bishu shanzhuang, a Mongol landscape in the northern part, a "natural" mountain landscape in the west, and a mostly Tibetan Buddhist landscape in the outer periphery to the east and north, where the Eight Outer Temples (Waiba miao) stand outside the wall.[27]

Organization of this book

This volume aims to contribute to the new Qing history by focusing on a single site: the palace, temple, and garden complex at Chengde. This is not a specialized study of the architecture or site itself – Anne Chayet and Philippe Forêt have already provided such studies, which all the authors here have drawn upon. This book, rather, uses Chengde as a vantage point from which to explore the importance to Qing history of Tibetan Buddhism, of the Mongolian peoples, and of the geostrategic struggles culminating in the conquest of Xinjiang. Also examined here are the role of ritual in Qing relations with Inner Asia and the nature of the emperorship itself, particularly under Qianlong. The artistic and architectural artifacts of the complex, associated texts, and the historical events that took place there all provide concrete illustrations of the themes of the new Qing history, especially its Inner Asian dimension. Most of the chapters in this book take a material artifact or specific text as the starting point for their analysis.

The book is organized into five Parts. Part I provides general background on the Qing empire at its height in the eighteenth century (Rawski, intended primarily for non-specialists), a concise primer on Tibetan Buddhism (Lopez), and an introduction to the architecture of Chengde and its interpretation (Chayet). These articles underpin arguments found throughout the rest of the book.

Part II examines how Chengde and the associated Mulan hunting ground functioned as an imperial capital. It is well known that Qing emperors spent a great deal of time in ritual functions – nearly as much as they spent on executive managerial duties (if, indeed, these activities can be clearly distinguished). Historians of imperial China have long appreciated the importance, for example, of the sacrifices at Beijing's ancestral and other altars, tours of south China, or birthday congratulations to dowager empresses. Scholars have taken less note of those ritual or ritualized activities directed not specifically at China but at the Inner Asian peoples of the Qing realm. Yet, these too were critical to imperial governance. Grand progresses to and from Chengde, examined here by Van Symons, took place almost annually during the long Kangxi and Qianlong reigns. And while Chengde was certainly a retreat from Beijing, the court in residence there was by no means on vacation. Rather, besides handling the voluminous day-to-day correspondence of the expanding empire, it also held diplomatic summits and lavish state banquets, here discussed by Renqiu Yu, and staged other events to impress Inner Asian visitors, confirm the loyalty of Mongol and Turkic nobles, and show respect to Tibetan lamas. Even hunting, Chengde's original *raison d'être* and a pastime much enjoyed for its own sake by the Kangxi and Qianlong emperors, had important ritual, diplomatic, and politico-military purposes analyzed here by Ning Chia and Mark Elliott. Hunts, fêtes, Buddhist ceremonies and other rituals served a strategic function in managing relations with Mongol elites, as described by James Millward, who also attempts in his chapter on the Torghuts' return to encapsulate "what all Qing historians should know about Mongolia."

The Qing emperorship has long fascinated students of the period with the grandeur – some would say grandiosity – of its multi-faceted imagery.[28] The Qianlong emperor, in particular, reigned longer than any other emperor in Chinese history, presided over an unprecedented expansion of imperial territory and population, and incorporated from the empire's recent conquests and quickening contacts with foreign lands a variety of new ideological tools and cultural points of reference. Thus, at Chengde, Tibetan

Buddhist iconography and Jesuit draftsmanship mingled with Manchu martial values, Confucian discourses on sagehood, and endless poetasting to produce, in Peter Zarrow's phrase, "the statecraft of Qianlong's self-expression."

The chapters in Part III survey the representations of the Qianlong emperor in their diverse media and cultural modes. Joseph Adler, in a study of texts associated with Chengde's Confucian temple (Wen miao), shows the Qianlong emperor establishing his bona fides as a Confucian commentator and reaching back to earliest Confucian tradition for the archetype of a sage king, a mantle which he dons himself. It is Tibetan Buddhism, however, that holds pride of place among the religions represented at Chengde. Elisabeth Benard examines the Qianlong emperor's practice of this faith, based on Tibetan accounts of his interactions with two incarnate high lamas, the second Jang gya Khutukhtu, Rolpai Dorje, and the Third Panchen Lama. The Panchen Lama's visit to Chengde in 1780 was one of the major diplomatic events in Chengde's history, and Tibetan sources (one of which is provided in translation by Nima Dorjee Ragnubs in Part IV) give a unique picture of the interaction between Qianlong and these two lamas, both of whom became his teacher and addressed him as the bodhisattva of wisdom, Manjushri.

An avid art collector, Qianlong commissioned many works, including portraits of himself as Manjushri, as well as the Chengde genre paintings discussed by Deborah Sommer. The ceremonial banquet in the steppe region of the Chengde complex featured regularly in the receptions of new tribal allies of the Qing, and the incorporation of Mongol groups under Manchu rule was critical to Qing success in the struggles for Inner Asia. Hence, the importance of this painting, which both documents the pageantry, and suggests how the court wished the event to be represented. Complementing Sommer's analysis of the painting itself is a translation of a letter concerning the Jesuit Jean-Denis Attiret's grueling work in Chengde in 1754, when demands for his services by Mongol princes and the emperor himself kept the court painter constantly busy (Sommer's translation in Part IV).

What emerges from the essays in this section and supporting translations (including Qianlong's Chengde poems, also in Part IV) is a portrait of a dilettante, but also that of a universal emperor simultaneously addressing multiple constituencies, each in their own idiom. One theme links these various materials: Qianlong's relentless urge to promote, commemorate, and justify his greatness and that of his imperial conquests.

Thanks to its status as a seasonal capital during the Qing empire's height, Chengde generated a good deal of writing. In addition to the large published and documentary record of both routine business and high-level diplomacy transacted at the Mountain Villa, there are reflective essays by emperors concerning the place and its significance, descriptive accounts by foreign visitors, and satirical legends conveyed through popular folklore. Besides Sir George Staunton's description of the Macartney embassy's sojourn at Chengde, however, little of this material is familiar to historians and none has hitherto been available in English.

The translations from Manchu, Tibetan, French, and Chinese in Part IV are selected for the fresh perspective they provide on the outlook of Qing emperors and the workings of Qing empire, in particular with regard to Inner Asia and Tibetan Buddhism. They furnish, moreover, concrete illustrations of points made throughout this book, including, for example, the implications of Qing multi-lingualism, here suggested by a parallel translation from Manchu and Chinese texts of the "Preface to the Thirty-six Views of Bishu shanzhuang" (Elliott and Lowe). If the account translated by Ragnubs gives a private, Tibetan viewpoint on the Qianlong emperor's engagement with Tibetan Buddhism, the Xumifushou stele inscription rendered here by Peter Zarrow provides an imperial statement on the subject meant for the public record. The imperial poems on Chengde themes which Scott Lowe translates show yet another facet of the Qianlong emperor, whose output of verse was allegedly superhuman.

We have also included two folktales concerning famous examples of Bishu shanzhuang and Eight Outer Temples architecture (Gernant). Because these stories were collected and compiled during the PRC period, their provenance is admittedly uncertain, as is the extent to which they reflect eighteenth- or even nineteenth-century popular feeling as opposed to Communist Party agendas. Nonetheless, they are fun, and not irrelevant to how the site is understood and enjoyed today. And finally, in Part V, James Hevia reflects upon those contemporary meanings of Chengde in his epilog to this collection.

Notes

1 Any introduction to Versailles (built in the 1670s) will tell of its many sun images to symbolize the Sun King, its references to Apollo and portraits of Louis XIV as the Roman sun god, its Orangery to recall Spain, and its Grand Canal and Little Venice. On Fatepur Sikri (1571–85), see Richards, *The Mughal Empire*, 29–30 and Nath, *History of Mughal Architecture*, vol. 1–2 supplement, *Architecture of Fatepur Sikri*.
2 Forêt, *Mapping Chengde*, 16.
3 Forêt, *Mapping Chengde*, 98.
4 In reviewing them for the *Journal of Asian Studies* ("Who Were the Manchus?"), Kent Guy refers to "the Four Books of Manchu studies": Rawski, *The Last Emperors*; Crossley, *A Translucent Mirror*; Elliott, *The Manchu Way*; Rhoads, *Manchus and Han*. However, one might add Crossley's first book, *Orphan Warriors*, to this list.
5 Bulag, *The Mongols at China's Edge*; Lipman, *Familiar Strangers*; Harrell, *Cultural Encounters on China's Ethnic Frontiers*; Hostetler, *Qing Colonial Enterprise*.
6 Ping-ti Ho, "In Defense of Sinicization."
7 Joseph Fletcher, "China and Central Asia, 1368–1884" challenged the "tribute system" model in the very volume where Fairbank put it forth most strongly. See also Rossabi, *China among Equals* and, most recently, Hevia, *Cherishing Men from Afar*.

8   Rawski, "Re-envisioning the Qing"; Millward, *Beyond the Pass*; Ning Chia, "The Li-fan Yuan of the Early Qing Dynasty"; Berger, *Empire of Emptiness*; Peter Perdue's forthcoming *China Marches West* will be a major contribution to the study of Qing empire in Central Eurasia.

9   Ross Terrill's reading of recent revisions of Qing history form the starting point for his analysis of the PRC today (Terrill, *The New Chinese Empire*), a state which he sees as retaining many imperial aspects, in particular regarding Uyghurs and Tibetans.

10 For a recent example, see Paul Kennedy, *The Rise and Fall of the Great Powers* or the final section of Jared Diamond's *Guns, Germs and Steel*.

12 Forêt, *Mapping Chengde*, 42.

13 Lecture by Heather Stoddard, Ann Arbor, July 22, 1994. This tradition is recorded in part of a story about the construction of the Pule si, recorded in the early nineteenth-century chronicle, *Amdo chos byung*. See note 23 below, on the Pule si.

13 Forêt, *Mapping Chengde*, 22, 36; Xiao Tian, *Chengde mingsheng*, 8.

14 Forêt, *Mapping Chengde*, 43–44; Chayet, *Les Temples de Jehol*, 19.

15 Forêt, *Mapping Chengde*, 45–46; Xiao Tian, 14–17.

16 On the uneasy relationship between the Manchu rulers and the cultural and commercial heartland of China in Jiangnan, see Kuhn, *Soulstealers*, especially ch. 3.

17 Forêt, *Mapping Chengde*, 48–49; Xiao Tian, 26.

18 Chayet, *Les Temples de Jehol*, 26–27, cf. Tianjin daxue and Chengde shi wenwuju, eds *Chengde gujianzhu*, 157.

19 Chayet, "The Jehol Temples and Their Tibetan Models," in Aziz and Kapstein, *Soundings in Tibetan Civilization*, 66.

20 Chayet, *Les Temples de Jehol*, 36. Because of the Anyuan miao's association with Xinjiang, it has folklorically been associated with Qianlong's Uyghur concubine, Xiang Fei (Rong Fei). In fact, the historical woman on whom the Xiang Fei legends are based came from Yarkand, a Muslim – not Buddhist – area, some 500 km south of Ghulja. For the folktale, see Xiao Tian, 216–19 ("Anyuan miao yu Xiangfei") and Zhu Yanhua and Yang Linbo, comp., X*iangfei de chuanshuo*, 147–52. Despite the title, this last work is a general collection of stories popular in the Chengde region, one of which concerns Xiangfei (on whom, see Millward, "A Uyghur Muslim in Qianlong's Court").

21 Chayet, *Les Temples de Jehol*, 39; p. 135 note 137 quotes from the dedicatory inscription by the Qianlong emperor.

22 This tradition appears in the *Amdo chos byung*, an early nineteenth-century Tibetan chronicle (Heather Stoddard, lecture, Ann Arbor July 22, 1994). The emperor received his Chakrasamvara initiation from Jang gya twenty years prior to the erection of the Pule si. See also Rawski, *The Last Emperors*, 258, and Berger, *Empire of Emptiness*, 60, 83.

23 Chayet, *Les Temples de Jehol*, 45; Sven Hedin, *Jehol, City of Emperors*.

24 The Third Panchen Lama's visit to China proved fatal, for he succumbed to smallpox (as Tibetan officials had feared) and died in Beijing, in November of that year. See Shakabpa, *Tibet, A Political History*, 155. In Chinese publications he is usually referred to as the Sixth Panchen Lama, the Chinese following the practice of posthumously entitling predecessors of the first lama to receive the title "Panchen."

25 Chayet, *Les Temples de Jehol*, 46–48.

26 See Rawski, *The Last Emperors*, 253, 260–61 and Berger, *Empire of Emptiness*, 161–64 on the importance of Wutai shan for followers of Tibetan Buddhism.

27 Forêt, *Mapping Chengde*, passim; Chayet, *Les Temples de Jehol*, 26.

28 Kahn, *Monarchy in the Emperor's Eyes*.

Part I
Chengde as Inner Asian capital

2 The Qing empire during the Qianlong reign

Evelyn S. Rawski

The Qianlong reign (1736–1795) represents the pinnacle of the Qing dynasty, "the most successful dynasty of conquest in Chinese history,"[1] which ruled China from 1644 to 1911. This empire, created by Qing arms, was the basis for the territorial definition of the modern Chinese nation state.[2] In contrast to their predecessor, the Ming dynasty, which had never decisively controlled even the Ordos, the arid region in northwest China lying within the northern loop of the Yellow River, the Manchu rulers of the Qing succeeded in incorporating northeast Asia, Mongolia, Tibet, the Tarim Basin, and Zungharia into their empire (Figure 1).

It was the Qianlong emperor who presided over the final phase of the territorial expansion which had begun in the late seventeenth and early eighteenth centuries, when Manchu emperors halted the Russian penetration of northeast Asia and signed treaties defining their mutual border. The Qing recognized that control of the Tibetan Buddhist establishment which commanded Mongol devotion was the key to controlling the Mongols. In 1720 rivalry between the Khoshuut and Zunghar Mongols came to a head in a dispute over the legitimacy of the Dalai Lama, who headed the Gelukpa order that ruled Tibet. A Zunghar invasion of Lhasa prompted a Qing counter-invasion, and a Qing garrison was established in the Tibetan capital, inaugurating a new period in Sino-Tibetan relations. Kham and Amdo (Mo. Kökö nuur or Kokonor, Ch. Qinghai) were placed under the administrative jurisdiction of Sichuan; in 1725 the Yongzheng emperor (r. 1723–1735) divided Khams into two, returning control of the western half to central Tibet, while administering eastern Khams through local tribal leaders. Meanwhile, alliances with the Khalkha Mongols strengthened the Qing efforts to subjugate the Zunghars, and a series of military campaigns finally brought the Tarim Basin (today's southern Xinjiang) and Zungharia (northern Xinjiang) into the empire in 1759. The Qing empire then stretched from the Pacific Ocean to the doors of Central Asia.

Several aspects of Qing rule are especially salient to the study of the Qing summer capital, Chengde. The Qing was a conquest dynasty with roots in the Inner Asian realm. Its founders were Altaic speakers from northeast Asia who claimed descent from the Jurchen Jin, who ruled north China during the twelfth and early thirteenth centuries. Nurhaci (1559–1626; the "ci" in Manchu is pronounced like "chee") and his son Hong Taiji (1592–1643) created a multi-ethnic force composed of Jurchen, Mongols, and "transfrontiersmen" which they organized into Manchu, Mongol, and "Han" banners. The banners were military units which also served as units of household registration for the Manchus and their allies. Manchus comprised only a fraction of the army that swept into China in 1644.

The conquest of the Ming territories was a difficult task which took almost four decades to complete. Having unified the northeast tribes and coerced Korea into subjugation, the Manchu forces were invited south of the Great Wall when Beijing was taken by the rebel Li Zicheng. Qing troops were welcomed into the Ming capital, but it soon became clear that they had no intention of restoring the Ming. After defeating the Ming loyalists, the Qing confronted the defiance of their own followers, who had been installed as regional military commanders in south and south-west China. The successful suppression of the Rebellion of the Three Feudatories (Sanfan) was finally accomplished in 1683, the same year in which Qing naval forces finally wiped out the last remnant of Ming resistance on the island of Taiwan. By that time, the framework of Qing rule had been set. Early attempts to cohabit with the Han Chinese population of the Ming empire had been unsuccessful and in 1648 the Qing ordered that the conquerors live apart from conquered subjects. In the capital, Beijing, and in strategically located cities and towns throughout the empire, bannermen were housed in walled garrisons that maintained a separate existence from the Han Chinese settlement.

Recent scholarship has challenged the thesis that the Qing dynasty should be seen as a Chinese or sinicized dynasty. The Qianlong emperor ruled a multi-ethnic state which applied different regulations to different subject peoples within its realm. Originally, in the seventeenth century, when the Manchus arose as a regional power in the northeast, the major boundary in Qing society was not ethnic but political. On the one hand were the Manchu, Mongol, and Han Chinese nobles and bannermen, the latter being persons who had voluntarily joined the Manchu cause, generally before 1644. All of these individuals belonged to the conquest elite, wore banner clothing, and were subject to banner law. On the other side were the subjugated populace, predominantly Han Chinese, who were governed by laws based on Ming precedents.

One of the most important tasks confronting the Kangxi emperor (r. 1662–1722) was to court the Han Chinese literati in order to obtain their acquiescence to Manchu rule. Studies of the imperial patronage of scholars in the project to compile the Ming history, the restoration of the civil service examination system, and the adoption of Chinese norms for death rituals illuminate various aspects of a multi-faceted policy that was extremely successful. The Manchu rulers learned to speak, read, and write Chinese. They studied the Confucian canon and patronized Chinese art and literature. Filiality became an essential prerequisite for rulership. The Manchu success at portraying themselves as Chinese rulers stimulated twentieth-century scholars to emphasize their sinicization.

In the tradition of the Liao, Jin, and Yuan dynasties, however, Qing rulers actively resisted sinicization, which they identified as the cause of the demise of non-Han ruling houses. The Manchu ruler Hong Taiji declared in 1635 that henceforth his people should be known as Manchus. Scholars have demonstrated that the Jianzhou Jurchen forebears of the Manchus were deeply influenced by their Mongol neighbors, many of whom were their allies in the conquest. Like their non-Han predecessors, the Manchus pursued a bilingual policy: Manchu and Chinese were the two official languages of government, although Mongolian was also used extensively in communications dealing with Mongolian administrative matters. Created in 1599 through state fiat, and revised in the 1630s, written Manchu became a security language for the rulers; until at least 1750, many military affairs were treated only in Manchu.[3]

The governance of the Qing empire was divided along two axes. The first was the political boundary dividing members of the conquest elite from the subjugated Ming population. The civil service, which administered the Ming territories, was characterized by "dyarchy" or shared rule. While Han Chinese, recruited through the examination system, staffed the lower and middle ranks of the bureaucracy, the top provincial and central government posts were split between Han Chinese and members of the conquest elite. The highest decision-making powers, however, were initially not evenly divided. Manchu nobles had dominated the councils of the conquest era. The Deliberative Council, the highest decision-making body during the Kangxi reign, was staffed exclusively by members of the conquest elite. During the Yongzheng reign, power shifted from the Deliberative Council to a variety of ad hoc bodies, manned by inner-court deputies and military specialists. Finally, from the Qianlong reign onward, the highest decision-making body became the Grand Council (Junji chu), which was staffed by Han Chinese and members of the conquest elite. The number of Manchus on the Grand Council exceeded Chinese for almost three-quarters of the Qianlong reign.[4]

The Qing policy with respect to non-Han groups living within the former Ming territories and Taiwan was sharply differentiated from its policy towards the major non-Han groups living along the Inner Asian peripheries of the empire. With respect to the southern and southwestern minorities, government policies followed the traditional Han Chinese formulation, namely that these were uncivilized (literally "raw") peoples who should be acculturated, i.e. "civilized" through sinicization. But different policies were applied to the peoples inhabiting the Inner Asian peripheries.

The empire was territorially divided into the "inner" (*nei*) domains of the former Ming provinces, and the "outer" (*wai*) domains of the Inner Asian peripheries. Local administration below the provincial level in the former Ming territories was largely in the hands of Han Chinese officials, while administration of the "outer" domains was largely in the hands of bannermen. The Manchu homeland in northeast Asia was administered by first one, then several, military governors appointed from the banner forces. Mongols who had submitted to Qing authority before 1644 were organized into banners and the banners grouped eventually under two leagues. Khalkha Mongols, who were divided into three federations during the seventeenth century, were also incorporated into banners and leagues: there were 200 banners and eighteen leagues by the end of the dynasty. The hereditary khans were given Qing princely titles, but the actual administration of the banners was handed over to an official, the *jasagh* (Ch. *zhasake*). All of the Khalkha leagues were put under the jurisdiction of a Qing military governor, appointed from the banners. Eventually, there were two military governors, one at Khobdo, to administer the western Mongols, and another at Uliyasutai, to administer Khalkha affairs. A third high official, the *amban* (Ch. *dachen*), was stationed at Urga (Ch. Kulun) to administer the affairs of the Jebtsundamba (Rje btsun dam pa) khutukhtu, the highest reincarnate lama of Mongolia.

The Qing presence in Tibet after 1720 was at first very indirect. The power and authority of the Dalai Lama, which had increased during the life of the Fifth Dalai Lama (1617–1682), was visibly diminished in subsequent decades. A council composed of Tibetan nobles was in charge of government; internal quarrels led to civil war (1727–1728) and Tibetan affairs were thereafter controlled by Pholhanas, the victor. Pholhanas died in 1747; his heir quarreled with and was killed by the two Qing *ambans* in 1750. They, in turn, died at the hands of a mob which stormed their residence. The Qianlong emperor was forced to intervene. He increased the size of the garrison in Lhasa and recognized the Dalai Lama as a secular as well as religious ruler. A new council of ministers was created, but the Qing *amban* were also granted increased powers of surveillance over Tibetan affairs. After 1792, *amban* were able to participate directly in government.

A similar approach was taken in the far west. The Makhdumzada Khojas who allied with the Qing were rewarded with princely titles and incorporated into the conquest elite. From 1759 to 1820, the Manchu court followed the Oirat Mongol precedent in the administration of Zungharia and the Tarim Basin. A Qing military governor was stationed at Yili, and he administered Zungharia. *Ambans* were stationed in the cities of Tarbagatai, Urumchi, Kashgar, Yarkand, Khotan, Aksu, Ush, Karashahr, and Kucha (Figure 1). Local notables, called *begs*, were permitted to govern the oases towns of the Tarim Basin according to Islamic law, but new regulations removed the hereditary right of the *begs* to office and limited their authority. Until the formal creation of Xinjiang province in 1884, Qing administration in this region remained substantively distinct from the administration of the "inner" domains.[5]

As Pamela Crossley demonstrates in *A Translucent Mirror*, the Manchu ideology of rulership reached a new level under the Qianlong emperor. His vision of a universal rulership based on the submission of divergent peoples, whose cultures would remain separate, was fundamentally at odds with the Confucian ideal of transforming (and culturally unifying) all peoples under a Confucian ruler. During the Qianlong reign, the court tried to cultivate each of the five peoples: the Manchus, Mongols, Tibetans, Uyghurs (Turkic-speaking Muslims), and Chinese whom the emperor identified as his major subjects. The languages of the "five peoples" were officially enshrined as the languages of the empire. The throne commissioned translations, dictionary compilations, and other projects to promote each language. The emperor himself, as the crucial link uniting these diverse peoples, knew Manchu, Chinese, and Mongolian, and studied at least some Tibetan and Uyghur.

The archival materials strongly support the argument that the Manchus disseminated different images of rulership to the five subject peoples of the empire. As noted earlier, the Qing emperors presented themselves as Confucian monarchs within the former Ming territories. Manchu princes hailed the emperor as "divine lord" (Ma. *enduringge ejen*), and their relationship to him was cast in the lord–vassal tradition of the pre-1644 period. Mongols referred to the Qing emperors as "great khans" (*boghdo khaghan*), on the Chinggisid model of rule. They presented annual tribute, frequently at Chengde, but were also part of a reciprocal exchange of brides and grooms with the Manchu imperial lineage.

The Tibetans' view of the Qing court was encapsulated in the relationship between the emperor and the highest Tibetan Buddhist prelates. Here, the framework of "dual rule," initiated in 1260 by Khubilai Khan, dominated perceptions of separate but equal rulers of the secular and spiritual realms. The Qianlong emperor represented himself to Tibetans as an emanation of Manjushri, the Bodhisattva of Wisdom, whose cult was centered on the temples at Wutai shan in north China. Only the Muslims were immune to such appeals by virtue of their religion. Qing rulers preached religious tolerance for Muslims, and bestowed tax exemptions on religious endowments, including those supporting the Yaghdu mausoleum, a shrine to Khoja Afaq, the founder of the "White Mountain" branch which had ruled the Tarim Basin.[6] Because Islam did not allow unbelievers to act as patrons of the faith, the emperor could never be fully accepted as the ultimate authority of the Islamic world under his direct control.

Even while they pursued policies of accommodation towards the peoples of Inner Asia, the Qing rulers artfully increased their control over these peoples, and exerted a profound influence on their societies and economies.

Eliminating opponents and rewarding allies, they restructured the social hierarchy in the peripheries. They eroded autonomous sources of power and prestige to establish the throne as the source of all secular authority. Many northeastern tribal peoples were incorporated into the banners as "new Manchus," and some were moved to garrisons in Shengjing (Mukden; pre-1644 capital), Beijing, and Xinjiang. Mongol noble titles were now conferred by the emperor, and could not be bequeathed to descendants without his approval. Qing patronage of the Gelukpa sect ensured its continued dominance in Tibet and among the Mongols, but in return the throne asserted its prerogative to recognize rebirths and approve appointments of high prelates. Despite earlier policies protecting the peripheral regions from Han Chinese penetration, the Qing were finally unable to keep Chinese merchants from moving into Xinjiang, Mongolia and the northeast, and these migrants quickened the pace of commercialization (and indebtedness) of these local economies. Banner schools, established in Mongolia and the northeast in the eighteenth century, increased the literacy levels of these societies, which became significantly "manchuized."

Many scholars have criticized the Qianlong emperor for his extravagance, but the Qianlong reign was an economic highpoint for the dynasty. Within China proper a growing population expanded cultivation, increasing the agricultural output, while foreign demand for tea brought new importations of silver into China throughout the eighteenth century. Foreign trade expansion went hand in hand with increased commercialization – the participation by peasant farmers and handicraft producers in local and long-distance markets – and gave weight to the judgment that the emperor presided over a "golden age." Outbreaks of what the emperor perceived to be "anti-Manchu" movements were quickly squashed. The self-confidence of the period was epitomized in the person of the emperor himself, a polyglot who attempted through his own life to personify the values and aspirations of his various subjects. His activities at Chengde reveal an important aspect of the Qing imperial persona, and one that has been neglected by Chinese historians.

Notes

1   Ping-ti Ho, "Significance of the Ch'ing Period," 191. Many scholars have treated the Qianlong reign and the Qing dynasty as "a debased era from which modern China still suffers." See Frederick Mote, "Intellectual Climate in Eighteenth-century China," 17. For Mote, Hungli (Ch. Hongli), the Qianlong emperor, was a man with "meanness of spirit" and "unbounded egotism" (23) who was responsible for the catastrophic literary inquisition that began in 1777 and did not end until 1796. In *The Immobile Empire*, Alain Peyrefitte expresses a Eurocentric view of the Qing empire during the Qianlong reign: a stagnant China is sharply contrasted to a dynamic Western Europe. The scholarship of the last two decades has produced more complex interpretations of both the literary inquisition and the Sino-European encounter of the eighteenth century, exemplified by the failed embassy of Lord Macartney (1793). In *The Emperor's Four Treasures*, Kent Guy

goes beyond the view that the "literary inquisition" was simply a product of Qing autocracy. The initial delegation of literary censorship to local educational officials produced meager results; only when the task was turned over to expectant educational officials, who were promised a "leg up" the list of prospective appointees for vacancies as a reward for diligence, did the pursuit of seditious writings really become a major activity. Guy concludes that the "literary inquisition" begun by the Qianlong emperor would not have succeeded had it not touched other deep social tensions and motivations among the Chinese literati. The stereotype of China as part of an unchanging Asian world, beset by the West, has undergone critical re-evaluation as scholars, influenced by historiographical debates on "Orientalism" and imperialism, have applied their new insights to Sinological data. James L. Hevia, *Cherishing Men from Afar*, ch. 1, thoughtfully reviews the major interpretive frameworks that have dominated previous scholarship on Qing foreign relations. Hevia's own theme, that the Sino-Western encounter should be re-interpreted as "one between two expansive imperialisms, the Manchu and British multi-ethnic imperial formations" (xii) complements the thrust of the contents of this volume.

2   Evelyn S. Rawski, "Re-envisioning the Qing."
3   Pamela K. Crossley and Evelyn S. Rawski, "Profile of the Manchu Language."
4   J. K. Fairbank and S. Y. Teng, *Ch'ing Administration*; Beatrice Bartlett, *Monarchs and Ministers*, 27, 49, 107, 178, and ch. 4 for a detailed description of the decision-making bodies created by the Yongzheng emperor.
5   See James A. Millward, "Uyghur Muslim in Qianlong's Court."
6   Millward, "Uyghur Muslim in Qianlong's Court," 440.

3 Tibetan Buddhism

Donald S. Lopez, Jr

Buddhism has both changed the cultures it has encountered and been changed by them, so that we speak of Indian Buddhism, Chinese Buddhism, Japanese Buddhism, and so on. Tibetan Buddhism is one of the major forms of Buddhism in Asia, with its influence extending far beyond the borders of Tibet, to the Kalmuk region of Russia near the Caspian Sea in the west, to Siberia in the north, to the western reaches of Mongolia and Manchuria in the east, and to the Sherpa regions of Nepal in the south. This religious tradition is properly referred to as Tibetan Buddhism, rather than "Lamaism," an anachronistic and pejorative term that mistakenly suggests that the religion of Tibet is not Buddhism. It is, therefore, perfectly acceptable to refer to a Mongol, for example, as a Tibetan Buddhist, much as one might say that a Spaniard is a Roman Catholic.

Buddhist thought, practice, and institutions were imported into Tibet beginning in the seventh century from the neighboring cultures of China, Central Asia, and most importantly, India. From that point, Buddhism in Tibet developed rapidly, with the early centuries marked by contacts with influential Buddhist figures of Kashmir and northern India. Tibetan Buddhist thought thus sees itself as an inheritance from India, although there have also been important influences from China and Central Asia.

The history of the introduction of Buddhism into Tibet is traditionally discussed in terms of two periods, referred to as the earlier dissemination of the doctrine and the later dissemination of the doctrine. The first period began in the latter half of the seventh century and saw the first translation of Buddhist texts from Sanskrit into Tibetan, the establishment of the first Buddhist monasteries, and the support of Buddhism by the noble families. The first dissemination ended with a suppression of monastic institutions by King Lang Darma (Glang dar ma) in 836. The second dissemination began over a century later, in the latter half of the tenth century, and was marked by the translation of many more texts, led by a steady stream of Tibetans who went to India to study, sometimes inviting their teachers back to Tibet. The lineages of teaching established between India and Tibet during this second period gave rise to the major sects of Tibetan Buddhism.

The relatively late date of the introduction of Buddhism to Tibet compared to China (first century CE) and Japan (fifth century) had important ramifications for the development of the Tibetan Buddhist tradition, the foremost being that the Tibetans had access to large bodies of Indian Buddhist literature that either never were translated into Chinese (and thus never transmitted to Japan) or which had little influence in East Asia. This literature fell into two categories: tantras and shastras (*śāstras*).

The origins of tantric Buddhism in India remain nebulous, with some scholars dating the early texts from the fourth century CE. Its literature, including all manner of ritual texts and meditation manuals, as well as exegetical works, continued to be composed in India for the next six centuries. This literature offered a speedy path to enlightenment, radically truncating the eons-long path set forth in the earlier discourses attributed to the Buddha, called sutras (*sūtras*). To this end, the tantric literature set forth a wide range of techniques for the attainment of goals both mundane and supramundane, techniques for bringing the fantastic worlds described in the sutras into actuality. Tantric practices were considered so potent that they were often conducted in secret, and aspirants required initiation. The practices themselves involved elaborate and meticulous visualizations, in which the practitioner mentally transformed himself or herself into a fully enlightened buddha, with a resplendent body seated on a throne in the center of a marvelous palace (called a mandala), with speech that intoned sacred syllables (called mantras), and with a mind that saw the ultimate reality directly.

A second body of literature, more important for Buddhist philosophy per se, were the shastras (treatises). Buddhist literature is sometimes divided into sutras, those texts traditionally held to be either the word of the Buddha or spoken with his sanction, and shastras, treatises composed by Indian commentators. In the case of Mahayana literature, sutras often contain fantastic visions of worlds populated by enlightened beings, with entrance to such a world gained through devotion to the sutra itself. When points of doctrine are presented, it is often in the form of narrative, allegory, or the repetition of stock phrases. The shastras are closer to what might be called systematic philosophy, with positions presented with reasoned argumentation supported by relevant passages from the sutras. East Asian Buddhism was predominantly a sutra-based tradition, with schools forming around single texts, as in the case of such as the *Lotus Sutra* and the *Avatamsaka Sutra*. Many important shastras were translated into Chinese. But the major project of translating Indian texts into Chinese virtually ended with the work of Xuanzang (596–664), by whose time the major East Asian schools were well-formed. Consequently, works by such figures as the Middle Way philosophers Candrakīrti (*c*.600–650) and the logician Dharmakīrti (seventh century), who flourished when the Chinese Buddhist schools had already developed, never gained wide currency in East Asia but were highly influential in Tibet. The works by these and other authors became the basis of the scholastic tradition in Tibet, which from the early period was a shastra-based Buddhism. Sutras were venerated but rarely read independently; the shastras were studied and commented upon at great length.

The eleventh and twelfth centuries, the period of the second dissemination of Buddhism in Tibet, was a period of active translation of numerous philosophical texts and the retranslation of texts, especially tantras, first translated during the period of the earlier dissemination. The eleventh century was a time of active travel of Tibetan translators to India, where they studied with Indian Buddhist masters in Bihar, Bengal, and Kashmir, and many of the sects of Tibetan Buddhism trace their lineages back to these encounters. For example, the Kagyu (Bka' 'rgyud) sect derives its lineage from the visits to India by Mar-pa the Translator (1012–1099), where he studied under several of the famous tantric masters of the day, including Nāropa and Maitripa. Mar-pa's disciple Milarepa (Mi la ras pa) is said to have achieved buddhahood in one lifetime (an achievement usually considered to require eons of practice) through his diligent meditation practice in the caves of southern Tibet, despite having committed murder as a youth through the practice of black magic. His moving biography and didactic songs are among the most famous works of Tibetan literature.[1] The Sakya (Sa skya) sect looks back to another translator, Drok mi ('Brog mi Shakya Ye shes, 993–1050), who studied in India under disciples of the tantric master Virupa. It was the Sakya scholar Bu dön (Bu-ston, 1290–1364) who systematized the various collections of Indian Buddhist texts circulating in Tibet into the well-known Kangyur (*bka' 'gyur*, literally, "translation of the word [of the Buddha]") and the Tengyur (*bstan 'gyur*, literally "translation of the shastras"). The most famous Indian scholar to visit Tibet during the second dissemination was the Bengali master Atisha (Atiśa, 982–1054), whose followers became the Kadampa (bKa' gdams pa) sect, regarded as a forerunner of the Gelukpa (Dge lugs pa).

The period of the thirteenth through fifteenth centuries was among the most consequential for the history of Tibetan Buddhism, with the development of distinct sects that evolved from the various lineages of teaching that had been initiated during the previous periods. These sects are traditionally divided under two major headings: those who base their tantric practice on texts translated during the period of the first dissemination and those who base their tantric practice on texts translated or retranslated during the period of the second dissemination. These two groups are referred to simply as the old (*rnying ma*) and the new (*gsar ma*), with the old obviously including the Nyingmapa (Rnying ma pa) sect and the new including the Kagyu, Sakya, and Geluk. The Nyingmapa sect traces its origins back to the first dissemination and the teachings of Padmasambhava who visited Tibet during the eighth century. "Treasures" (*gter ma*), texts believed to have been hidden by him, began to be discovered in the eleventh century and continued to be discovered even into the twentieth century; the fourteenth century was an especially active period for the text discoverers (*gter ston*). According to their claim, these texts were sometimes discovered in physical form, often within stone, or mentally, within the mind of the discoverer.

During the Mongol Yuan dynasty (1260–1368), Tibetan Buddhism played an important role at the court of Khubilai Khan, where the emperor's Buddhist preceptor was the famous monk Pakpa ('Phags pa, d. 1280) of the Sakya sect, and imperial titles were bestowed also on monks of the Kagyu sect. Under the Ming dynasty (1368–1644), Chinese emperors continued to confer gifts and titles on lamas of the Kagyu, Sakya, and Geluk sects. However, during the Qing (1644–1912), especially from the time of the Kangxi emperor (r. 1661–1722), imperial favor was directed especially toward the Gelukpas.

Unlike the other major sects of Tibetan Buddhism, the Gelukpas do not identify a specific Indian master as the source of their tradition, although they see themselves as inheriting the tradition of Atisha, the Bengali scholar mentioned above who arrived in Tibet in 1042. The preeminent figure for the sect (who may only retrospectively be identified as the "founder") is Tsong kha pa (1357–1419). While known in the west primarily as a reformer, apparently because of his commitment to monasticism, Tsong kha pa was also a creative and controversial interpreter of Buddhist philosophy. In his less technical works, he said that all of Buddhist practice could be encompassed under the categories of renunciation, the compassionate aspiration to liberate all beings from suffering, and the understanding that all phenomena are devoid of substantial or independent existence. He left a massive corpus of writings on a wide variety of topics, his most famous works being two compendia of practice, one detailing the esoteric path to enlightenment, the *Great Exposition of the Stages of the Path to Enlightenment* (*Lam rim chen mo*), and the other detailing the esoteric or tantric path, the *Great Exposition of the Stages of Mantra* (*sNgags rim chen mo*). Tsong kha pa founded the monastery of Ganden (dGa' ldan, named after the Buddhist heaven Tushita) outside of Lhasa in 1409, and his followers were originally known as the Gandenpas. This eventually evolved to Gelukpa, the "system of virtue." The Gelukpas established large monastic universities throughout Tibet and Mongolia, one of which, Drepung ('Bras spung), was the largest Buddhist monastery in the world, with over 13,000 monks in 1959. Tsong kha pa's stature, which was considerable during his lifetime (eliciting an invitation to visit the Ming court, which he declined), was only enhanced by the subsequent political ascendancy of his followers through the institution of the Dalai Lama.

It is a tenet of Tibetan Buddhism that enlightened beings are not limited to the form of the Buddha with which we are familiar; a buddha is able to appear in whatever form, animate or inanimate, that is appropriate to benefit the suffering world. Tibetans believe not only that enlightened beings take rebirth in the world out of their infinite compassion, but that such beings can be identified at birth. These beings, called incarnate lamas or tulkus (*sprul sku*), are said to have complete control over their rebirth, choosing the time, the place, and the parents in advance, so that a dying incarnation will often leave instructions for his disciples as to where to find the baby he will become.

Since the fourteenth century, all sects of Tibetan Buddhism have adopted the practice of identifying the successive rebirths of a great teacher; there were some three thousand lines of incarnation in Tibet (the vast majority of whom are male). The institution of the incarnate lama came to be a central component of Tibetan society, providing the means by which authority and charisma, in all of their symbolic and material forms, were passed from one generation to another. Indeed, the spread of Tibetan Buddhism can be mapped historically across the increasingly large geographical areas in which incarnate lamas are discovered, beginning in Mongolia, Nepal, and China, extending today to Europe and North America.

In the sixteenth century, one of the incarnate lamas of Tibetan Buddhism of the Geluk sect was named Sonam Gyatso (Bsod nams rgya mtsho), "Merit Ocean." He was believed to be the third incarnation of a great scholar of the previous century, Tsong kha pa's disciple, Gedun Drup (dGe 'dun grub, 1391–1474). In 1578 Sonam Gyatso was summoned to the court of the formidable Mongol chieftain, the Altan Khan. Translating Sonam Gyatso's name into Mongolian, the Altan Khan bestowed upon him the title of "Dalai" (meaning "ocean" in Mongolian) Lama. Only at this point did the two deceased predecessors of the third incarnation become retroactively the first and second Dalai Lamas. In recognition of his patronage at a time when the Geluk sect was being persecuted in Tibet, the Altan Khan was rewarded when, upon the death of the third Dalai Lama, the fourth incarnation was discovered to be the Altan Khan's grand-nephew.

The fifth Dalai Lama (1617–1682) was the first Dalai Lama to assume temporal control of Tibet, aided by the troops of the Khoshuut Mongol chief, Gushri Khan. He also consolidated his power mythologically, declaring himself to be not only the incarnation of the previous Dalai Lamas, but also as the incarnation of the great Tibetan kings of the seventh and eighth centuries who had established Buddhism in Tibet. In addition, the fifth Dalai Lama identified himself as the present incarnation of the bodhisattva Avalokiteshvara, the embodiment of compassion, who according to myth was the progenitor of the Tibetan people: Avalokiteshvara had taken the form of a monkey in order to mate with an ogress, their offspring the first Tibetans. By identifying himself with Avalokiteshvara, the Dalai Lama became the human manifestation of the cosmic Bodhisattva of Compassion. He was, in short, no longer just another Geluk tulku. He was a divine king.

According to ancient chronicles, Tibet had once been ruled by a lineage of kings, the first seven of whom descended from the heavens by means of a cord or ladder. Each king ruled until the time when his first son was old enough to ride a horse, at which point the king returned to heaven via the rope. As a literal descendant of heaven, the king was the embodiment and protector of the cosmic order and the welfare of the state. The king's stable presence on the throne thus insured harmony in the realm. There was a trinity of the king, head priest, and chief minister, with the active power of government in the hands of the head priest and the minister who represented the priestly hierarchy and the clan nobility. The king, endowed with magical power, represented the continually reborn essence of the divine ancestor, who was reincarnated in each king at the age of maturity and remained incarnated in him until his son reached the same age and ascended the throne.

With the fifth Dalai Lama's investiture, Tibet once again had a king, with the power and authority that had once descended in the form of the ancient kings arrogated to the Dalai Lama. This ancient model helps to account both for the institution of the incarnate lama and for the fact that after the fifth Dalai Lama, Tibet did not have a powerful divine ruler for two hundred years. During that period, the Dalai Lama was little more than a symbolic presence and, like the ancient kings, did not rule for long, ascending to the pure land (often aided, it is rumored, by the regent's poison), to descend again in the form of a child, during whose minority the regent continued to rule.

The fifth Dalai Lama also declared his own teacher to be an incarnation of Amitabha, the Buddha of Infinite Light, and Avalokiteshvara's teacher, bestowing upon him the title of Panchen Lama, establishing a new line of incarnation, which was to have its seat at Tashilhunpo (Bkra shis lhun po) monastery in Tsang province. From that point on, the Dalai Lama and Panchen Lama were to alternate as teacher and student in successive lifetimes. In practice, they were sometimes allies and sometimes rivals. The fifth Dalai Lama moved the capital back to Lhasa, the seat of the ancient kings, and built his palace there, a massive edifice called the Potala, taking its name from Potalaka, the name of Avalokiteshvara's palace.

During the eighteenth and nineteenth centuries, the Gelukpas maintained their political control over Central Tibet, with the occasional aid of the Manchu rulers of China. Especially from the time of the Kangxi emperor, imperial favor was directed largely toward the Gelukpas. For a variety of reasons, the leading Geluk figures, and hence the object of Manchu interests during this period, were the Panchen Lamas, notably the third Panchen Lama (1737–1780), who visited the Qianlong emperor at Chengde in 1780. A key figure in the arrangement of this important visit was the Geluk incarnate lama, the second Jang gya khutukhtu, Rolpai Dorje (Lcang skya Rol pa'i rdo rje, 1717–1786). His previous incarnation, known as the first Jang gya khutuktu (1642–1715), had been a religious advisor to the Kangxi emperor. The second Jang gya, born in the Tsongkha region of Amdo (near present-day Lanzhou), was taken as a boy to

Beijing on the order of the Yongzheng emperor (r. 1723–1735). He was raised at the court, where he became friends with Prince Hungli, who would become the Qianlong emperor. Jang gya remained an advisor and religious preceptor to the emperor throughout his reign.

Having provided a brief history of the development of Tibetan Buddhism, it is perhaps useful to offer a summary of some of its basic doctrines and practices. Tibetans share with all Buddhists a belief in a cycle of beginningless rebirth called samsara, where beings are reborn according to the law of karma. In brief, virtuous actions, such as charity and preserving life, result in happiness in the future, while non-virtuous deeds of body (such as murder), speech (such as lying), and mind (such as wishing others ill) result in suffering. The effects of these deeds not only determine the experiences of the present life but also determine where one will be reborn after death. There are six possible places of rebirth: the realms of gods, demigods, humans, animals, hungry ghosts, and hell beings. These realms vary in their degrees of pleasure and pain, with gods experiencing the greatest pleasure and hell beings the greatest pain. One is reborn as a god, demigod, or human as a result of virtuous deeds in the past. One is reborn as an animal, hungry ghost, or hell being as a result of non-virtue. Although rebirth as a human or a god is therefore regarded as relatively desirable, the goal of the Buddhist path is to take advantage of one's rebirth as a human to escape entirely from the cycle and to put an end to suffering and future rebirth forever. This state beyond suffering is called nirvana. In the early Buddhist tradition, the goal seems to have been for each person to strive for his or her own liberation from rebirth. With the rise of the Mahayana, the goal was expanded to include the liberation of all beings.

Although the various sects of Tibetan Buddhism derive their monastic regulations from the Indian schools known pejoratively as the Hinayana ("Lesser Vehicle"), all schools of Tibetan Buddhism identify themselves as proponents of the Mahayana, both in their practice and in their philosophy. Mahayana, a Sanskrit word which means "Great Vehicle," is the term used to distinguish a rather disparate group of cults of the book that arose in India some four hundred years after the death of the Buddha and which continued in India into the twelfth century. During these centuries, the followers of the Mahayana produced a vast literature of sutras that purport to be the word of the historical Buddha, as well as commentaries upon them. Reflected in these works are developments in Buddhist philosophy and practice. Among the factors characteristic of the Mahayana are the view of the Buddha as an eternal presence, associated physically with reliquaries (stupas) and with texts which embody his words, a belief in the existence of myriad buddhas working in multiple universes for the benefit of all beings, and an attendant emphasis on the universal possibility of enlightenment for all, monks and laypeople alike. It is from this last tenet that the term "Great Vehicle" is derived: the proponents of the Mahayana believed that their path was capable of bringing all beings in the universe to buddhahood whereas the earlier teachings were capable only of delivering the individual disciple to a state of solitary peace. Despite its claims to superiority and its massive literature, the reports of Chinese pilgrims to India suggest that the Mahayana remained a minority movement throughout its history in India.

Perhaps the most famous feature of the Mahayana is its emphasis on the bodhisattva, a person who makes the compassionate vow to become a buddha in order to lead all beings in the universe out of suffering and to the bliss of enlightenment. The Sanskrit term *bodhisattva* was rendered into Tibetan as "one who is heroic in his or her aspiration to enlightenment" (*byang chub sems dpa'*). The path of the bodhisattva is portrayed as one of extraordinary length, encompassing billions of lifetimes devoted to cultivating such virtues as generosity, ethics, patience, effort, concentration, and wisdom, the so-called six perfections, all of these deeds motivated by the wish to liberate all beings from the beginningless cycle of rebirth.

A common tenet of Buddhism is that all suffering is ultimately the result of ignorance. This ignorance is defined as a belief in self. Mahayana philosophy expands upon earlier teachings to see ignorance as not simply a misconception concerning the nature of the person, but as a misunderstanding of all things. According to the Middle Way school, the fundamental error is to conceive of things as existing in and of themselves – independently, autonomously, possessed of some intrinsic nature, some inherent existence. Wisdom, the sixth of the perfections to be cultivated by the bodhisattva, is the understanding that all things, including persons, are utterly devoid of such a nature and are, in fact, empty of an independent status, although they exist conventionally. Emptiness does not mean that things do not exist at all, but rather that they do not exist as they appear to the unenlightened. To say that things exist conventionally means, for example, that cause and effect remain viable and that things perform functions; one can sit on a chair and drink tea from a cup.

The practice of the Mahayana generally may be said to take two forms, both focused on the bodhisattva. The most influential of the Mahayana sutras, such as the *Lotus Sutra*, proclaim that all beings will eventually becomes buddhas and that, consequently, all beings will traverse the bodhisattva path. Thus, one form of Mahayana belief emphasizes practices for becoming a bodhisattva and performing the bodhisattva's deeds. As bodhisattvas advance along the path, they become increasingly adept at allaying the sufferings of sentient beings who call upon them for aid, often through miraculous intercession. Consequently, the other major form of Mahayana practice is concerned with devotions intended to procure the aid of these compassionate beings. The bodhisattva who is said to be the physical manifestation of all the compassion of all the buddhas in the universe, Avalokiteshvara, is the particular object of such reverence in Tibet, where it is believed that this bodhisattva takes successive human births as the Dalai Lama. Avalokiteshvara is invoked by the famous mantra *oṃ maṇi padme hūṃ*, which means, "O you who hold the jewel and the lotus [have mercy on us.]" Avalokiteshvara is depicted in a wide variety of forms in Tibetan art, two of the most frequent being with one head and four arms or with eleven heads and a thousand arms. The multiple arms are said to represent the bodhisattva's extraordinary ability to come to the aid of suffering sentient beings. Paintings of the thousand-armed Avalokiteshvara often show an eye in the palm of each of the hands. The bodhisattva thus serves as both role model and object of devotion in Mahayana Buddhism, functions that are by no means deemed mutually exclusive; it is quite common for persons who consider themselves to have embarked on the bodhisattva path to seek the assistance of more advanced bodhisattvas in their long quest for enlightenment.

In the realm of Buddhist practice, the Tibetans were able to witness and assimilate the most important development of late Indian Buddhism, Buddhist tantra. Tantra, known also as the *vajrayāna*, the "Diamond Vehicle" and the *mantrayāna*, the "Mantra Vehicle," was considered an esoteric approach to the Mahayana path whereby the length of time required to achieve buddhahood could be abbreviated from the standard length of three periods of countless eons to as little as three years and three months. As already mentioned, the chief technique for effecting such an extraordinary reduction in the length of the path was an elaborate system of ritual, visualization, and meditation, sometimes called deity yoga, in which the practitioner imagined himself or herself to be already fully enlightened with the marvelous body, speech, mind, and abode of a buddha. In addition to the ultimate attainment of buddhahood, tantric practice was said to bestow a wide range of lesser magical powers, such as the power to increase wealth and life span, to pacify the inauspicious, and to destroy enemies, both human and non-human. Yogins who developed these powers were known as *mahāsiddhas*, "great adepts."

An essential feature of Tibetan Buddhist meditation, especially in the realm of tantra, is the practice of visualization. In any tantric meditation rite, the meditator would begin by imagining an elaborate array of buddhas, bodhisattvas, and deities in the space in front of him or her, to whom would be presented (in imagination) wondrous offerings. In many forms of tantric practice, the meditator would eventually visualize himself or herself as a particular buddha or bodhisattva. It was essential that the visualization be carried out in precise detail, with each item of silk clothing and gold ornament appearing clearly. It was also necessary for the meditator to imagine the fantastic palace of the buddha, the mandala, which he or she inhabited, noting the particular bodhisattvas, protectors, gods, and goddesses located throughout the multi-storied dwelling.

Among the elements of tantric Buddhism most commonly identified in the west are its erotic and wrathful motifs, where male and female are depicted in sexual union, and bull-headed deities, adorned with garlands of human heads, brandish cleavers and skullcups. In Mahayana Buddhism, as already mentioned, wisdom and compassion (also referred to as method, that is, the compassionate means whereby bodhisattvas become buddhas), are the essential components of the bodhisattva's path to buddhahood. We have already noted that wisdom, especially the perfection of wisdom, is identified with the female. In tantra, the symbolism is rendered in more explicitly sexual terms, with wisdom as female and method male, their union being essential to the achievement of enlightenment. Buddhist tantra is said to be the "Diamond Vehicle" because wisdom and method are joined in an adamantine and indivisible union, bestowing buddhahood quickly. This is the chief symbolic meaning of the depiction of sexual union. However, part of the unique nature of the tantric path is its capacity to employ deeds that are ordinarily prohibited into practices that speed progress on the path to enlightenment, hence the great emphasis on anti-nomian behavior, such as the consumption of meat and alcohol, in the hagiographies of the *mahāsiddhas*. One such deed is sexual intercourse and many tantric texts, especially of the Unexcelled Yoga variety, prescribe ritual union as a means of unifying the mind of the clear light and the immutable bliss. Whether this intercourse is to be performed only in imag-mation or in fact, and at what point on the path it is to take place, has been a point of considerable discussion in Tibetan tantric exegesis.

Wrathful deities also populate the Tibetan Buddhist pantheon. Despite claims by nineteenth-century scholars which continue to be repeated, the most important of these deities are not of Tibetan shamanic origin, added to Indian Buddhism after its arrival in Tibet. It is clear from Indian tantric texts that these deities derive directly from Indian Buddhist tantra. Some of these deities are buddhas and bodhisattvas in their wrathful aspects, the most famous of these being Yamantaka, the wrathful manifestation of the Bodhisattva of Wisdom, Manjushri. His terrifying form is said to be intended to frighten away the egotism and selfishness that are the cause of all suffering. Yamantaka (especially in his "sole hero" aspect in which he has no consort) is a favorite tutelary deity of the Gelukpas, and monks imagine themselves in meditation as bearing his form. Other wrathful deities have the task of protecting the dharma, others are worldly deities with specific powers which may be propitiated.

An important part of the daily practice of a Tibetan Buddhist is the making of offerings to a buddha, bodhisattva, or a particular deity, and an image of that deity was therefore employed for that purpose. Images of wrathful deities were believed to offer protection to their owners and various deities, whose powers were of the more mundane variety, such as the god of wealth, were depicted and venerated for the boons they could bestow. Images were not considered to be merely symbolic representa-tions, because each statue and thangka after its completion would be consecrated, often in an elaborate ceremony, in the belief that the prin-ciple of enlightenment called the Truth Body of the Buddha (*dharmakāya*) would come to inhabit the image. In the case of statues, the consecration ceremony required that the inside of a hollow image be filled with scrolls of mantras and various sacred substances and then sealed.

It would be a mistake to see these beings as entirely symbolic, however. Tibetans have traditionally seen their world as populated by good and evil spirits who must be negotiated with through a variety of ritual practices. Nor was this a belief confined simply to the illiterate populace. The Tibetan authors who are regarded as preeminent scholars were, in most cases, Buddhist monks, much of whose lives were spent either in the performance of tantric ritual or in various sophisticated forms of meditation, in an effort to manifest a fantastic world of benign and malevolent forces, propitiating deities and repelling demons. What we might term "philosophy" or "art" was but one concern of these authors; a perusal of the titles in the collected works of any of Tibet's most erudite thinkers reveals that among the commentaries on Indian logical treatises and expositions of emptiness are myriad works devoted to tantric ceremonies and visualizations, along with instructions on techniques for drawing mandalas, making rain, stopping smallpox, and manufacturing magical pills.

Note

1   Mi-la-ras-pa, *The Hundred Thousand Songs of Milarepa*.

4 Architectural wonderland

An empire of fictions

Anne Chayet

Something happened in Jehol (Chengde),[1] north of the Great Wall, at the beginning of the eighteenth century. The Manchu emperors Kangxi and Qianlong built a summer residence consisting of a palace, a magnificent garden reproducing various famous sceneries of China, then eight temples surrounding its enclosure. Its many splendors, symbolizing the powerful empire, were meant to impress the Mongol princes invited to the imperial hunting parties, as well as Tibetan Buddhist lamas, and were part of the Qing dynasty's policy of conquest. By the mid-eighteenth century Tibet was a Qing protectorate.[2] Nevertheless, the strategic and political importance of Jehol did not endure long beyond the eighteenth century, when Qing emperors reached the zenith of their glory. Jehol was an instrument of their power, but it might also have been a factor in their decline.

Kangxi achieved the Manchu conquest of China in spite of the Rebellion of the Three Feudatories (1673–81). Rightly or wrongly, he suspected that Tibet had supported the rebellion. But he then faced another threat: Galdan, khan of the Zunghars, had attacked his Khalkha allies and endangered the empire. Kangxi may reasonably have feared an alliance between Tibet and Galdan;[3] and also an alliance between Galdan and Russia and even a triple alliance against the Qing. He negotiated with Russia, fought the Zunghars, then in 1696 defeated Galdan. The same year, he first discovered (or pretended to discover) that the Dalai Lama had died fourteen years earlier and that his successor had been chosen and brought up secretly.

A good hunter, Kangxi had thus successively caught all his prey: first Wu Sangui, then Galdan, while he played for time with the Russians and Tibetans. Then (in 1701) he sent the imperial armies to Tibet's eastern borderlands and initiated a policy of territorial annexation.[4] He undoubtedly had an expansionist conception of the empire.

In 1703, Kangxi ordered the building of the Bishu shanzhuang in Jehol.

It has often been said that Qing emperors considered the Bishu shanzhuang a reflection of the empire and, thus, that the mountains to the west of the Qing territory are figured by the picturesque hills that surround the summer residence. But Kangxi selected only classical Chinese models for the thirty-six views that he created in his park. He chose them after traveling in southern China following the end of the Three Feudatories rebellion. Did he view Tibet, Mongolia and the future Xinjiang as lying *outside* his empire and thus exclude their sceneries from a monument dedicated to the glorification of Chinese tradition? Probably not.

Another question arises as to why he built this summer residence in Jehol and not in the Beijing region, where earlier dynasties, including the Jin and the Liao, had their summer retreats, or in the favored hunting grounds of Mulan. In fact, since 1690 Kangxi had enjoyed the Changchun yuan residence northwest of Beijing and also the small hunting fields of the Xiangshan, not far from there. But Kangxi also kept the Manchu tradition of autumnal hunting parties in the mountainous region of Mulan, about 350 kilometers north of Beijing.[5] The Jiaqing emperor, who died in Jehol in 1820 and was the last Qing emperor to hunt in Mulan, wrote in his *Mulan ji* (Account of Mulan), "autumnal hunting is a tradition of our dynasty. Our purpose is the pacification of remote tribes."[6] With the Bishu shanzhuang representing the pacification of south China, the Kangxi emperor was considering new hunting fields, new fields of pacification. Hunting in Mulan, with an escort of 20,000 to 30,000 men, was a good opportunity to impress his guests (mainly Mongol princes) with the power of the Qing emperor. Mulan itself was not appropriate for a summer residence, lying too far from Beijing to allow regular supply of workers, and too close to the still unconquered fields of the Western Mongols and the new Russian settlements. Jehol, a convenient halting place halfway between the Great Wall and Mulan, while still clearly in the northern regions, was preferable in both these respects. The Jehol region was also a good place for hunting, and the climate was pleasant in summer (Figure 2).

In his Mountain Villa, Kangxi built simple and elegant pavilions of *nanmu* wood covered with plain grey tiles, blending into the surrounding woods (Figure 7). Manchu emperors received a classical Chinese education. They knew what *tianxia* meant, namely, the world, with China at its center. But *tianxia* also invokes images of the legendary Kunlun mountain, large at the top and narrow at the base, like the famous Bangchui rock of Jehol (Figure 11), and thus a sense of the periphery as well as the center. In this periphery around China was an outer circle of barbarians. The emperor's mission was to protect the empire against bad law and bad people, including barbarians, and to prevent their noxious activity.

The main features of the Jehol landscape are hills, alluvial plains and deserts; they are the features of the Bishu shanzhuang: wooded hills, a "plain" where yurts were disposed when the emperor received his guests (Figures 3, 8, 10), and lakes (in place of deserts), like the empty spaces of the classical Chinese painting. These also are the components of the empire.

A miniature garden is a landscape in the Chinese sense of the word: *shanshui*, mountains and waters. It is an enclosed composition of water, rocks or stones, often, but not always, including carefully chosen trees, which bear the deep symbolism of seclusion, longevity, fertility and immortality.[7] It is a reduction of what the world should be in an ideal order, in an ideal empire.

At first sight, Jehol, palace and park, seems to conform with this garden ideal. A second look, however, reveals that the walls enclosing the park are very imposing, certainly more so than the walls of the Yihe yuan (Summer Palace in Beijing). The Yihe yuan, in spite of its imperial importance, is built behind walls little different from those of an ordinary aristocratic pleasure garden. The Bishu shanzhuang wall is a miniature of the Ming period Great Wall, winding up and down the hills, visible from everywhere. Its meaning exceeds the mere intention to enclose a classical garden: Jehol is a reduced image of the empire pacified by Kangxi, and to protect its imperial host, includes its Great Wall. Later, another (real?) enclosure of the Jehol summer residence took form in the incomplete circle of the Waiba miao (Figure 4). By the end of Qianlong's reign, the Outer Temples formed an enclosure lying in the natural hills and sceneries surrounding the palace. From the highest hilltop pavilions in the park (Figure 10), the emperor could view the western mountains of his empire, at least symbolically.

The entire region speaks fluently in the idiom of the classical Chinese garden. There are many curious rocks and caves around Jehol, especially in the Yanshan Hills. The most famous of these formations is the Bangchui or Qingchui (Figure 11), resembling an inverted club, to the east of the Bishu shanzhuang. In a classical garden, a narrow margin separates what is good or ill-omen. It is dangerous to reveal too much of stones and rocks – reputed to be the bones of the soil.[8] Coming back to the Bishu shanzhuang park, the pines and the beautiful, fragrant *nanmu* wood of the pillars in the principal hall remind us that pine and rock are thought to share the same inner nature. The tree breaks its way out through the stone, which becomes dust; but after three thousand years, the pine becomes a stone itself.[9] We are led back to a scholarly sensibility and this other possible symbolism of the summer residence.

The original Chinese models of the thirty-six views established by Kangxi in his park are well known, as are those of the thirty-six views Qianlong added to his grandfather's scheme. It is possible to trace some lines of the geomantic organization of the park and between the Bishu shanzhuang and its hilly outer enclosure. There is a link between the Bangchui rock, the Pule temple and the Jinshan Pavilion in the residence (Figures 4, 18). In addition to the links between the inner and outer circles of the Bishu shanzhuang, between Kangxi's and Qianlong's creations, there are also links between the inner and outer circles of the empire; Philippe Forêt noticed such a connection between the Jinshan north of Mukden, the beautiful Jinshan pavilion in the Bishu shanzhuang park, and the Jinshan in Jiangsu.[10] The Jinshan thema can, then, be considered a rehearsal for the later Potala scheme (see p. 40), which likewise has multiple reference points both in China and Inner Asia. Kangxi – a barbarian Manchu in some people's eyes, but nonetheless emperor of China – wanted a Chinese temple to be built in his garden, a garden that lay outside the traditional frontier, in a barbarian land he made no longer barbarian. The model was Chinese but Kangxi already had a site of the same name in the ancestral country of the Manchus. Now where was the true Jinshan? Where was the fiction?

Many of the connections between the Bishu shanzhuang and the inner part of the empire – China – derive from classical tradition and allusions concerning the art of the garden, a common philosophy inherited from both Taoism and Confucianism. Buddhist elements in the tradition of gardens and miniature gardens are less numerous. Qianlong built three Buddhist temples inside the Bishu shanzhuang enclosure: Bifeng si; Zhuyuan si, with its bronze pavilion costing 65,000 silver taels; and Yongyou si (built between 1751 and 1764) with the Liuhe ta pagoda that collapsed and had to be rebuilt for 209,000 silver taels.[11] Qianlong also constructed a Confucian temple in the new town, west of the palace (Figure 20). In 1713, on the eastern bank of the Wulie River, Kangxi built only two modest Buddhist temples for his Mongol guests (said to have been built *by* the Mongol princes for the emperor's birthday – this fiction was the beginning of a diplomatic tradition).[12] If the Qing emperors had built only these temples (the Daoist Jinshan, the Confucian temple, and the Buddhist temples on the Wulie and Qianlong's inside the park) they would have done no more than prove their respect for the *Sanjiao*, the three (more or less) religious traditions of China.

But Kangxi's building of the first two "outer" temples for Mongols in 1713 provided a first indication that his policy was to rely, after strong military action, on the use of fictive forces, apparent tolerance and respect of faith. His son Yongzheng had no liking for Jehol and never used the place, but he did not give up the "temple policy" initiated by Kangxi, and himself established many Buddhist foundations in Mongolia, especially in Khalkha regions. One of the most important and most significant from an architectural point of view was the Amarbayasgalan monastery.[13] Qianlong had too much respect and veneration for his grandfather Kangxi to neglect his policies, hence he immediately played his part. We have already seen that he played it lavishly.

Peace with the Russians was restored after the Treaty of Kiakhta in 1727. But the Zunghars remained a dangerous nuisance. They invaded and plundered central Tibet in 1717–20, and to counter them the Qing had sent a rescue army. Two representatives (*amban*) of the Manchu emperor and a garrison took up permanent residence at Lhasa. At least from a military point of view, Tibet was to be part of the empire until the end of the dynasty. The Zunghars were not content with the loot from Tibet which they had placed in their temple in Yili (Ghulja), and their agitation exasperated Qianlong until he decided to put an end to it. The Qing destroyed the Zunghars, savagely, between 1755 and 1758. In 1759–60, the now nearly deserted Yili region was incorporated as part of what would be called the Xinjiang region.[14]

Qianlong also seemed partial to fictive forces. In spite of his merciless edicts, he never personally led a party to hunt the Zunghars. However, in addition to a new palace, thirty-six new views in the park and various temples in the Mountain Villa compound and in the boom-town of Jehol, between 1755 and 1780 he completed construction of the Waiba miao, fleshing out the scheme begun by Kangxi.

In spite of their number, the temples do not form a complete enclosure. There may be several reasons for this irregular layout (see Figure 4). As far as I know, there was no original and complete plan for the Waiba miao that might prove the fashionable theory that the palace and temple complex comprise a mandala (on mandalas, see Lopez, Chapter 3). As far as the main deities of the temples have been identified and are concerned, it would have been a really bewildering mandala in any case. In fact, other reasons adequately explain the disposition of the temples: there is not much room between the Bishu shanzhuang wall and the hills, and as the river Wulie has a bad record of sudden and destructive floods, this did not leave much convenient land to build on. The sometimes disconcerting imperatives of *fengshui* (geomantic rules) may be another reason for the irregularity of the general setting.[15] Finally, the fact that most of the temples were built to commemorate various unpredictable political and familial events provides further evidence that the temples were not part of a preconceived mandala.

In searching to explain the temples, we must remember that Qianlong was a student of Tibetan Buddhism. He was Manjushri – which was not new in China.[16] He probably appreciated the parallel drawn between his relationship with Jang gya and that of Khubilai Khan with Pakpa ('Phags pa). It is important to keep in mind the Tibetan notion of *mchod yon* (lama–patron) relations, including their evolution through time.[17]

But Buddhism was not the exclusive factor underlying the temples. As Qianlong built several temples, including one in Jehol for his beloved mother, filiality can also be set forth as a reason. Moreover, he frequently evoked as a major source of inspiration the attitude and policy of his revered grandfather Kangxi, who built temples for the Mongols in many northern parts of his empire.[18]

The Eight Outer Temples were, in fact, twelve in total; in order of construction they were Puren si and Pushan si (built by Kangxi), then Puning si, Puyou si, Anyuan miao, Pule si, Putuozongcheng miao, Guang'an si, Shuxiang si, Luohan tang, Xumifushou miao and Anguo si.[19] If we examine them in this order we can see very different sources of inspiration, very different political reasons, sometimes very peculiar amalgams, and an astonishing display of wealth. In 1755, the Mongol lands were close to complete pacification, and Tibet, after a rebellion immediately put down by imperial forces (1750) was, theoretically at least, a religious conservatory for the pious Mongol vassals of the emperor. Qianlong seems to have considered fictive forces as or more valuable than armed forces, for he spent lavishly on the Waiba miao.

Puning si (Figure 16) was built in 1755, by which time the complete destruction of the Zunghars (four years later), was easily predictable. The chosen model for Puning was Samye (Bsam yas), the oldest Tibetan monastery, founded by the end of the eighth century. The central temple in Samye, the Utse (dBu rtse), consists of three levels of which the ground floor is traditionally considered to be in Tibetan style, the second floor in Chinese style and, because Buddhism comes from India and rises above everything, the top floor in Indian style. In spite of the three-part stylistic division, the general model of Samye is said to be Indian. In his foundation inscription to Puning si, Qianlong insisted that the Indian and the Jehol plans were identical, while implying that the Tibetan version was ambiguous, as if insinuating that there was no more legitimacy in the Tibetan models than in the present building.

The door and first halls of the Puning si are built in "Chinese style," whereas the main hall (Dasheng ge) and surrounding pavilions are in more or less "Tibetan style." By "Chinese style," I mean to accentuate the contrast with Tibetan techniques and style of architecture. In fact, for Jehol the term "Qing style" (or even "Jehol style"), would often be more appropriate, to emphasize the decorative evolution here that was partly due to the influence of the increasingly syncretic Buddhist architecture of Tibetan origin, and partly to the re-introduction of plans of the Liao dynasty type, which, in turn, resemble earlier types in Central Asia and in Tibet. The Dasheng ge, described by Qianlong as Sumeru, is an impressive timber frame building, of which frontages suggest three decreasing floors, though there are no floors inside but rather a single room sheltering a gigantic (28.25 meters) statue of Avalokiteshvara. The Samye Utse in Tibet is composed of three concentric masonry structures, housing numerous chapels. The central structure has three floors, the third one timber framed. The main statue in its *cella* (ground floor) is that of Shakyamuni. Samye, with its central and adjacent structures in a circular enclosure, is considered a mandala. As picturesque as it may be, Qianlong's architectural interpretation of the mandala at the Puning si is mere décor.[20]

Four years later, the emperor built a smaller temple, the Puyou si, to the east of the Puning si. Very little is known about this temple; judging from old pictures (it is almost entirely destroyed) it was a good example of the syncretic architectural type of the northern and north-western Qing empire. The general disposition of the temple with the buildings at the rear end surrounding the square main hall on three sides as a gallery, recall Liao plans and structures.[21]

In 1764, Qianlong built what he called a copy of the Zunghar temples[22] destroyed in 1756 in Yili (Ghulja or Kulja, today's Yining, Xinjiang). This temple, the Anyuan miao (Figure 15), was meant for prince Dashi Dawa's tribe which had been resettled in the Jehol region. In a complex system of enclosures, Anyuan miao had a one-level gallery (destroyed) enclosing the main temple with a square structure. This plan also evokes Liao models. The surviving main temple appears from outside to be a three-level building with a massive masonry basement supporting two timber floors and the *xieshanding* roof.[23] In fact, the masonry merely conceals the lower part of the timber frame that bears the roof. Inside, there are two levels of surrounding galleries, with walls consisting of wood panels richly decorated with paintings, and a classical *tianjing* coffered ceiling. The main statue has been identified as Kshitigarbha.

In 1766–67, south of Anyuan miao, Qianlong built the Pule si for the Mongol tribes who came for the yearly tribute. The obvious model is the Temple of Heaven in Beijing; was there also an intended relationship with the altar of Heaven in Mukden (the old Manchu capital)? Pule si is aligned with the Bangchui rock to the east (whose shape its roof-bauble echoes), as if to follow the solar line, a straight line coming from Bangchui through the very center of the temple (Figure 18) and on into the imperial residence. Pule si is described as a stupa and a mandala. Its name contains the word *le*, one of the three ways to access nirvana, the other two being *an* (*An*yuan miao) and *ning* (Pu*ning* si). There seems to be a kind of inner organization in this line of three temples to the north of the Kangxi's temples.

A welter of other associations envelop the Pule si. Its western orientation recalls the oldest Tibetan temples, which all have an east–west orientation: the Jokhang in Lhasa opens to the west, Samye to the east (except for Anyuan miao, the other Outer Temples all face south, like Qing imperial buildings generally). The main temple of Pule si is a triple terrace of massive masonry, the lowest level being a surrounding gallery (destroyed). On the upper terrace is a timber mandala in Indian style, containing a statue of Samvara and protected by a circular pavilion under a conical yellow tiled roof. Pule si is the only case in which Qianlong mentions in his inscription the help of an advisor, the Jang gya (Lcang skya) khutukhtu. Jang gya, who played an important part among the Mongols, gave the emperor the Samvara initiation. In a previous life, Jang gya had been the translator Kawa Beltsek (Ka ba dpal brtsegs) who worked in Samye. Moreover, a Tibetan prophecy describes a special link with the East, often explained as symbolizing Manjushri, Wutai shan, and China, at least poetically. Samvara and his mandala[24] can symbolize the link between Jang gya and Qianlong as lama and patron (*mchod yon*). The tantric statue of the Yellow Samvara housed in Pule si symbolizes the union of wisdom and compassion (*prajñā* and *upāya*). As the temple was meant for the western Mongols, it also may symbolize their new link or union with the empire. In Pule si, the mixture of styles and allusions is a trifle jarring: but this deliberate confusion is part of the Jehol system. And the Samvara mandala is covered by a beautiful golden ceiling ornamented with an imperial dragon, whose symbolism here is unambiguous.

Then came the most glorious day. Between 1767 and 1771, Qianlong built his Potala, the Putuozongcheng miao (Figure 12), facing south, on the north side of the Bishu shanzhuang. He had it constructed for a solemn visit of the Mongol tribes upon the occasion of his own sixtieth birthday and his beloved mother's eightieth birthday. "Potala" refers to several places. It is the heavenly residence of the bodhisattva Avalokiteshvara, protector of Tibet. It is also the Lhasa Potala, legendary residence of the seventh-century Tibetan king Songtsen Gampo (Srong-btsan sgam-po), considered the "founder" of Buddhism in Tibet and an emanation of Avalokiteshvara, and later the famous palace (built 1645–48, 1690–93) of the Dalai Lama, also an emanation of Avalokiteshvara. There was still another Potala, in China, a sanctuary devoted to Guanyin (Avalokiteshvara) known as Putuo shan, on an island near Ningbo. But Qianlong did not like this place, nor the people there, and this southern Potala did not serve his purposes. Accordingly, the chosen model was the Lhasa Potala, and Qianlong noted this explicitly. The Potala had become a monument of civil and religious power in Tibet and in regions devoted to Tibetan Buddhism. The emperor's idea was that the Mongol princes would find in the Jehol Potala the same legitimacy they had looked for in Lhasa.

Qianlong's ambition was as large as the building he built; however the length of the main structure of this Jehol Potala is only about a third that of the Lhasa Potala, and this building bears little inner or structural resemblance to the original. The main building of the Jehol Potala, the Dahongtai, is an enormous quadrangular, blind fortress wall; it contains two inner courts surrounded by wooden galleries (recently rebuilt). In the middle of the main court stands the Wanfaguiyi Hall, a timber frame pavilion with its golden copper-tiled roof, typical of the Qing style (Figure 13).

When the building was nearly complete, there suddenly came an astonishing piece of news: the Torghut Mongols, who had left the Yili area in the sixteenth century (under Zunghar pressure) and settled in the lower Volga basin, had now returned to their native land (see Millward, Chapter 8). Their request for Qianlong's help seemed to indicate heavenly approval of the emperor's policies towards Xinjiang, Tibet and Mongolia. Qianlong wrote a new inscription in the Jehol Potala. He sent what would now be termed humanitarian aid to Yili and, of course, invited the Torghut princes to Jehol and gave them flattering titles.

Very little is known about the little Guang'an si which was built in 1772, west of the Jehol Potala, except the usual reasons for it (birthdays). It is said to have been in Tibetan style.

In 1774–76, following a pilgrimage with his mother to Wutai shan, Qianlong built the Shuxiang si, a temple to Manjushri, in that same valley north of the Bishu shanzhuang. One might be surprised that Qianlong did not put this temple inside the imperial residence, but instead placed Manjushri in the outer circle. Yet, while the links between the Manchus and Manjushri are well known, it is nonetheless necessary to underline the importance of Wutai shan for Qing history as well as in the Tibetan and Mongol traditions. The Buddhist confluence in Wutai shan, so important to the history of the diffusion of Buddhism in Eastern and Northern Asia, had to be represented in Jehol. Many architectural models created in the Wutai shan subsequently influenced Tibetan, Mongolian and Qing architecture. The Shuxiang si in Jehol is relatively classical, since the model was not chosen from the most "exotic" examples at the Wutai shan. The bodhisattva's statue in the Shuxiang si is said to be a portrait of the emperor himself – giving a divinity the appearance of a king is an ancient habit in Asia. The Shuxiang si was renowned for the quality of the scholarly work that was done there: as a true working monastery, it seems to have been rather an exception among the Jehol imperial foundations.

The Luohan tang, built in 1774, seems to derive more from fashion than from deliberate purpose. After several costly Tibetan-style buildings, with the Shuxiang si and the Luohan tang Qianlong built a temple and a chapel more typical of the syncretism of Qing architecture and ornamentation, with some Jehol particularisms (the glazed tile work on the gable of the *xieshan* roof in the Shuxiang si, for example). The cross-shaped plan of the Luohan tang is modeled on the Biyun si near Beijing. The Luohan tang no longer survives; and one can see some of its statues in the Puning si.

Of the last two temples, built in 1780, only Xumifushou miao (Figure 17) is documented and has survived. It was customary (and necessary in the Jehol case) to erect *xinggong* ("traveling palaces," or lodges) along imperial roads. The Qianlong emperor politely applied this custom on the occasion of the Panchen Lama's visit, rebuilding a part of the Huang si (Yellow Temple) in Beijing, and the Zhao miao in the Xiangshan, outside the capital. The Zhao miao was a reduction of the sumptuous Jehol Xumifushou, itself modeled of course on Tashilhunpo (Bkra shis lhun po), the Panchen Lama's own monastery. Tashilhunpo was damaged in the Gurkha War and even the ancient paintings do not give an accurate image of its eighteenth century aspect.

The main structure of the Xumifushou miao combines two rectangular reddish enclosures forming galleries surrounding the inner courts. In the middle of the western court is a beautifully decorated timber frame temple, the Miaogao zhuangyan dian, consisting of three levels of inner galleries. Its roof is covered with a golden copper-tile roof, ornamented with golden dragons.[25] The accommodation of the Panchen Lama was built at the north-western end of this structure. Except for the red color of the exterior walls, the resemblance to the Tibetan Tashilhunpo is limited.

Architectural confluences at Jehol and the Qing style

Much of what we see in Jehol, and in the northern half of the empire, speaks of the Qing use of architecture as a political tool of standardization and conquest. A stylistic evolution, visible especially in Buddhist architecture since the end of Kangxi's reign, arises from the natural intermingling of various influences, but the result is by no mean easy to decipher. Doing so requires, first, determining wherever possible how a synthesis was made and how possible models were applied. In this regard, it would be dangerous to underrate the importance of the earlier summer palaces in Beijing and various contemporary Qing foundations of northern China and Mongolia. Next, we must consider those "exotic" trends that might also have influenced some buildings in Jehol. Finally, a more surprising point: some important patterns of Buddhist architecture are missing at Jehol, although they are present in other parts of the empire and should be found in such a Buddhist context.

The models of the Jehol temples

Jehol buildings do not greatly resemble their models. In the case of the Anyuan miao, the model is nothing but a name; close examination has revealed that Liao plans are plausible models for both the Jehol Anyuan temple and probably also of the destroyed Yili temples on which it is ostensibly based. As for the "Tibetan" temples in Jehol (Puning si, Putuozongcheng miao, Xumifushou miao), it is worth underlining their many divergences from their original models (Samye, Potala, Tashilhunpo). We can speak of a fundamental difference of architectural conception between Tibetan and Chinese architectural approaches.[26] Since the resemblances are limited to a rather vague similarity of shape and façade, one is tempted to say that from a technical point of view the façades are Tibetan while the inner and secondary structures are Chinese.[27] This would be wrong, however, because most of the Tibetan façades in Jehol are in fact faux-Tibetan: massive blind walls or terraces, ornamented with the outline of Tibetan windows and cornices, and enclosing a purely Chinese pavilion built in the inner court. But, while traditional Tibetan technique is very seldom used, there are many technical details (especially ornamental details) that are no more Chinese than Tibetan. These might reveal the influence of recent Tibetan architectural evolution or more probably of the numerous creations in the emerging syncretic style of the early Qing period, found primarily among the Buddhist foundations of northern China and Mongolia.

We still know very little about the construction at Jehol, little about the workers who built the palaces and temples, even less about the architects, and comparatively little of the evolution of techniques (especially in Mongolia and Tibet). It has been said that Qianlong sent architects to Tibet to measure the height of the main buildings. This seems a rather charitable evaluation of Qianlong's basic interest and respect for Tibetan architecture, since the original dimensions (if they were ever measured) and their technical implications were *not* taken into account in Jehol.

In fact, Qianlong already had in Beijing every kind of specialist he needed. In 1743, specialists had been called from Tibet to transform his father Yongzheng's princely palace into the Yonghe gong monastery.[28] There was a medical college in the Yonghe gong, and "medical" lamas are usually well informed on architectural matters. Were these specialists the perpetrators of the astonishing differences between Jehol buildings and their Tibetan models?

Jehol Tibetan temples were part of the miniature image of the empire Qianlong wanted to achieve; their number might also suggest the extent of his personal interest in Tibetan Buddhism. But the temples were built primarily for Mongol princes, at least to impress them. What these princes knew and thought of architecture remains to be investigated. Many good Tibetan scholars and specialists of various techniques had been sent to Mongolia since the end of the sixteenth century; many Mongol monks had been sent to Tibet, and returned to their native land as accomplished scholars. There was intensive building activity in Mongolia in the eighteenth century; some, but not all, of the builders were Chinese. At least once already in its history, with the Khitan Liao, China had discovered that nomads could become great builders. In any case, we should try to determine whether the presence of Mongol religious dignitaries in Beijing and Jehol can explain some of the distortions of Qianlong's buildings.

If there were foreign specialists in the Qing court, like the Nepalese Anige in Khubilai's times, the emperor also had his own Chinese architects who were granted a special office in the Forbidden City. The Lei family is a good example, and an interesting one, because they had real connections[29] with the Jesuits Qianlong employed as painters, architects, and so forth. Numerous workers called to Jehol were Chinese[30] and many of them had worked before in the Yuanming yuan summer residence near Beijing, especially in the Xiyang lou, the European palaces built for Qianlong by the Jesuits (1747–59). This might also explain some stylistic details in Jehol.

Regardless of who the designers might have been, their temples in Jehol are odd. A visitor there who is familiar with Tibet must be struck by the fact that there is something conspicuously wrong in the Eight Outer Temples, at least in the northern line of them, from the Puning si to the Putuozongcheng miao: there is such a difference between the Jehol temples and their original models, that it seems impossible that the Tibetan temples could have influenced them directly. In fact, the original models of the Jehol temples were probably paintings. Murals and paintings representing famous temples or monasteries could be found everywhere in the area over which Tibetan Buddhism spread: murals illustrating the principles of monastic discipline, including rules for building, and more often paintings representing a specific temple, monastery or holy place. The temple is the Buddha's image and the same iconographical rules and measures are applied to the building or the picture made of it.[31] Several of these paintings existed in Jehol.[32] Such paintings are an old tradition in Tibet; for example, Tibetans asked in 824 for a "plan" of the Wutai shan[33] – in other words, a painting, probably similar to that of the Wutai shan which the monk Ennin brought back to Japan. Comparison of Jehol temples with *paintings* of Tibetan temples (as opposed to the physical temples themselves) reveals immediate similarities.

It is traditionally said that Asian painting ignores perspective; this is wrong.[34] Painting in China and in Tibet applied a form of perspective distinct from that of the European post-renaissance (although some extremely interesting examples of convergent perspective came earlier from the West into China).[35] As far as the representation of buildings is concerned, Chinese painting uses a kind of perspective that can be compared to our axonometric perspective: everything is visible, with no optical distortion, the buildings have the same dimensions on their front and rear sides, and are placed on top of the other as in a bird's eye view. Tibetan painting uses this type of perspective and also what can be termed divergent perspective, because the rear side of the building is larger than the front side. This gives the structure the aspect of a three-dimensional trapezium; in this case, moreover, structures are superimposed to give the impression of depth. (Of course, trapezoidal structures have never been built in Tibet, except in olden times, when many burial mounds were so shaped, but I doubt this is related to the later distortions in painting.)

Samye monastery lies on a flat piece of sandy land. Paintings representing the monastery show every building, in axonometric or divergent perspective, superposed in an ascending movement that almost gives the impression of a slope.[36] The circular outer wall is sometimes represented as a more or less circular broken line (a classical way in Tibet to represent the *cakravāla*, the mountains surrounding the Buddhist world). In 1755, when the Puning si was built in Jehol, the large flat fields where Anyuan miao was later built – the only large flat fields in the area – were still free of any construction. Had direct imitation of the Tibetan Samye been the goal, this location might have served best – although *fengshui* (geomancy) might have opposed this choice. In fact, the Puning si as we see it (Figure 16) is a more or less exact copy of a Tibetan painting representing Samye. It was built not on a flat piece of land, but on a moderate hill, where a quantity of earth and rocks were moved to give sufficient height and slope – a considerable and costly endeavor to create a likeness to paintings but not to the original model! Samye's central temple, the Utse, opens to the east; this is highly significant, but not visible on the paintings. Puning si faces the south. The various Puning si pavilions are built on superposed terraces; the outer wall jumps from one terrace to another, which gives the impression of a broken line, as in the paintings. The Dasheng ge, the central temple in Puning si, bears only a vague likeness to the Samye Utse, and to most of the paintings; it is much closer to the restorations of the *mingtang*, a very ancient type of building and symbol of central power in China, of which some examples were still built in the Tang times, corresponding to when Samye was built in Tibet. It combined a circular enclosure with a square central building.[37] The pavilions surrounding the Dasheng ge deliberately exaggerate the distortions of the paintings: for example, cubic structures shown in divergent perspective are rendered by hexagonal structures. This is not the result of an excessive or blind concern with accuracy. On the contrary, this rendering involves a keen knowledge of geometry and perspective and a kind of humorous detachment. Here, the Jehol builders were certainly not ordinary imitators.

The comparison between the Tibetan model, the paintings and the Jehol version is still more striking in the case of the Potala. The Lhasa Potala is an enormous building covering the greater part of a big grey rock, the Marpori (Dmar po ri), standing right in the middle of the Lhasa plain. The distant scenery, that is to say the slopes of the mountains overlooking the valley, is always a rather severe pale yellow and grey, sometimes splashed with patches of pale green in the first days of spring. On the flat land at the foot of the palace is a "village" (*zhol*) of simple terrace-roofed houses, enclosed by a wall. On the murals and paintings, on the other hand, the Potala is represented in a green grassy environment, surmounting a moderately sloped hill; the white buildings of the "village" are superimposed in order to suggest depth and perspective, as if they were situated on the very slope of the Marpori, which is not true. The Jehol Potala (Figure 12), surmounting a moderate grassy hill spread with little white buildings, is almost an exact copy of the thangkas.

One might object that Tibetan visitors and many of the Mongol princes, who surely knew the original Potala and Samye, would not have recognized these buildings in their Jehol version. Qianlong knew nothing of Lhasa, Samye, or Tashilhunpo. Perhaps what was built in Jehol sufficiently resembled the models he knew – paintings – to suit his goal, which was not to reproduce exactly but to surpass the models. It seems there were very few Tibetan visitors in Jehol, with the exception of Jang gya and such high religious dignitaries as the Panchen Lama, who probably were more impressed by the gorgeousness of their imposing foundations than by their likeness to their models. In their opinion, no doubt, there was only one Potala and one Samye in any case, but Jehol demonstrated the Qing imperial interest and generosity towards Buddhism. The Mongol princes were probably too taken by splendor and luxury to utter any criticism.

Jehol, with its "Tibetan look" was like a gigantic theater scenery. The visitors may have thought they had a part to play on this stage, but religious life in Jehol never reached a high level. Only Shuxiang si, the most "Chinese" of the Outer Temples, won a moderate reputation for learning. Only a few of the other temples housed a regular clergy, and most of their secondary buildings were nothing but barracks. Just as the Mulan hunts were seasonal, Jehol was a seasonal stage.

Sources of Jehol eclecticism

A somewhat delirious imagination is one of the most interesting characteristics of the summer residence. Qianlong gave the empire its largest extent. Jehol consequently gathered the reduced images of the central and remotest places of the empire. Some features of this astonishing collection of architectural types and decorative styles were, in fact, the result of a kind of inner maturation and became distinctive of the Qing syncretic style. Other features were considerably more distant borrowings. Qianlong did not escape the eighteenth-century universal curiosity for exoticism. As there were Chinese pagodas, and Greek and Egyptian ruins in European princely gardens, so were there European palaces in the imperial summer residence of the Yuanming yuan, just outside of Beijing.

In 1747, Qianlong was shown a European painting representing fountains. He ordered the Jesuit Giuseppe Castiglione to build similar fountains for him.[38] He was so pleased with the result that the Jesuits had next to build an entire residence in the same style, on a narrow piece of land in the northeast corner of the Yuanming yuan. The different pavilions and fountains, known as the Xiyang lou (Western Halls), were built between 1747 and 1759. The general plan and most of the details were conceived by the Jesuits, but with many imperial interventions. Workers were, of course, Chinese and possibly some Chinese architects provided help: this might explain the technical peculiarities of some of the buildings. These European palaces of the Yuanming yuan were highly criticized by right-thinking people, in and out the Court. Officially, they were the Jesuits' only contribution to the imperial buildings;[39] the Jesuits' presence at Jehol was limited to the tiring role of official painter, a role they played also in Beijing for the emperor and members of the court (see Sommer, Chapter 14). In fact, actual visitors in the Xiyang lou were very few and testimonies about this secluded imperial residence are scarce and often questionable before the British and French armies plundered and destroyed it in 1860.[40]

In 1873, Georges Ohlmer made photos of the still impressive ruins of the Xiyang lou European palaces.[41] The site has been slowly dismantled since, then recently rather unfortunately restored. The pavilions were a peculiar combination of an extremely rich European synthetic style and of Chinese details of technique and ornamentation, with the different parts of the garden divided by a majestic arched door in the same composite style. The architectural ornamentation of the façades was extremely rich and rather disconcerting for European eyes, for it combined plain marble and the brightest of ceramic, as shown by fragments of ceramic found on the site.[42] The shell motif and the foliage scroll motif, among others, were new in China; should we be startled, then, that we find some of them, slightly modified, also used in Jehol? These stylistic resemblances may be mere coincidences, however, for if there was an influence of the Yuanming yuan in Jehol, it was never systematic.

The European palaces of the Yuanming yuan offered an interesting display of large windows, for example in the southeast gallery of the Xieqi qu, or the southeast front of the Belvedere.[43] Tibetan architecture had favored wider windows since the seventeenth century. The Qianfo ge pavilion, situated on the middle terrace of the Dahong tai (the main building of the Jehol Potala; Figure 12) has three high rectangular doors with rich ceramic door frames and porch roof: is it a reference to the Yuanming yuan or, more likely, one of the many inventions of the builders?

An almost excessive use of ceramic has been made in Jehol, from ornamental details to screens, porches, window and door frames, gables and even complete façade. In the Yuanming yuan, ceramic might have been used so profusely to give colors to a colorless architecture. Glazed-tile factories around Beijing produced a great number of carefully classed components for roofs; also an increasing number of architectural components as required by screens, porches, and so forth, in such favor under the Qing. Very distinctive patterns were thus produced for the Yuanming yuan from ceramic, and such creativity also inspired the Jehol builders. Ceramic is an easy-to-use material and more solid than one might think. The glaze and colors are impressive, especially to barbarians. . . . It was the ideal material for a summer residence; might it have been used as a palliative, even as a coat of wrap, for the non-Chinese buildings, at the very moment technical specifications or native material were lacking, or when the emperor was dissatisfied with a colorless façade?

Most of the doors in Jehol are traditional northern Chinese triple-arched doors, some of them composed, in fact, of a single door and two lateral windows. But their carved ornamentation is by no means traditional. Carved stone friezes surrounding the arches suggest in places the foliage scroll motifs of the Yuanming yuan, although no definite model has so far been found. Such motifs are visible on the door of the Bifeng si (destroyed) inside the Bishushanzhuang, the main doors of the Puning si and Pule si, and the *pailou* of the Xumifushou miao. Neither the motifs nor the carving technique are typically Chinese, but are undoubtedly part of the Jehol style. Things are still more intricate with the lower front door of the Panchen Lama residence pavilion, Jixiangfaxi dian. The arch, in spite of three rather vaguely designed stupas surmounting the frieze, has a somewhat "oriental" look. But the technique and the complicated vegetal motif of the frieze reminds one strongly of some of the delicately carved motifs in the Yuanming yuan, for example the windows of the Xieqi qu and decorated panels between these windows. Once more, what is to be found in Jehol is not mere copy, but an adaptation.

What was definitely *not* a coincidence is a pair of small windows in the northern door of the Jehol Puning si. This pavilion is built on a square plan, corresponding to the northern area of the mandala, and covers a vaulted gateway. A double flight of steps gives way to the upper terrace. Windows open in each of the east and west walls. They have the Tibetan trapezoidal shape but are not open perpendicularly to the wall, probably in order to give a view on the mandala, south of the pavilion. But there is not a single straight line in these windows: they are an interesting example of a geometrical and perspective trick, and probably not a Chinese one.

The Jehol collection was not, in fact, complete. Three types of buildings, whose presence we would expect, are not represented on the site.

The most obvious missing monument in Jehol is the stupa. Of course, there are series of small stupas on the top of several pavilions of the Putuozongcheng miao and on the terraces of the Pule si, and there are miniature stupas on roofs or as decorative ornaments. But as far as it is known, there was no great stupa in Jehol like the great stupas in Wutai shan (Tayuan si) or in Beijing (Baita si and Beihai). Of course, the Pule si is a stupa, as it can be considered a mountain temple, but it is a different type. Stupas, especially great stupas, were once the most familiar Buddhist monuments in Tibet and Mongolia (most were destroyed in Mongolia in the 1930s and in Tibet after 1950). Perhaps Qianlong thought that the Beijing stupas (Baita si, rebuilt in 1272 by Khubilai and dedicated to Manjushri; and the Beihai stupa, built by Shunzhi at the occasion of the 5th Dalai Lama's visit), or even the Liuhe pagoda of the Jehol Yongyou si (a classical Chinese *ta* and not a Tibetan style stupa) were already a sufficient homage to Buddhism. But there is no sure explanation for this lacuna.

The second type of building lacking in the Jehol assemblage is the *wulangdian*, a vaulted masonry hall, of which the Wuliang dian (Ming period) in the Xiantong si at Wutai shan, or the Zhihuihai (1750) on the top of the Wanshou shan in the Yihe yuan are good examples. Jang gya spent many months of his life in Wutai shan, and even built a small temple there. Qianlong visited Wutai shan several times. He did build a *wulang-dian* in the Xiangshan as well as the one on the top of the Wanshou shan. The slope of the Xiantong si (Wutai shan), with buildings established on superposed terraces, suggests in a very different architectural style, the disposition of both the Jehol Puning si and the rear side of the Wanshou shan (where a *wulangdian* is crowning the hill). The great Ming architect Miao Feng (1540–1612), who worked in the Xiantong si, is often considered the inventor of the bronze pavilions; there is a beautiful bronze pavilion enshrined in the Xiantong si sloping composition. Qianlong himself, at high cost, built such a bronze pavilion in the Zhuyuan si of his Jehol residence, but no wulangdian, with which the bronze pavilion is closely associated. Why not? The *wulangdian* is often considered, even in China, as of non-Chinese origin. Perhaps Qianlong, as emperor of China, decided that the Wutai shan was, first and foremost, a *Chinese* sacred place, even if it was also sacred to the Tibetans and the Mongols, and thus decided that his Jehol evocation of the Wutai shan, the Shuxiang si, had to be purely Chinese.

There is a third type of building lacking in the Jehol collection. In the Tibetan tradition, the model of Samye monastery was Indian: Nālandā or Odantapuri, depending on the sources. In fact, the Mahābodhi temple (a famous temple in Bodh-Gaya, north India, where the Buddha attained enlightenment under the bodhi-tree) is often represented on murals and paintings in Samye or elsewhere. In Beijing there is an ancient (1465) and beautiful temple inspired by the Mahābodhi temple, the Wuta si; it was of course repaired by Qianlong. In 1513, the Biyun si, west of Beijing, was restored in the same style by a Ming court eunuch and again, later, by Qianlong. The model was used once more for another Wuta si in Hohhot (Inner Mongolia) – but not in Jehol. There was, apparently, no room for an Indian temple in the Waiba miao. These Indian monuments also present an important carved ornamentation whose style, although with conspicuous differences, is relatively longlasting. The style of the sculptures in these three temples built or repaired in Qianlong's time (Biyun si and two Wuta si) is not only comparable to the style of the carved ornamentation in the Qianlong's tomb, but also in a way to the style of murals in the Puning si at Jehol. It is an archaic style, a kind of revival that is also seen in Tibet and in Mongolia. Many bronze statues likewise support this analysis. Thus, again, the absence of an Indian temple at Jehol is curious, and possibly intentional.

Jehol seems to be a collection of architectural possibilities linked, or not, to political necessities. The resulting style is typical enough to be called Jehol style, a branch of the Qing style – which is usually despised for its lack of invention. But it is difficult to state conclusively whether components of Qing style in general were influenced by components of Jehol style. I would claim that the Zhao miao in the Xiangshan west of Beijing was also built in the Jehol style: it was a reduction of the Xumifushou miao, built the same year and for the same purpose. Similarly, the pavilions on the rear side of the Wanshou shan (in the Summer Palace, or Yihe yuan) are almost contemporary with the Puning si. It is difficult to find later examples of the Jehol style, however, because so many temples in Mongolia have been destroyed, and also because the temple policy ended with Qianlong. Later temples were probably built with less pregnant intentions.

There are many possible geometrical figures in the Jehol scheme, including the mandalas in the Puning si, Pule si and probably Anyuan miao, which combine square and circular shapes. Four empires met in Jehol: the everlasting cultural and economic power of Chinese empire, the warlike and once all-conquering Mongol empire, the religious Tibetan empire and the newly victorious Manchu empire. Jehol can be modeled, then, as a geometric figure with the Manchu emperor in the middle, China, Mongolia and Tibet forming a surrounding triangle – and some birds of prey on the sides, waiting for the future.

Not only has inventiveness been too hastily denied to Qing architecture, but its diffusion was broader than usually estimated, because it was an instrument of conquest. It gained some ground in Tibet, mainly in Kokonor (Amdo, Qinghai) and Labrang (Bla-brang; Xiahe in Gansu province) areas, but it made great strides throughout Mongolia. The Qing style, and part of the Jehol style, bulwarked the Buddhicization of Mongolia, and was still visible at the beginning of the twentieth century. During the nineteenth century, there were so many variations of temples inspired by Qing "synthetic" and composite style, that the Mongolian architecture, with a raving imagination but not always perfectly good taste, seems to have tried to achieve what Qing architecture had suggested but lacked time or will to do.

Notes

1 Official references to Rehe (Jehol in the Pekinese pronunciation, as altered by the French Jesuits) can be found on an edict dated 1723. The name Chengde appeared some ten years later, gradually superseding the name Rehe in official documents (see *Chengde Bishu shanzhuang*, 6). Although the present volume uses the term "Chengde" primarily, I retain the term "Jehol" (Rehe) adopted by the Jesuits in their letters and reports, because it may be considered a hint to the many foreign presences and influences in the place.
2 The word "protectorate" being the understatement traditionally used by Western scholars.
3 On the power the fifth Dalai Lama (1617–82) had on the Mongols, see Ishihama Yumiko, "A Study of the Seals and Titles Confered by the Dalai Lama."
4 It was in this year that the population of Dajianlu, the great tea market of Eastern Tibet, was first entered onto the *bantu* (Chinese population register); this suggests that these territories were not incorporated before this time. The following year (1702), Kangxi's armies entered the valleys of Nyag-rong (Kham).
5 See Hou Ching-lang and M. Pirazzoli, "Les chasses d'automne de l'Empereur Qianlong à Mulan"; Hou Ching-lang, *Mulan tu*; and also Forêt, *Mapping Chengde*.
6 Hou and Pirazzoli, "Les chasses d'automne," 41.
7 Stein, *Le monde en petit*; English translation, *The World in Miniature*.
8 The rule is that in a garden or in a miniature garden, the mountain or the rock that represents the mountain cannot be higher than the lowest part of any pavilion roof nearby. With regard to Jehol and the Bangchui rock, there is also a narrow margin between what is beautiful and what is exceedingly picturesque, possibly because it is part of a different scheme entirely.
9 Stein, *Le monde en petit*, 98.

10 Forêt, "Making an Imperial Landscape," 82–86. And in such cases, imperial authorities never objected to retroactivity in the explanation and justification.

11 From the old pictures and photos and from the surviving Liuhe ta, one can see that the architectural style of these buildings was very classical. The only elements of possible foreign influence seem to have been in the ornamentation of some doors and windows.

12 The plan of Puren si was typically Chinese: an enclosure with succeeding halls on the central line and some lateral buildings. As for the Pushan si, it is more difficult to see in the rather schematic plan and some photos dating back to the 1930s – all we have to recall the destroyed temple – any characteristics of more typically Qing architecture. See Sekino and Takeshima, *Nekka*, vol. 2.

13 See Chayet and Jest, "Le monastère de la Félicité Tranquille, fondation impériale en Mongolie," 72–81. This monastery, currently under restoration with an UNESCO grant, is in Selenge Aimag, north of Ulaan Baatar. It is dedicated to Zanabazar, and is considered the second most important monastery in the Mongolian Republic, after Erdeni Zuu.

14 See Petech, *China and Tibet*; Rossabi, *China and Inner Asia*; Millward, *Beyond the Pass*.

15 A significant point of comparison is the disposition, described as regular concentric squares, of the temples built by the Tibetan king Songtsen Gampo (Srong-btsan sgam-po) in the seventh century to nail down the Demoness. The actual disposition, as seen on the map, is extremely irregular. See Aris, *Bhutan, the Early History of a Himalayan Kingdom*, 15–20.

16 Farquhar, "Emperor as Bodhisattva."

17 See Seyfort Ruegg, "mChod-yon, yon mchod and mchod-gnas/yon-gnas" and *Ordre spirituel et ordre temporel*.

18 See Kahn, "The Politics of Filiality," 197–203.

19 For a more detailed description of these temples, see Chayet, *Les temples de Jehol*.

20 A similar group of pavilions was built in the Yihe yuan in Beijing, on the northern slope of the Wanshou shan.

21 See Steinhardt, "Liao: an Architecture in the Making."

22 There are very few documents concerning these temples and seemingly no picture of the model, Qainuq temple.

23 Compare, for example, the Ganden temple in Urga (Ulaan Baatar).

24 See also the Samvara mandala and discussion in the Yonghe gong (Beijing), published in Lessing, *Yung-ho-kung*, 130–38.

25 Similar dragons can be seen on the roof of the Yuhua ge (north-western part of the Gugong in Beijing), built in Ming times and restored by Qianlong, and also in Tashilhunpo; these may commemorate the tragic trip of the Panchen Lama who died in Peking in 1780.

26 Traditional Tibetan architecture shows big, thick, slightly sloping walls, made of stone, brick or adobe, bearing heavy beams supported by pillars (in the largest rooms), and terrace roofs. It did not provide much light to the rooms. In Chinese architecture, pillars set in the ground or in a terrace bear the roof timber framework; even in the frequent case of gabled houses, pillars are the essential component of the building, and light easily reaches the rooms. In other words, the Tibetan roof is supported by thick walls and occasional pillars; this requires a heavy structure and might be the reason why the upper floor in the Samye Utse was in timber work. The Chinese roof is supported by pillars; this means a light and more adaptable structure. Jehol and Qing architecture provide many examples of this adaptability.

In seventeenth- or early eighteenth-century Tibetan architecture, lighter structures using more timber work, and verandas and galleries opening on inner courts have been attributed rather unquestioningly to Chinese influence.

However, this gives short shrift to some genuine technical innovations in Tibetan architecture during the seventeenth century and possibly to other foreign influences. Some of the changes, moreover, should be credited to internal evolution under the influence of the active and powerful Gelukpa, which required impressive new buildings to project an image of their power and larger and better-lit rooms to accommodate increasing numbers of visitors, many from Mongolia.

27 Editors' note: During the Ann Arbor seminar, one participant dubbed the Putuozongcheng miao a "Potemkin Potala".

28 As mentioned, for example, in the biography of Jang gya Rolpai Dorje by his brother Chu-bzang Ngag-dbang thub-bstan dbang-phyug (R. Kämpfe, ed. *Die Biographie des 2. Pekinger lCan-skya Qutuqtu Rol-pa'i rdo-rje*, f.48.a). The result is more an example of the emerging syncretic Qing style than of the classical Tibetan tradition. See also Lessing, *Yung-ho-kung*.

29 See Hou and Pirazzoli, "Les chasses d'automne," 43.

30 Mainly from Hebei, Shandong and Shanxi. *Chengde Bishu shanzhuang*, 5, 207.

31 See Chayet, *Les Temples de Jehol*, 83–90 and "Remarques sur les représentations d'architectures dans la peinture tibétaine et chinoise."

32 Henmi Baei, *Chūgoku Lamakyō bijutsu taikan*.

33 See Chayet, *Les Temples de Jehol*, 86–90 and n. 260.

34 Chayet, *Les Temples de Jehol*, 91–93 and "Remarques."

35 The convergent perspective is particularly remarkable in the Tang paradise paintings in Dunhuang. Post-renaissance European perspective is more or less a development of convergent perspective, and it is still evolving. The Jesuits explained its principles to Kangxi and gave a lively demonstration of it in the chapels they built and decorated (often with *trompe l'oeil* effects) in Beijing. Kangxi judged this form of perspective technically interesting but not artistic. Giuseppe Castiglione (1688–1766), Jesuit, painter and later architect, worked at the Court under Kangxi and Qianlong, but was forbidden to teach perspective to his Chinese students. Nevertheless, a few Chinese scholars, artists and architects might have heard about this kind of perspective, owing to the translation of several treatises on perspective and geometry, especially an adaptation of the famous treatise by Pozzo.

36 For example, the thangka painting of Samye held by the Newark Museum.

37 See Liu Dunzhen, *Zhongguo gudai jianzhi shi*, 46–49.

38 See Pirazzoli-t'Serstevens, *Le Yuanmingyuan*, and, "A Pluridisciplinary Research on Castiglione."

39 In the case of the Xiyang lou, as in the case of the Queen's hamlet in Versailles, criticism was fueled by the cost of the buildings. Tradition tells that the bronze pavilion (1750) in the Beijing Yihe yuan was cast by the Jesuits.

40 The Panchen Lama visited the Xiyang lou in 1780 (Chayet, "Une description tibétaine du Yuanmingyuan").

41 See Thiriez, "Old Photography and the Yuanmingyuan," "Les palais européens du Yuanmingyuan," and "Ernst Ohlmer, ein Amateur-Fotograf im alten Peking."

42 London, Victoria and Albert Museum, fragments from the Dashuifa (?) façade (nos. 375–79).

43 See Pirazzoli-t'Serstevens, *Le Yuanmingyuan*, and Thiriez, "Les palais européens du Yuanmingyuan."

Part II
Rituals of empire

5 Qianlong on the road

The imperial tours to Chengde

Van J. Symons

The tradition of imperial "tours of inspection" (*xunshou*) is an old one in China, and one that the Qing emperors adopted enthusiastically in their rule over the empire. The Kangxi emperor (r. 1661–1722), for instance, led the court on a number of "Southern Tours" (*nanxun*) to the lower Yangzi basin, undertook pilgrimages to holy mountains and religious shrines, and frequently traveled north of the Great Wall to hunt and conduct diplomacy. These endeavors enabled him to escape the constraints of the Chinese capital and at the same time to discharge sacerdotal responsibilities and "soothe" his Han and non-Han subjects. Kangxi's grandson, the Qianlong emperor (r. 1736–95), too, was a peripatetic ruler who often spent time away from the Forbidden City and was also firmly in the spell of Chengde. Almost every summer, he would move the court there for one, two, or even three months, enjoying the rustic atmosphere of the Bishu shanzhuang palace complex and indulging in the pleasures of the hunt. However regular, the trips to Chengde eventually came to be portrayed in the same way as the emperor's travels to other parts of the realm, that is, as "tours of inspection" – extraordinary opportunities for the monarch to show concern and shower largesse on soldiers, local officials, and commoners along the route – rather than simply as vacation getaways.

This essay is divided into three sections. The first part provides historical context for understanding imperial movement. The second section describes the annual imperial progress to the summer retreat, noting the difficulties involved in the trip and the length of time it took. The third section examines the depiction of the excursions in the official record as tours of inspection. The goal here is to show how trips to Chengde fit into the larger discourse of touring in Qing emperorship.

The movable court

The early Qing emperors' love of travel contrasted greatly with the precedent left by the Ming emperors, who preferred a more static mode of rule. The Wanli emperor (r. 1573–1619), who surrounded himself with 20,000 eunuchs and a palace staff that included 3,000 women, is a well-known case. Because his ministers insisted that his first son succeed him rather than his third, Wanli broke off dialog with them and withdrew into the inner palace, ultimately becoming a captive in his own court.[1] While late Qing rulers ended up slipping into this rut themselves – it was reported that Empress Dowager Cixi's first prolonged exodus from the court in almost four decades occurred during the summer of 1900 as she fled the approach of Western armies toward Beijing during the Boxer crisis – the Qing emperors of the seventeenth and eighteenth centuries were very energetic, constantly roaming about the empire. In this they were closer to their Inner Asian predecessors, the emperors of the Liao, Jin, and Yuan dynasties, who, even as imperial masters of China, shunned its sedentary lifestyle, preferring instead to maintain a semi-nomadic existence as they shuttled back and forth between Beijing and their parallel capitals on the steppe.[2] We can see this pattern clearly exemplified by the Qianlong emperor.

The fourth Qing emperor to rule in China, Qianlong seems to have been unable to stay in the same place for very long. During his long sixty-year reign, Qianlong made six tours of Jiangnan, five visits to the Temple of Confucius in Qufu (Shandong province), five pilgrimages to Wutai shan, a Buddhist site in Shanxi province, and four excursions to Songshan and Kaifeng in central Henan, along with four "Eastern Tours" (*dongxun*), to the secondary capital of Shengjing (Mukden) in the Manchu homeland.[3] In addition, the emperor traveled regularly (semi-annually from 1741, annually from 1751 on[4]) to Chengde. Even when resident in the capital, Qianlong moved about constantly, preferring to stay at his suburban villa at the Yuanming yuan, which, with the help of Jesuit missionaries at court, he later famously adorned with Western-style buildings, gardens, and fountains. Moreover, Qianlong retained his active lifestyle until well into his old age: in the last year of his life, when he was eighty-nine, the emperor hosted foreign tributaries, imperial princes, and Mongol nobles on at least four occasions, visited, resided at, and prayed in a total of fifty-two palaces, halls, temples, gardens, and villas, and made the summer trip to Chengde one last time.[5]

To get a better sense of the rhythm of imperial life, let us take a closer look at the emperor's calendar of activities in 1780, the forty-fifth year of his reign.[6] Two extraordinary events occurred during this period. First, from February 16 to June 11, Qianlong conducted the fifth of his six "Southern Tours." Escaping the brutal cold of north China, he led his retinue quickly south through Shandong province and into the Jiangnan area, lingering at Suzhou, Jiaxing, and Hangzhou. On his way he visited temples, met with officials to personally examine the efficiency and integrity of local government, examined roads, dikes, and other public works, and rewarded local notables for their accomplishments. After offering sacrifices at the tomb of the first Ming emperor near Nanjing, the imperial party began the trip back to the capital, retracing some of the route taken earlier, but allowing more time, now that the weather had warmed up, to tour Shandong province.[7]

The second big event of the year was the visit of the Third Panchen Lama. Twelve days after returning to Beijing from the trip to the south, and having dutifully completed the rituals connected with the summer solstice, Qianlong departed Beijing again on June 23 for the Summer Retreat in order to prepare for the Panchen Lama's visit. He was, no doubt, particularly concerned to see that work on the Xumifushou Temple, modeled after the Panchen Lama's residence at Tashilhunpo and built specifically for the upcoming visit, was complete (see Zarrow, Chapter 15). The Panchen Lama arrived safely at Chengde on August 20. While there, the emperor met him personally and hosted him at numerous lavish banquets. (On the Panchen Lama's visit, see Benard (Chapter 10) and translation by Ragnubs (Chapter 16); on banquets, see Yu (Chapter 7).) He then left in late September for Beijing, arriving in the capital on September 29. The emperor, forsaking the annual hunt at Mulan, departed Chengde September 25 and arrived in Beijing on October 16, where he continued to fête this important guest.

Given these two major events, how much of the year did Qianlong actually spend in Beijing? One hundred and fifteen days spent on the Southern Tour and another 115 spent at Chengde left him with exactly 114 days to spend in Beijing. Of this, he spent fifteen days at the Yuanming yuan, meaning that in 1780 the emperor held court in the Forbidden City for a total of only ninety-nine days (see Table 1).

This year is not wholly representative, since a lengthy absence such as that occasioned by a Southern Tour did not occur every year. However, if we figure that in addition to the yearly visits to Chengde, during his reign the emperor made a total of nearly twenty major excursions of one sort or another outside Beijing, then it could be expected that every third

Table 1 The Qianlong emperor's whereabouts in 1780

Date	Place	Number of days
Feb. 5–Feb. 15, 1780	Beijing (palace)	10
Feb. 16–June 10	Travel (Southern Tour)	115
June 11–June 15	Beijing (Yuanming yuan)	4
June 16–June 20	Beijing (palace)	4
June 21–June 22	Beijing (Yuanming yuan)	1
June 23–June 29	Travel (Beijing–Chengde)	6
June 29–Sept. 25	Chengde	88
Sept. 26–Oct. 16	Travel (Chengde–Beijing)	20
Oct. 17–Oct. 21	Beijing (Yuanming yuan)	4
Oct. 22–Nov. 10	Beijing (palace)	19
Nov. 11–Nov. 17	Beijing (Yuanming yuan)	6
Nov. 18–Jan. 23, 1781	Beijing (palace)	66

year he would be away from the capital for an extended period of time. Even in years when he did not go on tour he would still go north for the summer, meaning that on average Qianlong was consistently absent from the formal halls of power for a good third of the year, and often more.

The way to Chengde

As evidenced in Table 1 travel time to and from Chengde (see Figure 2) could vary significantly. In 1780 the emperor's decision to visit the Eastern Tombs (where, among others, his grandfather, Kangxi, was buried) took him by a roundabout route that added fourteen days to the journey. This was considerably less than the time required when the Kangxi emperor first began visiting the Bishu shanzhuang site regularly after 1703. Kangxi, who reveled in the journey, sometimes took weeks to get to Chengde. Camping and hunting all along the way, he seems never to have been bound to a pre-determined route.[8] But by Qianlong's day, a line of imperial stations (*xinggong*, literally "travel palaces") at which the emperor could comfortably lodge linked Beijing to Rehe, and as a rule he moved in predictable fashion from one station to another in what was generally a seven-day journey. The measured pace from station to station may have been dictated by the needs of the emperor's mother, who almost always accompanied Qianlong to the summer palace complex; yet even after her death the seven-day routine was seldom changed.[9] Nor were either Kangxi or Qianlong in any hurry to return to Beijing once they left Chengde. Where Qianlong usually moved rapidly through to Gubei kou, the Kangxi emperor remained north of the Great Wall; but both of them found ways to delay their return to the capital, visiting the Ming tombs or hunting and sightseeing elsewhere.[10]

During the first half of the Qianlong reign, the court generally departed for Chengde in late August or even September. But beginning in 1772, the year after work on the Putuozongcheng Temple commenced, the court began to leave Beijing in late June, scheduling its departure around the summer solstice.[11] The return to the capital was generally defined by the ending of the fall hunt in Mulan (see Elliott and Chia, Chapter 6), with departure from Rehe occurring in mid- to late October and sometimes even November. In 1780, as noted, the emperor left for Chengde on June 23 (only two days after the summer solstice rituals and only twelve days after returning from the Southern Tour). The stages of the journey are carefully noted in the *Veritable Records (Da Qing lichao shilu)* and the *Diaries of Imperial Activity and Repose (Qijuzhu)*, but little information is given about the conditions of roads and bridges, distances traveled, the landscape, or the travel routine. Fortunately, a little more than a decade later, in 1793, Lord Macartney, the representative sent by King George III of England, was permitted to travel to Chengde to offer his respects to the Qianlong emperor. The seventy members of the British embassy, accompanied by some 200 porters, followed the same route utilized by Qianlong. The journals kept by Lord Macartney, his assistant George Staunton, and other participants in the embassy provide additional information on the journey from the capital to Chengde.

Macartney's entourage, like Qianlong's, made the trip in seven stages with six overnight stops. The British ambassador noted the distances traveled and the name of each imperial station en route, and determined that the distance from the Beijing city gate to Rehe was 131.5 miles (Table 2).

Generally Macartney's embassy departed early, at 5:00 or 6:00 a.m., traveled for two or three hours, averaging four to five miles each hour on the road, and then stopped at a designated place for breakfast. The trip then resumed, but lasted only a few more hours with the day's final stopping place reached by mid-day or early afternoon. Notables traveled on horseback or in carriages or palanquins and were supported by a huge staff of personnel.[12] The retinue was allowed to stay in the wings adjoining the imperial lodges, which, according to Macartney's description, were

> all constructed upon nearly the same plan and in the same taste. They front the south and are usually situated on irregular ground near the bases of gentle hills which together with their adjoining valleys are enclosed by high walls and laid out in parks and pleasure grounds with every possible attention to picturesque beauty.[13]

The trip was thus undertaken at a leisurely pace, and Macartney noted in his journal once he arrived that the "journey upon the whole has been very pleasant and, being divided into seven days, not at all fatiguing."[14]

Two well-developed roads connected Beijing and Bishu shanzhuang. One was reserved solely for the use of the emperor; the other was for his attendants and other authorized travelers. As he journeyed to Chengde in September 1793, Macartney noted working parties of ten men dispersed every 100 yards, and estimated that upwards of 23,000 troops were repairing the emperor's road in anticipation of the sovereign's return to

Table 2 Macartney's reckoning of the journey from Beijing to Chengde

Day	Distance traveled	Overnight stop
1	22.5 miles	Nanshi cao
2	20.5 miles	Miyun xian
3	21.5 miles	Yao tingzi
4	24.0 miles	Liangjian fang
5	13.0 miles	Changshan yu
6	8.0 miles	Boro hoton
7	12.0 miles	Chengde

the capital (supposedly the road was repaired twice each year). Another member of the embassy described the emperor's road as

> ten feet broad, a foot high, and made of a mixture of sand and clay, so evenly damped and so well packed that it becomes as hard as cement. . . . (It) is as clean and as smooth as the floor in one of our drawing-rooms. It is constantly swept, not only to remove fallen leaves, but the smallest grain of dust. On either side there are reservoirs, every 200 paces, from whence – often with great trouble – water is carried for damping the road . . . watch-posts are set up along the road and no one is allowed to step on it until the Emperor has passed.[15]

This description was almost certainly idealized.[16] For despite their attentiveness to maintaining it, for a number of reasons, the route from Beijing to Chengde was a continual challenge to governmental engineers. In the spring and summer, heavy rains turned the road into a quagmire, slowing, or even halting, all traffic.[17] (See the description of the Jesuit painter Attiret's journey, translated by Sommer, Chapter 14.) Several rivers, particularly those between Nanshi cao and Miyun xian, needed bridges or ferries to assure unhindered movement for imperial processions. Moreover, beyond Miyun xian, as the road begins to climb out of the North China plain towards Yao tingzi and from there to Gubei kou and beyond, it threads its way through narrow canyons and sharp defiles and is subject to landslides, torrential streams, and violent storms. Lord Macartney described the road there as "very rough" but "pleasant and romantic."[18] Staunton, somewhat more candid, admits that at one point the terrain was so rough and steep that the ambassador's carriage had to be emptied and hauled over a section of the road, "his Excellency traveling in the meantime in a palankeen."[19]

Apart from maintaining the necessary infrastructure, court officials faced the additional challenge of guaranteeing security. Macartney noted that guard towers or military posts, each with six to fifteen soldiers attached to them, stood about every five miles along the route.[20] On top of this was the burden of managing logistics (horses, fodder, carriages, tents, provisions),[21] while ensuring that the local countryside was not unduly disrupted by the imperial progress. Besides the emperor, the empress dowager, imperial wives, concubines, children and attendants, a large number of important government officials and bureaucrats also accompanied him – the business of the empire could not be neglected, after all – along with a sizable contingent of Eight Banner soldiers, invited to join the hunt. Even under the less extravagant Kangxi emperor, it was estimated that in 1711, out of a garrison of 30,000 troops at Rehe, 12,000 soldiers accompanied the emperor to Mulan.[22] Though no precise figures exist, the number of people journeying to Chengde in 1780 must have been quite large.

The Beijing-to-Chengde journey as a "tour of inspection"

Given the scale of the imperial party, it is no wonder that court officials were dispatched to "sternly investigate" the activities of all people who followed the imperial procession and to make certain that they did not trample underfoot the fields of the farmers or disturb their peace. Qianlong was especially concerned lest agricultural activities be disrupted in years when drought, flood, or other natural disasters had occurred.[23] He was well aware that each time he passed between Beijing and Chengde, local inhabitants faced possible hardship as a result. Hence, the emperor was gradually moved to cast his journey from the capital to the summer retreat as a "tour of inspection," in terms similar to those used for his other travels.

Howard Wechsler has shown that many classical texts speak of "tours of inspection." According to the *Classic of History* (*Shu jing*), the culture hero Shun embarked on a year-long *xun shou* to offer sacrifices at sacred sites, meet in audience with nobles, standardize weights and measures, and regulate ritual ceremonial. At the end of the tour, recognizing the difficulties inherent in undertaking them, Shun decreed that "tours of inspection" be carried out only once every five years. Wechsler suggests that such tours were undertaken by subsequent rulers as it suited their inclinations or the demands of governing. To justify them, rulers referred back to earlier texts which suggested that sage kings took them to ascertain local conditions and thus deter popular rebellion or the aggrandizement of power by regional lords or officials. *Xun shou* came to be viewed as a means to reinvigorate loyalty among the people and improve government. They enabled the ruler to break out of the center and move to the freer periphery. Furthermore, travel naturally allowed for greater interaction between the sovereign and his court, and even between ruler and commoner.

As this institution developed, so also did expectations of what a ruler should do while he traveled, such as inquire after the old and infirm and distribute honors or gifts to exemplary officials and commoners. Rulers often concerned themselves with questions of adjudication and it was anticipated that a ruler on a tour of inspection might reduce penal sentences or pardon criminals. Taxes were to be remitted, especially in areas passed through by the emperor and his entourage. Rulers and their officials were also expected to ask about local conditions and be attentive to roads, dikes, and bridges in the regions through which they passed.[24]

At first, the Qianlong emperor's peregrinations were not portrayed as classical tours of inspection. On his first four tours of Jiangnan, the emperor's motives were consistently framed instead in terms of filiality: he wished to show his mother the sights of Jiangnan. Indeed, it seems that the first Southern Tour, which took place in 1751, was delayed two years so that it would coincide with the sixtieth birthday of the empress dowager. The delay also helped underwrite the massive costs of the tour, which were ten times more than the amount spent by the Kangxi emperor.[25] What merchant or official commanded to offer monies or provisions to the entourage would dare deny the emperor the opportunity to show his filiality?[26] Such "exemplary, if conspicuous" filial piety also helps account for the presence of the emperor's mother on the next three tours of Jiangnan, as well as on three of the emperor's five visits to Wutai shan and three of his five visits to Qufu. The fourth and last tour south to include the empress dowager occurred in 1765, when she was in her mid-seventies. Because it was clear after its completion that she could no longer make another arduous journey, Qianlong announced that future tours were unwarranted, and took no more before her death in 1777.[27] Yet, three years later in 1780 (once the requisite period of mourning was up), the emperor embarked on a fifth Southern Tour. No longer able to justify the expenses involved on the basis of filiality, Qianlong chose instead to rely upon the older *xun shou* formula to justify the trip south, employing the tried and true rationale for the need to examine local government and public works. The emperor thus made a point while traveling to stop at temples and tombs to offer sacrifices, express interest in the aged and sick, and to reward the virtuous and the meritorious.[28]

The political touches put on Qianlong's journeys to Chengde followed a similar pattern. Until her death in 1777, Qianlong justified the excursions to the summer retreat as filial acts undertaken to please his mother. Indeed, records in the *Rehe zhi* of court journeys from Beijing to Chengde and back chronicle the trips of the empress rather than those of the emperor. After the prescribed mourning period had elapsed, Qianlong again initiated the excursions to Chengde. These continued until at least 1795 and possibly even until the fall before his death in 1799.[29] But since they could no longer be couched as filial undertakings, the emperor endeavored instead to project the aura of the tour of inspection onto them as well. Though there is little evidence to suggest that Qianlong coerced local officials and merchants to provision and fund the annual tours to Bishu shanzhuang, he did remit tax obligations for those areas traversed by the imperial party. In fact, a statement of tax remission was generally the first document Qianlong's officials entered in the official records for the day of departure to Chengde and the day of return to Beijing.[30] Besides cautioning travelers not to disrupt the local countryside, he insisted that they move in groups to minimize the disturbance. Encampments were to be peaceful, and local officials were to be warned of parties coming.[31]

Emperors on tours of inspection were also supposed to pay particular attention to the welfare of soldiers and officials in the areas they passed through. Qianlong took a keen interest in the soldiers in the strategic areas of Gubei kou and Rehe. For instance, when he passed through Gubei kou or arrived at Rehe it was not unusual for him to award bonuses to local bannermen as well as to soldiers from the Green Standard Army.[32] Sometimes eunuchs at Chengde were also rewarded in this way.[33] In addition, Qianlong showed concern for soldiers when there were natural disasters. In 1780, as the emperor began his return to the capital, reports reached him of massive flooding of the Yellow River and other areas of China, including Beijing.[34] The emperor's response was immediate. On September 30, he ordered investigations of the damage caused by the heavy rains, which revealed that the walls of many houses, including those of capital bannermen, had collapsed, leaving many destitute. The emperor awarded all bannermen in designated ministries one month's salary and provisions, and somewhat later made a more general announcement that all soldiers in the capital would be granted one month's salary and provisions, as would soldiers at Gubei kou.[35] As for soldiers at Rehe, the emperor stated that although he had already offered rewards to them, because they were still embarrassed for lack of provisions, he decided to grant them an additional one-half month's salary and provisions.[36]

Another type of inspection the emperor undertook on his way to or from Rehe was to visit temples, tombs, and other sacred sites, as when, for instance, he visited the Eastern Tombs in 1780 and ordered that the Grand Secretariat provide rewards to soldiers who had planted trees near the tombs.[37]

Conclusion

Like his grandfather before him, the Qianlong emperor was a peripatetic monarch, constantly in motion. During much of his reign, upwards of three months out of the year were spent by the court at Rehe or in Mulan, and some years he spent only one-third of his time in Beijing. While the annual excursion to Chengde was an integral part of the imperial routine, when he could no longer explain the trip as an act of filiality, Qianlong chose to conduct it as a "tour of inspection," on the model of the tours he had been leading around the empire throughout his reign. In this decision, one can see Qianlong acting as a conscientious Confucian monarch in the Chinese mode, even while his steadfast dedication to journey north of the Great Wall to hunt and feast with his Manchu, Mongol, and Tibetan subjects suggested that he likewise bore in mind the goals of the Inner Asian khan.

Notes

1 Huang, *1587, A Year of No Significance: The Ming Dynasty in Decline.*
2 This pattern was sustained most notably by the Khitan Liao. See Wittfogel and Feng, *History of Chinese Society: Liao, 905–1127.*
3 Kahn, *Monarchy in the Emperor's Eyes*, 88–89.
4 There were a few exceptions to these annual excursions. For instance, Qianlong did not travel to Chengde in 1777 and 1778 because he was mourning the death of his mother.
5 Kahn, *Monarchy in the Emperor's Eyes*, 250.

6   The forty-fifth year of the Qianlong reign corresponds to the period from February 5, 1780 to January 23, 1781 in the Western calendar.
7   For further information on the 1780 Southern Tour, see *QLSL* 1106: 16; 1918: 19.
8   For example, Kangxi's trip from Beijing to Rehe in 1705 took thirty days; in 1706 it took forty-two (*QDRHZ* 1: 478–82).
9   The Qianlong emperor could make the trip in three days if necessary. In the winter of 1754–55, he planned to enfeoff the Khoit *taisha* Amursana (a major Zunghar leader who defected to the Qing) at Bishu shanzhuang. However, the requirement that he conduct the Grand Sacrifice of the Winter Solstice kept him in Beijing until December 22, while Amursana waited in Chengde. Anxious not to offend his new ally, Qianlong then proceeded to Chengde on a forced march in three stages, starting on the 23rd, and Amursana and the other Western Mongol chiefs were fêted December 25–26 (*QLSL* 473: 3a–4a). Interestingly, the option of having Amursana come to Beijing was not entertained.
10 After leaving Chengde in 1705, the Kangxi emperor traveled another twenty-five days by a circuitous route westward to Zhangjia kou. After entering this pass on October 1, he traveled for thirty-one more days before reaching Beijing (*QDRHZ* 1: 478–80). In 1781, the Qianlong emperor moved from Chengde through Gubei kou in three days, but then spent forty-four more days meandering across the North China plain before reaching Beijing. In 1780, as mentioned, he visited the Eastern Tombs on his way back, taking eighteen days between Gubei kou and Beijing (*QDRHZ* 2: 736–52).
11 This is evident when one looks at departures in and around 1780 and their relationship to the June 21 date of summer solstice: 1776/June 28; 1777 and 1778/no departure due to death of the empress dowager; 1779/June 25; 1780/June 23; 1781/June 29; 1782/June 22.
12 In 1793, Staunton, who had a touch of gout, rode in a palanquin, while Macartney rode in "a neat English post-chaise," pulled by four horses. Macartney intended to present the carriage to the emperor as a gift. Once in China, the box on which the coachman normally sat had to be removed because driving the horses from such a position would have placed the coachman above the emperor. See J.L. Cranmer-Byng, *An Embassy to China*, 106 (hereafter "Macartney"); Sir George Staunton, *An Authentic Account of an Embassy from the King of Great Britain to the Emperor of China*, 164.
13 Macartney, 117.
14 Macartney, 116. Spelling modernized.
15 Cited in Hedin, *Jehol*, 12. See Staunton, 277, and Macartney, 117 for further descriptions of these same roads.
16 In his *Description . . . of China*, Du Halde engaged in similar hyperbole. Writing about the Gubei Pass, Du Halde noted that the emperor passed through here on the way to Rehe: "This Place is about forty leagues from Peking, always ascending towards the North: It is a mountainous Country, where he used to take the Diversion of Hunting: the Way to it from Peking is levell'd by Hand, and as even as a Bowling-Green" (vol. 1, 30).
17 Macartney, for instance, began his return trip from Rehe back to Beijing on September 21 after it had rained for six hours the night before. The twelve-mile trip, which normally would have taken two to three hours, took nine hours to complete.
18 Macartney, 109.
19 Staunton, 175.
20 Macartney, 117.
21 See *QDRHZ* 1: 195–96.
22 Ripa, *Memoirs*, 74.

23 *QDRHZ* 1: 520.
24 Wechsler, *Offerings of Jade and Silk*, 161–69.
25 For an excellent analysis of Kangxi's Southern Tours, see Jonathan Spence, *Tsao Yin and the K'ang-hsi Emperor*.
26 Kahn, *Monarchy in the Emperor's Eyes*, 89–97. The court was heavy-handed in coercing merchants and officials to remit grain and silver to provide for the fifth Southern Tour. However, it did promise tax remissions of up to 30 percent in the regions the entourage was to pass through. It also raised by one degree the rank of officials enlisted to host the visitors (*QLSL* 1918: 19; 1919: 4).
27 Kahn, *Monarchy in the Emperor's Eyes*, 88–92.
28 *QLSL* 1918: 19; 1106: 16.
29 Luo Yunzhi indicates that Qianlong's last journey to Rehe and Mulan was in 1795 (*Qingdai Mulan weichang de tantao*, 102–3), while Kahn, drawing on the *Diaries of Activity and Repose*, states that Qianlong traveled to Rehe in 1798 (*Monarchy in the Emperor's Eyes*, 250).
30 Normally Qianlong absolved the districts between Beijing and Rehe of 30 percent of their annual taxes. Though the figure was never less than this, it was sometimes higher in times of crisis (*QDRHZ* 1: 519–20, 538).
31 *QDRHZ* 1: 519–20.
32 *QDRHZ* 2: 675.
33 *QDRHZ* 1: 623.
34 *QLSL* 1114: 2–12; 1115: 2–3; *Qijuzhu* QL45.9.4, 45.9.16.
35 *QLSL* 1114: 2; *Qijuzhu* 45.9.3.
36 *QLSL* 1114: 8.
37 *Qijuzhu* 45.9.7.

6 The Qing hunt at Mulan

Mark C. Elliott and Ning Chia

Taking in the splendor of what the Qing emperors built for themselves at Chengde, it is easy to forget that all this – the imperial residence, the garden pavilions and rockeries, the artificial lakes and islands of *Bishu shanzhuang*, the temples in the surrounding Wulie River valley – all this came later. Before the temples, before the residence, before there was even a place called Chengde, there was a hunting ground. More than twenty years prior to any work on permanent buildings at the summer retreat, the Kangxi emperor made his first visit to the area, and he came to hunt. Hence, the answers to two questions underlying any consideration of the remarkable site that became Chengde – Why build a retreat? And why here? – lie in an appreciation of the Manchu hunt. The goal of this essay is to describe the role of the hunt at the Qing court, including the history of the establishment of the Mulan hunting preserve, its gradual institutionalization, the organization of the hunts, and the political and ritual importance of the hunt for the Manchu elite. Our sources for this study include institutional compendia and local histories as well as inscriptions in both the Chinese and Manchu languages.

Hunting in Inner Asian society

As an economic activity, hunting, of course, is as old as humanity itself, and hunting as politics followed right behind. The skills required for predation being not dissimilar to the skills required for war, the best hunters made the best warriors, and we can assume it was in this connection that the earliest links were established between hunting and politics. Leadership of the group often falling to its leaders in battle, demonstration of hunting prowess was a way to continue to prove one's qualifications as leader when other opportunities (such as the next war) were lacking. Even as it persisted as an occupation of ordinary people, hunting thus gained an association with elite politics ("The Sport of Kings") that it has shed only in the twentieth century. Of the hunt among the "Tartars," Gibbon wrote,

> To employ against a human enemy the same patience and valour, the
> same skill and discipline, is the only alteration which is required in

real war; and the amusements of the chase serve as a prelude to the conquest of an empire.[1]

In China, too, hunting was historically a way for the prince to show his mettle. In the fourteenth-century novel, *The Romance of the Three Kingdoms* (set at the end of the Eastern Han dynasty, 25–220 CE), one of the novel's main protagonists invites the emperor to join him in the hunt, reminding him that, "The kings and emperors of ancient times held four grand hunts yearly, riding forth from the capital each season to show the world their prowess."[2] That hunting was politically and militarily significant in the world of Inner Asia, whence the Manchus came, was therefore not unique.

Contrary to a widely held impression, the Manchus were not true nomads, roaming the steppe on horseback with their herds, moving with the seasons in search of fresh pastures. Rather, they preferred to dwell in fixed settlements, where they mixed sedentary agriculture with hunting, fishing, and limited herding. Although in this respect their way of life differed from that of steppe peoples such as the Mongols, it was similar enough that skill in the saddle and proficiency at hunting were always integral parts of the Manchu lifestyle. The importance of hunting in the Manchu way of life is well attested linguistically: the Manchu word for right, *jebele*, means "quiver," and the word for left, *dashūwan*, means "bow case," and there are also many specialized words in the Manchu vocabulary for equestrian and falconry gear, for particular types of arrows, and for different kinds of horses and dogs.

The Manchus shared this hunting culture with other peoples of the historic frontier zone north of China, such as the Xiongnu, the Khitans, and the Mongols. Because it was inextricably tied not just to economic production but also to social and military organization, for all of these groups the hunt occupied an arguably more central role in politics and society than it did among the sedentary Chinese. In 940, when Emperor Taizong of the Khitan Liao dynasty (907–1125) was criticized for excessively indulging in the pleasures of hunting, he angrily responded, "Our hunting is not merely the pursuit of enjoyment, but a means of practicing warfare!"[3] That this criticism was leveled by one of his Sinic subjects suggests that by this time the Chinese no longer regarded the hunt as an important vehicle for the display of kingly virtue. Indeed, by the Tang period, hunting was already associated with imperial extravagance and dissipation (hence the Liao emperor's defensive posture). But hunting remained a dynastic custom among all the nomadic and semi-nomadic peoples who ruled China. The discipline developed through hunting was highly valued by the rulers of the Jurchen Jin (1115–1234) and the Mongol Yuan dynasty (1260–1368). Of the Mongols, the Persian historian Juvaini wrote,

He [Chinggis khan] paid great attention to the chase and used to say that the hunting of wild beasts was a proper occupation for the commanders of armies. . . . They are ever eager for the chase and encourage their armies thus to occupy themselves; not for the sake of the game alone, but also in order that they may become accustomed and inured to hunting and familiarized with the handling of the bow and the endurance of hardships.[4]

The hunts referred to in both the Khitan and Mongol cases were large-scale exercises involving thousands of men divided into smaller units who fanned out to encircle a large area of forest. As the circle was drawn tighter, the game was driven out into the open where it presented a better target. Of course, animals were also more dangerous under these circumstances, and participants in the hunt had to demonstrate bravery and good horsemanship to avoid injury while keeping cornered beasts from escaping. Any who failed this test were subject to punishment. The organization of these massive, multi-day hunts, known in English by the French name *battue*, called for a high degree of cooperation between the "decimal" units into which soldiers were divided, which became the foundation of an elaborately articulated socio-military social order. This was the case among both the Jurchens and the Manchus. The Jin unit was called the *meng-an mou-ke*; the Qing unit was called the *niru*.

Born out of native hunting practices, the Manchu military *niru* (a Manchu word meaning "arrow," usually translated as "company") comprised about three hundred men. *Niru* were grouped together into successively larger units to form a corps called a "banner" (Ch. *qi*, Ma. *gūsa*), distinguished by the color pattern of its flags and uniforms. There were eight such corps, known collectively as the "Eight Banners," to which not just soldiers, but all the subjects of the Manchu khan belonged. The success of the Qing conquest of China is, in large measure, explained by the effectiveness of Qing military forces, who were molded by the strict discipline and warrior ethic imposed by the Eight Banner system through the hunt-oriented *niru* structure. Some sense of this comes through in the earliest Manchu records, where it is noted that:

Early on, when fighting or hunting, the rules were strict and there was no quarrelling or making noise. The Respected Khan [Nurhaci] always and everywhere instructed the soldiers by reminding them that, "If you make noise in [i.e., before] battle, the enemy will know where you are. If you are noisy while on the hunt, it will echo off the mountains and the animals will run away." Five *niru* being formed into one unit, when they went somewhere, everyone went to the same place; when they dismounted, they all dismounted one by one at the same place; when they attacked, they all attacked at the same place. The men in long heavy armor, bearing spears and heavy swords, led the attack, while those in lighter mesh armor, with bows and arrows, shot from behind them. The crack soldiers, on horseback, stood separately watching and gave assistance in places where the attack was not going well. In this way, every battle ended in victory.[5]

The intimate connection between hunting and warfare was something that Nurhaci supposedly even dreamed about.[6] Though increasingly bureaucratized over time, and progressively less vital militarily, the *niru*-banner system survived to the end of the dynasty as one of the bulwarks of Manchu identity. It is thus possible to say that the hunting tradition remained ingrained in Manchu society until the early twentieth century.

The establishment and administration of the Mulan hunting preserve

In the decades leading up to 1644, banner soldiers frequently went on organized hunts. Nurhaci's son and successor, Hong Taiji, even established a hunting ground in 1630 for this purpose, which was found east of the capital, Mukden.[7] During the actual conquest of China in the 1640s and 1650s, however, the hunt was temporarily abandoned, since most Manchus were engaged full time in the pacification of the empire. Although the first Manchu monarch to rule in China, the Shunzhi emperor (r. 1644–1661) hunted in a suburb of the imperial capital at Beijing (the Nanyuan, or "southern garden"), this was mostly for his own diversion and did not involve large-scale maneuvers. The real revival of battue hunting was left to his son, the Kangxi emperor (r. 1662–1722). Roughly a century later, the institution of the hunt had grown to such proportions that the Qianlong emperor (grandson of the Kangxi emperor, r. 1736–1795) proudly stated that the Qing imperial hunt was unprecedented in its scale; his successor, the Jiaqing emperor, boasted similarly that it surpassed the royal hunts of the Han and the Tang in magnificence.[8]

Kangxi's revival of the Qing hunting tradition can be traced to 1681, when he went hunting on lands belonging to the Kharachin, Aukhan, and Ongni'ud Mongols located in the march between the North China Plain and the Mongolian plateau, approximately 150 kilometers to the north of present-day Chengde, and very close to the thirteenth-century Mongol capital at Shangdu. He was accompanied by a number of Inner Mongolian princes and 3,000 mounted Mongol warriors, along with a few soldiers of the Eight Banners and a small entourage of officials who had traveled with him from Beijing. At the end of the visit his Mongol allies presented the lands to the throne as an imperial hunting preserve – apparently at the emperor's own request – and a banquet was held in celebration. By the time of the next visit in 1683, the lands had formally been constituted as the hunting ground known as Mulan, with a willow palisade marking its circumference (see Figure 2). Edicts of 1683 and 1684 expanded the participants in the hunt to include not just members of the royal family and court officials but also Eight Banner troops from the capital and from the Eight Banner garrisons in Nanjing, Hangzhou, Jingzhou, and Xi'an.

At first, protection and management of the preserve was the responsibility of one of the Mongol imperial sons-in-law. Then, in 1705, the Kangxi emperor created an official hunting office within the Eight Banners to manage the Mulan hunt. The highest-ranking official in this office was the Chief Controller of the hunting preserve (*weichang zongguan*), with his headquarters located at Tangsanying in the northwest of Chengde Prefecture.[9] Throughout the Qing dynasty, this position was always assigned to a Manchu, except during 1735–1745 when it was given to a Mongol bannerman.[10] Eight adjutants were appointed to assist him, four to manage security and four to oversee local Mongolian affairs.[11] Gradually, the area was incorporated into the Chinese administrative structure, being raised to the status of a department (*ting*) in 1723. Though Han immigration into the area did not begin in earnest until the middle of the nineteenth century, the removal under the Qianlong emperor of the four adjutants in charge of Mongolian affairs and the appointment of other kinds of officials such as the civil commissioner (*lishi tongzhi*), whose job was to mediate in disputes between banner people and Han Chinese, indicates that population was already becoming somewhat mixed in the eighteenth century.

In 1749 Mulan administration was switched for a short time to the Lifan yuan on the grounds that "the imperial hunting ground was the place of the Mongols, it should belong to the administration of the Lifan yuan. The chief controller of the hunting preserve should be a Lifan yuan position."[12] The Inner Mongolian Reception Bureau, one of the Lifan yuan departments, was authorized to make appointments to all of the official positions in the hunting administration.[13] The court's close interest in the proper management of affairs at Mulan can be seen in 1763 instructions issued by the Qianlong emperor regarding the specific financial support for hunting guards.[14] The emperor also augmented the number of officials at Mulan in 1753 and authorized the appointment of many more resident hunting guards, whose numbers rose from 191 in the Yongzheng reign (1723–1735) to 800 in the Qianlong reign (and later 950 under the Jiaqing emperor).[15] These hunting guards were selected from the banners in the capital. Under the direction of the chief controller, they guarded against poaching, squatting, and the illegal taking of timber. Perhaps their most important task was to supervise the rotation of the hunting ground's seventy-two hunting zones to ensure the balance and health of the animal population. To maintain the natural environment, the guards also implemented the dynasty's ban on any sort of permanent building or architecture within the preserve. Exceptions to this interdiction on construction were the East and the West Temple Palaces (*Dongmiao gong* and *Ximiao gong*), the Divine Stone Temple (*Shenshi miao*) for the emperor's worship during the hunt, and stelae.

In 1764, after fifteen years as part of the Lifan yuan, responsibility for the hunting preserve was returned to the Eight Banners, this time under the authority of the Rehe garrison lieutenant general, who was chief of what would become in 1778 Rehe prefecture.[16] Further tinkering of the administrative structure occurred during the last years of the Qianlong reign and under the Jiaqing emperor, but it is generally concluded that by this time the hunting administration could no longer effectively manage the area, or, in particular, prevent poaching of animals and trees.[17]

Transferring management of the hunt from the hands of Mongol lords outside the banner system and delivering it to imperial appointees changed the nature of the hunt, which became inexorably more bureaucratized. In this as in other areas (e.g., shamanic religion), Manchu ancestral practice was formally integrated into the dynastic system. While this system was heavily influenced by Chinese precedents, it is worth pointing out that from top to bottom the staffing of the imperial hunting bureaucracy was limited exclusively to Manchus and Mongols in the Eight Banners. So however institutionalized it became, the Mulan hunt remained literally and figuratively an Inner Asian preserve.

Why Mulan?

We have referred above to the hunting preserve as "Mulan." This reflects its use in the 1807 inscription by the Jiaqing emperor discussed below, but it is not how the preserve was known at first to the Manchus, who used its Chinese name for much of the 1700s and called it simply "the hunting ground in Rehe." The name Mulan (which bears no relation to the legendary warrior heroine) comes from the Manchu word *murambi*, meaning to hunt deer with a whistle (the Chinese expression for this is *shao lu*), and applies to one of the two kinds of hunting that took place here. *Muran* hunting, which usually took place in the early autumn, involved a relatively small party of hunters, one of whom would put on a modeled deer head and blow a wooden whistle to imitate the sound of a doe. This attracted the stag, bringing him within shooting distance. The *muran* hunt was primarily for sportsmanship and pleasure, and its spoils were divided by the emperor among the immediate party. It is a bit of a paradox that the name for the preserve was taken from this type of hunt, rather than from the other hunt that took place here, the large-scale battue hunt, or *aba* (Ch. *da wei*), described earlier, for which it was most famous. The modern Chinese name for the area, Mulan Weichang, combines a phonetic equivalent of the Manchu term *muran* with the Chinese word *weichang*, meaning "battue site."

Why establish a hunting preserve at Mulan? The most obvious reason is that the hunting here had always been good. When Khubilai built his capital at Shangdu in around 1260, he took care to include a hunting preserve. Though Marco Polo describes the preserve as populated mainly by tame deer, later in the reign it seems to have become the site of regular hunting by Khubilai and his court, which occurred on a grand scale.[18] Five centuries later this same area was still thickly forested and harbored a large and varied stock of game.[19] In addition, the region's terrain is notable for the north–south orientation of its many valleys, most of them opening up into small glens, thus lending itself naturally to the *aba* hunt, which required not only abundant game but clearings into which game could be driven. Altogether at Mulan there were 67 such clearings, called *hoihan* in Manchu. Each retained a Mongolian name or was given a new one (only two *hoihan* had Manchu names), a practice that emphasized the Mongol origin of the land. As mentioned, the hunt was held in a different part of the preserve every year in order to assure the continued supply of game both big (deer, antelope, tiger, bear, boar) and small (badger, hare, fox). In the early 1800s, the Jiaqing emperor noted sadly that the hunting ground had been seriously damaged by illegal tree cutting and poaching, and that the shortage of water, grass, trees, and animals made the imperial hunt very difficult. But in Kangxi's day the environment was thriving: over the years, the emperor is said to have shot 135 tigers, 20 bears, 25 leopards, 96 wolves, and several hundred deer, and it was recorded that the emperor once killed 318 hares in a single day.[20]

The Kangxi, Qianlong, and Jiaqing emperors showed an extraordinary devotion to the Mulan site. Between them they led the autumn hunt at Mulan on 91 occasions, often spending up to a month at a time living in tents, surrounded by Manchu and Mongol bannermen, together with Mongol princes and tribesmen and other followers. Only on rare occasions – usually those involving mourning, sickness, or some especially pressing business – was the annual visitation canceled.[21] Though the imperial complex at Chengde was officially known as a place to "escape the heat," to a degree this was a misnomer. For one thing, temperatures in Chengde did not vary that much from those in Beijing; only once in Mulan, at higher elevation, was there an appreciable difference in climate. Furthermore, when the Kangxi emperor established the custom of imperial visits to Rehe, he most often chose to come not during the time of greatest summer heat, but in September and October – just in time for the stag-hunting season. It is true that later, after the first buildings of Chengde had been completed, the emperor's visits generally began earlier, in July, June, or even May. However, it still does not seem that the heat is what drove him to Rehe, in that his visits extended well into the fall, often into November, and on seven occasions he returned for a month or two in the winter (though no hunts were ever held in that season). Sometimes the Kangxi emperor even returned twice a year.[22] One can conclude that the court kept coming back to Chengde, in part, because the emperors enjoyed the more relaxed atmosphere of the summer capital and the change of pace from the hectic, regimented life of the Forbidden City. They reveled in its natural beauty, its rusticity, and the diversity of activity the place afforded, most especially hunting and the chance to sleep under the stars. These sentiments are well-captured in a note written by the Kangxi emperor to a Manchu general in 1705:

> I am fine. Right now there is no business. At this cool place outside the passes, everyone, from soldiers down to errand-runners, has set up their tents. We've been living here eating game and fish from the mountains and rivers. At night I cover myself with just a cotton blanket. The rainfall has been just right. My mind and heart are tranquil.[23]

Mulan was, in many ways, a Manchu "Xanadu."

But hunting at Mulan was not only about relaxing. It was also about politics and military readiness. The preparations for removing the court to the backwoods and ensuring that the hunt proceeded smoothly required considerable organization. Once it was initiated by the Kangxi emperor in the 1680s, participants, who numbered in the thousands (one Jesuit account says 30,000!), were drawn from the same groups, primarily high court officials, bannermen,[24] and Mongolian nobles.[25] Discontinued for a time under the Yongzheng emperor (who nonetheless encouraged his sons to keep up their hunting skills[26]), the hunt was reinstituted by the Qianlong emperor, when the number of bannermen taking part in the hunt could top 12,000. This is not including participants drawn from almost all parts of Inner Asia, including inner and outer Mongolia, Qinghai (Kokonor), and Xinjiang.

Mobilizing for the chase

The Mulan hunt formally began with ceremonies held while the court was still in Beijing. On the day of departure, the emperor led members of the royal family and other members of the entourage, properly attired and equipped, to worship the Manchu ancestors. All promised the ancestors they would never forget the two most important aspects of the "old way," namely, Manchu language and mounted archery (Ch. *guoyu qishe*[27]). In return, they asked for the ancestors' blessing for the coming hunt. Tibetan lamas joined in to pray for the safety and success of the hunt.[28] After the ceremonies, the emperor and his hunting party moved out of the capital with the proper ritual items. These activities, and the words used to describe them such as "ritual" and "ceremony" (Ch. *li, dian, dianli*, or *lizhi*), seem to show that the Mulan hunt was viewed as a sort of imperial ritual by Chinese.[29] However, a preliminary review of Manchu records of the hunt does not show the same sort of preoccupation with categorizing this type of imperial behavior as "ritual." Moreover, that there was no fixed date upon which the court left for the north, and that in some years it never left at all, suggests that a certain informality, even an impromptu air, surrounded the hunt. We might better think of it not as ritual, but as rite. More on this will be said below.

Having assembled first at Chengde, the hunting party made its way further north to the hunting preserve, where everyone camped. Before dawn on the day the hunt began, the officers in charge led the participants for that day – usually about 3,000 people (2,000 Mongols and about 1,000 Manchu and Mongol bannermen), all grouped according to function (beater, archer, musketeer, etc.) – out of the encampment to the site chosen for the battue.[30] The men were divided into two wings, the left wing identified by a white banner and the right wing by a red one. Leaders of each wing then spread their men in two semi-circles over an area anywhere from thirty to eighty *li* around, with the temporary imperial encampment (called the *kancheng* in Chinese), at the north end. The penalties for breaking ranks were very strict. Once the wings had rejoined at the *kancheng*, blue banners were raised. The wing leaders then removed their hats, placed them at the end of long whips and held them up high, yelling the signal word *malagh-a* ("hat" in Mongolian) for the circle to begin closing.[31] The signal would be repeated three times up the line until it reached the central command post at the south end, where a large yellow pennant would be raised and movement begun inward. The circle would be closed until it was only two or three *li* around, with a second circle of marksmen having in the process formed around the circle of beaters.

All was now in readiness. By this time the emperor would have arrived at the *kancheng* from the main Mulan camp. Protected by expert marksmen from random attack by tiger or boar, the emperor ventured out on horseback into the midst of the scene and began the hunt. His was the first shot, and usually the largest stag was selected for him to pursue. On occasions when a tiger or bear had been trapped in the battue, the emperor might be privileged with the kill, aided by the specialized "tiger-gun brigade." Although highly staged, the emperor's performance in this spectacle – which was repeated many times during the month or so that the court usually spent at Mulan – was symbolically important. It was also an important place for imperial sons to demonstrate their worth: the bravery Qianlong showed as a young boy when confronted by a bear on the hunt is supposed to have won him favor over his brothers. A good showing on the hunt later appears to have become virtually de rigueur – in 1791, it was arranged for a favorite grandson of the Qianlong emperor to shoot a deer when he was only nine years old. In 1820 this grandson came to the throne and reigned until 1850 as the Daoguang emperor. This was only one way in which hunting and politics were intertwined in the Qing.

At the conclusion of the hunting season, the emperor threw a banquet for all participants, managed by the Lifan yuan. In addition to food, these events featured different entertainment programs, performed by the various peoples of the empire. After the general banquet, the emperor held a further special feast for the Mongol and Uyghur leaders (who, unlike the Kazakhs and Kirghiz, were Qing ministers), and issued them awards according to rank. The two Mongol league leaders whose territory encircled Mulan also offered a banquet.[32] Such a setting offered opportunities for the face-to-face contact that strengthened the ties between the court and Inner Asian peoples, many of whom feared traveling to China proper lest they fall victim to smallpox, which was largely unknown on the steppe, and to which they had little natural immunity. In particular, through joint participation in the hunt, the presentation of gifts, the bestowing of feasts, and the sponsorship of contests of martial and athletic prowess, the special nature of Manchu–Mongol relations was regularly celebrated and confirmed.

The politics of the hunt

The 1681 hunt that led to the foundation of the Mulan preserve was certainly not the first time that Manchus and Mongols had gone hunting together, and Kangxi's choice of the hunt as a means of demonstrating his ties with the steppe culture was hardly accidental. As early as Hong Taiji's time, the hunt was combined with diplomatic duties designed to intensify alliances with Mongol leaders.[33] But timing and geography made the 1681 hunt especially significant. In the early 1680s, with the Rebellion of the Three Feudatories over and resistance in Taiwan finally brought to heel, the emperor, then in his early thirties, was for the first time free to turn his attention to affairs in the north, where Qing rule was, as yet, quite tentative. Not only were ties between the Eastern, or Khalkha, Mongols, and the Manchu regime still uncertain, but the Western Mongols (Oirats), led by Galdan, were vying with the Manchus for the loyalties of Khalkha nobles as well as for the support of the Dalai Lama. Records show that the Kangxi emperor received Khalkha, Kharachin, and Dörböt leaders fourteen times in seven of the designated hunting sites. Later on, the Qianlong emperor held such meetings still more frequently, meeting with Inner Asian leaders in fourteen of the hunting sites and often taking the opportunity to proclaim edicts that affected them directly.[34] Thus, although the hunt was valued in part as a means of escaping Beijing, it hardly represented an escape from politics.

Indeed, even during the height of the hunting season Mulan served as a center of government. The imperial "palace" and "offices" were moved to Mulan and settled in the "traveling camp" (Ch. *xingying*), designed as a miniature tent city (called *huangman cheng* in Chinese), in which the location of tents corresponded roughly to the layout of offices and palaces around the Forbidden City.[35] To keep the government working during the hunting season, relays traveled between Mulan, Chengde, and Beijing once every three days. Thus, the emperor remained connected to all parts of the empire from his camp just as he did from the palace: he was able to receive official reports and memorials, give instructions, and issue edicts. Emergency matters sent by express courier took only slightly longer to reach him here. Moreover, court officials and clerks also worked in their tents as they worked in the imperial capital. The only difference was that the official documents from Mulan were additionally stamped with two special characters: *xingzai* ("at the hunting place").[36] The Qing official Zhao Yi (1727–1814), who witnessed office work at the "traveling camp" at Mulan, observed that there were no tables inside the tents and that the clerks either wrote lying on the ground or by using the wooden boxes in which memorials were packaged in transport as makeshift desks. Since the surface of the box was very limited, clerks had to write with their arms and hands unsupported in the air. Moreover, no lights illuminated the tents, so clerks labored by candlelight, candles stuck in simple frames of iron wire made by the clerks themselves.[37] With these rustic modifications, the bureaucracy kept humming.

The twin centers of Chengde and Mulan thus developed in the eighteenth century into a true summer capital, an assembly site on the other side of the Great Wall that mirrored the Liao, Jin, and Yuan maintenance of multiple capitals.[38] The *Gazetteer of Chengde Prefecture* emphasizes this, stating that the Manchu court designated Chengde as a "divine capital" (Ch. *shenjing*) to assist the main capital, Beijing, and held the annual hunt there as one way of providing this assistance.[39]

As an integral element of the summer palace complex at Chengde, the Mulan hunt increased the significance of the Mountain Villa in its interaction with the Inner Asian world. As already sketched above, Mulan as an imperial political center was rooted in the hunting tradition of the Manchus and other Inner Asian peoples. So it is not surprising that the reserve was the setting for several fateful moments in Qing history and of significant diplomatic activity concerning the Inner and Central Asian realms of the empire. In 1689 the Kangxi emperor, at Mulan on the hunt, signed the Treaty of Nerchinsk; just one year later, having assembled his troops on the northern border of the hunting ground, he led them in victory over Galdan, whose forces were threatening nearby. Again the next year, in 1691, the same area was the site of the submission of the Khalkha princes to the Qing at a momentous convocation at Dolonnor. Eighty years later, in 1771, the summer capital witnessed the reception of the Torghut leader Ubashi, who led his people back from Russia to the Qing fold (see Millward, Chapter 8).

The political importance of Mulan can also be seen in the way it represented the court's concern with what it called "unification." This was expressed in Chinese as *zhongwai yijia*, or *neiwai yijia*, both meaning roughly "interior and exterior as one family."[40] In Manchu, the phrase that is sometimes seen is *uherilembi*, "to unite." In modern parlance, these two phrases suggest that "Chinese and foreigners are one family." In the context of the Qianlong emperor's statements and poems, however, his use of this phrase indicates a unity of diverse peoples *within* the rule of the Qing empire. For example, *zhongwai yijia* is used repeatedly to describe the coming together under Qing rule of both the inner Mongols (Khorchin, Kharachin, Tümet,

Chahar) and outer, or Eastern, Mongols (Khalkha).[41] When, following the first pacification of Zungharia in 1755, the Qianlong emperor met with the newly submitted four Oirat (Western Mongol) leaders in Chengde, he expressed his joy again with the phrase *neiwai yijia*.[42] Elsewhere, the emperor used "one family" also to refer to the inclusion of Tibet in the Qing empire;[43] a similar, though not identical, sentiment is observed in a 1759 memorial to the emperor upon the incorporation of Zunghar lands into the realm: "Before the distantly radiating virtue and power of my sacred lord, the western marches have been pacified and the steppes, mountains, and rivers of the Zunghar Mongols have been unified with the territory of China (Ma. *dulimbai gurun*)."[44] The use of these phrases in the Chengde context underlines how the Mulan hunt worked for the Qing unification of the "inner people" (the Han Chinese) and the "outer people" (the non-Han) in the same "family-empire."

The Mulan hunt as "family training"

Located in Mongol territory at the geographic intersection of China, Manchuria, Mongolia, and at the spiritual intersection of these domains and Tibet, the political center that grew around the Manchu hunt well captured the diversity of the Qing imperial enterprise. It also gave the Qing dynasty a stage on which to assert its Inner Asian identity. The annual organization of the expedition "beyond the passes," the selection of bannermen participants and the issuance of summons to Inner Asian vassals, the physical transfer of the court north of the Great Wall to Chengde, the ritual affirmation of fraternal ties between Manchus and Mongols, the extravagant patronage of Tibetan Buddhism, and the grand autumn hunt – all were exercises that perpetuated what came to be heralded as a Manchu family tradition, the emblem of the warrior origins of the horse-riding, tiger-hunting Manchu nation.

Above all, it was the hunt that became a sacred Qing institution. The importance of the hunting tradition for the court and for Manchus at large was the subject of a valedictory written by the Jiaqing emperor in 1807, "The Record of Mulan."[45] The text, in Chinese and Manchu, was engraved on a stele 4.4 meters high that still stands in the valley at the more easterly of the two south entrances of the hunting preserve. It is placed a few hundred meters to the east (and somewhat lower) than another stele put up in the same valley by the Qianlong emperor in 1751. "The Record of Mulan" summarizes the importance of the hunting preserve to the dynasty from an early nineteenth-century viewpoint, near the very end of Chengde's "golden age" and is one of the most instructive of the texts associated with Rehe. The Chinese version of the inscription was included in a collection of imperial writings and has sometimes been cited in modern scholarship on Mulan.[46] Our interpretation of the poem relies, however, on the more obscure Manchu version, which provides a more Altaic – not to say more "authentic" – perspective on the place of the hunt in the Manchu imagination.[47]

The "Record" introduces the subject by stating plainly, "Mulan is our nation's hunting ground," and then enters into a lengthy description of the geography and history of the place. Observing that "when [the Kangxi] Emperor Shengzu visited here every year to hunt, all the different tribes would come together," the Jiaqing emperor noted the continuation of the tradition by his own father, Qianlong:

> Each time the inner and outer princes came in great numbers, followed by their retinues. As the imperial grace was deep and generous, after the genuinely valued far western lands were pacified, learning and civility was extended to the peoples of the Dörböt, Torghut, Kokonor, Uriyangkhai, and Muslim tribes, who were divided into rotations and came [here] to hunt in turn. Seeing that their sacred master never missed when he shot his bow, they were truly impressed, being both afraid and thankful. They became forever officials in the outer provinces of the great Qing dynasty. Truly, is not heaven exalted?

While on the one hand claiming that it was the extension of "learning and civility" to Inner Asian groups that assured their incorporation into the empire, at the same time the emperor implies that physical strength, virility, and warrior skills – both in the person of the emperor and in the field forces of the dynasty – were essential to Qing prestige and legitimacy. Without them, it could not be expected that the dynasty would be able to hold on to these territories or integrate them into the empire. This, presumably, is in contrast to the situation with regard to rule over China proper, where, in the long run, "civilizing" ability (*wen*) was valued over "militarizing" skill (*wu*).

The "Record" then goes on to affirm its author's intent to uphold this tradition:

> In order to perpetuate the lessons of my khan-father, every year I have been coming to hunt in the battue. Although I know that my shooting and riding fall far short, indeed, of the skills of my khan-father, it would not do if I were to dare not to apply myself to this wholeheartedly. I surely will not take up idle, leisurely ways.

Even taking filial humility into account, it is worth noting that a decline in the important Manchu skills of riding and shooting is taken for granted by the Jiaqing emperor. Yet, he perseveres in their practice and in inculcating the same belief in the importance of these skills in the next generation, emphasizing that "I took all of my household, as well as the grandsons and great-grandsons of the near branches [of the imperial clan] to Muran and made them practice the battue." The involvement of the larger imperial clan shows how the Mulan hunt had literally become a "family tradition" for the Aisin Gioro.

A few lines later, the "Record" returns to this same theme: "Hunting in battue-style is the family training of our nation, and the pacification of distant places is indeed a great and fundamental principle of our nation." Reflecting Qing consciousness of the historical roots of the battue hunt, the emperor suggests a direct connection between drill in hunting formations, military discipline (what he calls "family training") and the success of the empire led by the "nation" of Manchus.[48] This connection surely would have seemed very familiar to the Kangxi emperor, not to mention Chinggis khan. The imperialist bent of the Manchu empire is apparent here, too, as conquest (euphemistically known as "pacification") and the expansion of the frontier to include "distant places" are put forward as part of the basic philosophy of the Qing state.

The phrase describing the Mulan hunt as "family training" or "family teaching" (Ma. *booi tacihiyan*) is actually slightly different in Chinese, where the word is *jiafa*, meaning "family law" or "family tradition." The Qianlong emperor repeatedly referred to the hunt in these terms, identifying it as the "ancestral system" (*zuzhi*)[49] or the "family law" (*jiafa*).[50] In either the Manchu or Chinese case, though, "family" should be understood on two levels, both distinct from the meaning of the "family-empire" above. First, in a general sense, "family" referred to all Manchus, high and low, whether they were actually present at the hunt or not; a second, specific sense of "family" was in reference to the imperial clan. This "family" theme returns in the final lines of the "Record":

> As the peaceful days stretch on, it is possible that neglectful drifting may gradually occur. But the lord who watches over the making of rewards must not forget the founding way. Can the son who is heir to the house betray the aims of his ancestors? Hunting at Muran in the autumn is the eternal way that must not be forgotten, but preserved for all time by generation after generation of sons and grandsons.

We hear an echo of the words of the Kangxi emperor, who once wrote, "the sons and grandsons of later generations must respect the customs of their imperial ancestors by practicing the martial arts at Mulan so as to not forget the ways of the family."[51] The tenor of these comments indicates that the audience of the inscription was indeed the Manchu "family" – bannermen participating in the hunt as well as members of the imperial clan. Admission of "neglectful drifting" represented a realistic attitude on the part of the court regarding the toll that the assimilation process had taken by the early nineteenth century on Manchu martial vigor. Yet the emperor did not give up completely. At the very least, as the leader of the Manchu nation, the emperor continued to maintain the ways of the past by honing his riding and shooting skills annually. To do less, he was saying, would be a betrayal of the ancestors and of the Qing ideal of rule. The urgency of his exhortations can be seen to reflect a certain foreboding, and justifiably so: the Jiaqing emperor was the last Qing monarch to organize the Mulan hunt on a regular basis. Once he took the throne, his successor, the Daoguang emperor, ceased his visits to Rehe, and no further hunts were ever staged.

Conclusion

Under the Qianlong reign, with other aspects of Manchu cultural distinctiveness fading as bannermen became assimilated to Chinese ways, reenacting the Mulan hunt served as a crucial demonstration of the persistence of a distinctive Manchu *tradition*, even as the actual *custom* of hunting grew rarer and rarer. As such, the hunt at this time appears to take on the contours of what Eric Hobsbawm and Terence Ranger have famously called "invented tradition," the result of "a process of formalization and ritualization, characterized by reference to the past, if only by imposing repetition."[52] This transition is an important element in the evolution of the role of the hunt among the Manchus. Like other invented traditions, the Mulan hunt in the later eighteenth century represented an adaptation of an older practice for newer purposes, in this case the promotion of an ethnic awareness among Manchus and of the proposition that the way of the hunt was one of the ancient bonds tying the Manchus to the Inner Asian perimeter of their empire.

Such a consciousness was vital to the preservation of Manchu institutions, most especially the Eight Banners system and Qing-style emperorship. Court mindfulness of the element of tradition in the hunt – which by the end of the Qianlong reign was already tending toward the nostalgic[53] – has prompted the observation that the ritual bore a "magico-religious stamp" and that "by linking the emperor to his ancestors, the rite affirmed imperial legitimacy, supremacy, and power."[54] It is worth emphasizing again that as the embodiment of a historical tradition with links not only to the Qing past and present, but to Liao, Jin, and Yuan imperial precedents as well, the Mulan hunt pricked Manchu historical consciousness in a most decided way. As we have seen, the historical presence of "fathers" at Mulan was very marked. The proper reenactment of the hunt quite plainly played on the imperial conscience, making it at once a Manchu cultural performance and, at the same time, a filial act. In this sense, the Mulan hunt was the quintessential manifestation of the political and cultural amalgam characteristic of Qing rule so much in evidence in Chengde. Moreover, as part of the Qing imperial system, the institutionalization of the Mulan hunt was a vital component of the Manchu refinement of the Chinese imperial system through the insertion of Inner Asian lifestyles and customs into that system.

In historical perspective, it is not hard to see that the Mulan hunt specifically, and the Manchu hunting tradition generally, were strategic sources of power for seventeenth- and eighteenth-century Qing rulers concerned both to deepen the ties between the court and its Inner Asian subjects as well as to reinforce the martial aspects of Manchu identity. At the same time, the hunt also embodied some of the basic tensions that ran through Qing rule, in that the dynasty's Han Chinese officials seem not to have appreciated the importance of the hunt. In one passage of the "Record of Mulan," the Jiaqing emperor wrote:

> Annually in the autumn we go hunting for not more than twenty days, but [I still] take care of secondary matters, read memorials, and call upon and admit officials. All this is done just as it is in the palace. Since every matter is handled without the slightest delay, how is this like my having become addicted to extended excursions?

This defensive tone, reminiscent of the tenor of the Liao emperor's remarks cited at the beginning of this essay, suggests that the emperor was well aware that at least some Qing officials may have viewed the hunt as wasteful, self-indulgent, and an obstacle to effective government. The emperor's response, couched, as we have seen, in language that is both filial and proud, explaining the origins of this old Manchu tradition and the glory that it has brought the dynasty, reminds us of the gulf that separated the Altaic and Chinese worlds united by the Manchus under the Qing aegis.

Notes

1 Edward Gibbon, *The History of The Decline and Fall of the Roman Empire* (1905–1906), vol. 3, 77, cited in David Morgan, *The Mongols* (Cambridge, Mass.: Blackwell, 1986), 85.
2 Luo Guanzhong, attr., *Three Kingdoms: A Historical Novel*, trans. Moss Roberts (Berkeley and Los Angeles: University of California Press, 1991), 157. The four hunts referred to are those of antiquity: *chunsou* (in the spring), *xiamiao* (in the summer), *qiuxian* (in the autumn), and *dongshou* (in the winter).
3 Karl Wittfogel and Feng Chia-sheng, *History of Chinese Society: Liao, 905–1127*, 526, citing *Liao shi* 4: 48.
4 'Ata-malik Juvaini, *Genghis khan, the History of the World Conqueror*, 27.
5 Kanda *et al.*, eds, *Manbun rōtō* I, Taizu 4, 50–51.
6 Kanda *et al.*, eds, *Manbun rōtō* I, Taizu 4, 53.
7 Luo Yunzhi, *Qingdai Mulan weichang*, 1–2.
8 Hai Zhong and Lin Congshang, eds, *Chengde fuzhi* (1830) (hereafter *CDFZ*), *juanshou* 2: 30b, 3: 11a; Zhao Lian, *Xiaoting zalu*, 221. Note: *CDFZ* has a long introductory (*juanshou*) section in which *juan* are numbered separately from the fascicles in the main text. Where the *juanshou* section is cited in notes below, this is indicated. Otherwise, references are to *juan* and page in the main text.
9 *CDFZ*, 7: 2a, 10: 12b, and 25: 13b–14b; *Jiaqing chongxiu yitong zhi*, 44: 1b.
10 *CDFZ*, 25: 13b–15a and 33: 18a–20b.
11 He-shen (Hešen), Qian Daxin *et al.*, eds, *Qinding Rehe zhi* (1781) (hereafter *QDRHZ*), 46: 19b; *CDFZ*, 25: 13b–15a.
12 *Qianlong chao neifu chaoben Lifanyuan zeli* (1756) (hereafter *LFYZL*), 20.

13 *LFYZL*, 21; *Qingchao tongdian*, 26: 2176; *Gongzhongdang Qianlongchao zouzhe*, 26: 5b; *Qingdai bianzheng tongkao*, 42; Wei Yuan, *Shengwu ji*, 3: 11b.

14 *CDFZ*, *juanshou* 2: 18a.

15 *LFYZL*, 21; *QDRHZ*, 46: 19b; and *CDFZ*, *juanshou* 26: 14a–14b and *juan* 25: 14a–14b.

16 *CDFZ*, 3: 31b and 7: 2a–2b. This pattern is observed elsewhere that Chinese immigrants occupied Inner Asian or other frontier areas, such as Chengde, parts of Xinjiang, Taiwan or, later, Manchuria. In all these places, Qing military administration was incrementally complemented or replaced by an administrative system more similar, though not always identical to, that of China proper.

17 *CDFZ*, 25: 14a–14b.

18 Rossabi, *Khubilai Khan*, 33, 135; Rossabi, "The Reign of Khubilai," in Franke and Twitchett, eds, *The Cambridge History of China, vol. 6*, 472.

19 Forêt, *Mapping Chengde*, 91.

20 *Weichang wenshi ziliao*, 2: 121.

21 For the exact dates of all imperial visits, see the tables in Luo Yunzhi, *Qingdai Mulan weichang*, chapter 3. In years when he visited the imperial tombs in Mukden (e.g., 1754, 1778, 1783), the Qianlong emperor customarily called off the hunt. The arrival of important visitors at Chengde – Amursana in 1754, the Sixth Panchen Lama in 1780, Lord Macartney in 1793 – could also result in cancellation of the Mulan hunt.

22 In one eighteen-month period lasting from the spring of 1716 to the autumn of 1717, he spent only twenty-two weeks – less than six months – in Beijing. The remainder of the time he was in Rehe.

23 Elliott, *The Manchu Way*, 165.

24 To take part, bannermen had to be able to draw a bow of strength 10, the minimum deemed necessary to fell a deer; contests were held in the capital and in the garrison cities to select the strongest archers, whose expenses were borne entirely by the court. More details may be found in Elliott, *The Manchu Way*, 182–187.

25 *Weichang wenshi ziliao*, 4: 72.

26 The reasons for Yongzheng's abstinence from the hunt are not entirely clear. As a prince, the Yongzheng emperor was frequently present both at the Bishu shanzhuang compound and in the hunting parties at Mulan. Among the explanations one might offer are that he was too preoccupied with affairs of state; that he was too concerned with managing funds thriftily to spend the money to carry out the hunt; or that, given the suspicious circumstances surrounding his succession (it was widely believed that he had usurped the throne from his younger brother), he feared himself the victim of a hunting "accident" should he venture into the field.

27 Owen Lattimore once pointed out that *qishe* does not mean "riding and shooting," but "shooting while riding," i.e., mounted archery. See *Inner Asian Frontiers of China*, 65n.

28 *Qingdai huangjia lieyuan – Mulan weichang*, 4–5, 7; Wang Shuyun, *Qiandao beixun yudao he saiwai xinggong*, 26; *Weichang wenshi ziliao*, 2: 109–110.

29 CDFZ, *juanshou* 1: 21b; *juanshou* 2: 5a, 8b, 10a, 16b; *juanshou* 3: 8b, 12a; *juanshou* 6: 8b, 22a; also *juanshou* 16–21 under the title *xundian* (traveling rituals); *QDRHZ*, 45: 2a.

30 This description relies on Luo Yunzhi, *Qingdai Mulan weichang*, 151ff.

31 The reason for shouting "hat!" is not explained. Perhaps it referred to a type of formation.

32 *CDFZ*, *juanshou* 1: 22a–23a.

33 *Manbun rōtō* V, Taizong 57, 822–823.

34 *Weichang wenshi ziliao*, 4: 60–62.
35 *CDFZ, juanshou* 26: 15a–15b; *QDRHZ*, 48: 5a–6a. See the map of the Mulan camp design in Luo Yunzhi, *Qingdai Mulan weichang*, 144.
36 *CDFZ, juanshou* 2: 16b; *Qingdai huangjia lieyuan*, 5; Wang Shuyun, *Qiandao beixun*, 26–27; *Weichang wenshi ziliao*, 4: 57; Sun Wenliang *et al.*, *Qianlongdi*, 152–153.
37 Zhao Yi, *Yanbao zaji*, 1: 5a.
38 See the references to this in Franke and Twitchett, *Cambridge History of China*, vol. 6, especially the table on p. xxix.
39 See the prefaces in *CDFZ*: by Cheng-ge, 1a–1b; by Na-yan-cheng, 2a–2b; by Shen Weiqiao, 2a–3a; by Yu-en, 2a; by Hai-zhong, 1a; *fanli*: 11b, and *juanshou* 13: 32a.
40 For examples of the usage of *zhongwai yijia*, see *QDRHZ*, 16: 6b, 22: 7a, 48: 8b and 12b, and *CDFZ, fanli* 12:b, *juanshou* 6: 21b, *juanshou* 10: 13a, and *juanshou* 13: 28a. For *neiwai yijia*, see *CDFZ*, 19: 21a.
41 *CDFZ*, preface by Shen Weiqiao: 1b; also *juanshou* 2: 3a and 23a and *juanshou* 10: 13a.
42 *CDFZ*, 19: 21a.
43 *CDFZ, juanshou* 10: 12b–13a
44 The original reads: "*enduringge ejen erdemu horon goro selgiyebuhe de erei onggolo wargi jase be necihiyeme toktobufi jun gar monggo tala. alin bira de dulimbai gurun-i nirugan dangse de uherilebuhe*." First Historical Archives, Beijing: *Qianlong chao Manwen zhupi zouzhe* 308, Seksen, QL24.8.4.
45 In Chinese the title is given customarily as the *Mulan ji*, but this is an informal title; in neither text does the inscription itself bear a title as such (cf. the reproduction in Hebei sheng wenwu guanli chu *et al.*, "Qingdai Mulan weichang wenwu diaocha," 98, figure 9).
46 *Shiqubaoji sanbian* (Taipei reprint, 1969), vol. 9, 4373–4376; Hebei sheng wenwu guanli chu *et al.*, "Qingdai Mulan weichang," 95; Luo Yunzhi, *Qingdai Mulan weichang*, 212–213.
47 This text remains unpublished. Photographs of the stele were made during a visit to the site in October 1990 by Elliott, assisted by Philippe Forêt and James Millward, and a transcription made on the basis of these photos.
48 The translation of the Manchu term for "nation" here demands explanation. In the Chinese inscription, the word is *chao*, usually meaning "court," or in this case, more accurately, "dynasty." But the Manchu word *gurun* is much less clear in this respect, typically meaning "country" or "kingdom," though "dynasty" (as in *Ming gurun*) was possible, too. *Gurun* could also be used in expressions (such as *Manju gurun*), where the "country" referred to was not a geographical entity but an ethno-cultural grouping of people, in a sense close to the meaning of "tribe" or "nation." When combined with *boo*, meaning "house," the expression *gurun boo* provided an equivalent to the Chinese *guojia*, "state" or "country."
49 *QDRHZ*, 45: 2b and 47: 3b; *CDFZ, juanshou* 2: 11a and *juanshou* 11: 6b.
50 *QDRHZ*, 19: 2a and 21: 13a; 45: 14a, 46: 4a, 5a, 7b, 8b; *CDFZ, juanshou* 2: 8b; *juanshou* 3: 8b, 10b, 12a; *juanshou* 6: 12b, 24b; *juanshou* 8: 24b; *juanshou* 9: 10b–11a; *juanshou* 11: 8b, 16b; and *juanshou* 12: 16b, 18b.
51 Luo Yunzhi, *Qingdai Mulan weichang*, 123, citing *QDRHZ*, *juan* 25: 4b.
52 Hobsbawm and Ranger, eds, *The Invention of Tradition*, 4–5.
53 See the poem written by the emperor in 1789 during his penultimate hunting trip, cited in Luo Yunzhi, *Qingdai Mulan weichang*, 162.
54 Hou Ching-lang and Michèle Pirazzoli, "Les chasses d'automne de l'Empereur Qianlong à Mulan,", 39.

7 Imperial banquets in the Wanshu yuan

Renqiu Yu

After its completion in 1708, Bishu shanzhuang at Chengde became a location important to the Qing emperors in handling Inner Asian affairs, especially Mongol affairs. During the Kangxi (r. 1662–1722) and Qianlong (r. 1736–1795) reigns, each year the emperor and the imperial court spent several months at Bishu shanzhuang, making it a second political center of the Qing empire. As in Beijing, all sorts of imperial ceremonies were held at Chengde, including various banquets. This chapter, based mainly on Chinese sources, will discuss the imperial banquets at the Wanshu yuan (Garden of Ten Thousand Trees; Figure 8) within the Mountain Villa as a means used by the Qing emperors to assert their supremacy over the Inner Asian peoples.

When the Kangxi emperor initiated the construction of Bishu shanzhuang, he planned to use it, among other things, as a place north of the Great Wall to grant imperial audiences to the Mongol leaders, who were afraid of coming south to Beijing because they were vulnerable to smallpox. To cultivate goodwill and consolidate the Manchu alliance with the Mongols, the Kangxi emperor received their leaders at Bishu shanzhuang, conferring on them imperial clan titles and bestowing on them all sorts of gifts. Sumptuous imperial banquets became an integral part of these rituals: the Kangxi emperor regularly held them for the Mongols, and he also accepted the Mongol invitations to attend their banquets.[1]

We can assume that many delicious dishes were served at these imperial banquets, although available sources provide very few details about them. We know more about what the emperors liked to eat in ordinary days – for example, the Qianlong emperor's favorite dishes included different kinds of tofu and eggplant.[2] But the imperial records tend to focus on the banquet rituals and ignore details about the dishes served. As far as the Qing emperors were concerned, these banquets served to impress the Inner Asians with the Manchu empire's abundance and power, as well as with the emperor's benevolence and, thus, to win their loyalty. This was well understood by the compilers of the Qing official histories, who celebrated the emperors' accomplishments in obtaining the allegiance of the Mongols, Muslims, and the Tibetans, but mentioned almost nothing about the food served to the guests and at the imperial table.[3]

The Qianlong emperor regarded the imperial rituals as essential in establishing Qing political authority over the Inner Asian peoples, and he managed to have an image of himself as a master of these rituals shaped in the written record – either in the official histories or in his own poems and essays. A great admirer of his grandfather, the Qianlong emperor continued Kangxi's policy of building good relations with the Mongols through marriage, conferral of imperial clan titles, and regular imperial audiences in Beijing and Chengde. Several sets of rules for imperial banquets were codified during the Qianlong reign, and Bishu shanzhuang was rebuilt and expanded.[4] To provide a larger space where more Mongols could come to the imperial feasts and to create a more comfortable and harmonious atmosphere for guests from a nomadic culture, the Qianlong emperor ordered the construction of the Wanshu yuan and the Imperial Great Yurt.

The Wanshu yuan, located in the eastern part of the Bishu shanzhuang, was built in the 1740s, and in 1752 the Qianlong emperor held the first imperial banquet for the Mongols in the garden.[5] A tributary from Wulie River ran along the western side of the garden from north to south. In the eighteenth century, there were many trees and animals in the garden. According to Philippe Forêt,

> the fifty-seven hectares of the Wanshu yuan prairie were originally covered by a fairly sparse forest of elms and willows that sheltered deer and birds. . . . The Qing creation of a Mongol site [*menggu bao*] was consistent with the two effects desired for the Wanshu yuan landscape: flexibility in time and space. Yurts, tents, and low fences were erected for parties, concerts and receptions, and removed when these activities ended. The district was then restored to a natural landscape.[6]

The *menggu bao* mentioned by Forêt was clearly a construction of the Qianlong years. Commonly called *menggu bao*, or yurt, its official name was the Imperial Great Yurt (*Yuwo da menggu bao*). The imperial banquets hosted by the Qianlong emperor in the Imperial Great Yurt were thus known as Great Yurt banquet (*Da menggu bao yan*).[7] We do not know who actually initiated the idea of the Great Yurt.

The familiar appearance of the Great Yurt was probably meant to make the visiting Mongols comfortable; but its extraordinary size and colorful decorations also conveyed imperial magnificence to impress the guests. The Great Yurt was made of 765 pieces of wood, covered by layers of felt, wood chips, and white canvas. When imperial banquets were held in the Wanshu yuan, the Great Yurt would be erected right at the center of the feasting space marked by a low fence made of yellow canvas. Inside the yurt, an imperial throne, screen, and other imperial articles stood upon a large carpet. The space inside and outside the Imperial Great Yurt could accommodate more than a thousand people.[8]

On banqueting days, smaller yurts were also erected in the Wanshu yuan. Functioning in different ways, these yurts also served to give prominence to the Imperial Great Yurt. One of them was the Five-direction Yurt (*Wuhe menggu bao*), which contained an imperial bed for the emperor to rest on, placed conveniently behind the Imperial Great Yurt. South of the yurt there were two "patterned roof" yurts, one on each side of the road leading to the throne. These served as the waiting or resting places for high-ranking officials, Mongol princes, or foreign ambassadors awaiting the coming of the emperor. In addition, there were twenty small yurts in various locations, used by security guards, cooks, and servants.[9]

As movable houses, when not used, these yurts were stored in Yongyou si (Temple of Everlasting Blessings).[10] They occupied the space of twenty-five rooms in the temple. Four officers and forty soldiers were stationed permanently in the temple with the exclusive responsibility of cleaning and sunning the yurts. Taking care of these yurts was a serious matter. The humidity of Chengde could easily allow the felts to mold or become infested by moths if not properly cared for. Negligence would lead to various punishments. In 1776, for example, Yong-he, the supervisor-in-chief of Chengde, was demoted for "spotting the yurts."[11]

The banquet held in the Wanshu yuan, according to the Qing imperial statutes, was the second most important imperial banquet, surpassed only by the Taihe dian (Hall of Great Harmony) grand banquet held in Beijing on the emperor's birthday, New Year's Day, or upon the enthronement of a new emperor. The Wanshu yuan banquet was in the same category as the New Year's Eve banquet for Outer Mongols at the Baohe dian (Hall of Preserving Harmony) and those held in Yuanming yuan's Shangao suichang dian (Pavilion of High Mountain and Long River).[12]

The seating at banquets at the Wanshu yuan was strictly elaborated in the Qing statutes. According to *Illustrations For the Assembled Canon of the Great Qing*, the seats at the Imperial Great Yurt banquet were arranged as follows: within the Great Yurt, the throne was at the center, facing south, with a huge imperial dining table (*yuyan*) in front of it. Next to the throne, one single row on each side, were the seats for khutuktus and lamas. Below that were two rows of seats: the Mongol khans and princes sat in the front row, while the first and second rank Qing officials sat in the second row. The third rank Qing officials and young Mongol princes (*taiji*) sat in the open air outside the Great Yurt.[13]

The rituals of the Wanshu yuan banquet, according to *Comprehensive Rites of the Great Qing* (*Da Qing tongli*), were basically the same as those of the Taihe dian grand banquet. The following is a brief reconstruction: at eleven o'clock, all the Mongol khans and princes, Qing government officials in official uniform, and foreign ambassadors in their own national dress, gathered together in the Wanshu yuan awaiting the emperor. At twelve o'clock, as the court musicians began to play imperial music, the emperor came to the garden in a palanquin. After the emperor entered the Imperial Great Yurt through the northern gate and ascended the throne, the Mongols, Qing officials, and foreign ambassadors were ushered by officials of the Lifan yuan (Ministry Ruling the Outer Regions) and Honglu si (Banquet Office) to their respective seats. After performing the kowtow to the emperor, they sat down. Then the emperor bestowed on them tea, wine, fruit, and food. Each time they received bestowals from the emperor, the guests and the Qing officials knelt and kowtowed to the emperor. During the banquet, imperial musicians played different ritual music, performed only on such occasions. There were also performances by Mongol and Manchu wrestlers, Korean dancers, and various acrobats.[14]

Realizing in the 1750s that internal conflicts had weakened the Outer Mongol tribes, the Qianlong emperor believed that he had the opportunity to solve the Mongol problem that his grandfather, Kangxi, and his father, Yongzheng (r. 1723–1735), had failed to do (see Millward, Chapter 8). The Bishu shanzhuang became the primary place for handling Mongol affairs and the Wanshu yuan banquets were the occasions to celebrate the Mongol chieftains' acceptance of Qing supremacy. In the early 1750s, internal conflicts drove many Western Mongol tribes to defect from the Zunghars and to accept Qing overlordship.[15] In 1754, the leaders of the Dörböt tribe led three thousand households to defect to the Qing. The Qianlong emperor regarded it as a significant event marking the expansion of Qing influence into Central Asia, and he decided to grant the surrendered Mongol princes great receptions. In the fifth lunar month of 1755, the Qianlong emperor held a total of eleven banquets and receptions at the Bishu shanzhuang welcoming the Dörböt leaders, of which five were held in the Wanshu yuan. To record the historical event, the Qianlong emperor ordered the Jesuit painters serving at the Qing court to come to Chengde to witness and paint the scene of the Imperial Great Yurt banquet. The result was the famous painting *Ceremonial Banquet in the Garden of Ten Thousand Trees* (*Wanshu yuan ciyan tu*) (see Sommer, Chapter 11)[16]. Its marvelous depiction of the emperor, the Mongols, the Qing officials, and the musicians and cooks recreates the scene, but we should also bear in mind that this was specifically arranged by the emperor himself for us to see. In addition to this and other paintings, the Qianlong emperor also composed many self-congratulatory essays and poems to celebrate the event, stressing how his benevolence and generosity had won the trust and respect of the Mongols.[17]

It was at these banquets in the Wanshu yuan, the Qianlong emperor was delighted to note, that these Mongols learned to perform properly at the Qing imperial rituals. All the Mongols invited to these banquets were required to wear Qing official robes and to kowtow to the emperor at several points during the banquet. In the winter of 1755, the Qianlong emperor recorded in one of his poems what he perceived as awkward acts of the

Khoit Mongols headed by Amursana at the title-conferring ceremony at Bishu shanzhuang (in Zhanbojingcheng Hall of the main palace): "To pacify the land, our empire is more than generous / As they have come from afar, [the guests'] improper performance can be forgiven. / Their first time at the imperial ceremony, they don't know how to move; / But very happy they are, as new princes."[18]

Two days later, Qianlong hosted a feast for Amursana and his men in the Wanshu yuan, and the emperor found that once dressed in their official robes, these Khoit Mongols "seemed to have learned how to perform [ceremony]."[19]

We do not know how the Mongols responded to their treatment at Qing banquets, but the Qianlong emperor seemed to believe that the imperial privileges, such as the imperial music, food, and wine, had greatly impressed his guests, for he chose to record his impressions of the delighted Mongols overwhelmed by his magnificence.[20] In his poems, the emperor loved to paint a picture in which he was the center of the banquet distributing gifts and food to grateful guests.

The Tibetan Panchen Lama's visit to Chengde in 1780 is another case that illustrates the significance placed by the Qing on guest rituals. The Qianlong emperor devoted much time and energy to arranging the Panchen Lama's visit, and he seemed determined to use the Panchen Lama's enormous influence among the Mongol tribes in the western part of the Qing empire.[21]

In the Tibetan account of the Panchen Lama's visit (see Ragnubs, Chapter 16), the emperor emerges as a great patron of the Gelukpa sect who treated the Panchen Lama more or less as an equal. In his own poems composed in Chinese, however, Qianlong appears more assertive. On the day of the Panchen Lama's arrival, the emperor relished the Panchen Lama's grateful attitude, and he characterized the historic visit in this way: "By honoring one person, [I've] made tens of thousands happy / Both your name and mine will mark history."[22]

From the Qianlong emperor's poems about the Panchen Lama's visit to Chengde, we can see again that he was consistently concerned with the propriety of the ceremonial rituals that manifested imperial authority and supremacy. Three days after hosting the banquet for the Panchen Lama in the Wanshu yuan, the Qianlong emperor composed another poem stressing the Panchen Lama's voluntary submission and correct understanding and performance of the imperial rituals, and relating them to the Mongols and feasting:

> The divine monk took a rest in the Temple of Everlasting
>   Blessings [while waiting for the banquet in the Garden],
> His holiness has come and so many are eager to see him.
> A living Buddha, he said he should pay homage to the Old
>   Buddha,

– alas, even in ancient times such things were rarely heard.
The Mongol tribes, new and old all display increasing respect;
To entertain them, we host a feast.
Now, center and outer lands are one family extending beyond
     the Congling Mountains,
The Great Qing for ten thousand years will maintain Heaven's
     blessing.

In his own note to this poem, the emperor commented:

Our dynasty's family laws rule that when lamas come for an imperial audience, they only have to kneel (*gui*), not kowtow (*bai*) to the emperor. The Panchen Lama said, however, that "the emperor is an Old Buddha [*gufo*] and that I [the Panchen Lama] should kowtow (*bai*)". Thus [the emperor] allowed him [to kowtow] as he wished. This shows the Panchen Lama's respect and sincerity, and he is indeed worth praising.

The Qianlong emperor composed this kind of poem for more than four decades, reiterating the same notion that skillful use of such peaceful devices as banquets would help the Qing maintain good relations with Inner Asian peoples. He certainly hoped that his descendants would continue this time-honored Qing policy that he inherited from his grandfather Kangxi: every year grand imperial banquets were held in the Wanshu yuan, representatives from different subordinate peoples joined together to celebrate the glory of the Qing empire. These Qing imperial rituals served to establish and maintain a hierarchical power structure between the Qing central government and the Inner Asian peoples, and to strengthen Qing imperial authority. As long as these rituals were dutifully performed, the thinking ran, there would be peace and order in the empire. During his reign, the emperor Qianlong managed to do just that most years.[23]

But the Qianlong emperor's descendants failed to live up to his expectations. As a contemporary saying goes, quoted by a servant in the Qianlong era novel *Dream of the Red Chamber*, "You can put up a tent as big as you please, but there's no banquet that doesn't break up sooner or later."[24] After the death of the Qianlong emperor in 1799, the imperial banquets in the Wanshu yuan were less frequent; the last one was held by the Jiaqing emperor (r. 1796–1820) in 1819. After that, as the Manchu rulers grew increasingly busy with foreign and domestic problems quite different from those of the Qianlong emperor's time, there were no more banquets in the garden and the neglected Imperial Great Yurt and other smaller yurts gathered dust. In 1838, on the eve of the Opium War, the Qing court decided to auction off twenty-five small yurts that were severely damaged. Nine were sold at give-away prices – the court received a total of 108 taels. The other sixteen were in such bad shape that no one was even interested in them.[25]

Notes

1 *QDRHZ*, juan 13, 14; see also Jonathan Spence, *Emperor of China*.
2 Li Guoliang, "Bishu shanzhuang yushan zatan," 83–85; Wang Shuqing, "Qingdai gongzhung shanshi," 57–64.
3 *QDRHZ*.
4 Imperial preface to the *QDRHZ*.
5 *QDRHZ*, 15: 1b.
6 Philippe Forêt, "Making an Imperial Landscape in Chengde, Jehol," 46.
7 Zhao Lian, *Xiaoting zalu*, 1.6a–1.6b.
8 Zhao Lian, *Xiaoting zalu*, 1.6a–1.6b.
9 Yang Tianzai *et al.*, "Bishu shangzhuang de Wanshu yuan ji qi lishi zuoyong," 177–178; Yang Boda, "*Wanshu yuan ciyan tu* kaoxi"
10 Yongyou si, located in the eastern part of the Wanshu yuan, was built between 1751 and 1764. See Chayet, Chapter 4, and Sven Hedin, *Jehol*, 156–157.
11 Yang Tianzai *et al.*, "Bishu shanzhuang de Wanshu yuan," 178.
12 Zhao Lian, *Xiaoting zalu*, 1: 6b; *DQTL*, juan 37; for an illustration of the Baohe dian banquet, see K. C. Chang, *Food in Chinese Culture*, figure 27.
13 *Qinding Da Qing Huidiantu*, p. 1493.
14 *DQTL*, 37: 1–12.
15 Morris Rossabi, *China and Inner Asia from 1368 to the Present*, 146–147.
16 Yang Boda, "*Wanshu yuan ciyan tu*." The full painting is reproduced in ter Molen and Uitzinger, eds, *De Verboden Stad*.
17 *QDRHZ*, 23: 5a–9a.
18 *QDRHZ*, 23: 6a.
19 *QDRHZ*, 23: 6a. Elsewhere Qianlong noted that he also allowed the Mongols and Muslims to wear their ethnic dress at the imperial parties in Bishu shanzhuang. The surrendered Mongol tribes were allowed to keep their own customs, including hair and clothing styles. But it seemed that on most occasions the Mongols invited to the Baohe dian New Year's Eve banquet and the Wanshu yuan banquet were required to wear Qing official robes.
20 *QDRHZ*, 23: 2a, 8b, 9a. For imperial music, see Zhang Dongsheng, "Qingdi dongxun yu gongting yinyue" and *DQTL*, 37: 3b, 4b, 6a–11b.
21 Ya Hanzhang, *Ban-chan Er-de-ni zhuan*, 128–138.
22 *QDRHZ*, 24: 10b.
23 See Ning Chia, "The Lifan yuan and the Inner Asian Rituals in the Early Qing," 60–92; James Hevia, "Lamas, Emperors, and Rituals," 243–278.
24 Cao Xueqin and Gao E., *Honglou meng*, ch. 26. Editors' note: David Hawkes' translation of this passage ("You know what they say about the mile-wide marquee: 'Even the longest party must have an end?'" *Story of the Stone* 1.509) obscures the original image, which was of a banquet in a tent. The line is more literally translated here by Millward.
25 Yang Tianzai *et al.*, "Bishu shanzhuang de Wanshu yuan," 178.

8 Qing Inner Asian empire and the return of the Torghuts

James A. Millward

Although the rise of the Qing empire has customarily been described as a southern advance into China, it should also be seen as an expansion in a western direction. Gaining control of the lands and peoples of Mongolia and Xinjiang through diplomatic and military means was a major achievement of the Qing empire; it was possible in large part because, from the start, the Qing displayed a keen understanding of the political and sociological characteristics of the tribal peoples of the steppes.

This chapter provides an overview of Inner Asian politics and the historical background to the Qing annexation of the lands from Manchuria to the Pamirs. I have framed this survey with an account of the Torghuts (Torghuud), because the Qianlong emperor himself treated the eastward return of this tribe as the culmination of the long process of Qing westward expansion, and also because the reception of the Torghuts at Chengde epitomizes the role played by this Qing capital in Inner Asian affairs.

The Torghuts' return and its commemoration

Among the material artifacts of the Chengde palace and temple complex is a remarkable painting of a ceremony held in the Wanfaguiyi dian, the golden-roofed structure nested within the open atrium atop the Chengde Potala (Putuozongcheng miao; Figure 13). It depicts the official reception on October 27, 1771 of leaders of the branch of the Torghut Mongols who had migrated westward from Mongolia and Zungharia in the late sixteenth and early seventeenth centuries to escape, first, Khalkha expansion and then the rise of the western Mongol empire of the Zunghars. The Torghuts found new pastures north of the Caspian Sea, along the Volga, Emba and Yayik rivers – there they came to be and are still known as Kalmuks (Qalmuqs, Kalmyks). By the middle of the eighteenth century, however, they grew restive again under Russian taxes and military call-ups, and faced increasing conflicts with Russian and Ukrainian settlers colonizing the Don and Volga areas. Some 170,000 of the Torghuts, led by their khan Ubashi (Ch. Wo-ba-xi) and princes Shereng (Ch. She-leng), Tsebek-Dorji and others, then undertook a long migration back east, hoping to settle in lands newly depopulated by the Qing destruction of the Zunghar khanate in 1755–58.

Once the Russian authorities realized their erstwhile subjects had decamped, they sent forces in pursuit. The Kazakh nomads, too, harried the Torghuts as they passed. Thomas De Quincey described the Torghuts' (Kalmucks') harrowing journey in flowery terms:

> Far and wide the waters of the solitary lake were instantly dyed red with blood and gore: here rode a party of savage Bashkirs, hewing off heads as fast as the swathes fall before the mower's scythe; there stood unarmed Kalmucks in a death-grapple with their detested foes, both up to the middle in water, and oftentimes both sinking together below the surface, from weakness or from struggles, and perishing in each other's arms.[1]

In May of 1771, their livestock depleted and human numbers halved, the remaining 50,000–70,000 Torghuts arrived exhausted and unexpected on the Qing's westernmost frontier, seeking safe haven.[2]

The painting, like the event it commemorates, brings together many strands of Qing Inner Asia policy, and can be said to epitomize much of what the Bishu shanzhuang and Eight Outer Temples were all about. The Jang gya and Jebtsundamba khutukhtus, other Buddhist monks, Qing officials and Torghut Mongol nobles sit before an altar in the hall and in the galleries surrounding it. The Qianlong emperor presides over the proceedings from one side.[3] The people and the architecture are painstakingly detailed in the style of a Tibetan thangka and are clearly identifiable; even the imperial calligraphy labeling the Wanfaguiyi dian (Hall of All Dharmas Returning to One) in four languages is legible above the entrance. But despite its documentary aspect, the scene is also surreal: the emperor appears larger-than-life, the scene is painted from an impossible aerial perspective (see Chayet, Chapter 4) and is peopled with many more occupants than the real hall and surrounding galleries could accommodate. The hill behind the temple is depicted as the Buddhist Mount Sumeru, flanked by cloud-borne deities. The painting thus amplifies what the architecture of the Putuozongcheng miao was meant to signify: the confluence of Manchu imperial and Buddhist spiritual power in the interest of accommodating Inner Asian peoples as subjects of the benevolent Qianlong emperor within the Qing realm.

Though the event has been all but forgotten in histories of the Qing written outside of China, the Qianlong emperor considered the return of the Torghuts one of his reign's principal accomplishments, and commemorated it in several ways. Besides the painting, he composed poetry on the subject and had Hanlin academician Ji Yun do the same.[4] The Rehe Gazetteer and other official sources record the episode. In particular, Qianlong composed two essays on the subject to be inscribed in Manchu,

Mongolian, Tibetan and Chinese on steles erected at the entrance to the Chengde Potala.[5] His interpretation in these essays of the significance of the Torghuts' return is revealing.

> To first rebel and then obey is called "surrender" (*guixiang*). To come put oneself at our service of one's own accord is called "come to allegiance" (*guishun*). Now the Torghuts, who have with their whole tribe forsaken foreign lands, marched ten thousand leagues and given themselves over to be transformed, must be said to have "come to allegiance," and not to have "surrendered." The Western Regions [i.e. Xinjiang] are already pacified, and agricultural reclamation is flourishing in the northern region of Yili [i.e. northern Xinjiang] while taxes have been lowered to modest levels in the southern Muslim region [southern Xinjiang]. We have put the Kazakhs and Kirghiz on a loose reign as an outer boundary. We need not concern ourselves with the Andijanis and Badakhshanis,[6] since they [inhabit] a distant frontier. "He who is contented suffers no disgrace / he who knows when to stop is free from danger."[7] My way of thinking amounts to no more than this. Why must we make the whole world between the oceans all into [lands governed according to the principles of] lord-and-minister, into Our territory? The coming to allegiance by the Torghuts was granted by Heaven. Their return was unanticipated, yet it happened anyway. Thus I must make this record of it.

In the essays, the Qianlong emperor also refers to his grandfather and the original establishment of the Qing summer retreat at Chengde:

> The Mountain Villa was built by my Imperial Ancestor [the Kangxi emperor] as a place to win the hearts of people from afar (*rou yuanren*). Soon after fêting Tsereng and his men,[8] the Western Regions were thereupon pacified. Now, not many years later, we have this matter of the unexpected and unsummoned coming to allegiance by the Torghuts. With this, all the Mongol lineages are ministers (*chen*) of the Great Qing.[9]

The text of the second stele amplifies the comparison of Qianlong with Kangxi by equating Qianlong's aid to the Torghuts with Kangxi's assistance to the Khalkhas driven from their lands by Galdan after 1688. In a florid passage in the first inscription, the Qianlong emperor speculates that Kangxi's soul must be highly gratified by his grandson's fulfilment of his sagacious plan. Qianlong insists that all credit for the Torghuts' decision to come to the Qing rightly lies with Kangxi; nevertheless, despite the show of filial modesty, the Qianlong emperor's self-satisfaction is obvious throughout the stele inscriptions.[10]

The emperor (and his court), then, interpreted and contextualized the return of the Torghuts, first, as the culmination of a process which began with the Kangxi emperor's building of the Bishu shanzhuang and his policies toward the Khalkha Mongols and continued with the Qianlong policies towards the Zunghars and Muslims of Xinjiang. The return of the Torghuts served to vindicate the Qianlong era policies, both the military expansion into Xinjiang and the flexible, non-"tributary" diplomacy towards the Khazakhs and other peoples beyond Xinjiang.

Second, the emperor argued that Qing patronage of Tibetan Buddhism helped lead to the Torghuts' return, just as it contributed to the submission of the Khalkhas in 1691. The painting of the Wanfaguiyi Hall provides one indication of this; the emperor provides further evidence in the first stele, writing that "because Russia subscribed to a faith other than the yellow teaching [Gelukpa] . . . Ubashi raised his whole *aimagh* to flee to China (*Zhongguo*) where the yellow teaching flourishes.")[11]

Third, the fact that the Torghuts chose to "come to allegiance" uncoerced, unsummoned and unexpected resonates deeply with Chinese tradition. The sage ruler who could entice followers into right behavior by the example of his virtue alone is an ideal of classical Chinese (Confucian and Daoist) political philosophy. The Qianlong emperor wants us to know that by not attempting to impose direct Qing rule over all the peoples of Central Asia, he exercised Daoist "masterly inactivity" (he quotes the *Dao de jing* in the stele essay). Again, the Torghuts' return vindicates his policy of wise restraint.

In both its graphic and its textual forms, then, the Qing commemoration of the Torghuts' return and submission portrays Kangxi and Qianlong emperors as marrying judicious use of military strength with the moral magnetism of an ideal Chinese ruler. The Torghuts' flight to Qing territory thus demonstrated the Manchu rulers' embodiment of both Inner Asian and Chinese kingly virtues. It is no wonder the Qianlong emperor was pleased with himself.

The peoples of the Mongolian steppe and the rise of the Qing

We can readily sense the emperor's satisfaction from his stele inscriptions, but in order to fully appreciate the historical significance of this event, we must consider the relationships of Chinese with the peoples of Inner Asia over the longer term. Relations with these northerners, such peoples as the Xiongnu, the Turks, the Khitan, the Jurchen and the Mongols, had been a challenge to China-based states from the beginnings of Chinese recorded history. In times of peace, the relationship across the Sino-Mongolian frontier involved trading, elite intermarriage and diplomatic gift-exchange or appeasement (a flexible range of options often reductively and misleadingly called the "Chinese tribute system"). In troubled times, nomads staged small- or large-scale raids or even outright invasions across the frontier; likewise, some dynasties based in north China campaigned north to the steppe or west through the deserts to find and destroy nomadic adversaries, though direct control of the steppelands in Mongolia and Zungharia by Chinese regimes was rare and short-lived before the Qing.

There are many theories to explain the intersocietal dynamic along this frontier. The oldest views, common in traditional historiography but still echoed in popular histories today, consider the nomads aggressive "hungry wolves" innately or culturally predisposed to attack the civilized world. More recently, scholars have proposed more nuanced explanations based on structural factors: climatic change, military technology, the ecology and economy of pastoral nomadism, the sociological and political dynamics of Inner Asian society itself, and the relationship of Inner Asian peoples with China and other large agrarian states. Consideration of such factors provides a more complex, multi-causal approach to the rise of Inner Asian empires and their relationship with agrarian states.[12]

These approaches are often based on the kinship and social structures of Inner Asian pastoral nomadic peoples, which in most cases can be described as segmentary, with multiple levels of socio-political affiliation possible, though not always expressed or realized. At the lowest level, a camping group of several households would "nomadize" together, traveling from summer to winter camps and back as a group of a few tents. These groups understood themselves to belong to a larger unit as well, the clan or lineage, based on common descent from a male ancestor. For example, descendents of Chinggis (Genghis) Khan, founder of the Mongol empire in the thirteenth century, are known as Chinggisids.

On a higher level still is the tribe or extended lineage (*aimagh* in Mongolian, with a cognate term in Manchu). The *aimagh* was originally a confederation of clans bound by some notion of shared descent; at this level, the tie was likely to be putative and retrospectively asserted rather than genetic. Tribal history often begins with a totemic animal: the pre-imperial Mongols, one of several tribes inhabiting what is now Mongolia, believed in shared ancestry from the offspring of a blue wolf and a fallow deer; the Manchus venerated the magpie, which plays a role in both their creation myth and shamanic practices. Tribes were thus primarily politico-cultural, not familial, organizations. They became tightly unified only under certain circumstances, for certain purposes, under a strong leader.

The same is true for the next level of Inner Asian social organization, named the "supra-tribal polity" by Joseph Fletcher (also called an imperial or tribal confederation), under which multiple lineages and tribes allied, often under the name of one victorious tribe, accepting its leader as their own *khaghan* or khan (emperor or overlord). Such Inner Asian states then proceeded to conquer large areas of the steppe and often sedentary agrarian areas as well. Because of the openness of the grasslands and the portability of assets (livestock herds and belongings that could be loaded on carts or the backs of oxen or camels), a camping group, clan or tribe would only choose to join larger groupings and follow a particular leader after calculations of their own risk and benefit. A ruler who won battles, extorted trade opportunities and provided ample loot could attract large numbers of followers. If he or his successors failed in these ambitions, however, the followers could, with relative ease, pack up their camps and return to a more autonomous life with their herds, or cast their lot with a rival chief whose prospects seemed more promising. Competition for control of the steppe was, thus, more a matter of enticing followers to join and stay with a tribal or supra-tribal confederation under a particular dynastic leadership than one of capturing and holding territory. The charisma of chiefs and their ability to continually secure outside resources was critical to the maintenance of Inner Asian states.

While this general pattern still applied in many respects up to the mid-Qing period, the Mongol empire of the thirteenth through fourteenth centuries left important new legacies that later aspirants for control over Inner Asia took into account. One was the example of Chinggis Khan himself, who founded an empire that under his sons and grandsons came to control both steppe and much of the rich agrarian territory from China through the Islamic lands to Russia and the fringes of Europe. Because of this unprecedented imperial accomplishment, for centuries after the disintegration of the Mongol empire, direct descent from Chinggis Khan became a desideratum of rulership throughout Mongolia and Central Asia, and a prerequisite to taking the title "khan." The fourteenth-century conqueror Tamerlane (Timur), though he carved out a vast territory in Persia, Afghanistan, Transoxiana and the Kazakh steppe, refrained from calling himself "khan" because he was not a Chinggisid. When the fifteenth-century Oirat ruler Esen, though himself not a Chinggisid, did in fact assume the title "khan," other Mongols perceived this as illegitimate.

Despite this common Inner Asian reverence of Chinggis, there was little sense of an exclusive "Mongol" national identity as we would understand it today, and non-Mongol speaking peoples also bought into this source of legitimacy. One reason for the Manchus' early interest in cultivating relations with Mongol groups was to link their own dynastic patriline to that of the Chinggisids and thus become eligible to be great khans of Inner Asia.[13]

A second legacy of the Mongol empire inherited by the Manchus concerns religion. The Mongol rulers embraced Islam in the west and Tibetan Buddhism in the east, and exploited the political power of these faiths. As described by Donald Lopez (Chapter 3), Khubilai Khan's lama–patron (*mchod yon*) relationship with the Pakpa lama established a pattern in Mongol and Chinese relations with Tibet that was repeated in Ming and especially Qing dynasty patronage of Tibetan lamas.

Both of these factors, the Chinggisid example and the state patronage of religion, played a role in the struggles to reorganize Inner Asia after the disintegration of the Mongol empire. With the fall of the Yuan and rise of the Ming dynasty in 1368, most Mongols retreated from China. They were at that point still organized in "myriarchies" (*tümen*), the decimal groupings that had been imposed on the diverse tribes of the Mongolian steppe by Chinggis Khan. By the fifteenth century, these former military units came to serve as foci of identity, that is, as tribes in their own right, each under a Chinggisid khan. They included the Chahar (Chakhar), Khalkha, Tümet, Kharachin and Ordos. Further west, in Zungharia and the Altai Mountains, lived several western Mongol tribes collectively known as Oirats,[14] whose rulers were not Chinggisids and who spoke a dialect different from that of the eastern tribes. The Oirats vied with the (eastern) Mongols for control of the steppe. In the forests and plains to the east of the Mongolian steppe, meanwhile, lived Jurchen and other Tungusic peoples as well as some Mongol groups, many of whom served as frontier auxiliaries for the Ming dynasty.

Several of these northern tribal rulers succeeded in founding confederations strong enough to challenge the Ming. The first was Esen (r. 1440–54), the Oirat chief who, in the mid-fifteenth century, advanced from the Altai Mountains (on the border between today's Xinjiang and the Mongolian Republic) to the very gates of Beijing. The next contender was Dayan Khan (r. 1488–1533) of the Chahar, the senior Chinggisid descendent. He succeeded in reuniting the eastern Mongols temporarily and organized the myriarchies, each under the control of a Chinggisid prince, into left (eastern) and right (western) wings. Dayan led a series of successful raids across the length of north China around the turn of the sixteenth century, and later forced the Ming to open regular trade relations with the nomads.

Another Chinggisid, the Tümet chief known as Altan Khan (r. 1543–83), formed a confederation of Khalkhas and other eastern Mongols that pushed the Oirats back westward to Khobdo and Zungharia and launched frequent raids on Ming China. Altan's virtually unchallenged predations along the whole northern frontier of China led the Ming to begin constructing the massive series of frontier fortifications which we today call "the Great Wall."[15] This desperate and costly measure was of little avail against Altan Khan, however, who easily circumvented the walls and eventually forced the reluctant Ming to pay subsidies to him and other nomad rulers and to open trade markets where common Mongols could trade their livestock. Altan also promoted the conversion of the Mongols to Tibetan Buddhism by entering into lama–patron relations with the Gelukpa. At a meeting at Altan's capital in Hohhot (Mo. Köke Khota; Ch. Huhehaote) in 1578, the Tümet khan bestowed the title "Dalai" (ocean; universal) upon the Gelukpa reincarnating lama (*tulku*) Sonam Gyatso, who thus became the third Dalai Lama (his two previous incarnations received the title posthumously). In return, Sonam Gyatso announced that Altan was a reincarnation of Khubilai Khan, conferred upon him the title "Religious King, Brahma of the Gods," and prophesied that within eighty years Altan's descendants would rule over all of China and the Mongols.[16]

After Dayan Khan's death in 1533, the senior Chinggisid line passed through the khans of the Chahars to Lighdan (r. 1604–34?), the last Chahar khan and direct patrilineal successor of Chinggis. Lighdan Khan's reign corresponded to the rise of the Jurchens' Latter Jin dynasty under Nurhaci and Hong Taiji (see Rawski, Chapter 2), and by the second decade of the seventeenth century, Chahar and Manchu were competing for the spoils available from diplomacy, trading and raids on north China. When the Manchus allied with the Khorchins (1624) and launched a series of successful attacks on the Khalkhas, Lighdan Khan's people began to desert him for the Manchus. The Manchu advance drove Lighdan westward, where in 1627 he destroyed the Kharachin and Tümet khanates, accepted the surrender of the Ordos khanate, formed alliances with the Khalkha princes to the north, and established himself at Hohhot. In 1632, Hong Taiji seized Hohhot, then sent an army after Lighdan who had fled towards Tibet. Lighdan died of smallpox en route, but Hong Taiji's generals captured the Chahar khan's widows and his son Ejei, along with an imperial seal of the Yuan dynasty. Hong Taiji married the widows, incorporated the Chahars within the Latter Jin banner system, and took possession of the highly symbolic seal.

These events mark a watershed in the rise of the Qing state. After defeating Lighdan, the last Chinggisid khan, and accepting the personal submission of most of the princes of southern Mongolia, Hong Taiji changed the name of his people from Jurchen to Manchu (*Manju*), and proclaimed a dynasty known in Chinese as the *Da Qing* (in Manchu, *Daicing*), or Great Qing. By replacing names parochially associated with the Jurchens and their old Jin dynasty (1115–1234), Hong Taiji's new terminology better suited his new multiethnic empire with Mongol, Chinese and Korean as well as Manchu (Jurchen) subjects. Moreover, he adopted the title "sacred khan" (Mo. *boghda khaghan*; Ma. *enduringge han*), declaring in Inner Asian terms that he enjoyed heaven's support, and in so doing distinguished himself from the many Mongol "khans" who had proliferated since the sixteenth century. These changes in nomenclature thus reflect a universalistic Manchu claim to be rightful rulers not only of China but of Inner Asia.

The rise of the Qing dynasty must thus not be considered a simple conquest of the Ming by the Manchus. It was a multilateral struggle for which the stakes included not only China, but the legacy of the Mongol empire. This aspect is reflected even in the dynastic name "Da Qing" itself: in its Manchu pronunciation, *Daicing* is a near homonym with the Mongol word *daicin*, meaning "militant, warlike."[17]

Qing victory and the enclosure of Inner Asia

To the west, the early seventeenth century was a time of intense competition among the Oirat tribes for pasturelands and control over other tribes.

It was to escape these troubles that the Torghuts and some Dörböts migrated to their new pastures by the Volga. Eventually, a confederation of Oirat tribes arose under the name "Zunghar," or "left hand, left flank."[18] By the 1630s, the Zunghars had a capital city in Ghulja (Kulja), and an agricultural and manufacturing base in Zungharia, the northern part of today's Xinjiang. Asserting themselves on the broader Inner Asian stage, they attacked the Kazakhs, concluded treaties with Russia, and supported the fifth Dalai Lama as the Gelukpa expanded its secular power throughout Tibet. In 1640 the Zunghar Khan Ba'atur Khongtaiji convened the Oirats and the Khalkhas of Outer Mongolia in a congress (*khuraltai*) which established a law code and declared Tibetan Buddhism the official Mongol religion. This act summed up the dangers posed to the Manchus by a strong western Mongol confederation: using religion as a rallying point, the Zunghars threatened to unite the peoples and lands of Tibet, Kokonor, Zungharia and Mongolia into a pan-Buddhist front against the Qing empire.

Under Galdan (r. 1671–97), the Zunghars began to make good on this threat. Galdan, whose name is Tibetan,[19] spent his youth as a Gelukpa monk in Tibet and although not a Chinggisid was later (1679) granted the title Boshughtu Khan ("khan by divine grace") by the fifth Dalai Lama. In 1676, Galdan took control of Kokonor (also called Qinghai and Amdo) from the Khoshuut Mongols; he established Zunghar overlordship in the oases of Eastern Turkestan (today's southern Xinjiang) in 1678–80, ruling them as protectorate and tax-farm; and in 1688 he used a dispute between Khalkha chiefs and a supposed slight of the Dalai Lama's emissary as a pretext for an invasion of northern Mongolia. In all of these activities, Galdan had the support of the fifth Dalai Lama, and after 1682 that of the Tibetan regent who concealed the Dalai Lama's death and continued to act in his name. This regent, who ignored Kangxi's appeal to mediate the Khalkha quarrel and to restrain Galdan, may even have instigated the Zunghar aggression against the Khalkhas and their indirect provocation of the Qing.

Galdan's blitz into northern Mongolia forced the Khalkha leaders to choose between rising great powers of Inner Asia: Zunghar, Qing or Tsarist Russia. The Khalkha khans and the highest Khalkha lama, the Jebtsundampa Khutukhtu, bore nothing but bitter feelings towards the Zunghars who had routed them, burned their scriptures and looted their temples. Moreover, the Khalkhas also recognized that the Russian presence to the north was still slight. The Qing, on the other hand, shared many cultural similarities with the Khalkhas and avidly patronized Tibetan Buddhism. Thus, the Khalkha rulers sought refuge with the Manchus, leading over 140,000 destitute followers into Qing frontier territory, where the Kangxi court provided them with grain, livestock and other supplies. The Qing celebrated the incorporation of the Khalkha nobles and their people within the Qing empire with a grand ceremony in 1691 in Dolonnor (near the site of Shangdu, the old Mongol imperial capital), some 180 kilometers northeast of Chengde. This event, attended by the Kangxi emperor, Qing troops, high lamas, and Kharachin, Chahar and other Inner Mongol officials, was accompanied by feasting and games, much as the Torghuts' return would be eighty years later.[20]

Soon thereafter the Qing responded to Galdan's provocation with a series of steppe campaigns, defeating his forces decisively at Jao Modo in 1696. Meanwhile, Galdan's nephew rebelled in Zungharia, and Galdan was ultimately abandoned by his supporters, divine grace having by now clearly passed him by. His death the following year did not mark the end of Zunghar aspirations in Inner Asia, however, for there were further wars with the Qing in Mongolia in the 1730s, until the Zunghar and Manchu sides reached an uneasy truce in the fourth year of the Qianlong reign (1739). In the 1740s and 1750s, succession crises fractured the Zunghar confederation, and provided the Qing with an opportunity. When the Qianlong emperor prepared a new campaign against the Zunghars in 1754, many Zunghar leaders allied with the Qing, including Amursana, a Khoit chieftain. The defections to the Qing by these Oirat groups were the occasion of grand ceremonies at Chengde (see Figure 8; and Yu (Chapter 7) and Sommer (Chapter 11)).

With these defectors in the vanguard, Qing armies marched easily into Zungharia in 1755. After taking Ghulja (Yili) without a fight, the Qing initially planned to break up the Zunghar confederation and divide the region's pastures and people between four main Oirat tribes, each under their own khan; Amursana would have become khan of the Khoits. But Amursana hoped to control the whole Zunghar federation and turned on the Qing, slaughtering the remaining Qing forces in Yili.[21] The enraged Qianlong emperor ordered a massive retaliation to put an end to the Zunghar problem once and for all. After Amursana's death from smallpox and the near extermination by the Qing armies of those Zunghar groups who had sided with him, the Qing took direct control of Zungharia and Eastern Turkestan. The political term "Zunghar" was expunged; there are still Oirats living today, but no Zunghars.

Thus the Qing became rulers of Inner Asia as well as of China, victors in a contest ongoing since the fall of the Mongol empire and Yuan dynasty four centuries earlier. Subsequently, the Qing radically reorganized the peoples of the steppes, forests and deserts to China's northeast, north and northwest.

The earliest Mongol allies of the Jurchens and Manchus, including the Khorchins and Kharachins who enrolled with the Jin before 1635, had become "bannermen": members of the Mongol Eight Banners, a sociomilitary structure that, together with the Manchu and Han Eight Banners, made up what Evelyn Rawski has called the "Qing conquest elite." The Chahars, Khalkhas and other late-comers like the Torghuts, however, were incorporated within the empire with different administrative status. These tribes were reorganized into smaller groupings known in Mongolian as *khoshuun* (also *khosighun*), under the hereditary control of a *jasagh* (Ma. *jasak*; Ch. *zhasake*). (Confusingly, the term khoshuun is also translated as "banner" (Chinese *qi*), and thus jasagh becomes "banner prince," but khoshuuns must be distinguished from the Eight Banners, a different institution entirely.) Under Qing rule, the Khalkha and Oirat leaders initially retained the title of "khan," but they no longer enjoyed broad powers. Their lands and people, still formally known as *aimaghs* (translated as "khanates"), were subdivided into dozens of khoshuuns, and the khan's power was reduced to that of an ordinary banner prince. Over the course of the eighteenth century, moreover, the *aimaghs* increasingly took on geographic, as opposed to ethno-political, meaning: they became units of territory, not of people ruled by particular noble lineage. (Indeed, today an *aimagh* in the Republic of Mongolia is equivalent to a province; the *qi* in the Inner Mongolian Autonomous Region of China are equivalent to counties.) The Qing created leagues (Mo. *chighulghan*, Ch. *meng*) as new higher-level administrative structures under central government supervision to oversee the territories of the old *aimaghs*. Significantly, the leagues were named after the *place* where league officials met, and not after the khans as the *aimaghs* had been. On top of this, the Qing gradually overlaid a further system of imperial garrisons under Qing military officials known as *ambans* (Ch. *dachen*). These officials, some Mongol but mostly Manchu, governed from bases in the new urban centers of northern Mongolia: Uliyasutai, Urga and Khobdo. A similar administrative system applied to nomadic groups in northern Xinjiang.[22]

The final result of the incorporation of Mongol peoples by the Qing, then, was that after a century and a half of diplomatic and military measures, not only were the steppelands of Inner Asia under the control of the Qing emperor as Great Khan, but they had been politically reconfigured. Tribes were replaced by geographically defined entities. Loyalty to a charismatic leader gave way to an imperial subjecthood hemmed in by a multi-layered bureaucratic administrative system. These changes checked the fluidity of shifting tribal alliances and limited power to prevent the emergence of charismatic leaders who might rally nomads and challenge Qing authority. In this sense, the Inner Asian steppes had been effectively enclosed.

The Torghuts' return: the party and the morning after

This, then, was the new world to which Ubashi led his Torghut followers in 1771, though the Torghuts might not immediately have understood the implications of the new Qing order. In any case, after initial suspicion,[23] the Qing greeted the Torghuts warmly indeed. The Torghut nobility, summoned to imperial audience in Chengde, set forth from northern

Xinjiang in early August of 1771, less than two weeks after their arrival in Qing territory. Their journey to the Qing summer retreat took them through Urumchi, and then by a southern route through the Gansu corridor as far as Liangzhou, before turning northeast through Shanxi and Zhili provinces and finally to Chengde. Officials along the way accommodated the Torghuts' every need, and threw lavish banquets for the Torghut nobility.

The Torghuts reached the Mulan hunting grounds by mid-October. There Ubashi presented gifts to the Qing emperor and Qianlong directed "gracious inquiries" to Ubashi in Mongolian, before treating the Torghut khan to tea in a yurt. A feast the following day was attended by eighty-six Oirat, inner Mongolian and outer Mongolian nobles. Later, the Torghuts joined the emperor in a grand battue hunt (see Elliott and Chia, Chapter 6).

After several days of hunting, the entire party returned to Chengde and the Bishu shanzhuang for more festivities, including a banquet by lantern-light in the Wanshu yuan followed by fireworks. Next came the grand ceremony in the Chengde potala discussed above, for which the emperor had appropriate clothes specially made for the Torghuts. To complete his welcome to the refugees, the emperor granted their nobility Manchu and Mongol titles: Ubashi remained a nominal khan; other princes received the ranks *qinwang, junwang, taiji, beile* or *beizi*. Qianlong presented each with a generous gift befitting his new status.[24]

This sumptuous reception was most likely heart-warming to the Torghuts after their ordeal, but the real implications of their new position would have become clear to Ubashi only after the Qing plans for their resettlement were revealed. For though he enjoyed the title of "khan," he did not, in fact, retain leadership of his tribe. Rather, the Torghuts and others who had migrated back to Zungharia with him were to be ruled by several nobles, in lands well apart from each other. After the first winter, the Qing's final dispensation of Ubashi's Torghuts created ten banners in four leagues, under four league heads, settled in northern, southern, eastern and western "routes" (reservations) scattered across northern Xinjiang. Ubashi was now simply a league head in charge of four banners in the Karashahr area of Xinjiang. In addition to these four leagues of "old Torghuts," two banners of "new Torghuts" under Shereng were relocated near Khobdo in the Altai mountains, and four banners of Khoshuts who had joined the Torghuts were assigned to the shores of Bosteng lake, south of Karashahr (modern Yanchi). Moreover, these league heads were not autonomous, but had to answer to Qing *ambans* in Karashahr, Tarbagatai, Kur Kara Usu and Yili (Figure 1).

These resettlement conditions clearly raised great obstacles to the Torghuts ever becoming a unified, powerful tribal entity again. They were further weakened by smallpox, a frequent scourge of unexposed Inner Asian peoples who came into contact with Chinese. In late 1771 and early

1772, smallpox killed 3,390 of the Torghuts, including several members of Ubashi's immediate family.

The Qing government intentionally employed another, rather insidious device to keep the Torghuts from flourishing: they forced many of them to take up farming. Officials explained this reasoning explicitly. "If we allow them to engage only in multiplying their livestock and hunting, their strength will gradually increase. If they become powerful again, this will not be a good thing. . . . It will be better to let them expend more effort on agriculture."[25] Though given seed and tools, the Torghut nomads had no agricultural experience and made poor farmers.

Under these conditions, it is not surprising that the Torghuts failed to thrive. The Manchu traveller Qi-shi-yi, who encountered the Torghuts and Khoshuuts in the Karashahr area in 1777, describes the men as given to thievery and the women to prostitution. Moreover, Torghut children were often sold as slaves to Muslims of Xinjiang and western Turkestan, presumably by impoverished parents. A Chinese-compiled gazetteer from 1908 describes the Torghuts in the Jinghe area of northern Xinjiang as great drinkers and too lazy to farm (though such a depiction in a Chinese source may arise from simple stereotypes rather than observation). The Torghut population neither increased nor declined greatly by the end of the Qing period: in 1947, after a tumultuous century in Xinjiang and Chinese history, the combined population of the various "routes" of the resettled Torghuts numbered about 57,000.[26]

In the struggle for control of Inner Asia, the Qing had emerged victorious. This was due in great part to their control of resources from China proper, which gave them a military edge over their Zunghar rivals, but also to skillful diplomacy and their patronage of Tibetan Buddhism, which helped win Mongol adherence to their growing empire. The Torghuts left the Volga on a long migration in search of lands to live, worship and grow autonomously; nomad groups had often availed themselves of such migrations in the past, but the Torghuts' move would be the last such large-scale nomadic relocation in Eurasian history. Their journey ended – after ample Qing largesse and full ceremonial treatment with all the Chengde trimmings – with their total submergence within the Qing empire. The Qianlong emperor had a right to be satisfied with this unexpected turn of events: he had completed what his grandfather started at Chengde, and had changed the political and economic order of Inner Asia irrevocably.

Notes

1 De Quincey, *Flight of a Tartar Tribe*, 70. See C. D. Barkman, "The Return of the Torghuts from Russia to China" for a more reliable account.
2 In the stele inscription "Youxu Tu-er-hu-te bucong ji" (see note 5) the emperor estimates that of some 169,000 Torghuts who crossed the Volga (Ch. Eqile) River, only half reached Yili (Qi Jingzhi, 72). Hummel cites this figure (*ECCP*

660); Khodarkovsky gives a smaller estimate of 150,000 Torghuts setting out, *Where Two Worlds Met*, 232–34.

3 For an original reading of this and other Qianlong portraits, see Zito, *Of Body and Brush*, 17–26, 30. On Jesuit involvement in the production of this painting, see Wang Jiapeng, "Tuerhute donggui yu 'Wanfaguiyi tu.' "

4 The Qianlong emperor's poem, "Yan Tuerhute shichen" (Feasting the Torghut envoys) is in his *Yuzhi shiwen quanji*, j. 7, cited in Chayet, *Les Temples de Jehol*, 136, n. 144; On Ji Yun, see *ECCP*, 120–23.

5 "Tuerhute quan bu guishun ji" (record of the full Torghut *aimagh's* return to allegiance) and "Youxu Tuerhute bucong ji" (record of generous relief for the Torghut *aimagh*) are reprinted in Qi Jingzhi, *Waiba miao beiwen zhushi*, 60–82. I benefited from Qi's notes and translations into modern Chinese in rendering sections of the inscriptions into English for this article. Joseph-Marie Amiot, S. J., translated the first essay (or a version similar to it) from a copy he obtained "from one of those who was charged with writing it in Manchu," and attempted to preserve in the translation "that simplicity, that energy and that precision which the Emperor knew to give [the essay] in his native tongue" (Amiot, "Monument de la transmigration des tourgouths"). If Amiot is correct, the essay was originally written in Manchu, not Chinese. The version as he renders it is close to, though more elaborate than the Chinese text. Amiot does not mention the steles by the Chengde potala, but writes that a stele with this inscription was erected in Yili, "under the very eyes of the Torghuts" (404). For a discussion of the contents of the second stele, see John L. Mish, "The Return of the Turgut." For a reproduction of the Manchu, Chinese, Mongolian and Tibetan texts, see O. Franke and B. Laufer, *Epigraphische Denkmäler aus China*, mappe II, 63–70.

6 Andijan lies in the Ferghana Valley, in today's Uzbekistan. Qing sources used "Andijani" as a generic reference to Central Asians, including Kokandis, Tashkentis and Bukharans. The region known as Badakhshan now lies in Afghanistan and Tajikstan.

7 Qianlong here quotes Laozi, *Daode jing*, ch. 44. I use Wing-tsit Chan's translation of the line (*A Source Book in Chinese Philosophy*, 161).

8 Amiot's translation includes a line explaining that Tsereng (Tchering) and his followers were the only Dörböts to remain loyal to the Qing as opposed to the Zunghar confederation (421). Tsereng, a Dörböt prince, fled the Zunghar civil wars after 1750, bringing 3,000 followers to join the Qing. Gao Wende *et al.*, 541–42; *ECCP*, 10.

9 "Tu-er-hu-te quan bu guishun ji," reprinted in Qi Jingzhi, 60–62.

10 Qi Jingzhi, 74, 62.

11 Qi Jingzhi, 61.

12 See Owen Lattimore, *Inner Asian Frontiers of China* and "The Geographical Factor in Mongol History"; Joseph Fletcher, "The Mongols: Ecological and Social Perspectives"; Sechin Jagchid and J. Van Symons, *Peace, War, and Trade along the Great Wall*; Anatoly M. Khazanov, *Nomads and the Outside World*; Thomas Barfield, *The Perilous Frontier*; and Nicola Di Cosmo, "State Formation and Periodization in Inner Asian History" and *Ancient China and its Enemies*.

13 On Qing marital ties to the Mongol nobility, see Rawski, *The Last Emperors*, 135, 147–48.

14 This term has many variant spellings: Oyirat, Oyirad, Eleuth, Ögeled, Ölöd, Oelot, and in Chinese Wa-la, E-lu-te, E-la-te, Wei-lu-te, Wu-la-te. The Kalmuks and Zunghars were Oirats, and their names (and their variants) are sometimes used in the more general sense of Oirat. On the origins and early history of the Oirats, see Okada Hidehiro, "Origins of the Dörben Oyirad" and Miyawaki Junko, "The Qalqa Mongols and the Oyirad."

15 On the strategic and political background to the building of the Ming system of walled defenses, see Waldron, *The Great Wall*. Discussion of Altan Khan is on pp. 122–25.
16 Survey accounts of Dayan Khan, Altan Khan and this period of Mongol history may be found in Bawden, *The Modern History of Mongolia*, 23–80; Barfield, *The Perilous Frontier*, 243–50; and Rossabi, *China and Inner Asia*, 44–50. The prophesy is related from Tibetan sources in Shakabpa, *Tibet*, 95.
17 Elliott, *The Manchu Way*, 402–3, n. 118.
18 "Zunghar" appears as Jüün γar, Jegün γar, Dzungar, Jungar, Zhunghar, and in Chinese as Zhun-ga-er. Oirat (and its variants) and Kalmuk are also occasionally used, rather inexactly, to indicate the Zunghar confederation. On "Oirat," see note 14.
19 Specifically, dGa' ldan (pronounced "Ganden" in Tibetan) is the Tusita paradise of Maitreya, Buddha of the future, and also the name of the famous monastery founded by Tsong kha pa east of Lhasa (see Lopez, Chapter 3). It is also used as a personal name.
20 See Xiao Yishan, *Qingdai tongshi*, 1: 824–28, and Bawden, *The Modern History of Mongolia*, Ch. 2.
21 Chinese historiography treats Amursana as a villain, but Mongols in the Mongolian Republic have named a street in Ulaanbaatar for him.
22 For economic and social aspects of northern (Outer) Mongolia under Qing rule, see Bawden, *The Modern History of Mongolia*, ch. 3, "Khalkha in the Eighteenth Century"; Fletcher, "Ch'ing Inner Asia c. 1800," 48–58; and Sanjdorj, *Manchu Chinese Colonial Rule in Northern Mongolia*. On administration and the Lifan yuan in Mongolia, see also Ning Chia, "The Li-fan Yuan in the Early Ch'ing Dynasty," especially 108–20.
23 Shereng, one of the princes accompanying the Torghuts, had been among the Zunghars defending Zungharia (Yili) from the Qing in 1757. He fled to Russian territory, and Russia refused to extradite him, despite a mutual extradition agreement with the Qing in the Treaty of Nerchinsk (1689). Shereng resettled among the Torghuts (his fellow Oirats), and was a strong voice advocating the migration back to China (Khodarkovsky, *Where Two Worlds Met*, 231). At the time of the Torghuts' return, some Qing memorialists feared that Shereng harbored revanchist aspirations, but in the first Torghut stele the Qianlong emperor points out how unrealistic such hopes were. The emperor also uses the Russian failure to extradite Shereng as justification for granting asylum to the Torghuts – who were, after all, now themselves fugitives from Russia.
24 Ma Dazheng and Ma Ruheng, *Piaoluo yicheng de minzu*, 188–93. Ma and Ma base their account on published Qing sources and Manchu documents from the No. 1 Historical Archives in Beijing. Chinese translations of many of these Manchu memorials have been published: Zhongguo Shehui Kexueyuan Minzu Yanjiusuo, *Manwen Tu-er-hu-te dang'an*.
25 Ma Dazheng and Ma Ruheng, 199–201; quote from p. 201, citing a Manchu memorial from QL36.9.10, first *jian*.
26 Population figure from Xinjiang Military Headquarters surveys, cited in Weiwuer Zizhiqu Minzu Shiwu Weiyuanhui, ed., *Xinjiang minzu cidian*, 883. The Torghuts disappear statistically in data from the P.R.C. era, submerged in general figures for "Mongols."

Part III

The emperor's many faces

9 The Qianlong emperor and the Confucian "Temple of Culture" (Wen miao) at Chengde

Joseph A. Adler

When Qianlong and his entourage arrived at Chengde on June 29, 1780, the first thing he did was to stop at the Chenghuang miao (City God Temple), located just outside the southwest wall of the Bishu shanzhuang, near the Bifeng men (Jade Peak Gate).[1] He was, in effect, reporting to the local spiritual authority. From there he went to the adjacent Wen miao (Confucian Temple, or Temple of Culture; see Figure 20), to make ritual offerings to the "First Teacher," Confucius (Kong Fuzi, 551–479 BCE).[2] The temple had just been completed the previous year, when Qianlong had performed the first ritual libation, offering a stele inscription (translated below) and issuing an edict to announce the founding of the temple and the school connected with it.[3]

The temple and the school – the first government-sponsored school in the area – were two functions of the same institution, the purpose of which was to extend the "civilizing" (*wenhua*) benefits of learning to this former frontier area.[4] The Wen miao was, to be sure, overshadowed both in grandeur and in strategic significance by the Waiba miao (Eight Outer Temples) arrayed to the north and east of the imperial complex (see Chayet, Chapter 4). These Tibetan Buddhist temples were intended to persuade the emperor's Mongol and Tibetan subjects that the Great Qing was truly a universal empire, and thus was truly theirs.

But the Wen miao also played a symbolic role in the politico-cultural landscape of Chengde. It symbolized the continuity of the empire and this secondary capital with the Han Chinese cultural heritage. It thus represented the Han face of what was later called the empire of "Five Peoples" (Han Chinese, Muslim Uyghurs, Tibetans, Mongols, and Manchus) – a multi-ethnic construction of which the Chengde cultural and geographic landscape was a carefully designed microcosm.[5] While the primary audience for this extraordinarily expensive enterprise at Chengde was composed of Tibetans and Mongols and their Buddhist clerical establishments, the Han symbolism of *wen* (writing, culture) was absolutely critical to the Manchus' efforts to legitimize their conquest and continued rule of China – particularly in the eyes of the Han literati and officials, whose support was crucial to the regime.

This essay will synopsize and analyze Qianlong's involvement with the Chengde Wen miao from 1779 to 1782, based primarily on the *Veritable Records (Shilu)* of the Qianlong reign. It will include translations of some of the documents, in whole and in part, written by Qianlong regarding the temple. We shall focus on two topics that emerge clearly from Qianlong's writings on the Wen miao: *wen* (writing, culture) and *sheng* (the sage), both in connection with Qianlong's understanding of rulership and his efforts to reinforce the legitimacy of Qing rule in the eyes of Han Chinese literati and officials. We shall begin with a brief chronology of Qianlong's involvement with the Chengde Wen miao.

Qianlong 41

Summer, 1776: Qianlong's Minister of Rites proposes to him the construction of a school at Chengde. Orders are issued to build the school and the Wen miao.[6]

Qianlong 44

July 1, 1779: The imperial procession arrives at Chengde; stops at the newly-completed Wen miao to make offerings to Confucius.[7] The party then proceeds to Bishu shanzhuang, the imperial summer residence.[8]

July 7, 1779: Qianlong performs the first ritual libation at the temple; offers the stele inscription officially marking its completion.[9]

Qianlong 45

June 29, 1780: The imperial procession arrives at Chengde, the ritual offering is made, and the party proceeds to Bishu shanzhuang.[10]

August 30, 1780: Semiannual sacrifice to Confucius. Qianlong deputes Academician Ying Lian to perform the ritual.[11]

Qianlong 46

July 5, 1781: The imperial procession arrives at Chengde, the ritual offering is made, and the party proceeds to Bishu shanzhuang.[12]

July 9, 1781: The emperor issues an edict summarizing the regular schedule of rituals at the Wen miao.[13]

Qianlong 47

Beginning in 1782, there is no mention in the *Veritable Records* of Qianlong stopping at the Wen miao upon arrival at Chengde.[14]

Wen and the Chengde Wen miao stele

Wen has been a central concept in Confucian thought throughout its long history in China. The character *wen* originally denoted the marks of writing on bamboo or other surfaces, a meaning that it continues to carry today

– e.g. denoting a piece of writing (*wenlun*, an essay or thesis) or literature in general. But already before Confucius' time, it had also come to mean culture or civilization in general – particularly literate culture. Thus the modern word for culture is *wenhua*, literally "writing-transformation," i.e. the transformations wrought by literacy. In this sense it was complemented by the term *wu*, or military – as for example in the names of the first two kings of the Zhou dynasty (11th–3rd centuries BCE), Wu wang (the Military or Martial King) and his son, Wen wang (the Civil King).

Confucius used *wen* mainly in this broader sense, and the role it played in his thought was central. Living in a period during which the Zhou dynasty was fragmenting, he saw his historical role as that of a reviver of the moral excellence of the great founders of the dynasty. Only by reviving the cultural and political forms and values of these glorious sage-kings could the Zhou kingdom be re-unified, for unity depended on the moral power (*de*) of the king (*wang*), to which able and virtuous ministers and common people would be attracted of their own accord. The king's chief role was to act as the moral exemplar to the people, following the will or command of heaven (*tianming*).

Confucius believed that the way (*dao*) of the former kings was preserved in the cultural tradition, particularly in the classics, which recorded various aspects of this way. The several books of ritual (*li*), for example, purported to record, in great detail, not only the court and private ceremonies but also the manners, styles of clothing, daily routines, and sumptuary customs of the former sage-kings. Confucius believed that by re-instituting these forms of both ritual and ordinary practice (actually subsuming them under a broadened concept of *li* as "ritual propriety"), a truly virtuous king would emerge to fulfill his heaven-ordained role as the "pole star" around which a unified kingdom would revolve.

According to Confucius, then, the cultural tradition – both in its broadest sense, including various arts and music, and in its literary expression, especially the classics – was the embodiment of the way and the basis or source of political stability. It was for this reason that Qianlong found it politically useful to control and (within limits) to support the Confucian cultural-religious tradition.

The stele inscription offered by Qianlong on July 7, 1779 reveals his view of the cultural function of the school and temple. It also suggests that Qianlong understood *wen* to be crucial to his claim to be legitimate heir to the classical mandate of heaven (*tianming*). The complete text of the inscription is as follows:

Temple of Culture inscription[15]

In the summer of 1776, Cao Xiuxian, Minister of Rites,[16] who had accompanied the imperial procession to Rehe, was summoned to discuss current government [issues]. Xiuxian said, "Speaking in my official capacity, I consider this a suitable place to build a school to train literati." We replied, "Yes, this is the time." So the order to establish the school was made and the funds were appropriated. Once the school was established, a Temple of Culture would also be built. We ordered the siting of the land, the clearing of the area, the divining for an auspicious time, and the gathering of laborers. The temple and wall, pond and stream, hall and veranda, and ritual implements were all [built and installed] according to statute.[17] After two years, in the summer of 1779, We came on tour and personally offered the libation to complete it.

Rehe in the past was certainly a small, rustic place outside the passes. Although under the Jin and Liao it was called Xingzhou, nevertheless it alternately flourished and declined; it cannot be determined when it was an established place and when it was not. How could there have been a traditional teacher's mat and the sound of recitation [i.e. a school]? So, Our imperial ancestor [Kangxi] came here every year to escape the summer heat, and simply called it Mountain Village. Thus he referred [in a poem] to "the multitude of people approaching 10,000 families."[18]

We intend the flourishing of rites and music to last many years. Agriculture now is daily developing, and the number of households is daily growing. We estimate the size of the area as not less than several thousand *li*; the household registry claims about 100,000 people. Yet there has been no school to enlighten the people and advance their customs. How then could the way of sagely transformation be displayed to the ancestors and systematically spread? Moreover, now such western regions as Urumchi [in Xinjiang] are organized by commandery and county. Establishing a school will make [Chengde] even closer [to the model of China proper].

So the construction of this Temple of Culture at this time and this place should not be delayed. It should not be done only after people have requested it. We will call it the Rehe Temple of Culture, although we are now upgrading [the region] to Chengde Prefecture. This development will continue accordingly.

Formerly, Su Shi [1036–1101] wrote an inscription for Han Yu [768–824], saying, "The Duke's [Han Yu's] spirit is present throughout the world like water is present in the earth." I say that Han Yu perceived the way through culture [*wen*, i.e. through learning and self-cultivation]. Our master [Confucius] embodied the way and handed down culture. What Han Yu followed was just what the master had handed down. And yet, to perceive [the way] is to enact it in one's behavior; the substance [of the way] is the basis for this. Even when water is present in the earth it is still necessary to find it and get it out.[19]

Our master was the standard of heaven, the rightness of earth, the mountain's peak and the ocean's depth. There has not been a day when he has not been present in the mind's eye of every person. Throughout, [his way] has varied in development, yet it has not been lost. How can it depend on boring through [strenuous effort] to achieve it?

So, then, who says that the sound of the wooden bell clapper[20] cannot enlighten these people in their small, rustic place beyond the passes?

Qianlong forty-fourth year [1779], middle *xun* [ten-day period], of the second month of summer, by the imperial brush.[21]

Qianlong's conception of *wen* in this inscription is based on the theory of Su Shi, whom he quotes, and in one respect is contrary to the Cheng/Zhu orthodoxy that dominated the bureaucracy and the imperial Hanlin academy during the Qing. To understand what Qianlong is doing here, some background is therefore necessary.

Su Shi was one of the most prominent literati of the Song dynasty (960–1279). Famous to this day for his literary output, especially his poetry, Su was an active player in the controversies and political struggles of the Northern Song (960–1127), and was highly influential on contemporary and later literati. Yet he was excluded from the "orthodox" Confucian lineage, the *daotong* (succession of the way), by the formulator of that tradition, Zhu Xi (1130–1200).

One of the reasons for Zhu Xi's disapproval of Su Shi was Su's view that the way was brought into being through the creativity of literary and artistic expression (*wen*).[22] For Zhu Xi, the way was immanent and self-existent. But because of the ordinary human being's physical endowment (*qizhi zhi xing*), which obstructed one's ability to perceive the way, or the natural/moral order (*tianli/daoli*) inherent in one's own moral mind (*daoxin*), the way could only be realized through arduous moral cultivation and study of the words and deeds of sages (*sheng*). The sage is the extremely rare individual, born with a clear endowment of *qi* (psycho-physical substance), who can perceive the way directly in nature and in his or her own mind. The sage embodies the way in his or her behavior, thereby exerting a transforming influence on others (as well as, in most cases, by teaching).[23]

Zhu Xi had said that sages are few and far between. In fact there had been no true sages, in his view, between Mencius (Mengzi, 4th century BCE) and Zhou Dunyi (1017–1073), a contemporary of Su Shi. One sage per generation was about the best one could reasonably expect even in times when the way is being taught. The lineage of sages that Zhu Xi constructed continued from Zhou Dunyi to Cheng Yi (1033–1107) and his brother Cheng Hao (1032–1085), then through three generations of students to himself (although he never explicitly claimed to be a sage). The school or "fellowship" that adopted this lineage called itself *daoxue*, or "learning of the way," although a more objective term for it is the Cheng/Zhu school (indicating Zhu's role in codifying the teachings associated with the Cheng brothers, especially Cheng Yi).[24] This school came to define the "orthodox" version of the Confucian tradition when Zhu Xi's interpretations of the classics were made the basis of the civil service examinations during the Mongol Yuan dynasty.

During the Qing dynasty, the Kangxi emperor (r. 1662–1722), Qianlong's grandfather, was quite enamored of the Cheng/Zhu school, and some of his favorite Han officials – e.g. Li Guangdi (1642–1718) and Zhang Boxing (1652–1725) – were ardent and committed followers of *daoxue*.[25] Under Qianlong, though, the school occupied a more ambiguous position: it remained the required reading for the civil service examinations and the orthodoxy of the imperial Hanlin academy, but the emperor only paid lip-service to it, using it to maintain control of the literati and the bureaucracy.

Returning to the stele inscription, we have noted above that for Su Shi, *wen* (culture) embodied the way. But under the Qing, and especially during the Qianlong reign, the emperor controlled *wen*. By controlling the civil service examination system, by sponsoring the publication of acceptable works (and editing them to make them acceptable when necessary),[26] by censoring works that he perceived as threats to his political agendas, and by establishing schools such as the one in Chengde, Qianlong was implicitly assuming the role of the ultimate Confucian teacher, or sage. This gave him warrant to support the views of a scholar (Su Shi) who had been excluded from the Cheng/Zhu orthodoxy, without having to defend himself in Cheng/Zhu terms.

Qianlong had been thoroughly and rigorously trained in the Confucian classics and the learning of the Cheng/Zhu school. According to Harold Kahn, this continued "throughout his princedom and into the early years of his reign," when he reinstituted the "Lectures from the Classics Mat," or personal lectures to the emperor by Hanlin academicians.

His training in the classical canon did not make him a philosopher but it did make him an ideologue perfectly capable of drawing on the philosophers for the sanctions he needed to operate effectively as a king.[27]

His essays on Confucian topics (e.g. commentaries on passages from the classics) written after his succession to the throne differ markedly from those written before it, when he was more under the influence of his court teachers.[28] Not surprisingly, the earlier essays are very much in line with the interpretations of the Cheng/Zhu school, while the later ones usually take a critical stance in regard to all previous commentators, including Zhu Xi.[29]

Nevertheless, according to R. Kent Guy, Qianlong was convinced of "the importance of Confucian doctrine and the unity of *zheng* (governing) and *jiao* (teaching) in ruling China."

While Zhu Xi would never have claimed an emperor to be the sole sage of a generation (much less a sixty-year reign period), Qianlong probably saw himself in precisely those terms, and precisely in terms of Zhu Xi's arguments about the precariousness of goodness in human nature, the extreme difficulty of realizing it, and the consequent rarity of sages.[30] Again in Guy's words, "the association of wisdom, kingship and the articulation of cultural identity was a fundamental element of legitimacy in traditional China. Emperors of China were not only political leaders, they were sages and stewards of the classical canon."[31]

As non-Han (or non-"Chinese") rulers of a huge empire centered on traditionally Han territory, the Qing emperors' control of the classical canon, and of *wen* in general, was a major source of their legitimacy in the Han worldview. To win the loyalty of the Han population – especially the Han officials and literati – the Qing emperors drew on the Confucian ideology of rule by virtue or moral power (*de*). Since virtue was theoretically independent of ethnicity, they could stress their own moral qualifications in Confucian terms.[32]

Sagehood and rulership

Qianlong's understanding of sagehood and rulership is expressed in one of the essays he wrote between the years 1763 and 1785,[33] based on a line from the *Yijing* (*Book of Changes*), "The sage nourishes the worthy in order to reach the common people":[34]

> Heaven and earth nourish the myriad things. Human beings are one of the myriad things. Yet among human beings there are sages and there are the common [lit. myriad] people. Sages are not born regularly; people rarely achieve that status. But when one does achieve it, he has the responsibility of nourishing the people. How can he excuse himself from being a sage, from embodying the reason why heaven and earth gave him life? . . .
>
> Through the extent of the four seas and the multitude of common people, a single person's mind cannot have the power to reach everywhere. Therefore it is said that he "nourishes the worthy in order to reach the common people." But then there is the one with the responsibility to reach the people. How can he excuse himself from being a worthy, from embodying the reason why heaven and earth gave him life? . . . [And so on for the common people, whose responsibility it is to nourish the myriad things.][35]

"Sages" (*sheng*), "worthies" (*xian*), and "common people" (*min*, or here *wanmin*, "myriad people") are standard categories in Confucian discourse. Sagehood is the ultimate goal in this system of thought and practice. For Confucius, the sages were semi-divine figures, such as the mythic kings Yao, Shun, and Yu, who were too distant to serve as practical goals of self-cultivation – even for the educated *junzi*, or superior men, who constituted Confucius' primary audience. For Confucius, the goal towards which a junzi should strive was to be a man of *ren* (humanity): a humane person.

For Mencius, on the other hand, sagehood was a practical goal. He stressed that the sages were just like ordinary human beings, except that they had fully realized the potential for goodness that is innate in human nature. Furthermore, in Mencius' thought there is a clearer distinction between the model of the sage and that of the ruler. While most of Confucius' sages had been rulers, it is clear that, for Mencius, a sage is not necessarily a ruler and a ruler is not necessarily a sage. Although the ideal ruler would be a sage, Mencius, in his recorded dialogues with rulers of the various warring states, is not reluctant to treat them as imperfect human beings.[36]

The "Neo-Confucians" of the Song dynasty followed Mencius both in maintaining a clear distinction between the models of the sage and the ruler, and in claiming sagehood to be a practical goal. Zhu Xi, however, emphasized the extreme difficulty of achieving sagehood. This was the reason for his concentration on methods of self-cultivation, including his intense interest in providing access for followers of the way to the words of the true sages enshrined in the classical texts. Since ordinary people were obstructed from seeing the "order of the way" (*daoli*) in nature and in themselves, they needed the help of sages in their efforts to "perceive the way" and to perfect themselves. As mentioned earlier, sages were few and far between – sometimes even non-existent for many years. Hence the importance of texts, commentaries, and teachers in the Cheng/Zhu system.

In classical Confucian thought, the ruler's most important job is the selection of able ministers, who will make the government run smoothly and in accordance with the humane character and vision of the ruler. This is clearly the sage/worthy relationship described by Qianlong in his *Yijing* essay. Thus Qianlong assimilates the sage/worthy model with that of the ruler/minister, reaching back to the earliest model of the sage, that of the mythic sage-king – a model that had not really been current in Confucian discourse since the time of Mencius. A further implication of this identification of ruler and sage is that one of the functions of the ruler is to be a kind of universal teacher. This is one way in which Qianlong justified his tight control over literature and scholarship during the Qing.

Qianlong's view of himself as a sage in the ancient, superhuman sense should be seen alongside the other models of sacred rulership on which he drew: the Mongol/Manchu khan, the Buddhist chakravartin/dharmaraja, and the Tibetan Buddhist bodhisattva incarnation.[37] In adopting these multiple identities, it is clear that Qianlong did not see any contradictions among them. First of all, he was different things to different audiences. To the Mongols he presented himself as khan, or the universal "king of kings"; to Tibetans and Tibetan Buddhist Mongols he was a chakravartin, dharmaraja, or bodhisattva, and patron of the Gelukpa; to the Han Chinese he was a sage-emperor who performed the crucial sacrifices; to Manchus he was an avatar of a lineage linking the Qing to the Jin dynasty, and promoter of Manchu shamanic traditions. So occasions for potential contradiction did not often arise. Second, these multiple identities and practices may have been mutually reinforcing. For example, the compassion of the bodhisattva was certainly compatible with the benevolence or humanity (*ren*) of the Confucian sage. And in all cases, Inner Asian as well as Chinese, the notion that he enjoyed heavenly favor or mandate was equally salient.

Furthermore, to posit political reasons for these religious expressions is not incompatible with the observation that Qianlong seems to have been quite sincere in his Buddhist practice. His lifelong friend and teacher, Jang gya khutukhtu Rolpai Dorje (1717–1786), gave Qianlong several tantric initiations that required a considerable commitment of time, study, and practice (although we can probably never know whether Qianlong actually carried through on these commitments). Both Tibetan and Chinese sources suggest that Qianlong frequently went beyond what would have been necessary to show respect to Buddhism and to Tibetan lamas (see Benard (Chapter 10) and Ragnubs (Chapter 16)).

There is less evidence, however, that Qianlong took Confucian teachings seriously in the same way as many of the Confucian scholars of the Song and Ming dynasties. For the latter, Confucianism was a comprehensive and religious worldview and way of life for literati, as well as a social-political philosophy. For many of them (e.g. Zhu Xi and his school), being a Confucian was incompatible with being a Buddhist or a Daoist.[38] This alone suggests that the same kinds of needs were met by Confucianism as by the other two religious traditions.[39] Qianlong, though – despite (or because of?) having been rigorously schooled in the Confucian classics and the Cheng/Zhu commentaries – seems to have used Confucianism mainly as a way of controlling and legitimating Qing rule to the Han literati and bureaucratic establishments. On this point he differed from his revered grandfather, the Kangxi emperor, who seems to have been more seriously disposed towards the Cheng/Zhu school. As R. Kent Guy has put it:

> Whether he was cruising down the Grand Canal to show the imperial flag in the southeast, reminiscing boastfully of ten great campaigns on the boundaries of his enormous empire, or presiding over a regime which produced voluminous descriptions of its goals, methods and philosophical foundations, the Ch'ien-lung [Qianlong] emperor seems to have been a man concerned almost exclusively with the image and style of the monarchy.[40]

Immediately following the June 29, 1780 entry in the *Veritable Records* is an extended discussion by Qianlong on a passage from the *Analects* of Confucius. In it Qianlong makes rather creative use of the passage to argue that the Qing were not greedy in their conquest of China, Tibet, and Inner Asia. The placement of such a discussion at this point in the *Veritable Records*, where it is clearly associated with the Wen miao, supports the notion that the meaning and purpose of the temple were connected to Qianlong's efforts to legitimate Qing and his own rule. The passage being discussed is *Analects* 16: 7:

> There are three things the superior person guards against. In youth, before the physical body [lit. "blood and *qi*"] has settled, he guards against sex. Reaching maturity, when the physical body has hardened, he guards against strife. Reaching old age, when the physical body has declined, he guards against greed.[41]

Qianlong begins by quoting Zhu Xi's commentary on the passage and his grandfather Kangxi's statement on guarding against greed.[42] He then adds:

> Thinking carefully about what the imperial ancestor [Kangxi] said, it is that one should guard against greediness to expand the territory and incorporate distant lands. One should not overdevelop one's army at the expense of the people. Although Our imperial ancestor [Kangxi] had conquered Outer Mongolia, he also defended Tibet. He did not over-expand his army, as he had no choice.
>
> I, the child, have inherited my elder's will. I have pacified the Yili region [i.e. Zungharia], settled the Muslim tribes [i.e. the Uyghurs of the Tarim Basin], and put down the Jinchuan [rebellion]. This territorial expansion was far in excess [of Kangxi's]; the incorporation of distant lands was far more complete [than Kangxi's]. But I did not dare to depend upon my army's strength or my general's plans, and I did not overdevelop the army for my selfish desire. I too had no choice but to use them. But I received heavenly aid, and the various affairs were harmoniously completed.
>
> Now my long life is approaching seven decades, and I too am old. What has there been that was unfulfilled? Dare I not take Kangxi's warning as a warning?[43]

It is surely no coincidence that this disquisition was recorded about seven weeks before Qianlong received the Panchen Lama at the imperial summer residence in Chengde, on the occasion of the emperor's seventieth birthday.[44] Despite the fact that he had been assiduously studying Tibetan Buddhism with his friend and teacher, Jang gya khutukhtu, and had been learning to read and speak Tibetan for over a year so that he could communicate directly with the Panchen Lama, he apparently still felt it necessary to neutralize in advance any potential diplomatic friction that might arise during the visit. For the purposes of this essay, it is sufficient to note here how Qianlong makes use of the Confucian tradition (classics and commentaries) for his political and diplomatic purposes.

Conclusion

The cultural and geographic landscape of Chengde was a carefully constructed microcosm of the Qing empire. As such it was an idealized statement – or text, if you will – conveying certain messages about how the Qing emperors (especially Kangxi and Qianlong) conceived of their empire, its relations with its constituent cultures, and its neighbors. Situated as it was in the Manchu homeland, and established after the Qing had expanded its boundaries, the statements made by Chengde were especially focused on the cultural identity of the Manchus vis-à-vis their neighbors (and subjects), the Han, Mongols, Tibetans, and Uyghurs – and of these, especially the Buddhist Mongols and Tibetans.

But from the Han perspective, Chengde was far from homeland; it was more periphery than center. Qianlong fully adopts this perspective in his Temple of Culture inscription (translated on pp. 111–113). In this text (in the literal sense) he shows his command of the Han scholarly tradition by making well-educated use of the symbolic grammar of *wen*. According to this set of conventions, culture (Han culture, that is) spreads progressively from the center into the wilderness, making the world a human world that is, a "civilized" world "transformed by culture" (*wenhua*). This same statement is made in the symbolic "text" of Chengde itself by the construction and maintenance of the Temple of Culture, its school and its library. The temple honors Confucius, the patron deity or "first teacher" of this cultural tradition; the school initiates and trains new members of its civil society; and the library houses the written record of the sages and worthies who have mastered and furthered the tradition.

The political implication of this statement to the Han civil bureaucracy and the literati class is, in effect, that the Manchu emperors have not usurped the role of Son of Heaven; they have, instead, succeeded legitimately to that role, as shown by their successes in spreading the very culture that gives it meaning. As a legitimizing tactic this statement may not be especially remarkable. After all, political legitimization by the manipulation of religious symbols is at least as old as the *Epic of Gilgamesh*, and as contemporary as a US presidential State of the Union Address. Still, one cannot help admire, however grudgingly, Qianlong's chutzpah.

Notes

1 *Qijuzhu* (*Diaries of Activity and Repose*), QL45.5.27.
2 *QLSL*, 37: 16244, 1107: 11a.
3 For the edict, which mainly restates what he wrote on the stele, see *QLSL*, 37: 15967–15968, 1083: 14b–15a.
4 See Stephen Feuchtwang, "School Temple and City God."
5 See Philippe Forêt, *Mapping Chengde*.
6 For the 1776 edict ordering the construction of the school, see *QLSL*, 36, reprinted in Sekino Tadashi and Takeshima Takuichi, *Nekka: Supplement*, 103.
7 *QLSL*, 37: 15961, 1083: 2a.

120   *Joseph A. Adler*

8 *QLSL*, 36: 15962, 1083: 3b.
9 *QLSL*, 37: 15966, 1083: 12b. July 7 was the first day of *xiaoshu* (small heat), one of the twenty-four fifteen-day periods into which the year was divided. See Juliet Bredon and Igor Mitrophanow, *Moon Year*, 21. This would have been an auspicious day on which to initiate something, which probably accounts for the timing of the ritual. In Taiwan today, offerings of food, incense, and spirit-money are made by many people outside their homes and businesses on the first day of each of these periods, i.e. every fifteen days.
10 *QLSL*, 37: 16244, 1107: 11b.
11 *QLSL*, 37: 16295, 1112: 1a–1b.
12 *QLSL*, 38: 16561, 1132: 21b.
13 *QLSL*, 37: 16567, 1133: 5a–5b.
14 *QLSL*, 37: 16948, 1157: 3b.
15 *QLSL*, 37: 15966–15997, 1083: 12b–14b. See also *Qing Gaozong yuzhih wen erji*, vol. 1, 30.3; and Sekino and Takeshima, *Nekka: Supplement*, 104–105. For a photographic reproduction of the manuscript once preserved in the Cunjing ge (Honoring the Classics Pavilion) library at the Chengde Wen miao, see Sekino and Takeshima, *Nekka*, vol. 2, pl. 29–33.
16 See *Zhongguo renming dacidian*, 987. For further references see Zhou Junfu, *Qingdai zhuanji congkan suoyin* (Compendium of Qing biographical records), 3: 1683.
17 See Sekino and Takeshima, *Nekka: Supplement*, figure 9.
18 This poem has not been traced.
19 The point here is that knowledge of the way requires actively putting it into effect in one's behavior. The "substance" (*ti*) is useless without "function" (*yong*).
20 Alluding to *Analects* 3.24, "Heaven is about to use the master as a wooden bell clapper," i.e. the master's purpose is to spread the way through education.
21 The subscription is found in the manuscript preserved in the Cunjing ge library at the Chengde Wen miao (Sekino and Takeshima, *Nekka*, vol. 2, pl. 33). It is included in Sekino and Takeshima's transcription of the stele (*Nekka: Supplement*, 105), but not in the other printed versions of the text.
22 See Peter K. Bol, *"This Culture of Ours."*
23 The use of gender-inclusive pronouns is not as anachronistic as it might seem, given the traditional Confucian support of patriarchy. Women could be sages too, but only as exemplary wives and mothers; the way of the woman was different from that of the man.
24 See Hoyt Tillman, *Confucian Discourse and Chu Hsi's Ascendancy*, especially ch. 1 for the concept of "fellowship."
25 See Wing-tsit Chan, "The *Hsing-li ching-i* and the Ch'eng-Chu School of the Seventeenth Century."
26 See Kent R. Guy, *The Emperor's Four Treasuries*.
27 Harold Kahn, *Monarchy in the Emperor's Eyes*, 115.
28 The most influential of his teachers were Cai Shiyuan (1682–1734), Zhu Shih (1665–1736), and Fu-min (1673–1756) (Kahn, *Monarchy*, ch. 8).
29 See *Qing Gaozong yuzhih shiwen chuanji*, vol. 1; the pre-succession essays are collected in the *Luoshan tang chuanji* (ch. 1–30).
30 Guy, *Emperor's Four Treasuries*, 25–26.
31 Guy, *Emperor's Four Treasuries*, 10.
32 Guy, *Emperor's Four Treasuries*, 16. The theoretical independence of ethnicity and virtue (based on the thought of Confucius and Mencius) did not prevent later scholars – among them Zhu Xi – from asserting the impossibility or inappropriateness of a non-Han Son of Heaven. Zhu Xi, it should be recalled, lived his entire life during the Southern Song, when the northern half of China was ruled by the Jurchen (whom the Qing claimed as their ancestors).

33 The first collection of his prose writings as emperor was compiled in 1763; the second in 1785. See *ECCP*, 370. This is from the second collection.
34 *Yijing, Tuan* commentary on hexagram 27, *Yi* (Nourish), which contains the lines, "Heaven and earth nourish the myriad things. The sage nourishes the worthy in order to reach the myriad people."
35 *Qing Gaozong yuzhih wen erji*, 1: 9a–9b.
36 See especially his discussions with King Hui of Liang, which have their amusing moments (*Mencius*, D. C. Lau, trans.).
37 It is unclear whether Qianlong considered himself or was considered technically a chakravartin or a dharmaraja. The former is the more spiritual category, referring to a "king who turns the wheel of the law," i.e. one who is responsible for the propagation of Buddhism in a particular age or region. A dharmaraja is simply a secular king who sponsors Buddhism, such as Asoka in third-century BCE India. But the two categories are often not clearly differentiated. It is clear that Qianlong was often referred to as an incarnation of Manjushri, the Bodhisattva of Wisdom. See Benard (Chapter 10) and Ragnubs (Chapter 16) as well as David Farquhar, "Emperor as Bodhisattva."
38 This did not prevent them from "borrowing" ideas and practices from Buddhism, such as enlightenment and meditation.
39 This is by no means the only justification for understanding Confucianism as a religious tradition, but that topic is beyond the scope of this essay. Cf. Rodney Taylor, *Religious Dimensions of Confucianism*.
40 Guy, *Emperor's Four Treasuries*, 4.
41 *Lunyu (Analects)*, 16· 7.
42 Zhu Xi's commentary on the passage, partially quoted by Qianlong:

> Blood and *qi* are what the body depends on for life; blood is *yin* and *qi* is *yang*. *De* (to acquire) means greed (*tande*). We know what to guard against according to the time. We overcome it by means of order [*li*, principle]. Then we are not driven by our physical body.
> Mr. Fan (Fan Zhongyan [989–1052]?) says, "The sage is the same as other (ordinary) people in terms of the physical body (blood and *qi*). He differs from others in terms of the will. The physical body declines over time, but the ability to exert the will never declines. That which in youth is not yet settled, in maturity is hardened, and in old age declines, is the physical body. Guarding against sex, guarding against strife, and guarding against greed is will. The superior person nourishes his will; therefore he is not moved by the physical body. Thus as the years progress, his virtue increases.
> (Zhu Xi, *Sishu jizhu, Lunyu*, 8: 3a–3b)

Qianlong's quotation of Kangxi's comment:

> The imperial ancestor explained this as follows. "The learning of emperors and kings is not the same as careless recitation. So what is to be guarded against also must differ. Guarding against the unsettled and hardened [*qi*] need not be discussed further. What is to be guarded against is just greed. Yet how can greed be the same for all people? In the sense of desiring material goods, this can be guarded against. Desiring to attain infinite years and be eternally blessed with heavenly favor, this can be guarded against. Desiring the five winds and ten rains, and frequent comfort at all times, this can be guarded against. But if one desires to achieve such wealth as the excess of Qionglin [Imperial Garden near Kaifeng], or the selfishness of a noble's treasury, then this is like cutting out a piece of flesh to patch a sore; in one's haste one forgets what is important [i.e. this is too obvious and

impossible to waste energy worrying about]. Of old there was clarity on what to guard against – yet it has come to this. It is trivial."

(*QLSL*, 3716244, 1107: 12b)

43 *QLSL*, 37: 16244–16245, 1107: 11b–13b.
44 On August 20, 1780, according to *QLSL*, 37: 16282, 1111: 4a.

10 The Qianlong emperor and Tibetan Buddhism

Elisabeth Benard

The sixty-year Qianlong reign (1735–1795) offers a fascinating window onto the intertwined cultural and political histories of the Manchus, Mongolians, Han, and Tibetans. The sources for these histories are written in many languages; for the most part, however, scholars have understood the Qing only through Chinese-language materials, supplemented by European writings such as those of the Jesuits. Though there are understandable reasons for this, it accompanies an assumption that Chinese sources are plainly superior and that Inner Asian materials have nothing to add to them.[1]

Readers are urged to consider this for themselves. In Part IV, Nima Dorjee Ragnubs provides a translation of the first-hand Tibetan account of the Third Panchen Lama's visit to Chengde and Beijing, Chinese-language accounts of which are brief and stylized.[2] In general, the silence in Chinese sources on the question of the Qing emperor's religious faith has led to confusion over the meaning of the large number of Buddhist material artifacts produced by the Qing court, especially a group of paintings depicting Hungli in Buddhist settings.

The Qianlong emperor and Buddhism

Modern authors have tended to assert that Hungli did not really believe in Tibetan Buddhism, and cite as proof part of a 1792 stele inscription entitled "On Lamas" (Ch. *Lama shuo*), found in the Yonghe gong, a Tibetan Buddhist temple in Beijing:

> As the Yellow Church inside and outside (of China proper) is under the supreme rule of these two men (the Dalai Lama and Panchen Lama), all the Mongol tribes bear allegiance to them. By patronizing the Yellow Church we maintain peace among the Mongols. This being an important task we cannot but protect this (religion).

Qianlong later commented that protecting the Yellow Church (i.e. the Tibetan Gelukpa tradition) was "merely in pursuance of Our policy of extending Our affection to the weak."[3] Farquhar argues that Qing emperors had to cultivate both political and religious personas, but that the political component was paramount.[4] One art historian sees Qianlong's Buddhist portraits as dalliance in ego-boosting amusement.[5]

Contemporary Tibetan and Mongolian sources, on the other hand, typically portray the Qianlong emperor as a devout Buddhist.

Qianlong and Jang gya Rolpai Dorje[6]

Tibetan sources amply document the Qianlong emperor's commitment to Tibetan Buddhism. One excellent example is Tuken's (Thu'u bkvan) biography of the second Jang gya khutukhtu, Rolpai Dorje (1717–1786).[7] Rolpai Dorje was the Qianlong emperor's childhood playmate, schoolmate, religious teacher and artistic consultant. He supervised the translation into Manchu and Mongolian of the Tibetan canon of the Buddha's teaching (sutras) and monastic code of discipline (vinaya), the Kangyur (*bka' 'gyur*), along with its commentaries, the Tengyur (*bstan 'gyur*). A prodigious scholar, author, and diplomat, he exerted significant influence in the Qing imperial court, Mongolia, and Tibet.[8]

According to Tuken's biography, in 1725, the eight-year old Jang gya Rolpai Dorje was brought from Amdo to Beijing by the Yongzheng emperor. During the war in Amdo, the Yongzheng emperor was reminiscing about his father's and his own previous lama (the first Jang gya, Ngawang Losang Chöden), and became concerned for the safety of the young reincarnation (Rolpai Dorje). He had him transported to Beijing and lodged him at the Songzhu Temple in the imperial palace.[9] The Yongzheng emperor promised to support the Jang gya and his entourage with imperial treasury funds. Rolpai Dorje and the future Qianlong emperor (then known as Hungli and seven years senior to Rolpai Dorje) grew up, studied at the imperial palace school and spent much of their lives together.

The depth of Yongzheng's faith in either Chan or Tibetan teachings is hard to gauge.[10] A biography of Jang gya Rolpai Dorje by his younger brother recounts that Hungli gave Rolpai Dorje a cane used by his father, Yongzheng.[11] As Rolpai Dorje placed it in his "protector's" room, he recalled that Yongzheng was a great leader and did much religious work.[12] Then the emperor gave him a thangka, apparently of Yongzheng as Manjushri, and a weaving of Palden Lhamo. Rolpai Dorje hung these in his temple.[13]

In late 1735 Hungli became the Qianlong emperor and, in accordance with the Tibetan belief that Chinese emperors are emanations of Manjushri, the bodhisattva of wisdom, Rolpai Dorje began to address him as Great Emperor Manjushri.[14] In 1744, Qianlong indicated to Rolpai Dorje that he wanted to receive private religious teachings.[15] Rolpai Dorje remembered that his great teacher, the sixty-first Ganden Tipa (the head of the

Gelukpa sect) had advised him, "If the emperor asks you to teach him, then you must instruct him in the commentary on how to take refuge in the three jewels (the Buddha, his teachings [dharma] and the propounders of the teachings [sangha])." Rolpai Dorje thus taught Qianlong this as well as Tibetan grammar and reading. Qianlong studied diligently and quickly learned to read the language.

Later, Tuken relates, Qianlong requested further religious teachings and expressed his desire to understand the vast technical vocabulary of Buddhism, which pleased Rolpai Dorje greatly. Rolpai Dorje explained that the sutra path is the bodhisattva path and stressed its benefits. The emperor, enthusiastic, requested the teachings of this system. Rolpai Dorje taught him the commentary of the Graduated Path (Lam Rim) by Vajradhara Kunchok Gyaltsen, with a commentary by his predecessor, the first Jang gya khutukhtu (Ngawang Losang Chöden) as an aid to meditation. By studying these two texts, Qianlong developed great faith (*gong ma thugs dad gting nas khrungs*) and made a commitment to practice daily, which he kept despite his busy schedule.[16]

The biography emphasizes that Rolpai Dorje was the Qianlong emperor's root teacher, his spiritual superior. For a Tibetan tantric practitioner, one's root teacher is a spiritual parent who instructs and protects the practitioner. Chinese scholars doubt that the Qianlong emperor would cast himself in a position subordinate to Rolpai Dorje, and they dismiss the Tibetan texts as fabrications. While one might argue that Tibetan writers have a vested interest in portraying the lama's relationship with the Qing ruler as one of teacher and disciple, in matters of imperial image Chinese sources are no less freighted with an agenda to represent the emperor in a certain way.

In 1745 (the wood-bull year), Tuken's text continues, after Rolpai Dorje completed a retreat,[17] the Qianlong emperor asked him for the tantric teachings of his tutelary deity (*yidam*), Chakrasamvara (Demchok, the deity associated with the Pule si; see Figure 17).[18] As disciple and requester of the initiation, the emperor had to gather all the necessary materials and equipment. Rolpai Dorje conferred on the emperor the five deities with Chakrasamvara according to the lineage of the Indian siddha, Ghantapa.[19] During the initiation, Rolpai Dorje as vajra master sat on the throne and the emperor knelt to receive the initiation according to the prescriptions for disciples. The emperor offered 100 ounces of gold with a mandala (symbolizing the universe) to receive the initiation. Auspicious signs were noted. On the previous night the emperor heard the mantra *oṃ maṇi padme hūṃ* and, during the initiation, when he threw the flower to ascertain with which of the five cosmic Buddhas he was connected, his flower stood upright. This rare occurrence indicated that he would receive *vidyadhara* ("wisdom-holding") boons, qualifying him for advanced spiritual development.[20]

After the initiation, Qianlong said to Rolpai Dorje, "Now you are not only my lama, you are my vajra master." Tuken observes that the emperor took his commitment very seriously. Rolpai Dorje remarked that Khubilai Khan took the initiation of Hevajra (Kye Dorje) with the Tibetan Sakya master, Pakpa, in 1253 (the water-bull year). Though the element, wood, was different, both occurred in a bull year. These parallel events significantly linking the Mongol khan and Manchu emperor demonstrated an auspicious connection between the two powerful rulers and the beneficial aspects of Tibetan Buddhism for the emperors of China.

Qianlong received many other initiations, including those of the important goddess, Vajrayogini, a major protector, the six-armed Mahakala, and an entire set known as the Thirteen Golden Teachings, a central teaching in the Sakya lineage.[21] All these initiations involved a commitment to the daily recitation of the "essence syllables" (mantra) of a deity and usually a daily visualization practice that can take from fifteen minutes to several hours. Such practices argue for more than a passing or opportunistic interest in Tibetan Buddhism.

The Qianlong emperor and the Third Panchen Lama

The Qianlong emperor also received initiations from the Third Panchen Lama (1737–1780), whom the emperor invited to Chengde for his own seventieth birthday commemoration in 1780.[22] Qing emperors had invited other important Tibetan leaders in this manner;[23] frequently, the latter declined politely, citing the inclement Beijing weather and the risk of contracting smallpox. In fact, the Qianlong emperor had extended numerous requests to the Third Panchen Lama, who finally accepted the invitation to celebrate the emperor's seventieth birthday. The biography of the Third Panchen Lama describes in detail the lama's journey from central Tibet to Chengde and eventually to Beijing (on the visit, see also Ragnubs, Chapter 16; on its commemoration, see Zarrow, Chapters 12 and 15).[24]

When the two men first met in 1780 on the twentieth day of the Tibetan seventh month, the Panchen Lama greeted the emperor as Chakravartin Lhegyong (the Wheel Turner, Protector of the Deities).[25] The emperor inquired in Tibetan about his guest's long journey. The lama replied, "By the grace of the Emperor Manjushri, there were no difficulties." Then the emperor and the Panchen Lama both sat down facing each other on one long golden dais. They exchanged long white scarves (a Tibetan custom) and began to drink tea simultaneously. They conversed in Tibetan. The Panchen Lama gave a short speech about how indeed the emperor was the real Manjushri, the bodhisattva of wisdom.[26] Later, gifts were exchanged. The Panchen Lama's gifts to the emperor included a solid gold statue of Tsong kha pa (founder of the Gelukpa), a small Chakrasamvara statue, gold, amber, coral, 1,000 horses, and much more. The emperor's gifts to the Panchen Lama included a gold mandala, brocade appliqué thangkas

(Tibetan style paintings) of deities Guhyasamaja, Chakrasamvara, and Yamantaka (major tutelary deities of the Gelukpas).[27]

Noteworthy in the above account is the parity displayed between the Panchen Lama and Qianlong in their seating arrangement and simultaneous tea drinking. Moreover, Qianlong observed correct Tibetan protocol in exchanging white scarves and conversing in Tibetan. His gifts suggest attention to the Panchen Lama's interests and likes. The emperor gave him a gold mandala, an item presented only to important lamas or royalty. He also gave the Panchen Lama brocade appliqué thangkas (usually made in China), which Tibetans greatly esteemed.

On his third day at Chengde, the Panchen Lama performed a longevity ceremony for the emperor, during which Qianlong (patron) and the Panchen Lama (lama) sat on the same throne. The statues of deities and other costly religious objects exchanged on this day were predominantly items associated with longevity. As the objects were presented, Jang gya and six high-ranking lamas knelt and chanted long life prayers.[28]

On the fourth day of the Panchen Lama's visit, after a sumptuous banquet accompanied by Mongolian music, wrestling, acrobatic stunts, magic shows, horsemanship displays, and performances of historical plays and operas, the emperor praised his guest and asked him to teach the monks in the Chengde Potala (Putuozongcheng miao) and Tashilhunpo (Xumifushou miao) temples. When the emperor indicated his intention to attend the lectures, the Panchen Lama replied, "You, God of the Sky, Manjushri Emperor, who makes peace and happiness in the world, who spreads Buddhism ... you who bring religion, wealth, and happiness to all beings under the sky. . . ."

In the eighth month, with the stars in an auspicious formation, the Panchen Lama performed another long life ceremony for the emperor.[29] After chanting long life verses with paeans to Qianlong's previous lives and presenting gifts to the emperor, the Panchen Lama concluded by praising the emperor as a great protector of Buddhism. The gratified monarch promised to produce statues, books, and stupas and to build residences for monks, and he affirmed his faith in the God of the Sky and the Three Jewels.[30] Later in the eighth month in the inner palace, the Panchen Lama performed the white Chakrasamvara initiation, which also promotes long life.[31]

Further, states Tuken's biography, the Panchen Lama performed rituals for the benefit of the nation. When the Panchen Lama stayed in Beijing, he sponsored a long life ceremony for the emperor, as well as rituals to ward off sickness, starvation, and fighting and to attract wealth, luxury, and happiness for the empire. This ceremony was performed in the ninth month in the Yonghe gong, the sandalwood statue temple (Tsan Dan), and Rolpai Dorje's residence (Songzhu temple) in the imperial enclosure, and in twenty-eight other Tibetan monasteries in Beijing.[32]

One of the last ceremonies that the Panchen Lama performed for the emperor was on the twenty-seventh day in the ninth month.[33] Tuken does not name the ceremony, but judging from the statues and gifts presented to the emperor, it may have been a "protecting the nation" ceremony. Though ill, the Panchen Lama chose not to postpone the ceremony. The Panchen Lama, Jang gya's manager, the sixth imperial prince, and the Panchen Lama's cook went to one of the emperor's residences near the Ying Shugs Palace in Beijing. There they set up offerings and statues of Yamantaka (a main tutelary deity of the Gelukpas) and six-armed Mahakala. After the Panchen Lama finished the preliminaries, the great prince (probably Qianlong's sixth son, who had been the Panchen Lama's escort) and the emperor arrived. The Panchen Lama and the emperor exchanged scarves. Then the emperor presented a golden mandala symbolizing the universe to the Panchen Lama, who conferred the six-armed Mahakala blessing initiation upon the emperor and his retinue. Jang gya translated the initiation into Mongolian.

At the conclusion of the ceremony, the emperor presented the thanks-giving mandala as well as seventy-two bundles of Mongolian brocade and sufficient heavy cotton material to make nine chubas (*khyu pa*, a Tibetan robe). The Panchen Lama gave the Qianlong emperor the statues of a six-armed Mahakala, a Yama (lord of the Dead), and a Palden Lhamo (main protectoress of Tibet), all important protectors of a state or nation. He also presented Qianlong with two good quality Indian "fire brands" (*mei 'phrul 'khor*) and two swords with sheaths. The emperor was very pleased. The Panchen Lama and the emperor then presented scarves to the other participants. Before the emperor departed, he held a Tibetan style tea ceremony with dairy products (milk, butter, cheese, yoghurt) for everyone.

At the reception following the conclusion of the ceremony, the Panchen Lama confided to Jang gya, "I feel released and happy. All my work is done. Now I will take a few days rest and I will be fine." Then he smiled. Jang gya immediately responded, "How can you say your work is done? As long as there are beings in Samsara (cyclic existence) your work is not finished. Do not say such things. You have fulfilled all the emperor's wishes, but now [you must] go back to Tibet to help the countless beings. Do not say such things, even in jest!" "Yes, you are right," said the Panchen Lama. "I just made a kind of joke. There are many things to do."[34] The third Panchen Lama never returned to Tibet, however. Within three months he had died of smallpox in Beijing.[35] Jang gya presided over his funeral ceremonies and the bereaved Qianlong emperor established a memorial hall for him in the Pavilion of Rain and Flowers (Yuhua ge), a religious sanctuary within the residential sector of the Forbidden City.

The emperor's relationship with the Panchen Lama differed from his relationship with the Jang gya. First of all, the Panchen Lama knew the emperor for only some five months, unlike Jang gya who had spent most his life with the emperor. Second, since the emperor considered Jang gya his main teacher, he sought from him the highest (S. *anuttara*) initiations, which entail a serious commitment from both teacher and disciple.[36] In contrast, the Panchen Lama performed more generic long life and "protecting the empire" ceremonies. These rituals did not exact a commitment but did establish a connection between the Qing emperor and the Panchen Lama. Tibetan Buddhists believe that it is good to establish "connections" with important or powerful lamas who might be able to help you in particular circumstances, such as a prolonged sickness or dangerous enterprises. Thus Qianlong was acting according to Tibetan beliefs and through his actions endorsed their authority.

Both lamas were highly respected and the Tibetan texts make clear that the emperor treated them as equals when he requested them to share his throne during public receptions. In his role as their spiritual disciple, he accepted lower status by kneeling or sitting, while they sat on a throne with raised cushions. The emperor honored both Jang gya and the Panchen Lama with memorial halls in the Pavilion of Rain and Flowers (Yuhua ge) within the Forbidden City, not far from his own quarters. The Tibetan biographies detail the Qianlong emperor's solicitousness for the lamas, willingness to spend lavishly on Buddhist rituals and temples, and great faith in the efficacy of Tibetan Buddhism.

Portraits of the Qianlong emperor as bodhisattvas

Qianlong is depicted in many portraits ranging from the very formal, which were displayed more publicly, to the uncommon, such as Qianlong as a Daoist or as the bodhisattva Manjushri, which had a limited viewing.[37] Well known for his support of the arts, the Qianlong emperor established a large painting academy. Much has been written about the Chinese, Manchu, and Jesuit artists, but little about the Mongolian and Tibetan painters in the Qing court. Linked to the Palace Board of Works (Zaoban chu) was a Tibetan Buddhist Painting Academy in the Hall of Central Uprightness (Zhongzheng dian) that was responsible for religious painting and sculpture for the imperial family.[38]

It is significant that the Tibetan Buddhist Painting Academy dedicated its efforts specifically to the imperial family. Various sources attest that the empress dowager was a devout Buddhist and had great influence over her son. She lived in the southwestern part of the Forbidden City in the Cining Palace, which had a Buddhist temple, the Baoxiang Lou, as well as a complex of image halls in an adjacent garden compound; she is also credited with making an appliquéed thangka of Green Tara which now hangs in the Yonghe gong in Beijing. Her son, the Qianlong emperor, presented her with a set of nine Buddhas and a complete set of Amitayus Buddhas for her sixtieth birthday. On her seventieth birthday she received over nine thousand statues of the historical Buddha, bodhisattvas, Amitayus Buddhas, Taras and Arhats in multiples of nine. According to Chinese custom, certain homophones are auspicious, such as *jiu* ("nine"), homophonous with the character for "longevity," hence a wish for the recipient to live forever. For her eightieth birthday, celebrated in conjunction with the emperor's sixtieth birthday in 1780, Qianlong built the Chengde Potala and in 1781 she took part in its dedication. Continuing to commemorate this remarkable long life, in 1782 Qianlong had the Pavilion of Ten Thousand Buddhas constructed on the north shore of Beihai in Beijing. The sheer bulk of this material, most in the Tibetan idiom, attests to the sincerity of the dowager's belief.

Fond of having his portrait done in various styles, the Qianlong emperor had himself painted in numerous Buddhist guises. For our purposes the most interesting and least understood is a painting depicting the emperor as a Tibetan lama representing Manjushri (Figure 5). Of all the portraits, this one, which may have seven extant versions, has stimulated the most comment and has been misidentified as Qianlong representing the Buddha in a mandala, a residence of a deity.[39] As previously mentioned, the Tibetans considered Chinese emperors to be emanations of Manjushri and addressed them by this epithet; depicting the Qing emperor in a Tibetan style painting as Manjushri may be unprecedented, although it is very common for Tibetan lamas to be represented in this fashion. Since thangkas are not signed, they are difficult to date precisely, but this painting dates from the mid-eighteenth century.[40] It was probably completed after Qianlong received the highest tantric initiations, a process which began in 1745 and indicates that he took the time to maintain the obligatory practices. The actual portrait section of this painting appears to be in the style of European portraiture, while the remainder was executed by Tibetan or Mongolian monk painters.[41] Qianlong frequently had Jesuit artists – here, Giuseppe Castiglione – execute the faces in the paintings and Chinese, Mongolians, or Tibetans paint the rest. In the Tibetan art tradition, too, the face was reserved for the master painter and the less critical features reserved for the students to paint.

This painting places the Qianlong emperor in the center of the Gelukpa tradition. He is depicted as a Tibetan scholar in an emanation of the boddhisattva Manjushri. Over his shoulder to the right is a book and to the left is the sword of wisdom which cuts through ignorance. His right hand is in the teaching mudra. These implements and gestures are associated with Manjushri, as is the landscape in the background, the five peaks of Wutai shan in Shanxi. Qianlong wears the pandita's hat (T. *pan cha*) and in his left hand carries the wheel of Buddhist teaching that marks him as a dharmaraja – a great ruler who turns the wheel of Buddhist teachings, and the inscription reinforces this ideal:

> To the human lord (Qianlong) who is the sharp (minded) Manjushri manifesting as the great owner (of the world) and Dharmaraja. May

he live long who is firmly seated on the vajra throne and may wishes (of beings) be spontaneously fulfilled in this good era.

The emperor-bodhisattva is surrounded by 108 deities, representing the lineage of humans and deities linked in transmitting particular Buddhist (here, the Gelukpa) teachings from teacher to disciple. The Tibetan lama in the circle above Qianlong's nimbus is his root teacher, Jang gya Rolpai Dorje. Other figures in the assembly include the founder of the Gelukpa school, Tsong kha pa; Yamantaka, a tutelary deity who annihilates death and was a great favorite among the Gelukpa; and Chakrasamvara, the main deity of the first major tantric initiation that the Qianlong emperor received from Rolpai Dorje, in 1745. Chakrasamvara is also connected with a cave in the mountain which faces the prominent columnar stone known as Hammer Peak near Chengde. According to the *Amdo Buddhist History*, a great Nepalese scholar of Chakrasamvara, the youngest of the four Phamthing brothers, went to Luojia tun (T. Lo gya dung) near Chengde in China in the eleventh century.[42] He and his consort meditated on Chakrasamvara in a cave on the mountain that faces the massive column, which Tibetans believe to be a Shiva linga, an aniconic form of the Hindu deity Shiva, who frequently does battle with the Buddhist deity Chakrasamvara. It is believed that relics of Phamthing and his consort reside in a statue of Chakrasamvara in this mountain; Tibetans call this place "Luojia tun, place of the self-emanating Chakrasamvara" (Lo gya dung bDem mchog rang 'byung).[43] In this regard, it is significant that, at Qianlong's behest, Rolpai Dorje directed the construction at Chengde of the Pule si (Temple of Universal Happiness), dedicated to Samvara (Chakrasamvara), and that this temple stands in direct alignment with Hammer Peak and the cave (Figures 17 and 18; and Chayet, Chapter 4).[44] This painting thus also reinforces the strong connection between the Qianlong emperor and Rolpai Dorje and with his main tutelary deity, Chakrasamvara.

The bottom portion of the painting displays three main deities who are protectors of Tibetan Buddhism and of Tibet. From proper right to left these are Yama, lord of death, six-armed Mahakala, and Palden Lhamo, a protectoress of Tibet and especially of the Dalai Lama as ruler of Tibet. One of the last ceremonies performed for Qianlong by the Panchen Lama was "protecting the nation," wherein the Panchen Lama gave the emperor statues of Mahakala and Palden Lhamo, thereby implying that since Qianlong was a Tibetan Buddhist these protectors would guard his empire.

Clearly, these thangkas were not whimsical portraits of Qianlong play-acting as a buddha in a mandala but, rather, richly meaningful iconographic paintings which document his commitment to Tibetan Buddhist wisdom and power, within his personal faith and his public responsibility as an emperor.

The Qianlong emperor's tomb

Last but not least, it bears noting that Qianlong's tomb complex abounds almost exclusively in Tibetan Buddhist imagery and carved texts. Serious study has just begun of the precise significance of the Buddhist objects and decor in Qianlong's tomb.[45] Imperial tombs were, perhaps, the most personal and private arena of an emperor's life (and afterlife); monarchs typically planned their tomb complex many years before their death and access to the tomb was prohibited to the public. Tibetan sources state that Qianlong began construction of his burial place in 1743, in the water-pig year; it was completed in 1773. The Qing tombs remained undisturbed until July 1928 when they were looted by warlord Sun Dianyang and his troops.[46] Enough remains, however, to provide compelling evidence of Qianlong's personal beliefs.

At the entrance to the tomb, the mantra of the "Invincible Goddess with the White Umbrella" (S. Sitatapatra Aparajita or T. gDus dKar), dispeller of obstacles, is carved in stylized Sanskrit known as lantsa script. In the innermost chamber housing the coffin, incised on the wall is the famous "Ye Dharma" mantra, which sums up the major Buddhist teaching of dependent origination. Written in Tibetan script, it means, "all phenomena arise from the cause, that cause is explained by the Tathagata (the Buddha); and the cessation of the cause is explained by the great Sage." This popular mantra evokes the first teaching by the Buddha, the four noble truths; followers believe that repeating it, touching it, or writing it, will generate tremendous merit. Thus these two mantras, which dispel obstacles and generate merit, assure that the deceased Qianlong emperor will be reborn in a higher realm.[47]

These materials – biographies of Jang gya Rolpai Dorje and the Third Panchen Lama, Tibetan histories of Buddhism, portraits, and the tomb of Qianlong – demonstrate the emperor's deep involvement with Tibetan Buddhism and sustained relationships with its important lamas. In certain instances, such as the case of his spiritual teacher, Jang gya Rolpai Dorje, he treated lamas as his superior, or in the case of the Third Panchen Lama, as his equal. Moreover, though assessing personal faith through indirect sources is difficult, the materials presented here suggest that the Qianlong emperor pursued Tibetan Buddhism not only for strategic purposes, but also out of a personal commitment to the Tibetan Buddhist faith.

Notes

1 For a refutation of this view, see Pamela Crossley and Evelyn Rawski, "A Profile of the Manchu Language in Ch'ing History."

2 James Hevia compares ideological standpoints of the Chinese and Tibetan accounts of this meeting in *Cherishing Men from Afar*, 46–47.

3 See "Chien-lung's inscription on Lamaism" (*Lama shuo*) in Ferdinand Lessing, *Yung-ho-kung*, 57–62; quote from p. 59.
4 Farquhar, "Emperor as Bodhisattva," 34.
5 Hearn, "Qing Imperial Portraiture," 117.
6 On this subject, see also Wang Xiangyun, "The Qing Court's Tibet Connection: Lcang skya Rol pa'i rdo rje and the Qianlong Emperor."
7 Tuken (Thu'u bkvan) Dharmavarja (1737–1802) was an eminent scholar best known for his treatise on the history of Buddhist and non-Buddhist (including Daoist) doctrines; he was a disciple of Jang gya Rolpai Dorje. The biography, written in 1792, is found in the first volume (*ka*) of Tuken's *Collected Works* (ch. 21, pp. 611–638 of the edition we list in the bibliography).
8 For a brief description of his life and a description of an image of Rolpai Dorje, see T. Bartholomew, "Sino-Tibetan Art," 34–45. Jang gya Rolpai Dorje (not to be confused with Karmapa Rolpai Dorje, a teacher of the founder of the Gelukpa school Tsong Kha Pa (1357–1419)) has several biographies written by his contemporaries (e.g., that by his younger brother, Chu bzang Ngag dbang Thub bstan Dbang phyug). A summary of Jang gya's and Qianlong's relationship can be found in Chayet, *Temples de Jehol*, 60–64.
9 Thu'u bkvan, *Collected Works*, 1: 105. The Songzhu temple was built by the Kangxi emperor for the first Jang gya khutukhtu in 1712.
10 According to Anne Chayet, he showed more interest in Chan than Tibetan Buddhism (*Temples de Jehol*, 54) Also see Wills, *Mountain of Fame*, 242.
11 Hans-Rainer Kämpfe annotated this biography, *Ñi ma'i 'Od Zer*; this edition contains the original Tibetan and Mongolian texts.
12 Most Tibetan temples and houses have a "protector's" room where there is an image of the main protector and all sorts of war-like implements, armor, swords, etc. Rolpai Dorje probably put the cane in this room because it belonged to the emperor, who was, in his estimation, a defender of Buddhism.
13 The text is ambiguous. The portrait might be of Yongzheng, or of Qianlong. Kämpfe comments parenthetically, "*eine Erinnerung* [remembrance] *an die Zeit Kaiser Yung-chengs*" (52), suggesting the former. I have never seen such a thangka of Yongzheng, while there are at least seven thangkas depicting Qianlong as the bodhisattva Manjushri. Yet, the possibility certainly exists.
14 See Farquhar, "Emperor as Bodhisattva," and David Ruegg, "mChod-yon, yon-mchod and mchod-gnas/yon-gnas." This belief and its ramifications are discussed on pp. 129–131.
15 Thu'u bkvan, 318. This chapter (pp. 318–332), which concentrates on Jang gya's religious teachings, is poetically titled "Filling the great Emperor Manjushri's vase with nectar."
16 Thu'u bkvan, *Collected Works*, 319–321.
17 The text does not state what kind of retreat, but usually before an initiation the lama will do a retreat that concentrates on the deity of the initiation.
18 Thu'u bkvan, *Collected Works*, 323. According to Tibetan Buddhist custom, a disciple must ask his/her lama to confer an initiation. A lama will never bestow an initiation without a direct request. Also a lama can only give initiations that s/he is qualified to bestow.
19 Traditionally, each initiation must have an authentic and unbroken transmission lineage. This one is based on teachings given by the Indian yogi, Ghantapa. Rolpai Dorje was considered an adept of this Chakrasamvara lineage. Among Rolpai Dorje's works there are fourteen teachings (five attributed to Ghantapa) of Chakrasamvara which include retreats, offering food, performing a fire ceremony, singing praises, performing longevity rituals, and producing good wishes. See for example, Rol-pa'i-rdo-rje, Lcan-skya II, *Grub chen Dril-bu lugs kyi 'Khor-lo-sdom-pa'i lus dkyil kyi dmar khrid 'zal 'ses bde chen gsal ba'i sgron me 'zes bya ba b 'zugs*

so (Practical instruction for the esoteric visualization practices focussing on the kāyamandala of the Chakrasamvara Tantra as transmitted by the Mahasiddha Ghantapada).

20 Tibetans believe that such signs indicate a successful initiation.

21 Note that the Qianlong emperor received not only Gelukpa teachings, but also many Sakyapa teachings. His ancestors, Nurhaci and Hong Taiji, became interested in the Sakya teachings, as did the emperors of the Yuan dynasty. Hong Taiji founded the Temple of Mahakala at Mukden in 1635. See Grupper, "The Manchu Imperial Cult."

22 The title Panchen Lama combines part of the Sanskrit word for scholar, *pandita*, and the Tibetan word for great, *chen*, hence *panchen*. In 1601 the Fourth Dalai Lama gave this title to his teacher, Losang Chögi Gyeltsen, who was residing at Tashilhunpo monastery in central Tibet. Thus, successive reincarnations of his teacher were also known as the Panchen Lama, abbot of Tashilhunpo monastery. The Chinese consider Losang Belden Yeshe to be the Sixth Panchen Lama, since they include his previous rebirths before he was recognized as a reincarnation. The Tibetans only include previous lives after the reincarnation lineage was established, thus to Tibetans he is the Third Panchen Lama. There are numerous accounts of his visit to the Qing; see Cammann, "Panchen Lama's Visit."

23 The custom of inviting eminent Tibetan lamas to Beijing was established by Nurhaci's eighth son, Hong Taiji. Though Hong Taiji died before the arrival of the Fifth Dalai Lama, his son, the Shunzhi emperor, met the Fifth Dalai Lama in 1652 in Beijing and built the Yellow Temple (*Huang si*) for his stay.

24 This biography is appended to an autobiography covering the Third Panchen Lama's life until 1776. It was written in 1786 by Gonchok Jigme Wangpo (Dkon mchog 'Jigs med Dbang po (1728–1791), 'Jam Dbyangs Bzhad pa II, *Collected Works of dKon-mchog 'Jigs-med dBang-po* (cited hereafter as *DMJMBP*), vol. 4 (*nga*), ch. 3, 315–485). The Panchen Lama's autobiography may be found in the first volume (*ka*) of the Third Panchen Lama's *Collected Works* (Dpal-ldan-ye-'ses, Panchen Lama III, *The Collected Works (gsun 'bum) of the Third Panchen Lama of Tashilhunpo Blo-bzan-dpal-ldan-ye-'ses*). See also Nima Dorjee Ragnub's translation (Chapter 16) for an account of the events of the Third Panchen Lama's visit to Chengde.

25 This concept of the "wheel turner," an Indian epithet for a universal king, adapted by the Buddhists to refer to a ruler who turns the wheel of dharma, the teachings of the Buddha, is a frequent designation for Qianlong. See Ruegg, "mChod-yon, yon-mchod" and Farquhar, "Emperor as Bodhisattva."

26 *DMJMBP*, 4: 320–325.

27 *DMJMBP*, 4: 332.

28 *DMJMBP*, 4: 336.

29 Tibetans frequently perform rituals when the stars and planets are in a particular arrangement. In "Tibetan Astro Sciences" (192), Alexander Berzin explains "When a long life ceremony is offered to a lama, it is done in the early morning of his life force day. [For example] His Holiness the fourteenth Dalai Lama was born in the earth-pig year and his life force day is Wednesday." *DMJMBP*, 4: 379ff.

30 *DMJMBP*, 4: 387.

31 *DMJMBP*, 4: 407ff.

32 *DMJMBP*, 4: 468ff.

33 *DMJMBP*, 4: 481ff.

34 *DMJMBP*, 4: 483–484. According to Tibetan belief, each reincarnation returns to the world to do certain tasks. Once these tasks are completed, the subtlest consciousness abandons the body, i.e. dies. Jang gya was alarmed because he (correctly) sensed that the Panchen Lama was hinting at his own death.

35 He died in the second eleventh Tibetan month (1780). Since the Tibetan calendar is lunar, every three years there are adjustments, such as extra days or extra months; this is analogous to the Chinese *run* months, but the leap intervals do not fall in the same places.

36 The present Sakya Tinzin, head of the Sakya sect, once explained that a teacher and a disciple have mutual responsibility for maintaining the initiation commitment. He illustrated his point by holding an egg. Both the teacher and disciple should hold one side of the egg. If one gives up his/her side, it is acceptable but not ideal. However, if both abandon holding the egg, it breaks – a serious and perhaps irreparable infraction creating negative results.

37 See also Patricia Berger, *Empire of Emptiness.*

38 Yang Boda, "The Development of the Ch'ien-lung Painting Academy," 340. Yang adds that this was similar to the Buddhist Images Office (Fanxiang tizhu si) during the Yuan dynasty.

39 Hearn, "Qing Imperial Portraiture," 117.

40 For problems of dating a similar painting, see Ledderose and Buta, *Palastmuseum Peking*, 159, 161.

41 As interpreted in a paper delivered by Terese Bartholomew at a conference at SOAS in June 1994.

42 *Amdo Buddhist History (mDo sMad Chos 'Byung Deb Thar rGya mTsho)* 1849, 1: 550ff. This section was written by Baso rJe druang, wherein he states that according to different Tibetan sources, both the oldest and youngest brothers went there, but according to oral Chinese accounts only the youngest went. Confusion arises in *The Blue Annals* (Roerich, ed. and trans.) if you compare pages 227 and 381. However Brag sGom pa bsTan pa Rab rgyas, following the third Panchen Lama, favors the tradition that holds it was the youngest brother who went to Chengde.

43 Roerich, ed. and trans., *The Blue Annals*, 227, 381.

44 See Chayet, *Les Temples de Jehol*, 39–41.

45 Till, "The Eastern Mausoleums," and Nixi Cura, "Manchu Imperial Tombs: Interchanges in Iconography and Belief." Berger's analysis in *Empire of Emptiness* is extremely valuable.

46 Till, "The Eastern Mausoleums," 27–31.

47 According to Tibetan beliefs, many mantras exist but their power can only be efficacious if applied appropriately. For example, at a tomb complex, incising mantras for longevity would be inappropriate. However, mantras which dispel the obstacles that occur during the intermediary state between death and rebirth would be very helpful.

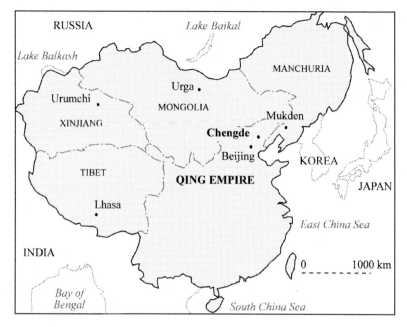

Figure 1 The Qing empire
Source: Philippe Forêt

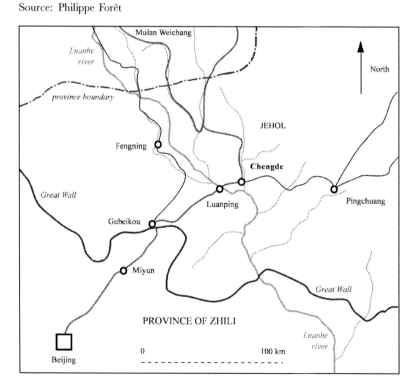

Figure 2 The road from Beijing to Mulan
Source: Philippe Forêt

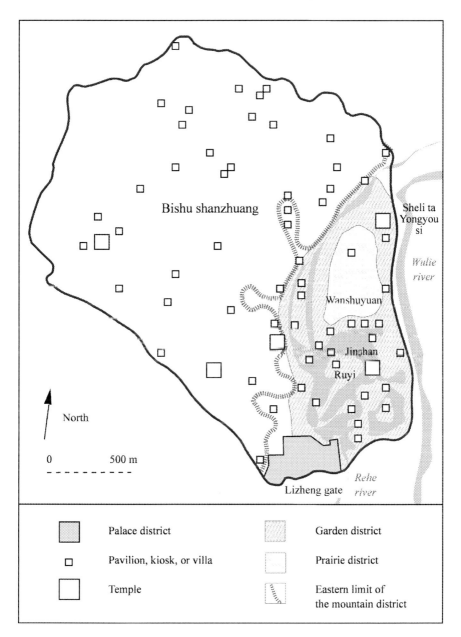

Bishu shanzhuang

Sheli ta
Yongyou
si

Wulie
river

Wanshuyuan

Jinghan

Ruyi

North

0   500 m

Lizheng gate

Rehe
river

Palace district

Pavilion, kiosk, or villa

Temple

Garden district

Prairie district

Eastern limit of
the mountain district

Figure 3 Bishu shanzhuang residence
Source: Philippe Forêt

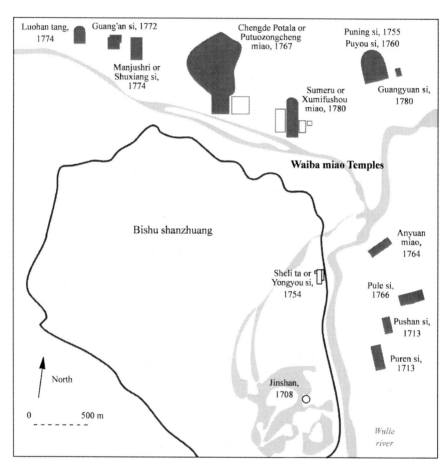

Luohan tang, 1774
Guang'an si, 1772
Manjushri or Shuxiang si, 1774
Chengde Potala or Putuozongcheng miao, 1767
Sumeru or Xumifushou miao, 1780
Puning si, 1755
Puyou si, 1760
Guangyuan si, 1780
Waiba miao Temples
Bishu shanzhuang
Anyuan miao, 1764
Sheli ta or Yongyou si, 1754
Pule si, 1766
Pushan si, 1713
Puren si, 1713
North
0   500 m
Jinshan, 1708
Wulie river

Figure 4 Waiba miao temples
Source: Philippe Forêt

Figure 5 Portrait of the Qianlong emperor as the bodhisattva Manjushri. Qianlong Emperor's Imperial Painting Academy; emperor's face painted by Giuseppe Castiglione (Lang Shining, 1688–1766)

Source: Freer Gallery of Art, Smithsonian Institution, Washington, DC: Purchase – Anonymous donor and Museum funds, F2000.4

Figure 6 The Bishu shanzhuang residence at Chengde

Source: *Rehe xinggong quantu*, landscape painting detail. Geography and Map Department,
Library of Congress

Figure 7 Detail of Zhenggong palace

Source: *Rehe xinggong quantu*, landscape painting detail. Geography and Map Department, Library of Congress

Figure 8 Ceremonial banquet in the Garden of Ten Thousand Trees (Wanshu yuan ciyan tu)

Source: Palace Museum, Beijing

Figure 9 Sheli ta, in Bishu shanzhuang
Source: Philippe Forêt

Figure 10 "Clouds and mountains on four sides" (Simian yunshan), mountain
district of Bishu shanzhuang with Potala in background

Source: Philippe Forêt

Figure 11 Bangchui feng, seen from garden district of Bishu shanzhuang today
Source: Philippe Forêt

Figure 12 Potala of Chengde (Putuozongcheng miao) in 1930
Source: © Sven Hedin Foundation

Figure 13 Hall of Ten Thousand Dharmas Joining into One (Wanfaguiyi dian)
Source: Palace Museum, Beijing

Figure 14 Xumifushou miao (Sumeru Temple) in 1930
Source: © Sven Hedin Foundation

Figure 15 Anyuan miao (Yili miao) in 1930
Source: © Sven Hedin Foundation

Figure 16 Puning si or Dafo si, Bangchui feng in background, 1930

Source: © Sven Hedin Foundation

Figure 17 Pule si in 1930
Source: © Sven Hedin Foundation

Figure 18 Pule si alignment with Bangchui feng

Source: *Rehe xinggong quantu*, landscape painting detail. Geography and Map Department, Library of Congress

Figure 19 Manjushri Temple in 1930

Source: © Sven Hedin Foundation

Figure 20 Wen miao, the Confucian Temple of Chengde in 1930
Source: © Sven Hedin Foundation

11 The art and politics of painting Qianlong at Chengde

Deborah Sommer

The Qianlong emperor was one of the most prolific collectors and patrons of works of art in late imperial China. Besides maintaining painting and craft ateliers in Beijing, he also sponsored the arts at his Bishu shanzhuang (Mountain Villa to Escape the Heat). Qianlong commissioned many paintings of life at Chengde and at the nearby Mulan hunting grounds, and these are valuable sources for historians interested in this place where the Manchu, Mongolian, and Han cultural spheres overlapped. Some of the paintings directly commissioned at the behest of Qianlong were historical genre scenes that record important moments in his political relations with neighboring peoples. As Qianlong's "imperial visage" (*yu rong*) appears in most of these works, they are a type of imperial portraiture and are thus important documents that reveal Qianlong's vision of himself as a sovereign over many peoples.

This essay focuses on one of the most important historical genre paintings Qianlong commissioned at Chengde: the enormous *Ceremonial Banquet in the Garden of Ten Thousand Trees* (*Wanshu yuan ciyan tu*), which commemorated a historic meeting Qianlong convened with Oirat (Western) Mongols on the grounds of the Bishu shanzhuang (Figure 8; see also Yu, Chapter 7). Focusing on the creation and the subsequent fate of this one important painting illustrates how Qianlong commissioned works of art to convey a certain image of himself to his political allies (and to his potential enemies). Linked to this essay is a translation of some correspondence by the French Jesuit brother who painted the early sketches for *Ceremonial Banquet*, wherein he provides a telling first-hand account of what it was like to work in Qianlong's service at Chengde (this is included in Part IV).

It may be impossible to discern whether the historical genre scenes of Chengde depict the realities, as opposed to the ideals, of daily life or political events there; nevertheless, as imperial portraits were granted the imprimatur of the emperor himself, these works at the very least indicate how Qianlong wanted himself to be seen by his subjects. Moreover, they incidentally provide many details of day-to-day life at the Bishu shanzhuang and at the hunting camps in Mulan. A survey of the art of Chengde reveals the diverse cultural influences – European, Mongolian, Manchu,

Tibetan, and Han – that shaped the aesthetic of the Qianlong reign. At Chengde, Qianlong commissioned European painters to document banquets with visiting Mongolians and record hunting expeditions with his Manchu colleagues; he had Tibetan painters depict him in the persona of a patron of the Buddhist dharma; and he personally copied out in his own hand not only entire Buddhist sutras but also the calligraphic works of Wang Xizhi (321–379), whose style represented the epitome of Han literati refinement. These works, exhibited in the halls and collected in the storehouses of the Mountain Villa, reflect Chengde's unique position at the confluence of several cultural systems. Surveying this art enriches our understanding of Qianlong's ability to interweave several worldviews simultaneously.

The *Ceremonial Banquet* work is but one of many historical genre paint-ings that depict the lifestyle of the court and its followers at Chengde. Favorite subjects of the artist's brush were hunting expeditions and the camp entertainment (wrestling, horse racing, and even picnicking) of the staff and soldiery who accompanied the emperor to the northeast. Of this genre, however, *Ceremonial Banquet in the Garden of Ten Thousand Trees* and its pendant piece *Horsemanship* (*Mashu tu*) are among the best documented. *Ceremonial Banquet* was placed in Qianlong's spirit-shrine for a time upon his death – further evidence of the painting's importance to him.

Extremely large in size (each measures approximately 400 by 200 cm, or roughly thirteen by seven feet), both paintings were executed in the *tieluo*, or appliqué, format. Many historical genre paintings were completed in the more common hanging scroll format, but some were produced in this newly popular medium of *tieluo*, literally, "paste-on lift-off" paintings. Appliqué paintings were not hung as free-standing hanging scrolls but were affixed directly to the surface of a wall from which they could later be lifted off and remounted.[1] *Ceremonial Banquet* is painted on silk perhaps manufactured in Hangzhou.

The Qing archives dryly document every step of the production of these two paintings, but their creation is described with considerably more élan in the correspondence of the Jesuit painters who served the Qing court. The cosmopolitan court at Chengde included visiting Europeans who recorded the events and ceremonies they witnessed during their stays at the Bishu shanzhuang. One of these visitors during the reign of Qianlong was the French Jesuit artist Jean-Denis Attiret (Chinese name Wang Zhicheng; 1702–1768), who had arrived in China in 1738.[2] Attiret lived with his fellow Jesuits in Haidian, near Beijing, and was engaged in Qianlong's service as a court painter, usually at one of his several palaces in and around Beijing.

On one occasion, however, he was commanded by Qianlong to go directly to Chengde to document an important historical event: a cere-monial banquet that commenced on July 5 of the summer of 1754 to commemorate Qianlong's recognition of a group of Oirats as his own subjects. In the mid-1750s, Qianlong held a series of banquets and enter-tainment for newly arrived Western Mongols who aligned themselves politically with the Qing. These secessions were of critical strategic impor-tance, for they reflected the weakening of the Zunghar federation, and were prefatory to the 1755 Qing campaign in Zungharia (see Millward, Chapter 8).

Attiret's work became the preliminary sketch for, if not the actual finished painting of, the famous *Ceremonial Banquet* (Figure 8). This painting depicts the moment at the start of the banquet when the emperor makes his entrance into the Wanshu yuan (Garden of Ten Thousand Trees), which has been decorated with yurts, trapezes for acrobatic performances, and open-air pavilions set with gifts. A large audience of Mongol immigrants, Qing officials, and Buddhist monks has lined up in attendance, awaiting the emperor's approach.

Attiret was ordered to go to Chengde, watch all these proceedings, and incorporate them into a composition to document the occasion. Attiret's visit to Chengde in 1754 is described in a letter to Europe by his fellow Jesuit, Jean-Joseph-Marie Amiot (1718–1793).[3] The section of that letter relevant to Attiret's stay at the Bishu shanzhuang is translated in Chapter 14. Amiot's account of Attiret's stay in "Chinese Tartary" begins with a description of the political events in Central Asia that sends a large contin-gent of Dörböt Mongols eastward to seek refuge under Qianlong and be accepted as his subjects. Qianlong sets out for Chengde from Beijing to receive them, taking a much larger retinue with him than usually accom-panies him to the Mountain Villa. This exodus initially gives the Jesuits stationed in Haidian some cause for relief, for as Amiot notes, "It is only when the emperor is absent that the people who work under his eyes have a little liberty," implying that Qianlong is a demanding patron. Attiret's plans for a spiritual retreat during this brief liberty are soon interrupted by an envoy delegated to take him to Chengde to paint portraits of the newly immigrated foreigners. Leaving in all possible haste to catch up with the imperial retinue that has already left for the northeast, he takes his painting materials and borrows from the envoy some clothes suitable for the event, for "here there are town clothes and travel clothes, determined by their length, shape, and by what is worn with what, and it would be the worst indecency to appear at court in clothing inappropriate to the occasion, place, and season."

Camping *à la tartare*, Attiret soon catches up with the slower-moving retinue, which is thrown into complete disorder by inclement weather. His description of this royal progress – which he calls an excellent model for an army in disarray, with human beings and animals crushed in a wild fracas – is hardly one likely to appear in the official Chinese sources. Arriving in Chengde, a "third-rate city," Attiret is given excellent rooms and is informed that he is to paint the coming festival. He attends the fête, watching everything with the gaze of an artist who must convey the essence of the entire celebration in one scene and present a sketch of it to the emperor that very evening. Under great time pressure, Attiret at first does not know where to begin, and Amiot relates the brother's psychological anguish with almost cinematic imagery – the reader sees Attiret anxiously sharpening his drawing pencils, stalling for time, waiting for inspiration. Attiret finally hits upon the plan for his initial sketch: the moment when Qianlong enters the site of the ceremony, "a moment flattering to this prince, where one saw at a glance all the magnificence of his grandeur."

Amiot's letter does not describe the actual festival that Attiret has witnessed earlier that day, for apparently the ceremony of 1754 was so similar to one convened by Kangxi in 1691 that Amiot, instead of describing it himself, refers the reader to an account of it recorded by Jean-François Gerbillon (1654–1707) in Gerbillon's third trip to Tartary. Gerbillon made eight trips to Tartary with Kangxi from 1689 to 1698 and participated in the negotiation of treaties with the Russians. Gerbillon's account is of interest in that it illustrates the continuity of ceremonial performances from Kangxi's to Qianlong's time. Amiot notes in his letter that Gerbillon's description is recorded in the fourth volume of an unnamed work by Père Jean-Baptiste Du Halde (1674–1743), no doubt Du Halde's four-volume *Description géographique, historique, chronologique, politique et physique de l'Empire de la Chine* (Paris, 1735) (a work unavailable to the translators). A secondary discussion of Du Halde's account, however, is included in the more readily available *Choix des lettres édifiantes, écrites des missions étrangères.*[4] This secondary account of the ceremonies Gerbillon witnessed in 1691 in Tartary (most likely in Dolonnor in Inner Mongolia) is found within the context of a discussion of the importance of Buddhism, particularly Tibetan Buddhism, to the Qing emperors. (A similar ceremony greeted the newly arrived Torghuts in 1771 – see Millward (Chapter 8); Ragnubs' translation from a biography of the Third Panchen Lama in Chapter 16, provides a detailed description of yet another such festival held in the Wanshu yuan in 1780.)

In the ceremony of 1691, Kangxi met with the current Jebtsundampa khutukhtu and his brother and received the homage of a group of Khalkhas. Gerbillon's account of the arrangement of tents, pavilions of gifts, and rows of dignitaries in ceremonial attire could equally describe the ceremony recorded in Attiret's much later painting *Ceremonial Banquet*, with the exception that Kangxi had four elephants brought in for the occasion. The Khalkha dignitaries expressed homage by repeated kowtowing, kneeling, and prostrating, but the khutukhtu and his brother were exempt from such acts of secular subordination and were allowed to remain standing throughout the entire ceremony. During the banquet that followed the kowtows and prostrations, Kangxi entertained his guests with acrobats, marionettes, and musical performances and offered the Khalkhas gifts of silver, silk, and clothing. Considering the similarity between

Gerbillon's description of 1691 and Attiret's painting of 1754, then, Qianlong's reception of the Oirats in 1754 was not a novel event but was a repetition of a ceremonial precedent established by his grandfather.

Attiret, pencils sharpened, creates a sketch of all the activities before nightfall, and Qianlong says of it that it is "*hen hao*," or very good. The next day, despite a serious chest cold, Attiret is enjoined to paint portraits of eleven of the most important Mongol nobles in attendance. The Mongol nobles watch him as he works, politely inquiring about life in France; marveling at the painter's art, they are mystified by Attiret's ability to capture their likeness with brush and ink.[5] Qianlong also dubs these portraits "*hen hao*" and honors the painter by having meals from the imperial table sent to him; he visits Attiret personally to watch him work and has him relocated directly to the throne room to create an enlarged sketch of the ceremony. All these imperial attentions incite the jealousy of the officials in attendance on Attiret, who make no attempt to disguise their sentiments.

Qianlong, dictating the subject matters himself, requires Attiret to create several more works and orders him to do an imperial portrait, posing obligingly for the painter. This life-size portrait pleases the emperor so much that Qianlong offers to make Attiret a mandarin of the fourth rank, much to the annoyance of the officials attending the Jesuit – and much to the chagrin of Attiret himself, who seeks heavenly rather than worldly honor. Qianlong is particularly pleased that in this portrait his head has been drawn sufficiently large. One eunuch in attendance during the emperor's portrait-sitting (one who knew of Qianlong's previously unspoken dislike of being painted with what the ruler considered too small a head) silently put his hands to his own head, spreading them apart and pointing at the emperor as if to suggest that the sovereign's head be made larger. (Note the size of Qianlong's head in Figure 13.) Attiret quickly understands, and produces a work that pleases the sitter.

Attiret sees Qianlong almost every day for the remainder of his stay at the Bishu shanzhuang, where he stays a total of about fifty days and completes over twenty portraits in oils, several large sketches, and a number of other works – an average of roughly one painting every other day. This workload harms Attiret's health so seriously that he is bedridden for two weeks upon his return to Beijing. He will be sent to Chengde again before long, however, to paint a new group of immigrants, but on the next trip his labors will be shared by his fellow painters Giuseppe Castiglione (Lang Shining, 1688–1766), and Ignace Siguelbarth (Ai Qimeng, 1708–1780).

Attiret certainly completed one or possibly two sketches of Qianlong's banquet for the Oirats, but whether he actually completed the extant painting of the *Ceremonial Banquet in the Garden of Ten Thousand Trees* is uncertain. Chinese records indicate it was most likely completed the following summer with the cooperation of Castiglione and Siguelbarth. The signature in the lower left corner of *Ceremonial Banquet* says "Respectfully painted in the twentieth year of Qianlong," which would indicate it was completed in the year following Attiret's first journey to Chengde, or 1755.

Yang Boda has examined the history of the *Ceremonial Banquet* and its companion painting *Horsemanship* at some length and has attempted to sort out its complicated history and content by exploring the Chinese records (he also availed himself of Amiot's correspondence).[6] Two works once listed as *Large Paintings of the Imperial Visage at Ceremonial Banquets* (*Yurong yanyan dahua*) in the *Official Qing Records of the Activities of the Bureaus and Workshops in the Palace Board of Works in the Hall of the Cultivation of the Mind* (*Yangxindian zaobanchu gezuo chengzuo huoji*) are most likely the paintings *Ceremonial Banquet* and *Horsemanship*. This can be deduced, Yang asserts, from the content of the works and from the paintings' signatures. The available data may be summarized as follows. On the ninth day of the fifth month of the twentieth year of Qianlong's reign, or 1755, an imperial commission to paint two *Large Paintings of the Imperial Visage at Ceremonial Banquets* was given to Castiglione, Attiret, Siguelbarth, and others. The paintings were completed on the twenty-sixth day of the sixth month, mounted on the tenth of the seventh month, taken to Chengde on the eleventh of the seventh month by the official Bai Shixiu (which indicates that some of the work on the painting was done outside Chengde), and adhered to the eastern and western end walls of the Zhuan'a shengjing dian (Scenic Winding Hills Hall) at the Bishu shanzhuang on the twentieth of the seventh month.

Yang carefully describes the content of *Ceremonial Banquet* and attempts to identify the almost 140 people it depicts. He notes that the actual background scenery behind the garden has been artificially adjusted somewhat to accommodate the composition of the painting. In looking at the painting, the viewer faces north. In the northeast, or upper right-hand corner of the painting, rises the Pagoda of the Six Harmonies (Liuhe ta), which is built in imitation of a structure in Hangzhou. In the upper left, or the northwest, are two peaks topped with two pavilions that were included in Kangxi's thirty-six famous views of the Bishu shanzhuang. In order to emphasize the voluminousness of the central yurt, the artists have de-emphasized these peaks, the Jin mountain in the northwest and Hei mountain in the northeast. The composition of the painting accords with the canons of western perspective, and space seems to recede into the distance. There are two main focal points: one is the small finial atop the acrobatic trapeze in the foreground, and the second, more important one, is slightly above the main yurt in the background. Almost all the straight lines in the painting converge on these two points. Such a composition accords well with the canons of perspective Castiglione translated into Chinese for the benefit of his fellow court painters.[7]

In the area where the banquet is to take place, a Mongolian yurt with a three-pillared entrance is centered before a "wall" created by a length of yellow cloth. On either side of the main yurt stand musicians dressed in red. The main yurt is carpeted with a colorful rug with a winding lotus design; a throne sits in the back of the yurt, which is lined on both sides with tables for a banquet; outside are two more lines of tables to a side, six tables to a row. In the foreground before those tables kneel two rows of people on a side, fifty-four people in all, ranging from royal princes to officials of the second rank. At the end of each row are leaders of the new immigrants.

Two smaller yurts flank either side of the main pavilion. In front of the smaller yurt on the left, eleven people dressed in the garb of Tibetan monks kneel at attention. In front of the small yurt on the right stands a large pavilion with fourteen tables of gifts of silk, porcelain, jade, and enamel to be distributed to the Mongolians. On the west stands a large contingent of kneeling men: forty-nine men (some of them Mongols) dressed in Qing official costume fill the first three rows. Ten of these men are painted in the western style, and Yang Boda believes that these may be the Oirat – former Zunghar – officials of whom Attiret painted portraits earlier. Behind these men kneel five more rows of seventy Oirats (wearing Mongolian-style hats and large earrings) who are to be enfeoffed. Farther to the west, outside the cloth wall, are three small tents where servants are making the preparations for the feast. In the southeast corner, Qianlong, then forty-four years old, enters in a palanquin, dressed in a summer hat, yellow gown, and blue robe – and, one might notice, his head seems somewhat larger than that of anyone else in the painting. He is accompanied by rows of civil and military officials of the second rank. In the center foreground stand several trapeze frames for acrobatic performances; a small table beneath them holds five golden vases.[8]

Attiret, as he noted in his account of his sojourn at Chengde, has chosen the moment most likely to flatter Qianlong, the moment when all the eyes of the visitors are turned toward the sovereign as he enters this carefully staged tableau, carried on the shoulders of his servants. The Mongols and Tibetan lamas kneel motionlessly as the imperial entourage walks sedately onto the stage, parasols fluttering faintly in the breeze. What better scene could show a calm and ordered empire at peace, an empire to whom all peoples pay homage as guests pay homage to a generous host?

Qianlong's role as host is reiterated in *Horsemanship*, the companion painting to *Ceremonial Banquet. Horsemanship* depicts a large contingent of Oirat dignitaries dressed in national costume who are watching a show of equestrian skills performed by Manchu bannermen. This event took place in the late fall or early winter, judging by the leafless trees and red foliage of the natural setting.[9] Standing in a neatly squared group of linear rows near the center of the composition, the guests immobilely observe the equestrian skills of their Manchu hosts as they gallop past in the foreground, performing handstands and other acrobatic stunts on horseback. Behind the visitors stands a row of Qing officials who form a kind of fence or boundary in the background; on the right side of the composition, Qianlong (painted slightly larger and taller than anyone in the composition) rides at the head of a contingent of men dressed in Qing court attire; all in this group are mounted and thus rise above the heads of the Oirats standing on the ground. Although this painting is hailed by some modern Chinese art historians as a visual paean to ethnic harmony,[10] a less sanguine observer might interpret a different message: that *Horsemanship* depicts Qianlong as the gracious host and lord of a "captive audience" of Oirats, who are corralled into a neat square by the requisites of ritual guest behavior, bounded behind by a "living fence" of Qing officials, and reminded before their eyes of the active power of the Qing. The Oirats can only watch this show of strength, passive and motionless; they stand afoot, that is, horseless, in a world where military power is exerted from horseback.

Ceremonial Banquet and *Horsemanship* were created to be hung in the Zhuan'a shengjing dian, one of the imperial residences located inside the southern walls of the Mountain Villa complex. It was one of the more important buildings of the imperial complex, for it was here that Qianlong's mother resided when she accompanied her son to Chengde, and it was here that Qianlong entertained Mongol leaders again in the fall of the twentieth year of his reign to celebrate the acceptance of the Mongol leaders into the Manchu fold and to celebrate military victories in Yili. As the Qing records above indicate, the paintings were rushed to completion in the late summer of that year, just in time for the celebrations. *Ceremonial Banquet* was hung at the east end of the hall; *Horsemanship*, on the west;[11] both would demonstrate Qianlong's military prowess to his mother and to all his guests.

The *tieluo* format of the paintings suggests that *Banquet* and *Horsemanship* were meant to be a permanent part of the hall's decor, and it is interesting to consider the possible connections between the paintings themselves, the structure that housed them, and the associations the hall's name invoked to those who entered it. The title of the hall itself is very revealing of Qianlong's vision of himself as a sovereign, and this vision is echoed in the content of the two paintings installed there. The phrase *zhuan'a* in the hall's name appears at first glance to be a transliteration of a Manchu word (*juwan* means "ten" in Manchu), but it is actually the title of the verse "Winding Hills" from the *Book of Odes*. This ode praises a virtuous (but unnamed) sovereign of Chinese antiquity, and Qianlong obviously intended to draw parallels between himself and this model of Han classical propriety by naming this hall after the ode. (On Qianlong's use of the classical Chinese tradition, see Adler, Chapter 9.) The ancient Han ruler resided among a region of "winding hills" whose topography was not unlike that of the Bishu shanzhuang; he arrived from the south like a whirlwind (a phenomenon ascribed to the ancients' supernatural powers). Similarly, Qianlong arrived in Chengde from the same direction on his annual visits – although Attiret, in witnessing such an approach, "did not distinguish in any fashion that majesty, that economy, that order that characterized all Chinese ceremonies." The report of this Jesuit detractor notwithstanding, the classical allusion is supposed to invoke in the visitor an image of a contented ruler securely supported by his allies. The ode reads,

> To the winding hills comes a whirling wind from the south;
> [. . .]
> Your lands are vast and extensive, stretching far and wide;
> [. . .]
> You have received a long-lived mandate, wealth, and happiness;
> [. . .]
> You have supporters and helpers, filial and virtuous people who bear you up like wings;
> [. . .]
> Such is our gracious sovereign,
> Considered a paragon by all in the four quarters,
> [. . .]
> The sovereign's chariots are many; his horses, trained and fleet . . .
>
> (excerpted from ode 252)

The two paintings that hung in the Zhuan'a shengjing dian visually portray the text of this ode: *Ceremonial Banquet* depicts the "gracious sovereign" Qianlong just as he arrives in the park in a sedan chair to enfeoff his "supporters and helpers," that is, the new Oirat subjects; *Horsemanship* depicts him again with Zunghar leaders, enjoying an equestrian show performed on horses "trained and fleet." In the naming of the Zhuan'a shengjing dian pavilion, Qianlong thus styled himself after the sage kings of Chinese antiquity by evoking traditional poetic imagery from Han classical literature. He interpreted those images visually with the help of European painters who accommodated his desire to be depicted as "a paragon by all in the four quarters" of the empire. Thus did Qianlong put European painting styles and classical Han literature into service to promote his political relationships with the Mongols.

What was the eventual fate of these two paintings? Yang Boda believes both hung in the Zhuan'a shengjing dian for almost forty-five years, although some believe they may have been replaced earlier. Nonetheless, upon Qianlong's death, both paintings were sent to Beijing as memorial souvenirs and placed in Qianlong's spirit-shrine in the Jingshan shouhuang dian. When the last Qing emperor abdicated, the paintings became part of the Palace Museum collections. Most secondary sources by modern-day Chinese art historians point to these paintings as visual proof of the long history of harmonious coexistence among China's many ethnic groups. Both works were publicly exhibited for the first time in 1975 in an exhibit of paintings about the Mountain Villa. This was during the Cultural Revolution, and one wonders if the exhibit was intended to demonstrate the proper place of minority peoples (a certain myopia perhaps beclouding the fact that Qianlong was a "minority" Manchu sovereign over the Han people). *Ceremonial Banquet* underwent some restoration for the 1975 exhibit and was remounted then; its blue and gold colors had flaked and it was somewhat mildewed, but it was otherwise restored to good condition. In 1981, a symposium on the *Ceremonial Banquet* painting in China was attended by various international scholars.[12] *Ceremonial Banquet* has thus played a role in art and politics in both the Qing dynasty and in modern times, outlasting both the fall of the imperial dynastic system and the Cultural Revolution.

Notes

1 This medium is described in English in Zhu Jiajin's "Castiglione's *Tieluo* Paintings" and in Chinese in Yang Boda, "*Wanshu yuan ciyan tu*," 15.
2 For a bibliography of sources regarding Jesuits in China, see Joseph Dehergne, *Répertoire des Jésuites de Chine*.
3 Besides creating paintings for the imperial ateliers, the Jesuits also composed music for the Chinese court. Musical works by Amiot and other Jesuits resident in China in the seventeenth and eighteenth centuries have recently been interpreted by the group Musique des Lumières; see recording of Teodorico Pedrini, *Concert baroque à la Cité Interdite*. I am grateful to Josef Kyburz for drawing this work to my attention.
4 *Choix des lettres édifiantes*, 180–184.
5 For a reproduction of a portrait of a Mongol noble attributed to Attiret and dated to 1754, see Ka Bo Tsang, "Portraits of Meritorious Officials," 70. A Chinese version of this work includes color plates of other Mongol nobles; see Tsang's "Ji feng gong, shu wei ji [Record of the portraits of ten martial heroes]."
6 The following several paragraphs summarize the main points of Yang Boda's "*Wanshu yuan ciyan tu* kaoxi [An Analysis of *Ceremonial Banquet*]," and "Guanyu *Mashu tu* [On *Horsemanship*]."
7 For Castiglione's work on perspective, see Cécile Beurdeley and Michel Beurdeley, *Giuseppe Castiglione*.
8 See Yang Boda, "*Wanshu yuan ciyan tu* kaoxi."
9 For a discussion of this painting, see Yang Boda, " Guanyu *Mashu tu*.'"
10 Jinling Chen and Zheng Guangrong, "*Mashu tu* [Horsemanship]."
11 Yang Boda, "*Wanshu yuan ciyan tu* kaoxi."
12 Yang Boda, "*Wanshu yuan ciyan tu* kaoxi."

12 The imperial word in stone

Stele inscriptions at Chengde

Peter Zarrow

The Kangxi and Qianlong emperors who built the Bishu shanzhuang (Mountain Villa to Escape the Heat) and the Waiba miao (Eight Outer Temples) inscribed their reasons for this vast building project on large stone tablets. These steles were a form of self-expression and one means by which the emperor related events in Chengde to larger questions of his rulership. They thus formed an important part of the Qing's general claim to legitimacy. At Chengde, Mongols, Tibetans, Manchus, and Chinese mingled and provided the emperor with an audience he was at pains to awe. Exactly who could enter each part of the Mountain Villa and the Outer Temples cannot be determined exactly. Some visitors could roam around the palace complex (the mission of Lord Macartney did so in 1793), but this was probably rare; other visitors were taken to specific spots. The temples do not seem to have been centers of monastic life, but several did house monks and the rest were used as temporary military camps. The "audience" of the stele inscriptions was certainly limited. However, the stele records were published, both in collections of imperial writings and in the *Rehe Gazetteer* (*Qinding Rehe zhi*) of 1781, and were thus accessible to the literati. It may be that very few actually read the emperor's works, though the steles remain of interest even if only as imperial monologs. Most steles were written in at least two languages (Chinese and Manchu) and many in four (Chinese, Manchu, Mongol, and Tibetan). Other inscriptions at Chengde included a fifth language, Uyghur (Eastern Turkic in Arabic script).

The use of several languages symbolized the extent of the Qing domain and the nature of its rule. There was no thought of making everyone learn Chinese (or Manchu); rather, the peoples of the empire were incorporated as distinct peoples and welcomed as such. Yet, the imperial goal was not to turn a completely different face to each people. The Chinese-language tablets would not have been kept secret from important visitors, who might know Chinese or at least have translators at their disposal, though their primary audience would have been Chinese officials and educated Manchus. Unfortunately, it has only been possible to consider Chinese versions here. It may be surmised that the versions in other languages differ in certain details and emphases. For us, "reading" the Bishu shanzhuang is a multi-layered project which must include literally reading stone inscriptions which were probably written – in part – precisely for later historians to decipher. This essay is a preliminary attempt to introduce the Chengde steles.

In their stele inscriptions the Kangxi and Qianlong emperors proclaimed their virtue, power, and hospitality. Since one of the main functions of the Chengde palaces was to entertain Mongol princes on their visits to the court, hospitality, imperial benevolence to those "from afar," and, conversely, the love and respect for the emperor of those who were coming from afar were constant motifs. The legitimacy of the Qing house was, if not crassly advertised, nonetheless strongly and repeatedly implied in a variety of imperial comments. The Qing house was especially favored by heaven and held its mandate.[1] Occasionally, Qianlong expressed the fear that his descendants would not continue to work hard and live frugally, thus risking heaven's abandonment. But this still, of course, amounted to claiming these virtues for himself – and his ancestors. The founders of the Qing royal line were repeatedly praised. Such praise could take the form not only of references to specific qualities like industry and sagacity, but also comparisons to the various buddhas. Qianlong claimed to rule as a chakravartin – a universal ruler, protector of Buddhism, and temporal counterpart of buddhas. He associated the Qing line with Amitabha, the Buddha of Eternal Light, and with Manjushri, the Bodhisattva of Wisdom, whose icons Qianlong himself adopted.[2] Tirelessly recounting his efforts to "nurture" and take care of the people, Qianlong compared himself and his predecessors to the mythical sage-kings of old, perfect men favored by heaven (see Adler, Chapter 9). He enumerated the different forms of Qing dominion: the "tax lands" where the Qing ruled directly, the borderlands where peoples were brought under Qing suzerainty through enfeoffment, and the surrenders of recalcitrant peoples. As a ritual and practical matter, the visits to the Qing court by the leaders of various people constituted Qing rule by acknowledging personally the suzerainty of the emperor.

In addition to the ideological claims to legitimacy made in the inscriptions, the Qing's sheer physical presence north of the Great Wall was important for claiming sovereignty over territories outside China proper. Kangxi and Qianlong made occasional imperial progresses to southern China for similar reasons, but it was their nearly annual trips to Chengde and Mulan which recalled the Manchu origins of the Qing and symbolized the irrelevance of the Great Wall in the imperial point of view (Figures 1 and 2; on Qianlong's trips to Chengde, see Symons, Chapter 5).

The vast majority of the stele inscriptions at Chengde were written by or for Qianlong, though several important ones were written by his grandfather, Kangxi, and a few by his son, Jiaqing. His father, Yongzheng, did not visit Chengde. The Chengde steles may be divided into those erected inside the imperial complex itself and those erected in the temple complexes outside. This essay will first discuss the steles in the Mountain Villa and then discuss those of the Eight Outer Temples, focusing on the statecraft of Qianlong's self-expression.

The steles in the Mountain Villa

The steles in the Bishu shanzhuang came in all different sizes and shapes, and they were scattered around different sites in the complex.[3] Most were in Chinese, though some added Manchu and a few added Tibetan and Mongol. The inscriptions of the texts dominated the steles, but they also held carvings of dragons, phoenix, deer, flowers, trees, and sometimes humans. The present-day scholar Yang Tianzai has cataloged five aspects of the steles worth our attention:

1   they explain the physical conditions of the palace complex, giving a sense of being there two hundred years ago that no picture can convey;
2   they illustrate something of the emperor's life and thought, especially as the emperors were, perhaps, more relaxed and hence more expressive in Chengde than Beijing;
3   some steles explain why and how a building or pavilion came to be erected, and hence are important for architectural history;
4   some steles reflect specific historical circumstances (such as the Panchen Lama's visit to Chengde in 1780); and
5   the steles reflect the historical flux of the Qing dynasty, its self-glorification and its doubts.[4]

Here, we will focus on the question of Qianlong's thought and self-presentation.

The steles include a number of poems as well as brief prose pieces (on Qianlong's poetry, see Lowe, Chapter 17). The prose pieces, like those on the steles at the Waiba miao, explicitly explain the purpose of a building and how it came to be constructed. They provided the occasion which Qianlong used to make various other points. The poetry inscriptions, however, were less bound to occasion and apparently more spontaneous. In general, Qianlong's poetry is considered orthodox and competent. It is perhaps rather academic poetry, more remarkable for its allusions than its beauty. His poems at the Mountain Villa complex, however, are more notable for their direct references to imperial glory than for such themes as nature or friendship. The "occasion" of the poem may simply have been Qianlong's awe at the loveliness of some particular spot, but he used these occasions to make political points. In 1781, for example, he wrote of the beauty of the "green carpet," the lawn on the south side of the Wanshu yuan (Garden of Ten Thousand Trees) where he often met foreign dignitaries (Figure 8). The green carpet, he noted, was not made by a westerner (a reference to Central Asian or Persian carpets?) but was once a Mongol pasture. Of course, the point made silently was that the Qing had asserted control over Mongol lands, indeed had actually taken possession of them. Qianlong also used the carpet trope to reproach the Han and Tang dynasties – with their expensive carpets – for luxury and decadence. He piously hoped his descendants would maintain his own standards of frugality. In another stele poem Qianlong implied a claim to the territories of the north and west when he noted that under the Qing the agriculture and pastures of Yili had been developed.[5]

More than once Qianlong used the steles to speak to his descendants. He wanted to impress upon them that the Bishu shanzhuang complex was no mere pleasure garden, but with the Mulan hunting grounds was a place to practice the martial arts and obedience to the family laws (see Elliot and Chia, Chapter 6).[6] Qianlong hoped that his descendants would heed the mistakes of previous dynasties. The summer residence could become a trap of luxury and selfishness; Qianlong warned himself and his descendants not to disgrace their ancestors. The possibility was always present that heaven would abandon the Qing if it neglected its duties. Both civil and military arts were crucial for the dynasty, Qianlong reminded his descendants, and Chengde was the place to practice the latter.

Most stele inscriptions contained a mix of separate messages conveying Qianlong's image of himself and his desires for the realm. Here is a translation of Qianlong's poem, "Climbing the Heights," from a stele found near Bangchui feng (Hammer Peak). It was a common literati practice to go climbing on the double ninth festival (the ninth day of the ninth lunar month), and Qianlong used the occasion to play with the word high.[7]

Climbing the heights on the double ninth is a custom of old,
And today I desired to chant the Du Fu poem.[8]
I was amused at his ignorance of the wonder of this place,
How can the Ba river and Jade mountain match it?[9]
The mountains outside the pass are crisp and green,
Heaven is clear and vast,
The lakes are crystal, and the Wulie river flows with silver waves.
Looking all round, we can see everything,
What need is there to descend for close inspections?
Asked how we can see everything:
The meaning of the word "high" explains it.
Heaven is high, and the sun and moon move through it,
On the earth, Mt. Tai is the highest point.
The third highest point is the ruler (*jun*),
Whose height still depends on the people.
If he relies only on his height and lacks compassion for those
    below,
There is danger! and the high will fall.
Those whose fame is high may well collapse,
Those whose words are high cannot easily behave accordingly.
Few are those who harmonize with the six high notes,

While tall towers ultimately rest on low [foundations].
Countable on one's fingers, these are minor cases,
So what is the virtue of height?
Using these seven words to hurriedly make a poem,[10]
Here is the interaction: climbing high and coming down.
(Qianlong, 46th year, 9th month, 9th day)

A number of important themes were conveyed in this poem. First, Qianlong's grandiose modesty. Highest of the high, he gloried in his height, and he pronounced the view good, ridiculing the need to descend for a closer look at the ordinary. Qianlong compared the emperorship to the sacrality of heaven and earth. Yet, he not only noted, in good Confucian fashion, that the emperor in some sense depended on the support of the people; as well, he ironically observed that the high frequently fall low. His enigmatic answer to the question why one should seek to become high seems to stress the interrelationship between high and low. These are relative terms, obviously, which only have meaning in relation to one another. The implication is that height itself leads to falling. Why do those with great fame eventually fall? Perhaps because their very fame incites criticism and attack. Why do those who make the most promises and boasts fall? Qianlong explicitly said it is because their behavior cannot match their words.

Second, the political point of the poem nonetheless located the emperor as one of the three sacred points of the cosmos. The height or glory of this role "depends" on the people, as in a later metaphor tall towers rest on their foundations. The foundation must be stable; that is, the people must be taken care of. This Confucian paternalism reflected an important element of the Qing's claim to legitimacy. It was also a matter of objective political calculus that Qianlong wanted his heirs to remember: if people rebelled because their living conditions were miserable, then the dynasty was in trouble. The rulers had an interest as well as a moral obligation in assuring the stable livelihoods of the people. An earlier poem inscribed on another hill noted that the sage towers above other men,[11] but here Qianlong played with the notion of sagehood in a more nuanced fashion (on the emperor as sage, see Adler, Chapter 9).

Qianlong here also displayed his grasp of geography and culture, "possessing" Du Fu as it were and so possessing the heart of China while simultaneously glorying in his own non-Chineseness. Emphasizing the beauty and wonder of the landscape north of the pass (through which the Manchus had moved in 1644 to conquer China), Qianlong spoke to a kind of Manchu patriotism. The trope he used was to contrast the openness and grandeur of Inner Asia to, by implication, the cramped, sullied, and built-up conditions in China proper. He was able to use the motifs of Chinese nature poetry precisely to criticize China. Somewhat bizarrely, Qianlong also condescended to Du Fu. It may be that here again, the real point was political. Du Fu's dispirited poem reflected the great An Lushan Rebellion of the mid-eighth century, which nearly brought down the Tang dynasty and caused Du much personal hardship. The Qing, Qianlong was suggesting, was even stronger than the once-glorious Tang.

Here we see the tension between Qianlong's tasteful modesty and his overweening pretensions. Both qualities, of course, are fitting for an emperor. Another stele poem from 1781 wrapped the Qing in the mantle of Mencius. Mencius (372–289 BCE) was considered the foremost philosopher-sage after Confucius himself. Qianlong noted that Mencius used the term "dawn" as a metaphor for the natural goodness of people and that Mencius warned people not to lose their natural goodness, which needed constant nurture. In highly allusive and heightened language, Qianlong indicated his own self-restraint – a prime Confucian virtue – and wondered at Mencius's foreknowledge of the Qing. For with the Qing had come peace, the flourishing of life, pristine mornings with cool dew, clean scents, and the development of natural goodness: so did the Qing create conditions of which Mencius would have approved.[12] Qianlong is not so crass as to say all this directly, but he uses the indirect language of poetry to get these points across. Similarly, in a series of three poems written between 1775 and 1779 and located at the Yue tai (Moon-viewing Terrace; see Gernant's translation of "The Pond of the Companion Moon," Chapter 18), Qianlong used the moon in a way suggestive of the Qing itself.[13] The moon shines eternally in all directions, and Qianlong recommended moon-gazing as a sublime experience.

Praise for the beauty and wonder of the summer residence ran through Qianlong's Chengde poetry. If the Bishu shanzhuang reflected the glory of the Qing, it also represented a respite from the labors of rulership. On a large stele in the woods through which he often traveled from the summer residence itself to the northwest gate of the complex and the Outer Temples, Qianlong inscribed six poems between 1775 and 1798.[14] Considered collectively, the poems complain of the burdens of state, speak of the desire to become a hermit in the woods, and even look forward to retirement from office. At first, Qianlong spoke of retiring in twenty years (when he would be eighty-five), and then in ten years, anticipating the cool and green of the Bishu shanzhuang. Qianlong also spoke of his sense of growing old and tired; for once, he called himself a lesser man than the ancient sage-kings.

Finally, the last two poems (1796 and 1798) announced his abdication, though Qianlong added that he still must train his son in the skills of rulership. If he thought only of his own comfort he would abandon his responsibilities, but he must help his son evaluate the officials and make sure the people have sufficient food and clothing. In 1798 Qianlong took note of the White Lotus Rebellion, impatiently awaiting news of its suppression.[15] In 1806 Qianlong's son and successor, Jiaqing, added a seventh poem in remembrance of his father. Like his father, Jiaqing noted the burdens of office.

A different kind of self-presentation is found in the prose inscriptions of the Mountain Villa complex. A good example of these may be the 1752 stele commemorating the building of the Yongyou si (Temple of Everlasting Blessings) in the northeast part of the Wanshu yuan.[16] Here, Qianlong made certain religious claims for the Qing dynasty:

> In ancient times the Buddha ruled the world as a dharma king and comprehensively saved humans and heaven.[17] He appeared everywhere and stopped everywhere. The ritual sites he established were all on sacred mountains and precious spots such as the Vulture Peak and the Deer Garden. These august temples are all the traces of the Buddha's stops, and so blessings accumulate especially in these places. Our grandfather the Kangxi emperor appeared as Amitabha, and he was chakravartin.[18] He had great fortune and wisdom, and his charismatic holiness was unsurpassed. He went everywhere on inspection tours and to see historical relics, and since he loved Chengde, he built the Mountain Villa here to refresh himself from summer's heat. He followed the natural shape of the cliffs and ravines to build on the principle of simplicity. Here in this spot [we] can nourish our natures, revive our spirits, and in a free and easy manner deal with affairs. The rousing excitement of a thunderstorm and the freshening of raindrops engender magic transformations which penetrate to every place, not violently but rapidly, like the Buddha idly sitting in the woods emanating spiritual peace, preaching the law to affect the universe, and raising up living souls to treat all life with charity.
>
> When We were young We served Our grandfather. His pastimes and pleasure trips were not for the purpose of enjoyment, though they gave him pleasure, and he nourished things according to the season: this is the flow of heaven and earth. Thirty years have passed in a flash. When We go hunting in the fall, We also often camp in this place. The pines and clouds are as of old, the beams and rafters soar. Here We remember the silent protection of the ancestors on high, and so We thought to repay [them] and garner blessings [for the later generations of the dynasty]. We thus erected this temple by the Wanshu yuan and called it "Everlasting Blessings." The sounds of bells, fish-clappers, and sutras being sung were not necessary to bring fame to the thirty-six scenes.[19] Since Our grandfather shone as a sacred sun, even after a thousand and ten-thousand ages, all his children, officials, and the populace will forever remember him as if he were still alive. So the Golden Dharma Altar of Mt. Qidu [Vulture Peak] of the Shakyamuni Buddha is protected by heaven and the dragon spirits in eternal perfection.[20] We have succeeded to the ancestral throne, We calm their hearts, pray for blessings, sustain their wishes, and this way entrust Ourselves. We only hope that We may without shame recount Our former desires, and that is all.
>
> (Qianlong, seventeenth year [1752], first day of the seventh lunar month)

Qianlong's extravagant praise for his grandfather is striking. He virtually never mentioned his father, Yongzheng, in the Chengde inscriptions;
however, this was appropriate since Yongzheng did not travel to the
Mountain Villa in Chengde or to the Mulan hunting grounds. Qianlong
had a strong sense of place.[21] In the inscription for the Yongyou si he
focused on his grandfather, Kangxi, again calling him Amitabha and a
chakravartin. Qianlong associated himself with Manjushri, and the combination of Manjushri, Sakyamuni, and Amitabha suggested wisdom,
compassion, light, and charismatic trans-historical powers.

Qianlong connected Chengde the place with the transformative powers
of buddhas and bodhisattvas. Although the Mountain Villa complex
contained Confucian and Daoist temples, all the Outer Temples were
Buddhist.[22] When Qianlong claimed that the workings of nature at
Chengde were like the Buddha's teachings, this was no mere metaphor
but a deliberate association of the two. He claimed that Kangxi and the
Buddha were actually alike in their eternal qualities. It is also interesting
to note Qianlong's references to ancestral support. This comes not from
outside spiritual beings but is transmitted genetically, as it were. At the
same time, regardless of any personal flaws he might have possessed,
Qianlong claimed the protection of still-potent ancestors. The whole
inscription is, of course, a demonstration of the filial piety of the grandson
for his grandfather. In a 1782 stele Qianlong noted that his father,
Yongzheng, under the press of affairs, never visited Chengde or Mulan
but, later regretting this, urged his descendants to follow Kangxi's example
instead.[23] Qianlong's love of Chengde was thus filial. He insisted, "Staying
at the Mountain Villa, every day We tremblingly obey heaven and the
ancestors and make sure that Our rule benefits the people and provides
peace to the interior by soothing the borderlands."

Kangxi had built up Chengde precisely to deal with the outlanders,
according to Qianlong, and in this way too Qianlong justified his own
love of the place. There was nothing exclusive about Qianlong's justifica-
tions for Chengde or, for that matter, the entire Qing regime: "Although
Confucianism and Buddhism take different routes, their basic principle is
the same."[24] Qianlong argued that Chengde both expressed the love of
the Qing for all its peoples and represented a strict barbarian-subduing
policy of *realpolitik*. Qianlong outlined the role of the Bishu shanzhuang in
the system of Qing domination in the larger context of Confucian legitimation as follows:

> My imperial ancestor [Kangxi] built the Bishu shanzhuang outside
> the pass not for his own pleasure but to pass down the basis of govern-
> ment to later generations. The realm is held by heaven's mandate
> (*guojia cheng tianming*) and [We the Qing] kindly possess outer lands not
> previously held, and We have entered them on the household regis-
> ters and maps,[25] while states which had not previously surrendered

are now enfeoffed.[26] The Mongols of the forty-eight banners living far outside the frontiers submit [to Us] with special respect. They come to us every year bearing tribute while We feast them in return, all in accordance with the ancient customs. It is simply the case that some have never had the smallpox, and so they fear to enter within the borders. Yet like those within the borders they deeply and sincerely hope to see the emperor and to understand the idea of imperial virtue.[27]

Thus did Chengde allow these loyal and sincere subjects to see their emperor in a relatively safe place. The fact of submission, as we will see again below, is a sign of the mandate. His grandfather, according to Qianlong, met the wishes of the Mongols every year at the mountain palaces. The mobs came flowing in and were satisfied. In this respect the Qing was like the "three dynasties" – the classical Xia, Shang, and Zhou dynasties which provided the model of perfect kingship. Qianlong noted the greatness of later dynasties, namely the Han, Tang, Song, and Ming, but also noted that they all fell into chaos through the fault of men. Thus did his grandfather learn the lessons of history. After the Rebellion of the Three Feudatories (1673–1681) Kangxi did not dare to indulge in his own pleasures: he lived frugally, preserved the common people, protected the borders, and united the hearts of all the subjects of the realm – central and peripheral peoples alike. Qianlong personally served his grandfather and learned from his diligence and self-sacrifice. He calmly observed that imperial virtues have to come from within the emperor since no one can force an emperor to be good:

If [Kangxi] truly had gone out to pursue pleasures, or if he had hidden deep in the palace, partied with officials, indulged himself sensuously, and ignored government business, then who could have prevented him? But in fact he wandered in remote, desolate borderlands, powerless to avoid the hardships of travel, and unable to eat at regular times [to keep the Mongols in order]. . . . Therefore, since We succeeded to the throne, We have strictly maintained the tradition of regular tours [hunts]; especially in these times of universal peace, We truly dare not to allow the civil or military officials to indulge themselves in idle pleasures lest We destroy the family laws of our sacred ancestors. Every time We come to the Bishu shanzhuang, I recall my sacred predecessor [i.e., Kangxi, but also an allusion to the mythical sage-kings Shun venerating Yao]: like looking at the sun, it hurts but one cannot stop oneself.[28]

The Outer Temple steles

The inscriptions on the steles of the Waiba miao all dealt with a single subject: the peoples to the north and west of China proper, Tibetans and especially the Mongols. If the steles of the Bishu shanzhuang dealt with a wide variety of subjects and displayed different tones of voice, the temple steles outside the wall of the summer residence reflected rather the Qing's preoccupation with the need to impress the Mongols. Of the twelve outside temples, built between 1713 and 1780, six were built completely in Tibetan style or contained Tibetan elements. Kangxi and Qianlong both proclaimed that their temple-building was an act of hospitality for visiting Mongols, who followed the Gelukpa sect of Tibetan Buddhism. Most of the temple steles were inscribed in four languages: Chinese, Manchu, Mongol, and Tibetan. Chinese historians have emphasized that the success of the nation-alities policies of the Qing can be seen here.[29] In this sense the temples foreshadow how China became a multinational state after the Qing collapsed in 1911. One may certainly say that the Outer Temples were an instrument of Qing foreign policy, at least as related to the states and confederacies to its north and west. Feng Mingzhu has pointed out that Qing border policies were completely new, abandoning the Ming dynasty's use of the Great Wall as a defensive barrier.[30] In Feng's view, the Qing, as Qianlong himself virtually stated, simply used the Gelukpa sect as a technique to control borderland peoples.

However, both these views – the emphasis on foreign policy and the search for the origins of the multinational state of China – read the present back into the past. From the point of view of the Qing royal house, the issue was not "foreign" policy but how to run an empire which included both China proper and the Mongolian plains and Tibetan massif. The fact that the emperors proclaimed they were "cherishing those from afar" in order to restrain the aggressive natures of "barbarians" is not proof that this was all they were doing, or even their primary motive. The temples reflected imperial attitudes toward the peoples of the northern and western borderlands, and certainly they played a role in building what is, today, a multinational state, but in the eighteenth century they created a stage where the roles of empire were acted out.[31] The loyal princes of Mongolia and clerics from Tibet visited the center, thereby acknowledging the supremacy of the emperor, enjoying his benevolence, and perhaps getting something in return, not only gifts but the intangible gratification of having reached the center of things. In any case, the temples were a sign of imperial benevolence, a concrete symbol of the emperor's wealth, glory, power, and religious sanctity, as well as of his generosity. A concern with how Mongols and the Qing were to understand each other ran through the stele inscriptions. At the same time, however, it appears that another "audience" for the stele inscriptions was critical Chinese bureau-crats worried about the bottom line. The emperors wanted to justify their expensive building projects, and foreign policy provided a convenient ratio-nale for doing so (on the Outer Temples, see Chayet, Chapter 4).

In his stele inscription for the first temple at Chengde, the Puren si (Temple of Pervading Benevolence, 1713), Kangxi set the pattern later followed more sumptuously by his grandson. Kangxi noted that various Mongol princes had come to celebrate his sixtieth birthday and wanted to erect a Buddhist temple. This Kangxi would do for them. "Our view is that in ruling the empire (*tianxia*) We do not rule for Our own benefit but for the benefit of all; we pacify (*an*) not just for Ourselves, but We pacify to provide peace everywhere."[32] Kangxi then noted his accomplishment of the task, difficult since ancient times, of pacifying those far away and making them like the near, or in other words, obedient. Kangxi grandiosely proclaimed that even though the ancient sage-kings (the "three *huang*" and the "five *di*") had never pacified the Mongols, now there is "no difference between the peoples of the center and those of the periphery (*zhongwai wubie*)." The Mongols deserved the temple they wanted, since, as Kangxi noted with a mixture of condescension and practicality, Mongols were a solid and brave people, and as Buddhists they were law-abiding.

Kangxi's fundamental pose was that of the host offering hospitality. Since the Mongols wanted to visit the emperor, as proper vassals should, providing them with a temple was a simple act of proper imperial behavior. Without making a direct declaration of faith, Kangxi proclaimed his munificence and desire to spread his magnanimity across the land, along with the light of Buddhism to insure the people's health and longevity. All of this was related to the glory of the Qing:

> As We look at past history and remember the former dynasties, their populations were limited and their geographical extents were still circumscribed. Chengde is located on the bend of a river, on wondrous bluffs above the Great Wall. It was not known to the government's border affairs agencies in the past, nor could it be found in any atlases. Now, Our virtue is inadequate, but We nurture the whole realm (*wanfang*). All of the lands outside the borders have become imperial lands.[33]

The themes of imperial benevolence and hospitality, adoration from outsiders, the Buddhist faith, the infinity of the imperial dominion – and the emperor's birthday – all appeared again in Qianlong's stele celebrating the erection of the Xumifushou miao (Temple of the Happiness and Longevity of Mt Sumeru; Figure 14). This was the last of the great temples at Chengde, which Qianlong built in 1780 (for a complete translation of the stele inscription, see Zarrow, Chapter 15). Here, Qianlong celebrated the visit of the Panchen Lama from Tibet. Qianlong's appreciation for the history of the Gelukpa sect, so important and potentially volatile in the politics of the entire territory to the west and north of China proper, no doubt stemmed from his need to prevent unrest among the Mongols. Qianlong insisted that the initiative for the visit came from the Panchen Lama, though in fact the Qing had cajoled him into coming. Qianlong underscored this fiction by explicitly contrasting the Panchen Lama's current trip to the visit of the Dalai Lama in 1652, which came in response to an invitation from Qianlong's great-grandfather. In any case, the occasion of the visit was Qianlong's seventieth birthday, and Qianlong was again doubtless dissimulating when he insisted that he wanted no fuss and that only the Panchen Lama's own desires to honor him persuaded him to allow a celebration. As Qianlong contrasted the Panchen Lama's own desire to visit to the invitation extended by his great-grandfather to the Dalai Lama, so he contrasted the still-troubled times of the late seventeenth century to the absolute peace of the eighteenth. The Mongol tribes which were still resisting the Qing in the earlier era had since surrendered.

Indeed, Qianlong included the usual formulaic phrases about peace and prosperity in the rhetoric about the Panchen Lama's visit, not ostensibly as his own imperial claims but as features of the Qing which the Panchen Lama wished to see. Yet the point was, of course, clear that Qianlong claimed to be a sagely emperor.

When he condescended to the Mongols who were welcoming the Panchen Lama's visit ("This all stems from their perfect sincerity and happened without anyone telling them how to behave"), he was not only commenting on the innocent, childlike nature of the Mongols, but also demonstrating the effects of the peace and prosperity of his realm. The notions of "one family" and cultural transformation – "becoming civilized" with its connotation of assimilation – that Qianlong seems to favor have to be understood in the context of a frankly racialist framework. Although the image of the emperor as father runs through the political culture, there is no hint of organic nationalism with the emperor as head of a single body. Rather, the criterion for civilization is simply a people accepting the overlordship of the emperor. From the point of view of the Qing, no people need lose its own identity or change its customs except in this one regard.

Between his assumption of the throne in 1737 and 1780, Qianlong built eight temples, most, like the Xumifushou miao, designed to look Tibetan.[34] The courtesy of inviting Mongols and Tibetans to a familiar architectural landscape was another act of imperial hospitality. Inside the Mountain Villa imperial complex the architecture and decoration were more traditionally Chinese. The Outer Temples, however, reflected the imperial obligation to encourage the peoples of the empire to pursue their own ways of life.[35] Qianlong found that Buddhism comforted the peoples of the west, who lived hard lives.

Of all the Outer Temples, the Potala Temple (Putuozongcheng miao, or Temple of the Potaraka Doctrine; Figure 12), built between 1767 and 1771, was the largest. Looking like a small-scale version of the Potala of Lhasa, the Chengde Potala Temple was built, Qianlong proclaimed, as a sign of the good relations between the Qing and the Mongol peoples, whose leaders would be present for the celebration of his sixtieth birthday and the eightieth birthday of his mother the empress dowager.[36] Again, in a stele erected for the Qianfo ge (Hall of the Thousand Buddhas) in the Putuozongcheng miao complex, Qianlong protested that the insistence of Mongol princes overrode his desire to avoid fuss. This was their custom and since it manifested their sincerity, Qianlong said, he ordered this hall built.[37] In the main Potala Temple stele Qianlong recorded his extreme satisfaction with his accomplishments.

The theme of outsiders voluntarily and even spontaneously coming to pay homage to the Qing was extremely important for Qianlong. It did not particularly matter if it was true – the Panchen Lama, as noted above, came with a hint of coercion. When, however, a people really came to Qianlong of their own volition, he gave even greater notice to the fact. The return of the Torghuts to China was, in his own estimation, perhaps the most significant event in Qianlong's entire reign. It confirmed the Qing's powers of attraction. The most sacred sense of the Chinese emperorship lay in its passivity, passive but still compelling submission and magically providing order (see Millward, Chapter 8).[38] The Torghuts arrived in Qing lands just in time for Qianlong's birthday; although this was not in fact a consideration of theirs, the emperor regarded this as a particular sign of heaven's favor. He recorded the fact in the Potala Temple stele and in two special steles erected in the Potala complex in 1771 as well as again in the Xumifushou miao (Temple of the Happiness and Longevity of Mt Sumeru) stele a decade later. In the Potala Temple stele itself, Qianlong began by citing the universality of Buddhism, the suitability of building a Potala in Chengde, and its symbolic aspects as a sign of the Qing's generosity to its Mongol vassals.[39]

Qianlong listed the tribes which had surrendered a long time before, tribes like the Zunghars which he had conquered, and finally the Torghuts. Their return just as the Potala was finished was an amazing example of the law of karma, according to Qianlong. The Torghuts had been forced out of western Zungharia (the Yili region) and settled along the Ural River and then the lower Volga River in the early 1600s, becoming subjects of the Russian tsar. Facing political and religious pressure, however, they fled back to Qing territory in 1771. Their population was decimated in the flight, but Qianlong welcomed them and granted them land in Mongolia and Xinjiang. According to Qianlong, they had suffered especially from the absence of the Buddhist sangha. In the two stele inscriptions devoted to the Torghuts, Qianlong emphasized that they were not rebels who had been forced to surrender but on their own account had "returned to submit" (*guishun*) to the Qing.[40] The Torghuts' story was recorded at length in four languages. The crux of Qianlong's interpretation of its significance was mystical:

> How could it be that the entire world to the farthest oceans certainly desires to submit to Us, becoming our servants and vassals? Yet the return and submission (*guishun*) of the Torghuts is precisely the will of

Heaven and men. It happened without our foreknowledge, and so We must make a record of this event.[41]

Qianlong concluded that defeating peoples without battle was better than through fighting; and peoples' submitting through natural inclination was better than through surrender. He noted that his imperial ancestors built the summer residence at Chengde precisely to soothe distant peoples. He himself had pacified the Zunghars in the far west (through fighting) but had never expected the return of the Torghuts. Qianlong modestly denied that his virtue was a factor, and he acknowledged that in this time of limitless success, danger lay in complacency. He pointed with pride, nonetheless, to his overriding his advisers' fears that welcoming the Torghuts carried the risk of offending Russia.

The return of the Torghuts marked the complete vassalage of the Mongols to the Qing. It is interesting that Qianlong focused not on his sagely attractions – beyond a prudent benevolence – but claimed that heaven and the ancestors themselves were active agents supporting the Qing. This was a theme Qianlong had enunciated in the inscription on the stele for the Puning si (Temple of Universal Peace; Figure 16).[42] Here, Qianlong congratulated himself for defeating the Zunghars. He announced he was following his ancestor's example in building a temple to celebrate the pacification of a recalcitrant tribe with enfeoffing ceremonies, feasting, and hospitality. But the particular point he stressed was that "august heaven aids those who possess virtue." Similarly, in his Yili stele on pacifying the Zunghars, Qianlong began with the claim that heaven had given all it covered to the Qing.[43] Here, Qianlong also advanced an evolutionary theory of the Qing: its founders built the military basis of the empire, its later emperors (Kangxi and Yongzheng) constructed sound government, and Qianlong himself gave it peace and prosperity. He felt only pity for the rebellious Zunghars. After all, "Those whom Heaven supports cannot be killed even if people want to overthrow them. Those whom heaven opposes cannot be established even if people want to support them."[44]

This essay has not attempted to determine what Qianlong thought. Rather, it has discussed what Qianlong said and tried to determine what those words meant. There may, for example, have been an element of fear when Qianlong compared his reign to that of Tang Xuanzong, a reign which was marked by many glories but which ended in disaster. (Not unlike Qianlong's own reign, which saw a massive rebellion arise before his death.) Of course, Qianlong did not "utter" these words; rather, he had them chiseled in stone. They were not remarks lightly tossed off but almost sacred records. The physically imposing steles marked the even more physically imposing temple complexes outside the summer residence in Chengde, while inside the palace grounds, steles commanded not only buildings but vistas of nature. Regardless of the inscriptions, then, the steles were part of the Qing's claim to dominion. The inscriptions made its claim more specific even while the imperial words covered every possible ground for legitimation from good government to awesome power, from the mystical favor of Heaven to imperial benevolence, and from the potency of the imperial ancestors to the submission of peoples from afar.

Steles of the Mountain Villa complex consulted for this essay

1 Yongyou si (Temple of Everlasting Blessings) – in the northeast part of the Wanshu yuan (Garden of Ten Thousand Trees); in Chinese, Manchu, Mongolian, and Tibetan, 1752 (Qianlong)
2 Chuifeng luozhao ting (Hammer Peak Sunset Pavilion) – on a hill to the southwest of the Mountain Villa complex, forming the twelfth of the thirty-six landscapes of Kangxi; stele inscription is a poem written in Chinese after a climb by Qianlong in 1754 (Qianlong)
3 Yongyou si sheli ta ji (Commemoration of the Stupa of the Temple of Everlasting Blessings) – on south face; Preface to the *Hundred-rhyme Poem of the Mountain Villa* (*Bishu shanzhuang baiyun shi*), on north face, 1765 (Qianlong)
4 Wenjin ge (Literary Ferry Pavilion) – designed to house the Four Treasuries (*Siku quanshu*) and erected in 1775; the record was written in 1774 and three poems were written between 1775 and 1779 (Qianlong)
5 Yue tai (Moon-viewing Terrace) – an artificial hill in front of Wenjin ge, 3 poems 1775–1779 (Qianlong)
6 "Linxia xiti" (Playing in the woods) – seven poems, on the imperial road from palaces to northwest gate, 1775–1798 (six by Qianlong, one by Jiaqing)
7 "Lütan bayun" (Eight rhymes on a green carpet); "Pingdan" (Dawn) – north shore of Lake Deng, 1781 (Qianlong)
8 "Jiuri denggao zuoge" (Poem on climbing high on the double ninth) – stele found near Chuifeng luozhao ting, 1781 (Qianlong)
9 "Bishu shanzhuang houxu" (Later preface to the Mountain Villa to Escape the Heat, called "later" since Kangxi had written a record of the Mountain Villa in 1711) – near the Yongyou si, 1782 (Qianlong)

Steles of the Outer Temples consulted for this essay

1 Puren si (Temple of Pervading Benevolence), 1714 (Kangxi)
2 Puning Si (Temple of Universal Peace), 1755 (Qianlong)
3 Jieyan (Praise-Buddha), erected in the Puning Si, 1755 (Qianlong)
4 Pingding Zhun-ga-er leming Yili (The Yili stele carved upon the pacification of the Zunghar Mongols), erected in the Puning si complex, 1755 (Qianlong)

5 Pingding Zhun-ga-er hou leming Yili (The Yili stele carved upon the second pacification of the Zunghar Mongols), erected in the Puning si complex, 1758 (Qianlong)
6 Anyuan miao (Temple of Pacifying Distant Lands), 1765 (Qianlong)
7 Pule si (Temple of Universal Happiness), 1767 (Qianlong)
8 Putuozongcheng miao (Potola Temple), 1771 (Qianlong)
9 Qianfo ge (Hall of the Thousand Buddhas), erected in the Putuozongcheng miao complex, 1770 (Qianlong)
10 Tu-er-hu-te quanbu guishun (The return of all the Torghuts), erected in the Putuozongcheng miao complex, 1771 (Qianlong)
11 Youxu Tu-er-hu-te buzhong (The good treatment of the Torghut tribe), erected in the Putuozongcheng miao complex, 1771 (Qianlong)
12 Shuxiang si (Manjushri Temple), 1775 (Qianlong)
13 Xumifushou miao (Temple of the Happiness and Longevity of Mt Sumeru), 1780 (Qianlong)

Notes

1 The Mandate of Heaven was an ancient legitimating device; briefly, the emperor was perceived to be chosen by heaven to rule on account of his superior virtue, and he ruled as the Son of Heaven – a universal king ordering the cosmos. Similar notions of heavenly favor were employed by Inner Asian states, such as that of the Mongols under Chinggis Khan, to justify their rule.
2 See the Qianlong stele commemorating the building of the Yongyou si (Temple of Everlasting Blessings), translated on p. 152.
3 There were a total of over twenty imperial steles in the Mountain Villa complex, two by Kangxi and the rest by Qianlong, with a few additions by Jiaqing. Of these, eleven have survived, nine in fairly complete form, all by Qianlong. This count is offered by Yang Tianzai, "Bishu shanzhuang de beike jiqi lishi jiazhi," 217–218 (hereafter cited as "*BSSZ beike*").
4 Yang Tianzai, "*BSSZ beike*," 228–229.
5 "Lütan bayun" (Eight rhymes on the green carpet), in Yang Tianzai, *Bishu shanzhuang beiwen shiyi*, 6–10 (hereafter cited as *BSSZ beiwen*); "Yongyou si shelita" (Stupa of the Temple of Everlasting Blessings, 1765), in Yang Tianzai, *BSSZ beiwen*, 101.
6 "Bishu shanzhuang houxu," in Yang Tianzai, *BSSZ beiwen*, 90–99.
7 "Deng gao bei," in Yang Tianzai, *BSSZ beiwen*, 76–81.
8 Du Fu (712–770), one of Tang dynasty's premier poets, wrote a poem called "Climbing the Heights":

> When winds rage and the sky is high, gibbons cry mournfully;
> Over white sands on a clear riverbank, birds fly and whirl.
> Leaves fall from deep woods – rustling and soughing;
> The Long River rolls on, forever, wave after wave.
> Ten thousand miles away in sad autumn, I often find myself a stranger;
> My whole life afflicted by sickness, I mount alone the high terrace.
> Beset by hardships, I resent the heavy frost on my temples;
> Dispirited, I have by now abandoned my cup of unstrained wine.
> (trans. Wu-chi Liu, in *Sunflower Splendor*, 140–141)

9 Both the Ba river and Jade mountain are in Shaanxi Province in China's north-west, where Du Fu spent much of his life.

10 For example, heaven, earth, ruler, fame, behavior, music, towers.

11 "Chuifeng luozhao ting" (Hammer Peak Sunset Pavilion, 1754), written after Qianlong climbed the Hammer Peak southwest of the Mountain Villa, which was one of the thirty-six scenes of the Kangxi era, in Yang Tianzai, *BSSZ beiwen*, 71–75.

12 "Pingdan" (Dawn), in Yang Tianzai, *BSSZ beiwen*, 11–15.

13 The Moon-viewing Terrace (Yue tai) stele, in Yang Tianzai, *BSSZ beiwen*, 63–70. The Moon-viewing Terrace was an artificial hill built in front of the Wenjin ge (Literary Ferry Pavilion).

14 "Linxia xiti" (Enjoying the woods), in Yang Tianzai, *BSSZ beiwen*, 16–35.

15 The White Lotus Rebellion was the most massive of several uprisings which shook the last years of the Qianlong reign, arising in central China in 1795 and spreading to the provinces of Sichuan, Hubei, Shaanxi, and Henan before it was finally put down by Qianlong's successor in 1803.

16 "Yongyou si" (Temple of Everlasting Blessings), in Yang, *BSSZ beiwen*, 82–89; *cf.* Sven Hedin, *Jehol*, 156–159.

17 An alternative translation might be that the Buddha ruled the world through dharma kings.

18 Amitabha (or Amida) was the Buddha of Infinite Light; the Panchen Lamas were considered the incarnation of the Amitabha Buddha. Associated with the Pure Land, Amitabha was extremely important in China. Chakravartin or "wheel-turning" kings were universal rulers who were the temporal counter-parts of buddhas and equally powerful (on Tibetan Buddhism, see Lopez, Chapter 3).

19 The thirty-six scenes refer the scenic spots in the Mountain Villa complex which were Kangxi's favorites. Qianlong's point is that his construction of the Yongyou si was a gesture only.

20 Shakyamuni is the historical Buddha.

21 Qianlong's glorification of his father is found rather in the Yonghe gong in Beijing. This was Yongzheng's residence when he was a prince, before he ascended the throne. Qianlong erected massive steles in the Yonghe gong, in Chinese, Manchu, Tibetan, and Mongol, with eulogies to Yongzheng. Qianlong there claimed his father was an enlightened buddha, specifically Shakyamuni. See Ferdinand Lessing, *Yung-ho-kung*, 8–14.

22 These are not exclusive categories in China's syncretic tradition, but there is no doubt of the overwhelming Buddhist influence at Chengde.

23 "Bishu shanzhuang houxu," in Yang Tianzai, *BSSZ beiwen*, 90–99.

24 "Yongyou si shelita," in Yang Tianzai, *BSSZ beiwen*, 101.

25 Lands Chinese and foreign which no previous dynasty completely controlled were officially incorporated into the tax and census system.

26 Outlying territories had been brought into the Qing system through enfeoff-ment – something like vassalage ties between the Qing emperor and "native rulers" – but were not taxed.

27 "Bishu shanzhuang baiyun shi xu" (Preface to the *Hundred-rhyme Poems of the Mountain Villa to Escape the Heat*, 1765?), in Yang Tianzai, *BSSZ beiwen*, 107.

28 "Bishu shanzhuang baiyun shi xu," in Yang Tianzai, *BSSZ beiwen*, 108.

29 Qi Jingzhi, *Waiba miao beiwen zhuyi*, 1–2.

30 Feng Mingzhu, "Waiba miao de xingjian yu Qingchu de xibei bianfang" (Early Qing defense in the northwest and the construction of the Outer Temples), 511–513.

31 For the state as a metaphor of the rituals of rule – and more than a metaphor – see Clifford Geertz, *Negara: The Theatre State in Nineteenth-century Bali*.

32 "Puren si beiwen," in Qi Jingzhi, *Waiba miao beiwen*, 1.
33 "Puren si beiwen," in Qi Jingzhi, *Waiba miao beiwen*, 2.
34 The architectural models for the Xumifushou Temple, the Putuozongcheng Temple, and others were derived from specific Tibetan sources, but the Tibetan elements were largely superficial, arranged to create the appearance of their original models from a distance. See Anne Chayet, Chapter 4, and "Jehol Temples and Their Tibetan Models," 65–72.
35 Qianlong made this point explicit at the Anyuan Temple (1765) and Pule Temple (1766) complexes. The role of the Qing was not to make all peoples the same but to allow or even encourage their differences.
36 Technically, Qianlong turned sixty *sui* in 1770 and his mother turned seventy *sui* in 1771: but his intention was to celebrate both birthdays together.
37 "Qianfo ge beiji" (1770), in Qi Jingzhi, *Waiba miao beiwen*, 83–90.
38 See the Confucian *Analects*: "The Master [Confucius] said, among those that 'ruled by activity' surely Shun may be counted. For what action did he take? He merely placed himself gravely and reverently with his face due south; that was all." "The Master said, He who rules by virtue is like the pole-star, which remains in its place while all the lesser stars do homage to it." (*Lunyu* 15: 4, 2: 1, following Arthur Waley's translation in *Analects of Confucius*, 193, 88.)
39 "Putuozongcheng zhi miao beiji" (Record of the Potala Temple), in Qi Jingzhi, *Waiba miao beiwen*, 51–59. Hedin offers a partial translation of the Putuozongcheng Temple stele in his *Jehol*, 17–18.
40 "Tu-er-hu-te quanbu guishun ji" (Record of the return of the Torghuts) and "Youxu Tu-er-hu-te buzhong" (The good treatment of the Torghut tribe), in Qi Jingzhi, *Waiba miao beiwen*, 60–82.
41 "Tu-er-hu-te Quanbu guishun ji," in Qi Jingzhi, *Waiba miao beiwen*, 60.
42 "Puning si beiwen," in Qi Jingzhi, *Waiba miao beiwen*, 8–21.
43 "Pingding Zhun-ga-er leming Yili," in Qi Jingzhi, *Waiba maio beiwen*, 22.
44 "Pingding Zhun-ga-er hou leming Yili" (The Yili stele carved upon the second pacification of the Zunghar Mongols), in Qi Jingzhi, *Waiba miao beiwen*, 30.

Part IV
Voices from Chengde

13 Preface to the "Thirty-six Views of Bishu shanzhuang"
Record of the Mountain Villa to Escape the Heat

Translated by Mark C. Elliott and Scott Lowe

Here we present two translations of the preface to the "Thirty-six Views of Bishu shanzhuang," a collection of poems describing the most beautiful scenes at Chengde, credited to the pen of the Kangxi emperor. The poems, together with their woodblock illustrations, were first published in 1712, the date of this preface, with editions in Chinese and Manchu. Later they were reprinted by the Qianlong emperor, who added another thirty-six poems of his own composition. The Kangxi emperor expounds here on the main reasons behind the selection of Rehe – meaning both Chengde and Mulan – as the site for the summer residence of the Qing court. One might note that his vision of the area was simpler than that of his grandson (see Chayet, Chapter 4).

Working independently, we have translated both versions of this preface, the Chinese (by Lowe) and the Manchu (by Elliott), which we present below. It is suggested that readers read the two versions and consider which comes from a Chinese and which from a Manchu original. Are there any differences traceable to influences of Chinese versus Inner Asian cultures? The versions are identified in the endnote.

"Record Written by the Emperor on the Mountain Villa to Escape the Heat" – Version 1

Gold Mountain sends forth [dragon] veins, warm rapids divide the springs, clouds and pools are clear and deep. [There are] rocky ponds and dense green vegetation, broad rivers and fertile grasslands, yet nothing harms the fields and cottages. The wind is clear, summer bracing; it is an ideal place for people to be nourished. Arising from heaven and earth's inborn qualities, it is the sort of place where people can commune with nature.

We have gone on many inspection tours south of the Yangzi river, and deeply know the beauty of the south. Twice We have gone to Shaanxi and Gansu and have a growing understanding of the western lands' exhaustion. To the north, We have passed through the Dragon Sands. To the east, We have traveled to the Long White Mountain. The grandeur of the rivers and simplicity of the people truly cannot be recounted fully. Yet all these places are not what I have chosen [for the summer palace].

Only here in Rehe is the road near the capital; one can come and go in no more than two days. The land is open for development, wasteland and wilderness; if I cherish the intention [to build here] how could it harm anything? Therefore We have gone up high, smoothing out the differences of near and far and revealing the influences of the natural peaks and mountain vapors. In harmony with the pine forests, We have built studios; then caves and cliffs embellish [the landscape]. We have channeled water by pavilions so that tangled mists emerge over the watery ravines. All this is not what human strength can accomplish, but is done through the aid of fragrant plants, nature itself, without the expense of carved rafters and cinnabar pillars. Being fond of forests and streams, cherishing simple sentiments, I peacefully gaze out over all things on earth. Looking down, I observe many species. Refined birds play on the green water and do not hide. Deer reflect the setting sun as they form herds. Eagles fly [up above], fish leap [down below], complying with the high and low of their heaven-given natures. The earthly versions of auspicious vistas emerge from distant purple mist.

Traveling about or resting, it is always the details of agriculture [that consume my thoughts]. Whether day or night, I never forget the warnings of the classics and histories. I encourage tillage in the southern acres; hoping for a copious harvest with overflowing rice baskets. Stopping in the west we make music, celebrating timely rains and sunrises.

This is a rough sketch of living at the Mountain Villa to Escape the Heat. When it comes to enjoying irises and orchids, then I love virtuous conduct. When I gaze at pines and bamboo, then I think of pure and chaste conduct. Overlooking clear currents, then I value incorruptibility. Looking at luxuriantly growing grass, then I despise venal dissipation. What I do here is in accord with the ancients' practice of studying nature to understand human character. This, one must know.

What the ruler receives is taken from the people. One who does not love [them] is surely confused. Therefore, We have written this in the records, so that morning and evening [We] will not alter. Respectfulness and sincerity lie precisely in this.

"Record Written by the Emperor on the Mountain Villa to Escape the Heat" – Version 2

From Gold Mountain a vein in the earth broke through, and from the hot water was formed a spring. The clouds [of steam] forever filling the valley, the stones and pools turn green. Grass grows luxuriantly everywhere, and there is no fear that harm will come to one's fields or home. The wind is pure, and the summers are cool, easily suiting and nourishing people. All things born or possible on heaven and earth fall into the category of creation.

Many times have I gone to inspect the rivers, and I know well the fresh beauty of the southern provinces. Having twice been to Qinlong [Shaanxi], all the features of the western lands are even clearer to me. I have crossed the northern deserts, and I have gazed eastward up toward the White Mountains. Though I cannot fully express the firmness of the mountains and rivers or the simplicity of a man or a thing, I also cannot praise them too much.

Then there is this place, Rehe. The road is close to the capital, and to go back and forth does not take two days. The land is spread out, wild and untilled. If you fill your mind with it, the myriad cares cannot but be driven away. When from here you weigh the appearance of high and low, far and near, the views of the mountains and peaks open themselves up before you. If you make your abode by a pine tree, the colors of the uneven river bank appear strikingly. If you lead water down to the pavilions, the fragrance of the hazelnut trees fills the valley. All this is not within the power of man to make. He can [only] move to an attractive place and adapt to it. Nothing has been squandered on carving the poles of my tent; one is content in one's thoughts, having embraced the simplicity of the springs and the forests. Looking peacefully at the myriad things, contemplating deeply their every type, one cannot escape enjoying the colorful birds and the green water. In the rays of the setting sun the shining deer flock together. Birds flying, fish leaping, following the high and low of heaven's nature. In distant colors and purple mist, the epitome of a beautiful vista stands unveiled.

[Yet] in going together on an excursion and enjoying it in each other's company, I cannot help thinking about planting, harvesting, resting, and suffering. No matter whether it is early or late, I do not forget the peacefulness and danger [spoken of] in the sutras and the histories. Encouraging the planting of the fields, I hope for a year of plenty, with the filling of boxes and baskets. The prospect of a completed harvest is approaching, and I rejoice when rain and sun combine in the right way.

This is the general situation at the Mountain Villa to Escape the Heat. Also, observing the iris, I prize virtuous acts; seeing pine and bamboo, I think of firmness and discretion; leaning forward to watch the clear current, I value honesty and sincerity; seeing the dense grass, I despise greed and filth. One must not fail to know that these were things that the ancients also compared and composed into poetry.

As the ways of the one who has become lord are taken from the people, if he does not cherish them, he will be led astray. Therefore having written this note, truly, let respect for this, night and day, not be changed.

(Written in the last decade of the sixth month
of the fiftieth year of "Universal Peace")[1]

Note

1 There is no sure way to identify which was the original text from which the other was translated; very likely they were composed independently, yet simultaneously, with reference to each other. Version 1 above is translated from the Chinese version of the preface, version 2 from the Manchu version. Most readers will note the reference in version 2 to "uncarved tent poles" as one of the giveaways of the less formal, "greener," more naturalistic Manchu style. Version 1's Chinese text, on the other hand, speaks of the absence of "carved rafters" and "cinnabar pillars," and despite an overt insistence on the power of "nature itself," reveals a greater interest in changing and dominating the landscape. Alert readers will also identify other differences, as well as some crucial similarities.

14 A letter from a Jesuit painter in Qianlong's court at Chengde

*Translated by Deborah Sommer**

This letter, a record by Jean-Joseph-Marie Amiot of Jean-Denis Attiret's stay in the Bishu shanzhuang in the summer of 1754, is included in the "Mémoires de la Chine" section of the *Lettres édifiantes et curieuses écrites par des missionaires de la compagnie de Jésus collationnées sur les meilleures éditions et enrichies de nouvelles notes.* My treatment of Chinese terms that cannot be clearly identified follows Amiot's eighteenth-century French romanization.

The translators have attempted to preserve the original tone of this eighteenth-century missive, which sounds somewhat florid and overwrought to modern ears; it nevertheless engages modern readers as it no doubt engaged its original intended audience with tales of the Great Wall and dialogs with the exotic and distant Emperor of China himself. This document provides a unique perspective on the personality of Qianlong and on everyday life at Chengde, as it relates an almost hour-by-hour description of Attiret's visit there. It intimates both the seriousness of the pressures concomitant to choreographing an important political event and the occasional pettiness (and, more often, attentive courtesy) of the bureaucrats in Qianlong's service, those gentlemen who, Amiot remarks, "received our dear Brother with all the demonstrations of politeness and graciousness that these gentlemen know how to provide so well when they believe themselves to be conforming to the intentions of their master." Amiot relates Attiret's sojourn in Chengde with vivid imagery, cutting characterization, and an almost manipulative dramatic flair that evokes in the reader an empathetic appreciation of the physical and psychological rigors Attiret experienced in Qianlong's service. This description of Chengde was recorded outside the official bureaucracy by foreigners who probably believed their correspondence was secure from Han or Manchu eyes, for otherwise Amiot would never have satirized Qianlong's journey to Chengde as a bumbling comedy of errors. Since the Jesuits expressed fealty only to their own Christian god, it is hardly surprising that this letter scarcely portrays Qianlong as a bodhisattva in human guise; he appears instead as an uncompromising but appreciative taskmaster, at times almost comically vain but always marvelously wily and not ungenerous.[1]

Letter from P[ère] Amiot, Missionary in China, to P[ère] de la Tour, of the same order. Peking, October 17, 1754.

My reverend Father,

. . . I am going to tell you about some things that personally concern Brother Attiret. I will tell of his travels in Tartary in the retinue of the Emperor, of his nomination to the mandarinate, and of his generous refusal of a dignity that, by giving him a rank in the empire, would have allowed him to forget, at certain moments, the state of humility to which he has consecrated himself for the love of our sovereign Master, and to which he has with a good heart sacrificed his talents in being the simple Brother of our order.

The reason the Emperor wanted to have Brother Attiret in Tartary and then compensate him by making him a mandarin of the tribunals of his house demands some explanation. I will give it to you, adding some necessary preliminaries, accompanying them with all the circumstances that have some bearing on the topic.

At long last a revolution occurred in the country of the Zunghars, among the Tartar sovereigns whose states are bordered in the middle by Tibet; bordered on the east by Tartars who are tributaries of China, the Khalkhas, and the Mongols; bordered on the west by Muslim Tartars and nomads; and bordered on the north by a part of Siberia. After the death of the last Zunghar, a lama of royal blood placed himself at the head of a powerful faction and came finally to be recognized, despite his contenders, particularly those who wanted, naturally, to occupy the throne.

This new sovereign, an agitated and turbulent man, fearless and inflated with his first successes, wanted new conquests, and he was confident in his ability and good fortune. He found it distasteful that the Khalkhas, his neighbors, were tributaries of China, and he convinced himself of subjugating them. He submitted to the Emperor the ridiculous proposition that he [the emperor] cede them to him, alleging that it was a right owed to his crown that Zunghars of old had enjoyed, and alleging that he was well resolved to employ all his forces in order to enjoy them himself.

The Emperor responded to these pretensions only by inviting him to become a tributary of the empire, offering to make him an official of the first rank and maintain him upon his throne. The lama-become-Zunghar felt his pride offended at such a proposition. He responded that he was in his state as sovereign as the Emperor was in his, that he cared nothing for official rank, that he was declaring war, and that arms would decide who of the two would receive homage and tribute from the Khalkhas.

Of course there were many malcontents among the subjects of the usurper, and as their discontent was only waiting for a favorable occasion to explode, the most enlightened of them concluded that they must profit from the good will that they supposed the Emperor would show to those who declared themselves enemies of that tyrant. They secretly formed their plot; ten thousand of them fled their country and came with their families and all their baggage to present themselves before the Emperor and recognize him as their sovereign and master.[2]

The Emperor received them with open arms; he gave them a site in Chinese Tartary where he permitted them to establish themselves. He named some mandarins to check to see that they did not lack anything – or, more likely, to check on what they were doing. He sent them great sums of money and provisions of all kinds in great quantity; in a word, he put them in a position to lead in their new home much more comfortable lives than they had enjoyed in their own country. There were among the immigrants a good number of people of distinction. The Emperor ordered them to come to Jehol [Chengde], a place in Chinese Tartary where he went each year to enjoy hunting and where he had palaces almost as beautiful as the ones he had in Peking. His Majesty's intention was to receive them in a ceremony where he would consider them his subjects, giving a great banquet governed by the rites for these kinds of occasions, and to decorate them with the same dignities that, according to birth and according to the rank they occupied, they would have hoped to have had in their own country, had they been in favor.

The new settlers went without delay, with a number of people determined by the Emperor, to the place where they had been ordered to go, and when everything was in place, the Emperor himself then set out from the Yuanming yuan and headed for Jehol, accompanied by all his court, officials, counts, and all the great officers, with the exception of a small number who stayed in Peking to take care of his affairs in his absence.

It is only when the Emperor is absent that the people who work under his eyes have a little liberty. Brother Attiret wanted to take advantage of this at the outset by renewing in fervor, through going on retreat (which we do each year for eight or ten days), the spiritual forces that one needs here more than anywhere else. He went into retreat on the evening of the sixth day of the fifth moon, not the slightest bit aware of what was to come. The next day, around four o'clock in the morning, Count Te [i.e. De], a great courtier of the Emperor,[3] arrived at Haidian with a posting, with the order from His Majesty to bring Brother Attiret to Tartary. This dear Brother, as I have already said, had gone to Peking to go on retreat; thus he had to come here again to receive the order to set out. Two mandarins had been deputed for that, and Count Te waited in his lodgings in Haidian, where he wanted to stay to get a little rest. Brother Attiret, who had been happy to have had eight whole days to spend with only his God, drew himself out of his solitude the day after he had started it and left at once to go to the Count, to discern more clearly His Majesty's intentions. As soon as the Count saw him, he told him that he was only ordered to tell him that they should start without delay, that the Emperor wanted them with him within three days at the latest, and that other than that he did not know what was wanted of him, but that it was probable that His Majesty wanted him to draw portraits of some of the most important foreigners that he would receive in a ceremony as his own subjects. "Don't bother with anything," added the Count; "here are fifty taels that the emperor has ordered me to give you; think only of setting out as soon as possible. It would be best if we could set out today. I've been ordered to furnish you with all that is necessary for you and your servants. I will give you my own horse; from among my clothes choose those that fit you best, and use those." One must note that here there are town clothes and travel clothes, determined by their length, shape, and by what is worn with what, and it would be the worst indecency to appear at court in clothing inappropriate to the occasion, place, and season.

As for the horse, Brother Attiret thanked the Count, telling him that the mule that he rode every day to go to the palace would service him just as well for travel; but he accepted the clothing, because it was impossible for him, as well as for us, to make in such a short space of time what he needed. Thus this dear Brother gave no more thought to ordinary preparations. He stayed in our house at Haidian, where he spent the rest of the day preparing his colors and other art supplies in the event that he might need them. It was a good thing, we will see later, that he took such precautions. He wrote us a note to tell us that the next day he would set out. I went with P[ère] Benoist to bid him farewell, and on the eighth day of the fifth moon (June 26), we accompanied him before three o'clock in the morning as far as the lodgings of the Count, where this gentleman was waiting for him to mount his horse.

The twenty-eighth of the same month, our travelers passed through *Nan-ting-men*, which is the first entry into the mountains, and at noon they crossed the Great Wall. "This title is too simple," Brother Attiret wrote me, "for such a beautiful thing. I am astonished that, as many Europeans as have seen it, they have left us unaware of the immense work that it entailed. It is one of the most beautiful works in the world, regardless of the age, the place, or the nation that imagined or executed it. I am firmly resolved to make a sketch of it on my return."

Despite the fact that many missionaries had spoken so much of the Great Wall, all they said paled before the image Brother Attiret conceived of it. Artists see the world with eyes different from those of ordinary travelers. It is to be hoped that this dear Brother would, in his moments of leisure, paint for us a work of what had struck him so vividly. But it seemed that he would not be able to do it soon, being charged with other matters more important and more pressing for him.

The same day, they arrived at *Leang-kien-fang*, where the court had stopped for a few days of rest. The *te-kong* [i.e. Count Te] had given an account of his mission, and he was ordered by the Emperor to give the care of Brother Attiret into the hands of the Count Minister, which he did without delay. The latter received our dear Brother with all the demonstrations of politeness and graciousness that these gentlemen know how to provide so well when they believe themselves to be conforming to the intentions of their master; but he did not tell him the reason he had been brought there; he informed him that he knew nothing. He ordered that a tent be put up near his own at once, for along the route there were neither lodgings nor houses for anyone; the palaces that were found at some distance from one another were only for the Emperor and his women. As night was falling, things had to be done quickly, scarcely providing the stability necessary to prevent the various accidents that could happen in the event of a storm. In fact, as soon as Brother Attiret was settled, the sky, which had been overcast, discharged a deluge of water that inundated the whole area. The steward of the Minister, who had come himself to see if anything was needed, reassured the poor Brother, who, little accustomed to camping *à la tartare*, began to be worried lest the double canvas of the tent eventually succumb under the enormous weight that had already begun to make it sag. He told him that he could relax, that he must not touch anything, and that the water would flow off itself, after which he retired. The rain grew heavier each moment, however, and soon the tent shook. Our traveler's two servants, as green as their master and no less embarrassed than he was by their ineptitude, began to shout that it was going to fall. Brother Attiret saw in effect that the poles or stakes that had been fixed in the ground to keep the tent up were coming out of their holes little by little. He rushed to hold one, ordering one of the servants to hold up another while the other servant went for help. They were not long in this predicament; one of the Minister's people arrived just in time with a dozen slaves, and in a few moments all was in good order. Thus our Brother got off only slightly shaken.

Nothing in particular happened to him during the remainder of the journey, which continued a little more smoothly than in the first few days. He was in the retinue of the Emperor, and he was not going faster than His Majesty. The march of the prince, as he envisioned it, inspired picturesque images, but he admitted that, if he were painting an army in disarray, he would have had an excellent model before his eyes. He did not distinguish in any fashion that majesty, that economy, that order that characterized all Chinese ceremonies. He saw nothing but a confused mass of people of all ranks going hither and thither, pushing, shoving, running, some to dispatch orders and others to execute them; some searching for masters they had lost in the crowd; some looking for their section or going to join the ranks of the Emperor, from whom they had become separated. All that he saw seemed a tumult, a confusion, an obstruction; there were only pitiful, lamentable, and tragic creatures that inspired in him fear, horror, and compassion. Here were overturned carts that people tried vainly to upright, camels stretched out with all their baggage, heaving anguished cries with each blow struck to get them up; here were destroyed bridges, exhausted horses, men dead, dying, or injured, trampled by the feet of horses or crushed under the wheels of carts that ran over their bodies; perplexed riders in the fracas trying to extricate themselves from the mess: such are the images that, coming out of his brush, he never would have dared title "The March of the Emperor of China." One must not believe, however, that all the travels of the Emperor were like this; this was an extraordinary event, and never had the prince had so many in his retinue. He wanted to give to the foreigners who had delivered themselves to him as his own subjects an idea of his power and greatness, and he wanted do it in such a way that if some among them took a fancy to leave, they would, in recounting to their compatriots what they had seen, inspire in them a just fear of troubling him or draw them under his allegiance: an artifice that succeeded perfectly, because ten thousand people were still behind him wearing his colors.

As soon as Brother Attiret arrived in Jehol, the Minister housed him in his own lodgings, where he gave him the best room. He paid him the honor of visiting him in the evening and extended all kinds of obliging assistance; he promised, among other things, that he would serve him maigre on the days that our religion does not permit us to eat meat. What was infinitely gracious on his part is that despite all the affairs he was in charge of, he wanted to take care of everything himself to the last detail. He added, before ending his visit, that the Emperor probably wanted Attiret to make a drawing of the fête that was going to take place, although he was not sure. It was the second of July; the Brother rested until July 4, without knowing what was wanted of him.

After his return he was able to tell me that Jehol was little more than a third-rate city that had nothing of beauty except the Emperor's palace. Jehol is situated at the base of a mountain and is watered by a river that is quite small but that enlarges from time to time in a terrible manner, either through snow melt or by an abundance of rain; it then becomes a furious torrent that no dam can stop. A few years ago a part of the palace was destroyed; the damage came to great sums as much because of the quantity as of the quality of the furnishings that were lost or ruined.

Jehol began to amount to something under Kangxi; since then, it has always grown and is becoming a sizable place under the current Emperor, who comes each year for several months with his court and who has built a number of buildings and other works that embellish the place and make it a very agreeable abode during the three months of great heat that we have here.

On July 4, at eleven o'clock in the evening, Brother Attiret was notified of an order of the Emperor: this was to go the next day to the palace, where the Count would tell him what to do. He obeyed, and he learned that the intention of His Majesty was that he paint or at least sketch all that would occur in the ceremony that was going to take place. It was strongly recommended that he locate himself where he could see everything, lest something be forgotten from his sketch and so that the Emperor would be satisfied.

A capable painter would not be at all perplexed by a similar order in Europe, where he is permitted some embellishment and where, in keeping to the truth, he could give free rein to his genius, less in fear of being disavowed than sure of being applauded. But it is not the same here: one does only what one is told and does what one is told to the letter. It is not genius that is valued. The most beautiful lights must be snuffed out as soon as they appear if they lead to something that is not positively asked of one.

All these thoughts in mind, and filled with a great store of goodwill, Brother Attiret gathered all his fiber, went to the place of the ceremony, assisted to the end, saw everything with his own eyes, and, in spite of all that, didn't know how to approach his subject. He was confused and confounded by all the choices he had to make. He saw everything and saw nothing. The order to go to work at once was given as soon as the ceremony had ended. He was told by the Emperor that the sketch had to be delivered that same evening to Count Te, who would take it to His Majesty, who wanted to see it. He had nowhere to turn, as the Brother realized all too well. He took the path back to the lodgings of the Minister, retired soundlessly to his room, and set himself to executing his orders. He sharpened several pencils like a man trying to gain time, and still nothing came to him. Finally he seized upon his point of approach. This was the moment of the Emperor's entry into the site of the ceremony, a moment flattering to this prince, where one saw at a glance all the magnificence of his grandeur. He rapidly sketched all that this offered, and several hundred figures of many different types appeared in rough outline. Time passed more swiftly than he wanted, and Count Te was at his door. He had to deliver the work before nightfall, which required some effort. He went to the palace himself to find out His Majesty's response. He was most flattering. The Emperor told him, by way of the Count, that everything was "*hen-hao*," that is, "very good."

Here is the place to describe this ceremony, or at least to give a brief outline of it. I would do this with pleasure, if, after having seen the sketch that had been done for the Emperor, and after having heard the explanation from the mouth of Brother Attiret, I had not learned that the ceremony in question is very nearly the same as that done under Kangxi in the year 1691, which P[ère] Gerbillon has described in detail in his third voyage to Tartary, which you will find at some length in the fourth volume of P[ère] DuHalde. Thus, my Reverend Father, it is to this account that I take the liberty of referring you. I can say nothing better or of greater circumstance than you would read there.

The next day, the Brother, being inclined to retouch his design, was interrupted suddenly by a messenger from the Emperor, who notified him of an order to go to the palace, where His Majesty had decorated with the titles of Dignitary, Count, and Grand Lord, eleven of the most important immigrants, who, with all of their retinue, were sanctioned as members of the state and subjects of the prince who governed it. It was to do the portraits of these eleven lords on whom this honor had been bestowed that the painter had been summoned. One of these portraits was finished the same day and shown at once to the Emperor. He found it a marvel. His Majesty informed Brother Attiret that, before the fête ended in the next six days, he had to complete the portraits of the others. He would have liked to have had a little time to himself to take a breather and to rid himself of a malady that he had contracted by the change of climate and diet, and he would have liked the leisure to get rid of it entirely, or at least to alleviate it a little. He had been attacked by a chest cold, accompanied by a course of wind and a very violent fever. Despite this triple discomfort, which lasted for some time, he had to go to the palace each day, working from morning to night in a place that was virtually a public space, since it was the hall where the courtiers assembled to attend the performances and other events they took part in. "What made my malady infinitely worse," said Brother Attiret, "is that they were on my back all day, asking me a thousand questions, all different, which I had to answer while working at the same time." A single word would have delivered him of all these importunities; but he dared not say anything, because these were none other than the dignitaries, counts, and the highest grand lords of the empire. He felt moreover that these lords did this only to honor him, for the greater part of their questions were about France or about those things they believed would please him. This state of constraint, combined with forced labor and his three maladies, soon drained him of his strength. The mandarin who served as an attendant for him seriously warned Count Te to present a supplication to the Emperor to inform him of Brother Attiret's condition. Count Te himself saw that this was indeed the case and hastened to act accordingly. The Emperor ordered that his painter rest and sent him one of his doctors to care for him. After a day of rest, the patient believed himself strong enough to continue his work. He returned to the palace, where he finished, within the set time, the eleven portraits with which he was charged.

It is said that the Tartars [i.e. Western Mongol defectors to the Qing], little accustomed to seeing themselves reproduced thus, marveled at recognizing themselves on canvas and seeing themselves with all their accouterments. They laughed at one another until, after a few strokes of the brush, they perceived a little resemblance; when they were finished, however, they were ecstatic. They little understood how this could be done: they could not keep themselves from watching the palette and brush; none of the painter's actions escaped them. The Chinese and Manchu lords who were present laughed also with all their hearts, not at the copies, but at the originals themselves, whose faces, appearance, and every mannerism had so little in common with Chinese politesse and manners. Probably of all those there, only the painter was not at ease. He had to respond to several people at once; he wanted the Emperor to be satisfied with his work, and he had to seize instantly each feature he wanted to paint. Even had he been in good health, I do not think he would have laughed.

As each portrait was done, however, it was presented to the Emperor, who examined it at his leisure and made his judgment upon it, which the Eunuchs of the Presence announced immediately to the Brother when they returned the painting. As all the judgments were flattering and honorable to the painter, of which each time it was said "*hen-hao, hen-hao*," that is, "very good, very good," they elicited all kinds of compliments and marks of affection from the great ones who amused themselves by watching him paint. What increased their estimation of him even more is that each day a mandarin in ceremonial attire brought him meals from the table of His Majesty, bringing them in front of everyone, most of whom would have been very happy to have enjoyed the same honor. The matter went so far in this regard that Count Te grew jealous. He was unable to hide it: and, as if he wanted to avenge himself of some wrong that had been done to him, or because he wanted to diminish the joy he imagined was in Brother Attiret's heart, he often said, mockingly, "Sir, here it is quite different than in Peking or Haidian, where one cannot see the Emperor so easily; I am offended that His Majesty does not come to enjoy himself by watching you paint."

If this courtier had known the true sentiments of the person he wanted to annoy, he certainly would not have entertained such a discourse, because at the very time this dear Brother was heaped with courtesies and honors by the grandees and by the Emperor himself, he wrote me with an open heart: "I would prefer that this comic act finishes: far from the house of God and deprived of spiritual succor, I have difficulty persuading myself that this might be for the glory of God."

After the eleven portraits were finished and approved by the Emperor, the painter received an order to enlarge the sketch of the ceremony, which he thus far had made only in a smaller version. Another room in the palace was assigned to him, and it was Count Te who had to take him there and set him up. It seems as if this Count scarcely suspected the Emperor would visit this place, because when he entered he spitefully addressed the Brother, saying: "And you won't see him today, either; this is scarcely a place His Majesty frequents." The Brother did not respond but set himself to work. He had barely started when a Mandarin of the Presence came ceremoniously to give him two pieces of silk from the Emperor. A moment later the Emperor himself entered and good naturedly asked the Brother if he was free of his malady, watched him work for a moment, asked him some obliging questions, after which he left; but in leaving he told the Count that Brother Attiret should not be there but should be placed at once in the *ta-tien*, that is, in the throne room.

He had to obey. The Count himself took some of the painter's gear and helped him move so that he could do so more promptly. Arriving in the hall, Brother Attiret saw a mandarin coming toward him, carrying in his two hands, which were raised to the level of his eyes, a paper of a special kind, and which the Emperor used sometimes for painting. The mandarin told the painter, in giving him the paper, that the intention of His Majesty was that he draw a certain Tartar gentleman on horseback pursuing a tiger, bow drawn, about to let the arrow fly; he added that the Emperor wanted to do the painting himself. Brother Attiret did what was expected of him. The next day he received an order to prepare four pieces of the fine, gummed silk that the Chinese use for painting water-colors. He was then to take them to the garden to find views and scenes to serve as backgrounds for the paintings he would do of the games and amusements of the actual celebration, with the exception of the perfor-mances and bright firework displays; these games were for the most part just acrobatic performances, horse races, and military exercises. Reading the third voyage of P[ère] Gerbillon in Tartary, which I have already told you about, will give you an idea of what these were.

Brother Attiret did all that was ordered of him each time. Arriving at the garden with Count Te, who never left him, he put some of his ideas on paper and sketched everything he thought he could use in his drawing. The Emperor saw him from afar, came over to him, examined what he had just done, changed what was not to his taste, and added what he judged proper. He did him the honor of asking him whether he was tired and specially advised him to walk slowly. When he finished, the Brother returned to the palace to work on his drawings. Two entire days passed without him seeing His Majesty and without being disturbed. He took advantage of this to continue his work.

On the morning of the third day, the Emperor honored him with a visit. He wanted to see all that had been done and found that the figure of his person, which had been drawn on horseback in one scene and carried in a chaise in another, leaned a little too far backward in both instances. He wanted this mistake corrected at once, and in order to facil-itate this he sat on his throne, which was right there; he acted out what he had in mind, and a drawing was made of his position. As it was very hot, he had the goodness to order the Brother to remove his hat and sit down – a singular favor that he accorded none of his other subjects, who had either to kneel or stand in his presence, even while working.

The Emperor returned the next day. A eunuch carried in his hands the painting His Majesty had done himself over the sketch of the Tartar on horseback, of which I have spoken above. He displayed it before the Brother and ordered him to retouch the posture of the rider, who was just about to let his arrow fly. After that slight correction, the painting was returned to the chambers of His Majesty, who wanted to work on it some more. But that same evening it was sent to Brother Attiret, with the order to finish it. There only remained the quiver, the horse's tail, and the rider's boots. I forgot to say that the Emperor early that morning had asked Brother Attiret whether he still had some Korean paper, oiled and ready for the application of colors – without saying, nonetheless, what he wanted to do with it. As the Brother responded that he had none left, the Count was ordered to dispatch a courier to Haidian immediately to request a sheet from Brother Castiglione, who had some prepared.

While the courier was on the road, Brother Attiret lost no time. In addition to the sketches I have mentioned, he still had to do the portraits of the most important lords who were to be included in the painting of the ceremony; all the portraits had to have the approval of His Majesty, which augmented his difficulties not a little. He had to redo two of them several times, as the Emperor did not find them to his taste; that of the Count Minister was completely off because of the desire that he resemble it so closely. The Emperor wanted the eyes done in a certain way that flattered the man most, wanted his head to be more or less leaning forward, and wanted him to have such and such a posture; but all this was not forthcoming from the imagination of the painter, who exerted all his efforts to comply with the prince's wishes. But he was so bewildered by all these difficulties that he lost sight of his model, no matter what he did to finish the painting. The Minister offered some less-than-subtle criticism, giving him to understand, nevertheless, that it was not his fault. All the other portraits were considered marvels, His Majesty acclaimed them highly, and hence the entire court lavished praise on them as well.

But all this was just the beginning, so to speak, for the painter. The courier returned with the canvas – or more correctly, the prepared paper – that he had procured in Haidian. As soon as the Emperor was apprised of his return, he betook himself to the room where Brother Attiret was working; he sat upon the throne and ordered that he be painted life-size. The Brother had not yet had this honor. Since the Emperor and all his court thought the other portraits were good, this one had to be excellent. And the painter surpassed himself. Since he had to do it on the spot, there was more imagination in the painting. Before he brought forth a single brush stroke and before the first sketch was even done, the Emperor exclaimed, as he arose, "This is very good! This is very good! I have been here for two hours, and that is enough for today!" What the prince found most flattering in the portrait was to see himself with a large head that seemed a size larger than usual. He had hinted more than once that he wanted to be painted thus; in all his portraits he had always found his head had been made too small. But not a word had been heard about this before, and no one was aware of his views on this matter. It had been thought enough to increase his natural size with a few lines, and even then one thought one had overdone it. His Majesty did not think it fitting to explain himself on those other occasions more clearly, and he did not explain himself in this last instance, either. Just as Brother Attiret took up the palette and brushes, a eunuch opposite him put his two hands upon his head and spread them far apart; he pointed with his fingers, when the Emperor was not looking, as if he wanted to tell the

Brother that His Majesty wanted to be painted with a very large head. Another eunuch made it known in so many words in a tone of voice loud enough that the Emperor could hear, and His Majesty confirmed, with a sign of approval, what he had just said. The painter needed no more prompting, for it was as good as said; he acted accordingly, and brought off what was in all senses a marvel.

As soon as the Emperor retired, Brother Attiret worked later on the portrait and did all the brush work he believed necessary for a perfect resemblance, employing all his skills to enhance it. Some days later, His Majesty having seen it and finding it much more to his liking than the first time, complimented the painter and patted him affectionately. The desire to be reproduced in color increased in him as soon as these colors represented his person as he wished to be. He sent the Brother to the garden to get some ideas for the background of a scene where he wanted to be depicted shooting an arrow. After the Brother had sketched in the landscape and all else he believed necessary to embellish his subject, the mandarin who oversaw these kinds of works carried it to His Majesty, who approved it with acclaim. Now the Count had just been charged with another errand, and he had to carry out His Majesty's orders at some distance. He left on the eleventh of the sixth moon, but before his departure he went back to the lodgings of the Minister to take his leave of him. As he went out, Brother Attiret heard him and ran ahead to wish him bon voyage. The former did not respond to his greetings except for some perfunctory compliments of felicitation. The Brother did not doubt in any way but that all these compliments were heaped upon him because the Emperor's portraits had succeeded so well. He replied with the usual responses; but when some moments later a lower-ranking mandarin congratulated him in almost the same terms and in what seemed to him to be a somewhat singular manner, he had the curiosity to ask why, specifically, he was proffered these felicitations. The man complimenting him, greatly astonished, told him quite simply that he rejoiced with him that the Emperor had made him a mandarin. "Me, a mandarin?" replied Brother Attiret. "Yes, you, a mandarin," he replied coldly. "What! All the court knows, and you have not been told yet!" And so on. The poor Brother was a little dismayed at this news; but as he had been prepared for this for quite some time, he thought only of finding some means of parrying this blow without offending the Emperor. . . .

[Attiret learns that because Qianlong is so pleased with his work, particularly with the life-size portrait, that he is to be made a mandarin of the fourth rank. The Jesuit Attiret, not concerned with worldly rewards, tactfully declines this honor. He nevertheless continues to paint for Qianlong and sees him almost daily at Jehol for the remainder of his sojourn there.]

Although Brother Attiret did not enjoy very good health, he was obliged nevertheless to paint from morning to night with no rest other than that afforded at meals and at night. Still he was obliged to get up from his sleep to devise different compositions in his sketches and paintings. He was in Tartary only fifty-odd days, and of those only forty were devoted to work, and during this short space of time he made twenty-two portraits in oils, four large sketches, both of the ceremony and of other events, and a quantity of other things, each of which itself would have demanded, even in more favorable circumstances, one or two days of work. Thus he was so overwhelmed and so dispirited that he was unrecognizable on his return. We found him thin, pale, bent over at the back, and walking only with great difficulty and pain. He had contracted, as much by the fatigue of Jehol as by that of the journey, a kind of sciatica that obliged him to stay in his room more than fifteen days after his arrival here; but thanks to the Lord, the rest returned his strength to him, and he is in good health today. He must make the same journey again before long, because the Emperor will perform the same ceremony for new immigrants who number almost ten thousand, as I have said above. It seems that he will have things a little easier than the first time, because P[ère] Siguelbarth and Brother Castiglione, painters like himself, must accompany him; moreover, it is very probable that the three painters will not be called on to do anything more than draw the portraits of the most important of the new arrivals, since all the rest have already been painted by Brother Attiret.[4]

Notes

*   The translator is grateful for the assistance of Louis Dupont with some of the eighteenth-century French terminology.
1   Notable correspondence by Jesuits in overseas missions was published by the order in collected volumes titled *Lettres édifiantes et curieuses*, which were reprinted in various later selected editions. This letter is from the "Mémoires de la Chine" section of just such a collection, the *Lettres édifiantes et curieuses écrites par des missionaires de la compagnie de Jésus collationnées sur les meilleures éditions et enrichies de nouvelles notes*, vol. 36, 246–299.
2   The malcontents referred to here include Tsereng, with his Dörböt followers. Amursana had not yet, or had only just, allied with the Qing. For background on these Mongol affairs, see Millward, Chapter 8.
3   The editor has not been able to establish the identy of "Count Te" definitively, but the best guess is that Attiret's escort was Delge (Ch. De-le-ke; ?–1794), a Mongol Borjigid descendent from the Barin *aimagh*. Eldest son of second-rank Prince (*junwang*) Lin-qin, in 1750 Delge married the Hewan hošoi gungju, a second-rank princess, the daughter of the Qianlong's younger brother, Hongzhou. Because his health was poor, Delge did not inherit the rulership (*wang*) of the *aimagh*, but lived in Beijing, where he used his noble status as *gong* (usually "duke," but here evidently translated by the Jesuits as "count," as in Amiot's "*te-kong*") to maintain his presence at court (hence Amiot's "courtier" rather than "minister"). He did some translation work in the Manchu Classics Translation Office. It seems that such a hanger-on imperial son-in-law, with rank but not much to do, would be just the sort of person designated as Attiret's handler. It would also explain Count Te's grumbling at the imperial honors bestowed on

Attiret. Gao Wende *et al.*, *Zhongguo minzu shi renwu cidian*, 599; Evelyn Rawski, personal communication, February 15, 2000.

4   Editors' note: These new arrivals were very important indeed, for they included the Khoit *taisha* Amursana, a major defection from the Zunghars, whom the Qianlong emperor went to great lengths to honor. Because ceremonial duties kept him in Beijing until December 22, Qianlong traveled in a three-day forced march to the Bishu shanzhuang, where Amursana and other Western Mongols had already arrived. The banquets and enfeoffment ceremonies for these Khoit and Dörböt leaders were held December 25–26, ensuring that the Jesuit painters passed a cold and cheerless Christmas that year. *QLSL*, 19.10.18 *guihai* (473: 3a–4a); 19.11.12 *dinghai* (476: 12a); 19.11.13 *wuzi* (476: 12a–13a).

15 Qianlong's inscription on the founding of the Temple of the Happiness and Longevity of Mt Sumeru (Xumifushou miao)[1]

Translated by Peter Zarrow

The rise of the Gelukpa sect began with its founder, Tsong kha pa. He had two major disciples, Gedun Truppa, whose eighth incarnation is today's Dalai Lama, and Rgyal tshab dar ma rin chen, whose sixth incarnation is today's Panchen Lama, Losang Belden Yeshe (1737–1780).[2] These two lamas transmitted religious principles to each other [over the generations] and learned together as teacher and disciple, and thus they invigorated Buddhism. The Panchen Lama is thus today the teacher of the Dalai Lama. The Potala where the Dalai Lama lives is called in Chinese the Putuozongcheng miao. The Tashilhunpo where the Panchen Lama Losang Belden Yeshe lives is called in Chinese the Xumifushou miao.[3] Thus is Tibet divided into the nearer Ü (dBus) and the farther Tsang. In 1771 We built a Putuozongcheng miao on a hill to the north of the Bishu shanzhuang for blessings as well as to mark the return of the Torghut people.[4] Since the Sixth Panchen Lama, Losang Belden Yeshe, wanted an audience with Us, today We have constructed the Xumifushou miao (Temple of the Happiness and Longevity of Mt Sumeru) on the left side of the Putuozongcheng miao and modeled it on his residence in order to give him a restful place for meditation. Also, We are following the precedent established by Our Imperial Ancestor Shizu [the Shunzhi emperor, r. 1644–1661], who built the Northern Yellow Temple in the capital to house the Fifth Dalai Lama.[5] However, the visit of the Fifth Dalai Lama in fact came at the emperor's sincere invitation, while this visit of the Panchen Lama is not in response to Our summons but came from his own desire to visit the capital in order to witness the flourishing of the Gelukpa sect, [Our] nurturing and teaching, the ubiquitous peace and happiness, and the plenitude of goods in China (*huaxia*). At the same time, his visit has coincided with Our seventieth birthday and it is a time for celebration. Now, We had not intended to allow extravagant ceremony and had prepared an edict to forestall this; however, with the visit of the Sixth Panchen Lama, we should not hinder [his wishes to honor Us]. Our realm (*guojia*) has enjoyed peace and harmony for over a hundred years, and so the peoples of the center and the peoples of the periphery are one family.[6] It has also been over a hundred years since the visit of the Fifth Dalai Lama. At that time, when Our Dynasty was first established, the Khalkha Mongols and the Oirat Mongols still included some obstructionist elements, but today there is complete peace and harmony. The Khalkha submitted a long time ago, and all of the Oirat are now obedient. As soon as they heard of the visit of the Panchen Lama, they rejoiced and all wanted to serve him and adore him. This all stems from their perfect sincerity and happened without anyone telling them how to behave. Thus the higher goal in the building of the Xumifushou miao is to exalt accomplishments planned through the ages which have pacified and protected the realm (*bang*), while the basic goal is to answer the absolutely sincere desire of the vassal peoples to become civilized. Can We be perfunctory about this?

(Qianlong, forty-fifth year [1780] sixth month, first week)

Notes

1   Dated first week, sixth month, 1780. The Qianlong emperor built the Xumifushou miao (Figure 14) to the east of the Putuozongcheng miao specifically to welcome the Panchen Lama. Mt Sumeru ("Xumi" in Chinese transliteration) is the mythical mountain where the gods lived to the north of India, a translation of the Tibetan "Bkra shis lhun po" (Tashilhunpo), and the Xumifushou miao was architecturally based on the Tashilhunpo temple of the Panchen Lama in Tibet. It is also called the "Ban-chen Xinggong," or "Panchen's palace while traveling," in Chinese. The translation of this inscription is based on Qi Jingzhi, *Waiba miao beiwen zhuyi*, 97–102.

2   Tsong kha pa (Ch. Zong-ha-ba; Tsong kha pa Blo bzang Grags pa in complete Tibetan transcription, 1357–1419) founded the Gelukpa sect in Tibet, which came to dominate Tibet politically. The Chinese called this sect the Yellow Church after the yellow hats worn by its monks. Gedun Truppa (Ch. Gen-dun zhu-ba, T. Dge 'dun Grub pa, 1391–1474) is considered the first Dalai Lama. Rgyal tshab Dar ma Rin chen (Ch. Kai-zhu-bu ge-lie-ke ba-le-zang, 1364–1432) is usually considered a major disciple of Tsong kha pa, though Tibetans regard Losang Belden Yeshe (called E-er-de-ni in the Chinese here, 1737–1780) as the Third Panchen Lama. Tibetans consider Losang Choki Gyaltsen (T. Blo bzang Chos kyi Rgyal mtshan, 1567–1662), teacher of the Fifth Dalai Lama, to be the First Panchen Lama. E-er-de-ni is a Chinese transcription for the Mongol (borrowed by Manchu) "Erdeni," or "precious," which is a translation of the Tibetan *rin po che*, found in the Panchen Lama's complete title. Qianlong's unorthodox version of the origins of the Dalai and Panchen lamas acted to raise the status of the Panchen Lama who was visiting him.

3   "Putuozongcheng" refers to the Potaraka Doctrine. The temple, modeled after the Potala (built 1645–1695 in Lhasa), was built to the north of the Bishu shanzhuang between 1767 and 1771 and was sometimes called *budala* in Chinese transcription. The monastery of Tashilhunpo (Ch. Zha-she-lun-bu; T. Bkra shis lhun po) had been founded in Shigatse (Ch. Rikaze, T. gZhis ka rtse) in 1447 by the first Dalai Lama, Gedun Truppa, and became the home of the Panchen Lamas in the time of bLo-bzang chos-kyi rgyal-mtshan. See note 2 above.

4   Qianlong is claiming that the ancient Tibetan provinces of Ü and Tsang (Ch. Wei and Zang) reflected a political split between the Panchen and Dalai lamas. It is true that the great monasteries of Tashilhunpo and Potala became the political centers of their respective provinces, but only after the seventeenth century. (On the Torghuts, see Millward, Chapter 8.)

5   The Fifth Dalai Lama, Ngawang Losang Gyatso, visited China between 1652
    and 1653, during the Shunzhi reign. With the conquest still unsettled, the Qing
    correctly felt that good relations with the Dalai Lama were critical both because
    Tibet had considerable power of its own just to the west of Chinese territory
    and especially because of the Dalai Lama's influence over the Mongols.
    Qianlong's claim that the Panchen Lama's visit of 1780 was without the Qing's
    entreaties and even threats is disingenuous.

6   The phrase "*zhongwai yijia*" refers to two contrasting elements as "one family";
    these two elements may be rendered as: (1) center and periphery; (2) Chinese
    and foreign; and (3) the central plain (along the Yellow River) and outside the
    central plain. Qianlong emphatically believed that the emperor was, by defini-
    tion, the central point of a realm sheltering diverse peoples who made up "one
    family" not by a common identity but by harmonious coexistence. The present
    effort may represent an over-translation but at least conveys some of the ambi-
    guity of the original. To translate as "Chinese and foreign" is probably the best
    single option but is inadequate to explain the position of the Qing royal house,
    which was clearly not *sino*centric. For further discussion and textual citations for
    this and similar expressions, see Elliott and Chia, Chapter 6.

16 The Third Panchen Lama's visit to Chengde

Translated by Nima Dorjee Ragnubs[1]

Seventh month, twenty-second day (Chinese calendar seventh month, twenty-first day; August 20, 1780); first day of visit

(315) According to the Tibetan lunar calendar, the Panchen Lama departed from the *xinggong* [i.e. Xumifushou miao, his "travel palace"] in the iron bird year, seventh month, the twenty-second day [August 20, 1780]. The emperor sent his high and low ranking ministers to receive him. They ran with their horses, did three prostrations, and ran back, after which more horsemen came to greet and welcome him. The Tibetans found it amusing that some would come to greet him and would run back, then others would come and do the same thing. When the Panchen Lama arrived at a distance equivalent to two arrow-shots, the emperor sent eight people to carry the sedan chair. These bearers wore hats with peacock feathers. (316) The Panchen Lama rode in the sedan chair, and when they reached a small pass you could see the entire area of Chengde. This area had beautiful mountains and valleys as green as malachite and fresh green grass abounded with many fruit trees and fields of grain. There were waters with eight pure qualities and beautiful buildings. There were many "Yellow Hat" monasteries and Ho shang (Chan) monasteries. The east side of Chengde on top of the rocky mountain is called Panthuhu shan, an awesome sight. In the wide plain there were many different colored parrots, many ponds, villages, and towns surrounding this area. Above was the Jewel (Shiva linga) and many palaces. When he descended to the plain, [he was greeted by] the highest minister Eng Ephu Gung [i.e. *efu gong*, imperial-son-in-law, duke Eng.?] and two others, Hos Ta Shin [He-shen dachen?] and nephew Gung Phhing Sheji Lon, etc., and many other high ranking and low ranking ministers as well as the excellent Lord of all Beings, the truthful Jang gya Rolpai Dorje, and Tsenpo Mingrol Nomon Khan, and Ta Zhag Je Tung (rTa Tshag rJe Drung) Tulku [main lama of Pashu monastery]. (317) In addition, there was the abbot of Chengde Potala, members of Tashilhunpo [i.e. Xumifushou miao], Ta Phu Zi [i.e. Dafo si or Puning si, Chengde's Samye; Figure 16], the Manjushri Temple (Shuxiang si), and Yili temple (Anyuan miao), and others, abbots of all

the monasteries, Jasag lamas, Ta lamas, Sul lamas, chanting masters, and many lamas and lay people with horses.

Eng Efu Gung and Hos Ta Shin and the two home ministers presented a welcome scarf from the emperor. When the Panchen Lama saw them approaching, he wanted to descend but they insisted that he remain in the sedan chair. They relayed the emperor's message, "When I think that I will meet you now, I am very happy. How is your health? No difficulties during the trip, no sicknesses?" Speaking to the ministers, he said, "Bring him with welcome musical instruments with '*phithan*,' victory umbrellas and banners, carry this swift sedan chair." The emperor also said, "Bring Panchen Erdeni in my sedan chair." The Panchen Lama seemed very happy, gave everyone a scarf, and he sent a message with scarf to the emperor that he would arrive soon. After receiving the scarves from the ministers, the Panchen Lama blessed the ones who wanted to be blessed [by putting his hand on their heads].

The sixth prince and two home ministers rode horses in front of him to the great Ta Phu Zi monastery,[2] (318) On the road there were young men carrying insignias and symbols of the emperor, umbrellas, banners, military flags, victory fans, many were wearing different colored robes. The monks lined up on the sides of the road. Also there were people from Gyalmorong, Chamdo, Dayab, Ba, Li thang, Gyalthang, and eighteen small nations from Kham as well as from Mis Tsang Junge, Oirats and Zunghars. Hundreds of people came to receive him and he blessed each one. He spoke a few words to high ranking people. In front of Puning temple was the emperor's tent. The sixth prince and two home ministers brought him into the tent where he was served tea and yogurt. Then they brought the emperor's daily sedan and related the emperor's request that he should sit in the sedan to go the palace, so the chair would be very blessed, and he would be very pleased.

The Panchen Lama said, "I am a very low ranking monk, I cannot use the Manjushri emperor's daily sedan." The ministers replied, "The emperor wishes to show great respect to you, you must use this. You should not hesitate, you have been using the emperor's sedan since the Blue Fort [i.e. Köke Khota, Hohhot?]. (319) This is the custom for close relatives." The Panchen Lama accepted, went to Ta Phu Zi, and then went to Jang gya's residence. Fruits, cookies, and teas had been set out, and they rested there. While they were resting, the sixth prince and two home ministers, said, "The emperor is eager to see you so we should leave soon." They left immediately and he allowed most of his retinue to return to Tashilhunpo monastery (Xumifushou miao).

Fifty horsemen went with him to the emperor's palace. Tens of thousands of people were kneeling down as they were proceeding to the palace but the crowd was very quiet. (320) The emperor's men were holding the weapons to defend the royal laws and banners. Many musical instruments – big drums, small strings, bamboo flutes, flat drums, round drums, long trumpets, horns, and many different cymbals – fantastic, beautiful, and frightful looking – were being played simultaneously. They also held the seven royal symbols and all other symbols for the chakravartin king. Reaching the outside main gate, [named] Tsangti (Gtsang 'khris), and entering the courtyard, the fifty horsemen entourage descended from their horses. Officials in various uniforms and young men carrying offering objects and fans were there to receive them. They went through many enclosures to the emperor's residence palace.

When they reached the reception room, Panchen Lama descended from the sedan because he saw the emperor in the receiving hall. As the sixth prince and home ministers held his hands, the Panchen Lama and his cook went to meet the emperor. (321) The emperor was surrounded by luxuries indicating that he had accumulated much merit in previous lives. His queens were wearing white brocade robes. He considered himself the ruler of the earth and a great leader with many intimidating army battalions to protect the country. Many other nations admired him and sought his protection. As a chakravartin he had the Four Requisites (*sde bzhi*), the Seven Royal Symbols, and all other necessary implements. He was called by Tibetans, "Chakravartin Lhegyong (Protected by the Gods)."

The Qianlong emperor was standing with his retinue in the main hall. This was the first meeting of the *mchod yon* (lama–patron): of the Manjushri emperor Qianlong and the Panchen Lama. The Panchen Lama presented him a very long white silk scarf with a bronze statue of the Buddha, inlaid with pearls and other jewels. As the greetings started, the Panchen Lama began to kneel down but the emperor took his hand and made him rise, saying in Tibetan, "Lama, please do not kneel." Then the emperor presented a very long and spotless silk scarf to Panchen Lama and said in Tibetan, "How are you, lama? The long journey must have been difficult and tiring."

(322) The Panchen Lama replied, "By the kindness of the Manjushri emperor there were no difficulties. Wherever it was cold I was warm and wherever it was hot I was cool. I faced no problems." The emperor said with delight, "That is good fortune!" and led the Panchen Lama by the hand into an inner room. They began to converse after sitting down facing each other on a wide golden throne. . . .

(324) Soon after the conversation started, Jang gya Rinpoche offered scarves to the *mchod yon* (the lama and the patron). The Panchen Lama's older brother and manager, as well as the chief cook, Gangcen Khempo, and other members of the entourage offered scarves to the emperor. The emperor had a brief conversation with them; in a joyous mood he gave scarves to each. At tea time the emperor asked the Panchen Lama to drink the tea first but they decided to drink simultaneously.

As they had tea, they conversed [in Tibetan]. Qianlong emperor asked, "How is the Dalai Lama? How old are you, Panchen Erdeni? What is the sign of your birth year? I am very happy and fortunate that on my seventieth birthday you have come to visit. (325) It has been very beneficial to the people and for the Buddhist teaching in Amdo and here; they are happy that you are here." The emperor was in a joyous mood and had a long conversation. The Panchen Lama answered the emperor's questions and gave a little speech explaining that the emperor was the real Manjushri. Then the emperor addressed Jang gya Rinpoche, "Khutukhtu, today is very fortunate." Jang gya agreed, saying, "Today the lama and patron are together, and enjoying good weather; it seems to me that everything is beyond compare."

They left the room together with a few people from their entourages to view the inner palace rooms and shrines. The Panchen Lama blessed and chanted for good luck in these rooms. Within the courtyards between the rooms were beautiful trees of different colors and flower gardens. (326) As they walked, Qianlong invited Panchen Lama to look up, pointing out more palaces, temples, and residence rooms. He asked Panchen Lama, "Please visualize and bless them as well."

They came to a large palace courtyard with many bushes and plants. In this palace room there was a high golden throne and on this throne the lama and patron sat together facing each other and were served tea. Qianlong said, "One visualizes lamas and one can see them through this method. But today you are here and I can see you [in person]. This makes me very happy. The reason we are able to be together like this must be because of good prayers in our previous lives." They were both pleased with their conversations and togetherness.

Then the emperor began to present gifts: a necklace of pearls as big as apricot pits which he was wearing, a rosary decorated with gems, a wide yellow brocade flat-brimmed hat with a large pearl in a gold setting on top, and a large pearl in front, and a jade *ruyi* scepter. The weather was beautiful as the emperor presented the gifts, and he announced his happiness and commented that the sun was out, and made other remarks expressing his pleasure. (327) Then they walked out of the north back door hand in hand, with the Panchen Lama's hand resting on top of Qianlong's hand. The emperor then wished Panchen Lama a happy evening and promised to see him tomorrow.

Seventh month, twenty-second day; second day of visit

(340) Tea was served, simultaneously to each of them, by their own cooks. As the two cooks were pouring the tea, the emperor asked to be given the Panchen Lama's cup. Then the cook put the cup into the emperor's hand and the emperor passed it to Panchen Lama himself, smiling happily. The Panchen Lama asked the emperor's cook, Amban Phu Lihuye, to bring the emperor's cup to him and then presented it with his own hand, addressing the emperor as Manjushri emperor. The emperor said, "You drink before me," and Panchen Lama said "You drink before me," and finally they decided to drink at the same time. During this conversation,

the emperor said, "I sent the sixth imperial prince to receive you. Did he serve you well?" (341) Panchen Lama replied, "He did a wonderful job." ... The emperor said, "This year is my seventieth birthday, and you have arrived here healthy and happy. This is of great benefit to the teachings of Buddhism and to the happiness of all beings. I studied a little religion over the years with Jang gya khutukhtu. (342) But this Buddhism is deep and wide as the ocean and I have been busy working for the nation. Therefore I could not attain the goals of meditation I learned from Jang gya. But I am almost there! Our meeting here is the result of previous lives' prayers and wishes. I hope that the good connection we have will allow me to receive many dharma teachings and initiations from you. During the time of the Fifth Dalai Lama, my ancestor [the Shunzhi] emperor built a Yellow Temple, so this time I have built a monastery that is a replica of Tashilhunpo for your residence. I have built many temples and monasteries in this summer place. When you are visiting these places and having a pleasant time, if you could also bless them, it would be most fortunate for me. I did not know how to speak Tibetan before, but when I heard you were coming here, I immediately began to study colloquial conversation with Jang gya. I tried hard but I am still not fluent in the language. Religious teachings in Tibetan can be translated by Jang gya."

They continued to have this sort of excellent conversation. (343) The Panchen talked of politics and religion in a manner that pleased the emperor. They both enjoyed the conversation. The emperor then began his departure to his palace. The emperor said "Do not see me out." So the Panchen Lama did not accompany him. The Panchen Lama's entourage, however, did proceed to the front gate of the monastery to watch the emperor depart.

The Panchen Lama then blessed Jang gya and the court lamas by placing his hand on their heads. They then had tea and conversation. Jang gya then said, "This is a great day, as if the stars were in conjunction; everything went very well. The weather was good and the emperor took great pleasure in your company. I have been with this emperor [from childhood] until my old age and I have never seen him in such a joyous mood. It is a good omen that the lama and patron should be together so happily serving the teachings of (344) Tsong kha pa. Therefore I would like to give you a scarf in thanks." He presented a scarf, and the rest of the court lamas followed suit. The court likewise presented scarves, as well as the Mongolians, etc., who were present. From this day the expenses for the Panchen Lama and his entourage [of 300] were covered out of the imperial treasury.

Seventh month, twenty-third day; third day of visit

The emperor's family, the sixth and eighth (345) princes, five princes and princesses and his daughter Gurun Hexiao [1775–1823] each presented the Panchen Lama with scarves, and collectively they presented a mandala of ten srangs of gold. They also presented twenty double silk scarves, ten bundles of red "*masham*" brocade, twenty bundles of red brocade, ten bundles of orange brocade, ten bundles of velvet, altogether seventy bundles of brocade along with ten bundles of red and yellow heavy wool. Offering these various gifts of high quality, they wished the lama long life. The lama gave them a hand blessing and they all drank tea together. The Panchen Lama then reciprocated with scarves, a Buddha statue, one "*sharpa*" coral necklace, and five bundles of weaving for each one. As a collective gift for the group he gave five statues, seventy bundles of incense, five bundles of fine weaving and twenty-five bundles of common weaving.

When the [six-year-old] princess Gurun Hexiao visited the Panchen Lama, the emperor sent a message: "This princess is very interested in the dharma. I treat her equally with my sons in gifts and love. This daughter's good tendencies must be a result of her devotion to Buddhism in her previous life. So she has strong faith in you, and is very interested in visiting you. I send her to you with my princes. (346) Please bless her for benefit in her life, Panchen Erdeni." When they had the tea ceremony, the Panchen Lama engaged the princess in conversation, asking her questions. He asked, "Princess, please sit cross-legged [rather than kneel]." The princess answered, "I cannot sit cross-legged before my father, so it would not be good to sit in front of a lama that way. I am more used to this so it is more comfortable for me." The Panchen Lama said, "Even though this daughter of the bodhisattva emperor is very young, she is able to make these distinctions. She must be a bodhisattva, a manifestation of the dakini. How interesting!" The princess asked the Panchen to teach her and give her a name in Tibetan. The Panchen Lama gave her the transmission teaching of Amitayus, White and Green Tara, and White Tara's mantra. He gave her the name Sonam Belgyi Dolma (Savioress of Glorious Merit). Immediately she asked one of the ministers to bring a pen and paper saying, (347) "It is not good to forget the name the lama gave me" and she wrote it in Manchu. The Panchen Lama also performed an exorcism that entailed visualizing Vajrapani against future obstacles for her. He then gave her a protection cord. He also gave her a Buddha statue, a coral necklace, five bundles of weaving, fifteen bundles of incense, and one bundle of fine weaving suitable for robe-making. The princess then removed her own special rosary made of medicinal wood and inlaid with jewels and offered it to the Panchen Lama, asking him, "Guide me for many lives."

Seventh month, twenty-third day; fourth day of visit

(350) Accompanied by the sixth imperial prince and the home ministers, the Panchen Lama went on horseback to the palace. He left his own entourage outside the main gate of the wall and proceeded only with his cook. He rode a sedan chair carried by eunuchs, with an escort of fifteen.

It was almost two miles to the Garden of Ten Thousand Trees. The Garden is huge and green, and in it there was a large Mongolian tent. . . . In the center of the tent is a big square throne . . . with three sets of stairs, one each on left and right. On the main throne platform was an extra throne. The backrest is high and covered with dragons and jeweled finials. In the middle of the backrest are painted clouds. In front of the formal jewelled throne is the Manjushri emperor's throne, very wide, with cushions and armrests, facing south. To the right side of the throne is another throne, likewise with cushions and a backrest – this was the Panchen Lama's throne.

(352) They met in the Great Tent. The emperor held the Panchen Lama's hand and escorted him up the three levels of stairs to the throne. The Panchen Lama stood, waiting for the emperor to sit. The emperor then said, "take a seat." The Lama and Patron sat down at the same time . . . [other lamas and princes were arranged to their left, behind and below and in front of them].

(353) Lama and Patron were served from 100 golden dishes, on yellow tablecloths. Everyone else had 50 silver plates on white tablecloths. Before the emperor tasted his food, he presented three of his dishes to the Panchen Lama. The Panchen Lama's cook, his chamberlain, manager, two lay officials, and the Tibetan abbot of the Yonghe gong were in attendance. During two servings of tea, there were performances of Mongolian music. Then Manchu and Zunghar boys wrestled. Acrobats climbed wooden ladders and performed tumbles. Magicians did tricks, followed by displays of horsemanship. Many eunuchs performed historical plays and sang opera. There were many and varied performances, just as would be in the Pure Land.

The emperor talked with the Panchen Lama. "The weather is very hot. Are you bothered by the hot weather?" The Lama replied, "No, not at all. The weather is neither hot, nor cold, but perfect. I have no problem with the water here. I am content, my mind is clear, and I am happy here." (354) The emperor replied, "That is wonderful. I see that the Lama looks very healthy, which makes me happy. Today is a fortunate day, because, thanks to the kindness of Panchen Erdeni, God of the Sky and the Three Jewels, my kingdom is happy and peaceful. The teachings of the Yellow Hat have spread. The Manchus and the Inner Eight Banners, the Outer Forty-nine Tribes of Mongolia, and the seven tribes of the Khalkha, the Aoslod, Torghut, Zunghars, and so on who join us here – they also enjoy strong faith and happiness. Sometime I would like you to attend prayers with the monks in the Potala Temple and in Tashilhumpo to teach them. I will attend too. This year, on my seventieth birthday, you were able to come and I was able to see you. This is good fortune for me."

The Panchen Lama answered, "You are the God of the Sky, the Manjushri Emperor, who brings peace and happiness to the world, who spreads Buddhism and the special teachings of Tsong kha pa. For all beings under the sky, you bring (355) religion, wealth, and happiness. Thanks to your kindness, an insignificant lama like myself is able to attend your seventieth birthday and meet you. I cannot repay this, but I will follow your golden orders and visit Potala and Tashilunpho [i.e. their Chengde models] to pray for your long life and a long reign over your kingdom." After that, they had a long, happy discussion of Buddhism and politics.

Seventh month, twenty-fifth day; fifth day of visit

(358) Starting on this day, there were ten days of Chinese opera. The emperor invited the Panchen Lama to attend at least the opening, but said the lama did not have to attend the rest. The emperor's daughter, the princess [Gurun Hexiao], presented the Panchen Lama with a pearl necklace, saying that when she had received his teaching a few days before, she had brought nothing to give him. The Panchen Lama accepted the necklace, and blessed her in return.

The sixth imperial prince went to Tashilunpo to receive the Panchen Lama and accompany him back to the palace on horseback. ... (359) When they reached the shore of the lake, the Panchen Lama, the prince, the Jang gya khutukhtu, along with other imperial court lamas, all embarked on a yacht. The opera was to be held at the emperor's mother's residence. Curtains had been erected in front of the throne. ... [The seating arrangements for lamas, princes, etc. are given in detail.] (360) The emperor sent home minister Efu Gung to say, "this place is my [late] mother's, the empress dowager's, room. That the Panchen Erdeni is here will benefit my mother. ... I am not coming today because when I go into that room I get upset and miss my mother. Pray for my mother. The performance is in the Chinese language. Even if you don't understand it, stay there and have a rest."

[The following sections describe the Long Life ceremony which the Panchen Lama performed for the emperor. The titles and gifts exchanged are given in great detail.]

Eighth month, fourteenth day; twenty-fourth day of visit

(398) The Panchen Lama wrote to the emperor thanking him for his frequent gifts. He included a present and sent it to the emperor. That same day the Panchen Lama, the sixth prince [and others, making a party of fifteen] (399) left for the palace at the emperor's invitation. Yurts were set up around the palace, decorated with "*ganjera*" yellow tops. Many ministers and officials turned out in their uniforms and waited on either side of the road on the way to the tents. They held umbrellas and weapons and played music. The Panchen Lama arrived at the tent in a palanquin.

. . . As soon as the Panchen Lama sat down [on a small throne], ministers and eunuchs came to receive hand blessings. Some eunuchs and ministers requested a "teaching-connection," so the Panchen Lama gave transmissions of the mantras of Mig se ma, Rigsum Gonpo, White and Green Taras, and Amitayus. Then they heard musicians, (400) and the emperor arrived at the yellow screen, where the tents were. The emperor and the Panchen Lama exchanged scarves as equals (*mjal dar rtse sprod*). The emperor held the Panchen Lama's hand in such a way as to indicate that he was taking the Panchen Lama to the tent [with his palm up, and the Panchen Lama's hand facing down]. They sat down on the same throne, the emperor facing to the south and the Lama facing to the East. In front of the throne, fifteen feet away, sat the emperor's court lamas, the Panchen Lama's retinue, and Mongolian leaders. To the left sat the emperor's family and inner ministers. From their knees, the emperor's servants offered tea with dairy products – butter, cheese, milk, and yogurt – along with sugar, honey, and brown sugar. After serving the emperor and the Panchen Lama, they served everyone, kneeling to all. While tea was being served, wrestlers wrestled as entertainment; boys from Rjyal Mo Rong sang and danced. Chinese boys did circus stunts, such as flips, cartwheels, and standing on each other's shoulders, as well as many magic tricks. Other boys danced dressed as yaks and snow lions. People from Lha Tang gave a puppet show. . . . Then, on the south side of the garden, Byand nkang rtse pa and others held an opera until sundown.

After sunset, the emperor (401) said, "Pingkogs!" Immediately, He Tsi Ting, in charge, brought enormous lights and placed them in the center of where they were sitting. The fire took on many different shapes – some trees, some bushes, 35 hands high. It was magic for the eyes. Not only were [the flames] shaped like trees, but they had many different colored leaves. Then the emperor said "Chikogs!" and the ministers came in front to the left of the throne and placed cotton rope in the fire. The fire circled around and took the shapes of the Eight Auspicious Symbols. In the front of the garden appeared fireworks in the shapes of different people dancing together. Some of the shapes turned into the shapes of the people who handled the fireworks. Then all the fireworks went off in the air, creating a great noise. In the middle of the firecrackers were hundreds of people dressed in red brocade uniforms, (402) holding firecrackers in the form of bells. Some were sitting, some standing, facing in all directions. Sparks emanated from the bell-shaped fireworks, making Chinese letters, which the emperor translated in Tibetan as *Ku Tu Bda Wai 'gling*, Place of All Happiness.

While they were watching the fire performance, both *mchod* and *yon* [Lama and Patron] were very happy, making constant conversation, especially about the Eighth Dalai Lama's health, studies, efforts in learning, what initiations he had taken, and his debating classes. The emperor asked, "When he debates, is he calm and quiet or brash and fearless? What is he studying now?" . . . [After further discussion of the young Dalai Lama's curriculum, the emperor asked what special things he could do for the Dalai Lama in the future. The Panchen Lama replied,] "The Dalai Lama is omniscient and an emanation of Avalokiteshvara. He does not need to depend on studying and practicing to attain his goals, [but] to set a good example for his students and followers, he makes a great effort. His learning is extremely vast. (403) In the year of the fire bird, he studied with me the Lam Rim Chenmo, Vajra Mala [a collection of Tantric deities], Mitra Brgya Tsa, many mandala initiations, Dubthab Gyamtso [the Ocean of Sadhanas], Bari Brgya Tsa, many empowerments and blessing initiations. He received many deity initiations from me. After all, whatever I've received from my lama, Vajra Dhara, and the Seventh Dalai Lama, I give back to him entirely and I honor him as holder of all teachings of all Buddhism" . . . .

Ninth month, twenty-seventh day; sixty-sixth day of visit (now in Beijing)

(481) In the early morning, his cook asked the Panchen Lama, "How are you today?" [The Panchen Lama replied,] "I have no appetite but otherwise nothing else is wrong. My urine is not changing color." Everyone went to the emperor's palace, called Gyd shugs kung. The great [sixth] prince and Jang gya were present. The Panchen Lama received the same lunch as the emperor, but he did not eat much. (482) The great prince and Jang gya inquired about his health. Jang gya took his pulse, and said that he did not see anything serious in the diagnosis. "But there is a great difference between Tibet and here in terms of climate, water, and environment, so we must pay close attention to your health. Also, the great prince should tell the emperor about your health and ask to postpone your teachings." The Panchen Lama refused. "I am not seriously ill. Please do not tell the emperor, and do not worry, great prince."

[The Panchen Lama gave the emperor the blessing-initiation of six-armed Mahakala, following which many gifts were exchanged, and the emperor hosted the Panchen Lama to tea. After the emperor left the room], (483) the Panchen Lama said to Jang gya, "I feel released and happy. All my work is done. Now I will take a few days rest and I will be fine." Then he smiled. Jang gya immediately responded, "How can you say your work is done? As long as there are beings in Samsara your work is not finished. Do not say such things. You have fulfilled all the emperor's wishes, but now [you must] go back to Tibet to help the countless beings. Do not say such things, even in jest!"

(484) "Yes, you are right," said the Panchen Lama. "I just made a kind of joke. There are many things to do. So, I will pray as you wish."[3]

Notes

1   Translation from Dkon mchog 'jigs med dban po, 'Jam Dbyangs Bzhad pa II (Gonchok Jigme Wangpo, 1728–1791), *The Collected Works of Dkon-mchog-'jigs-med-*

dban-po II, the Second 'Jam dbang bzad of Bla brangfa bkra sis shis 'khyil (DMJMBP).
Page numbers from this edition are indicated in the translation. In preparing
this translation, I am grateful for editorial assistance from Angela Zito, Donald
Lopez, and James Millward. Editors' note: In the excerpted passages, names
and terms transcribed in Tibetan have, where possible, been changed to the
standard spellings used in the present volume. Names, terms, and utterances
(such as Qianlong's "Pingkogs!") that cannot be identified have been left in the
form suggested by their Tibetan transcription and/or placed in quotation marks
in the translation.
2 Puning si is also known as Dafo si or "Great Buddha Temple," for its enormous
statue of Avalokiteshvara (see Chayet, Chapter 4).
3 The Panchen Lama died of smallpox a few weeks later, on November 27, 1780.

17 Five poems by the Qianlong emperor

Translated by Scott Lowe

In Chinese accounts, the Qianlong emperor is sometimes credited with writing more than 40,000 poems over the course of his long, exceptionally literate life. The emperor himself modestly conceded that perhaps only half the poems compiled under his name actually emerged from his brush. Even if we assume the emperor to have erred in his own favor by a factor of two, he was still the author of more than 10,000 poems, a truly astonishing total for any mortal, much less for one actively managing the affairs of one of the greatest empires the world has known. Below, I translate five poems especially relevant to Chengde.

Shooting Bears[1]

> Silent, deserted, the Jade Emperor's fairyland is caressed by fall
>   breezes
> Paw-shaped frosted arrowheads are good for shooting bears
> But [I] laugh at Han Gaozu, [supposedly related to] the
>   Vermilion Emperor
> Merely sending women to be married – you're a hero?![2]
>   (1743, written on an eastern inspection tour
>   to the Mukden hunting grounds)

Red Leaves[3]

> Serried peaks of dark clouds dispel the clarity of dawn
> [I] suddenly see red leaves on a horizontal branch
> Hesitating, pacing, gazing at the scene, it is hard to complete a
>   sentence
> At several spots the rugosa roses set off the fine green jade
>   (1758, ninth month, while holding
>   court at Bishu shanzhuang)

Seventieth Birthday Celebration[4]

> A decade ago in the imperial palace [the dowager's] person was
>   not yet [gone]

[Now] at the mountain village [one] somehow hears rejoicing
   over "hills and mausoleums"[5]
Seven decades! [I] count on my fingers the six emperors, both
   recent and ancient
[who have lived as long as I][6]
Following the heart, [I] have experienced for myself their ways
   and warnings
From the northern borders people come without break for
   audience at the courts
West heaven welcomes the dawn, celebrating the "divine monk"[7]
We ought to speak of auspicious days, not speak of sad ones
Gazing east to the Pine Study,[8] the melancholy is unbearable.
                                     (1780, Bishu shanzhuang)

Written on the Road to Mozhou[9]

Earthen outer walls still stand at old Mozhou[10]
People's homes huddle tightly up against them
In the fourth month of every year they gather at the medicine
   market
Customs ought to accord with what is advantageous to the
   people.
                                     (1780, on the road)

Another Poem on Capturing Deer[11]

Autumn – deer gather in herds in this season
Taking advantage of free moments, [We] occasionally go hunting
Iron ball threading through [a pair of deer], the female falls first
Gunpowder smoke lingers, as the [mortally] wounded male
   gallops off
Can't say the eyes are as sharp as in former days
[We] distribute as usual [the meat], making many happy
Those Miao rebels,[12] one shot will hit two traitors
[This is] an omen that we may hope soon to be perusing victory
   reports.
                                     (1795, fall, Bishu shanzhuang)

Notes

1 Sun Piren and Pu Weiyi, eds, *Qianlong shi xuan*, 41. Sun and Pu have collected
   the original commentaries, written soon after the poems were completed, and
   identified most of the allusions.
2 Qianlong is referring back to a well-known exploit of his childhood: his facing
   down of a charging bear wounded in a hunt in Mulan, whereby he greatly
   impressed his grandfather, the Kangxi emperor, with his bravery. Qianlong
   contrasts his own heroism not only in bear hunting but in dealing with Inner

Asian nomad adversaries to that of the Han dynasty emperor Gaozu. Whereas the Han infamously appeased the Xiongnu with gifts and Chinese princesses, Qianlong here crows that his own more assertive means have proven more effective. Or, in the context of the last lines of the poem, perhaps he is hinting that bears, like rebellious subjects and bordering peoples, need to be met with sharp weapons and firm resolve.

3 Sun and Pu, *Qianlong shi xuan*, 174.
4 Sun and Pu, *Qianlong shi xuan*, 302–303.
5 The "hills and mausoleums" rejoiced over here are a metaphor for the longevity and high position of Qianlong, and a rather oblique reference to the birthday celebrations taking place in the distance as the poet writes.
6 The "six emperors" are the six sovereigns of Chinese history who managed to live past seventy. Qianlong seems to marvel at his own exceptional longevity. Of these other long-lived sovereigns (Han Wudi, Liang Gaozu, Tang Minghuang, Song Gaozong, Yuan Shizu, and Ming Taizu), the original commentary suggests that only the latter two were worthy role models. The other four appear to have served a cautionary function, by providing warnings of the results attendant upon ill-considered actions.
7 "Divine monk" (*shen seng*) indicates the Panchen Lama. "West heaven" evokes images of his paradise (S. Sukhavati, Ch. Jingtu), believed to be located in the far distant west.
8 Former residence of the dowager empress, Qianlong's mother.
9 Sun and Pu, *Qianlong shi xuan*, 301.
10 Mozhou was the birthplace of the reputed founder of traditional Chinese internal medicine, Bian Que, who lived during the Warring States period (403–221 BCE). Bian Que was elevated to divine status, so that in the time of Qianlong he was worshipped in Mozhou as the Medicine Emperor (Yao Wang), with a festival in the fourth month of the traditional calendar.
11 Sun and Pu, *Qianlong shi xuan*, 345–346.
12 The two deer killed are taken as representing the two leaders of the Miao, who were, in fact, captured soon after this poem was written. The Miao uprising was one of many in the closing years of Qianlong's reign.

18 Two folktales from Chengde

Translated by Karen Gernant

"The Pond of the Companion Moon"[1]

In front of the Wenjin Pavilion[2] at the Mountain Villa to Escape the Heat is a pool, called Pool of the Companion Moon. When travelers come here, they discover an odd thing: the bright, blazing sun is high in the sky, but the pond reflects only an image of the crescent moon. . . .

Legend has it that the Qianlong emperor came every year to the palace at Chengde to escape the summer heat. Each time he was in good spirits, he wanted a large banquet. . . . One year in the 6th month, he received news of more victories on the borders, and he was overjoyed. So there was a banquet where he and his crowd of officials drank their fill in the "Invite-the-Moon Tower" behind the large opera stage. At the banquet, while Qianlong listened to the officials' compliments, he was gazing at the scenery, which rivalled that of the Yangzi delta lands. Feeling very satisfied, he drank several large cups of wine one after another. When the crowd of officials saw that the emperor was happy, they, too, drank large cups of wine. After three rounds, Qianlong felt a little tipsy. The sun was beginning to set. The setting sun's bright rays were reflected on the gold inscribed plaque of the Invite-the-Moon Tower. Looking at the inscription he himself had written, Qianlong suddenly thought of the immortal poet Li Bai's poem, "Invite the Moon to Share the Wine" and began to recite it softly. . . . The official He-shen said drunkenly, "It's a pity that we have night and day, and that the moonlight can't shine for a long time on the golden wine vessel."

By this time, Qianlong was already 80 or 90 percent drunk. He was confused. He suddenly recalled that the Tang Empress Wu Zetian was able to order a hundred flowers to blossom in the winter. "I am also the Son of Heaven. My wealth is the whole country. Is it possible that the moon can't be reflected in my wine cup in the daytime?" When he reached this point in his thinking, he drunkenly put his wine cup on the table, and said loudly, "He-shen, listen to my decree."

Startled, He-shen . . . immediately knelt down on both knees and said, "Long Life, I'm here."

"Pass along my decree," Qianlong began. "I want to see the moon in the daytime, too. There must be no mistake." It made no difference that the emperor was talking drunken nonsense. If you didn't do this, you would be killed. The He-shen who was ordinarily arrogant and domineering in front of the officials now was just a "hen" (*caoji*). Thinking it over, he knew there was no way out of this one. When he got home, he blew up, frightening the servants so much that they all took cover.

He-shen had an old retainer, who was expert at offering rotten advice. When this servant understood the reason for He-shen's anger, he immediately came up with a devilish idea. He . . . asked, "Why are you so annoyed?"

He-shen hung his head and said sorrowfully, "Old Long Life drank until he lost his wits, and told me to issue an edict telling the moon to come out in the daytime. Isn't this the wildest fantasy? But if it isn't done, I'll be killed."

The old retainer . . . laughed and said: "You needn't worry. I have a plan." He-shen immediately asked what it was, and the retainer said: "It is foolish talk to order the moon to come out in the daytime. But the proverb says, 'One hundred skilled craftsmen will go first.' You can order a hundred craftsmen to figure out a way to create the moon. If they can do this, then you can stall Old Long Life. If they can't, you can just say that they made a fake moon and that the moon's essence went away. Denounce them. Isn't this a good solution?"

He-shen was delighted. He immediately summoned one hundred skilled craftsmen who were building the Eight Outer Temples. He dangled a reward: whoever could create a moon visible in the daytime – and do so within three months – would receive one thousand ounces of silver. If they couldn't do this, they would all be executed.

Everyone knew that He-shen – this scoundrel – had a black heart and methods like poison. Whatever he said, had to be done. But who had this abilty? Everyone discussed it from every angle. But no one thought of a way to do this. The days were passing one by one. Everyone looked at each other; they were all very worried. Those who were a little younger lay on the table and began weeping. Soon everyone was weeping and wailing. The sound of crying could be heard from far away.

One day, all of them cried until their throats were hoarse. Their tears also dried up. Dozing on the *kang*, they tossed and turned. Suddenly, outside someone was calling: "The moon for sale! The moon for sale!" Everyone thought this was odd. How could anyone sell the moon? They rushed out to look. It was a crazy old water porter. As he shouted, he asked the craftsmen: "Do you want the moon?"

Everyone . . . said, "Where does the moon come from? We are all going to die of worry soon. And you still trifle with us?" . . .

But the old man said, with enthusiasm, "There really is the moon. It fell into the well over there. I dredged for it for a long time with my wooden bucket, but I couldn't dredge it up. If you don't believe me, come with me to have a look!"

Everyone thought, since it was just noon, how could the moon have fallen into the well? But . . . two craftsmen went along with the old man. They reached the well. Hey! It was a circular rock covering the well opening that was reflected in the well. It was like the moon. The two raised their heads to question the crazy old man, . . . but he had disappeared.

When they returned and told the others of this, an old carpenter slapped his thigh and said: "Hey! This is Lu Ban's guidance. We'll make a pond. Beside the pond, we'll build an artificial mountain of rocks from Lake Tai[3] to cover the sun. Out of this artificial mountain, we'll chisel a crescent moon shape. It will reflect in the pond. Won't this moon be visible in the daytime?"

Everyone's spirits rose. They found He-shen and told him they needed rocks and other materials. They began their work at the lotus pond in front of the Wenjin Pavilion. Before three days had passed, the moon had been created. Everyone invited He-shen to look at it, and he was happy, too. But he also put on an act and gave some advice: a crescent moon wasn't as good as a full moon. He unyieldingly told the stonecutters to change the crescent moon into a full moon.

Then He-shen invited the Qianlong emperor to admire the full moon. When he saw the moon reflected in the pond, Qianlong was absolutely amazed. . . . He exclaimed, "This wonderful craftsmanship truly excels nature!"

When He-shen saw that Long Life was happy, he tried to ingratiate himself. "That gang of stupid craftsmen at first created a crescent moon. . . . I issued an order to create a full moon."

For a while, Qianlong was deep in thought. . . . Then he cursed, "That was truly stupid: How can a full moon be as good as a crescent moon!" He heaped a string of abuse on He-shen, and immediately ordered the craftsmen to change the full moon into a crescent moon.

. . . Qianlong wrote an inscription – "Pond of the Companion Moon" – and had it engraved on a stone tablet, which was placed on the artificial mountain in front of Wenjin Pavilion.

(Recorded by Wang Qi)

"The Dragons on the Roof of the Travel-Palace Temple"[4]

Among the travelers visiting Chengde, there was no one who did not pronounce the golden tiles and lifelike golden dragons on the roof of the [Xumifushou] temple wonderful. But an observant person notes . . . that there are only eight dragons, not nine. What happened to the other one?[5]

Legend has it that – in order to welcome the Tibetan Panchen Living

Buddha coming to pay his respects at Rehe – the Qianlong emperor had chosen an auspicious and wonderful place in Lion Gully for large-scale construction. He had a new temple built exactly like the Tibetan Potala – a small Potala palace.[6] More than 30,000 ounces of gold went into the golden tiles on the roof alone. The great [Miaogao zhuangyan] hall was decorated with gleaming gold and jade. Qianlong was very happy when he saw this.

Suddenly he noticed that the roof of the hall was missing some ornamentation. So he pulled out another 10,000 ounces of gold. He himself drew nine dragons, and he ordered that nine dragons should be made for the roof.

When the craftsmen received this order, they began casting dragons like the ones the emperor had drawn. These dragons were drawn oddly: they were like dragons jumping to the clouds and they were also like pythons running along the eaves. Moreover, each of the nine dragons was different. One was large, while eight were small. Some of their heads were raised to Heaven, some lowered toward Earth. Some ran ahead, some looked back. The workers wasted a lot of effort before they got this right. . . .

When they cast the first dragon, it came out as just a lump of metal. They cast another, and it was also just a lump of metal. More than 300 people worked for a year on the casting – and not one dragon was successfully cast. The Panchen Living Buddha would soon arrive to pay his respects, and the dragons hadn't yet been finished. The emperor was furious, and set a deadline of one month. If the casting still wasn't finished, all of the craftsmen would be killed. The craftsmen were very worried. Now there was nothing for it but to wait to die.

One day, the troops seized an old goldsmith and brought him to the site. This old goldsmith looked and looked at the furnace, and said, "To work this much metal, only if you sacrifice twins – one young boy and one young girl – to the furnace can you finish the casting." But no one had twins. Only the old goldsmith himself had a daughter and a son, who were already 4 *sui* old. In order to save the lives of all of the others, the old goldsmith resolved in desperation to sacrifice his own son and daughter to the furnace.

Everyone knew that it was not until the old goldsmith was fifty that these twins had been born. He loved them like his very life. Now, hearing that he would sacrifice his own children to the furnace, they all knelt before him and said they'd rather die themselves. They wouldn't allow the twins to be sacrificed to the furnace.

Holding back tears, the old goldsmith said: "We can try one more time. If we're successful, we won't sacrifice to the furnace." The people all believed him. . . . The old goldsmith saw that the metal had already melted in the furnace. He said he was going outside to relieve himself. After a while, he carried a large package back in. When no one was looking, he threw it into the furnace. The fire suddenly changed to a golden-red color.

Everyone thought this strange. The old goldsmith said, "The fire is ready. Open the furnace!" The nine dragons were all completed. After they had been gold-plated, they were even more beautiful.

The emperor looked extremely pleased, and at the travel palace there was a great celebratory banquet. But behind the hall, the old goldsmith knelt on the ground and picked up earth to use as incense to sacrifice to his son and daughter. As he did so, he was weeping. The flowing tears trickled . . . into a small creek.

Just as the emperor was raising a cup to the nine golden dragons he had designed, he suddenly felt rain on his face. He was greatly astonished. The sun was red, the sky blue: Where did the rain come from? A eunuch suddenly shouted: "The dragons are alive! The dragons are alive!" When the old goldsmith wept, the dragons all turned over in sorrow. They were crying. The emperor blanched in astonishment. When he heard the sound of weeping behind the hall, he immediately sent someone to investigate. Only then did he learn that it was the old goldsmith crying.

Furious, the emperor ordered the military to behead the old man. Just then, the largest golden dragon flew down from the eaves. It swept away several of the soldiers with its tail. Riding the golden dragon, the old goldsmith flew away. So, today, the temple of the Panchen Lama's Chengde residence is missing one dragon.

(Recorded by Zhu Yanhua and Wang Qi)

Notes

1   "Banyue chi," *CDDCS*, 10–12.
2   The Wenjin Pavilion (Wenjin ge) was built in the Bishu shanzhuang in 1774 to hold a copy of the enormous compendium of Chinese written works, the Four Treasuries (*Siku quanshu*).
3   Fantastically-shaped limestone rocks from Lake Tai in Jiangsu province are commonly used in Chinese garden landscaping.
4   "Xinggong miaodingdi long," *CDDCS*, 76–78.
5   In China, dragons traditionally come in nines (the Hong Kong district Kowloon, for example, is *Jiulong*, or "Nine Dragons" in Cantonese). There is an expression, "nine dragons wriggle on a roof" (*jiu long pan ding*), from which the issue of the "missing" dragon arises.
6   The story-teller confuses the Chengde Potala, or Putuozongcheng miao, with the Chengde replica of Tashilhunpo, the Xumifushou miao. The latter was the Panchen Lama's residence – his lodge or "travel-palace" (*xinggong*) in Chengde.

Part V
Epilog

19 Chengde today

James L. Hevia

In 1929, the noted Swedish explorer Sven Hedin began a search in north China for a perfect example of Chinese Buddhist architecture. He had received financial support for this venture from Vincent Bendix, a Chicago industrialist of Swedish extraction, who seems to have had an interest in Buddhism. Once Hedin had located such a specimen, he was to have two replicas built, one to be shipped to Chicago and the other to Stockholm. In the winter and spring of 1929–1930, Hedin led an expedition that examined a number of Buddhist temples in Inner Mongolia, not one of which, he later wrote, "measured up to our demands."[1] Aware of the Qing emperor's palace and temple complex at the Chengde Mountain Villa, Hedin arrived there in the summer of 1930, where he found what he described as "a gem of Chinese architecture and construction." This was the Wanfaguiyi Hall (Figure 13), the central temple located within the Potala reproduction (Putuozongcheng miao; Figure 12). Hedin dubbed it the "Golden Pavilion," and thereupon set about reproducing it![2] He also had extensive photographs taken of all the outer temples.

It is from this photographic record (and others from Japanese researchers) that we have some idea of what the Mountain Villa looked like after the fall of the Qing dynasty. The exteriors of all the main temples were in great disrepair and the facade of the Putuozongcheng Temple had lost much of its dark red stucco. The insides were in equally bad condition. The four-story wooden galleries that had once surrounded the Golden Pavilion were gone and the bright red enamel of the temple's pillars was almost completely worn away. We can assume that the palaces and pavilions in the inner part of the Mountain Villa were also in disrepair. Japanese scholars who followed in Hedin's wake provided similar accounts of decay,[3] but no efforts were made by any organization, private or public, to preserve the site at that time.

Meanwhile, the reproduction of the "Golden Pavilion" that Vincent Bendix had commissioned was shipped to Chicago, where it appeared in the 1933 Century of Progress Exposition. In a souvenir booklet prepared for the Exposition, Sven Hedin noted that "when the original Golden Pavilion of Jehol has become a pile of crumbling ruins and its glory is no more, its faithful replica on the shores of Lake Michigan will still with-stand the ravages of time." Given conditions in China in the 1930s, Hedin's prediction appears completely justified – perhaps the sole record of Chengde's glory would be the Golden Pavilion on a faraway shore. Soon, however, it too ran into difficulties. After appearing at the 1939 New York World's Fair, the temple was taken apart, sold to the Harvard Yenching Institute, and placed in storage for the next four and a half decades.[4] Hedin seems, therefore, to have been only partially correct – both the original palace-temple complex and the fragment of a copy that he made of it had slipped into obscurity as monumental events transformed East Asia and the rest of the world from 1937 forward.

After the Chinese Communists came to power in China in 1949, the Mountain Villa became part of the preservation agenda of the People's Republic. Little, however, appears to have been done to restore it to its former glory during the first three decades of Communist rule. With the economic reform program that began in the early 1980s, however, all this changed. The palaces and temples at Chengde were soon recognized not only for their historic value, but also as a possible source of tourist revenue.

If the English-language pocket guidebook series entitled "Discover China's Cities" is any indication, Chengde had entered the arena of inter-national tourism by 1988. According to the guide, Chengde boasted "the most magnificent classical imperial garden-palace complex in China, second only to the famous Forbidden City in the capital."[5] In the spirit of openness to the outside world, a catch phrase of the reform era, the book provided thoughtful advice about sightseeing, shopping, accommo-dations (including a yurt hotel that had been put up in the Wanshu yuan (Garden of Ten Thousand Trees; Figure 8), and opportunities for joint-venture investment in developing Chengde's mineral resources. The guidebook's advice was complemented by color-photographs of famous sites in and around the Mountain Villa, including one of a deer herd that roamed the inner park. The deer herd recalled not only the hunting tradi-tions of the Manchus, but also referenced wild game specialties to be found in the city's restaurants, several of which were mentioned in the guide. The most famous of these displayed a poem composed by the Qianlong emperor in praise of the restaurant's mastery of dishes from north of the Great Wall. Finally, the guidebook reviewed local festivals and indicated that there were a number of active religious communities in Chengde, including Muslims and Christians, as well as the Buddhist temples, some of which contained active monastic communities. These references to the open practice of religion was in keeping with the Communist Party's national policy of relaxing restrictions against religious worship, a policy which had became part of the reform program by the middle of the 1980s.

It was this guidebook that I carried with me on my first visit to Chengde in 1991 with several American research scholars based in Beijing.[6] At that time, the Putuozongcheng Temple was undergoing massive reconstruction.

The center of the structure, where the Golden Pavilion stood, was completely closed off, while other portions were only partly accessible. It was clear, however, that the restoration staff had to rebuild parts of the structure from scratch. Most notably, this included the inner galleries, the weight-bearing parts of which were then being constructed out of reinforced concrete. In contrast, the Xumifushou miao (Temple of the Happiness and Longevity of Mt Sumeru; Figure 14) was completely open. Although restoration work had yet to begin there, it was clear that it was in far better condition than the Putuozongcheng Temple. Even though they were in serious need of paint, the temple's inner galleries, for example, were intact. After visiting the rest of the outer temples, it appeared that the worst cases of structural damage indicated in the Hedin photographs had been addressed and a concerted reforestation project was evident in the hills surrounding the Mountain Villa. At the same time, however, there were few images or thangkas on display in any of the temples, and only minimal signs of worship. But this may have been related to the fact that there were few visitors in town at this time of the year.

On my second visit, things were quite different. In the fall of 1993, I returned to Chengde with a group of Chinese, European, and American scholars to participate in a conference commemorating the two-hundredth anniversary of the first British embassy to China. The conference was being held here because this was where the British ambassador, Lord Macartney, had been received by the Qianlong emperor in 1793. Although restoration was still underway, the Putuozongcheng Temple, with the exception of the Golden Pavilion, was almost completely open to visitors. The pavilion could be viewed from various levels of the rebuilt galleries. Moreover, in contrast to 1991, all the temples were bustling with visitors, many of whom had left offerings at the various shrines or were in the process of doing so as we passed through the temples.

The restored Putuozongcheng Temple also contained a message not visible in 1991. On one level of the gallery along an inner side wall, there was a painting of the Potala at Lhasa, in front of which was a text in Chinese and English. It told a brief story of the liberation of Tibet and of the support of Tibetan Buddhism by the government of the People's Republic of China. In addition, a shop had been opened and one could buy Chinese and English language books on Tibetan Buddhism, Sino-Tibetan relations, and the history of Tibet. One of them had essays that discussed the relationship between the Jang gya khutukhtu Rolpai Dorje and the Qianlong emperor, an analysis of the Chinese name for Tibet (Xizang), and "facts" about the 1959 rebellion in Tibet written by Tibetan and Chinese officials and historians.[7] These developments all suggested that Chengde had become caught up in the Chinese government's on-going international struggle with the exiled Dalai Lama. For those foreign tourists who could not venture to Lhasa, the restored Chengde Potala served as a staging site for the government's claims about its "liberation" of Tibet.

At the same time, other parts of Chengde were producing different kinds of messages. On Ruyi Island in the inner gardens (Figure 3), where restoration was also in full swing, a building for the performance of Chinese opera reminiscent of one in the Forbidden City contained a museum of opera props and Qing memorabilia. On the second floor in an L-shaped gallery, wax figures of each of the Manchu emperors in ceremonial court robes had been arranged. The significance of this particular element in the restoration project seemed to signal a re-evaluation of the Qing dynasty period in Chinese history, a situation that was mirrored by some of the papers presented at the anniversary conference. While the Qing were still taken to task for having missed an opportunity to import European science and technology into China, they were also lauded for having resisted aggressive European encroachment represented by the British and for representing the last moment of China's greatness before the disasters of the nineteenth century. This last theme was more broadly played out in the huge increase of publications in China about the Qianlong reign. The emperor was, himself, ever more present in Beijing between 1991 and 1995, appearing in wax effigy at the Temple of Heaven and the Yonghe gong, the Tibetan Buddhist temple he patronized in Beijing, and in a staged performance of the Winter Solstice Grand Sacrifice in 1991.

The image of the Qianlong emperor as a symbol of China's greatness was even more pronounced on my next visit to Chengde. When I arrived in July 1995, Chengde, along with the Potala in Lhasa and a few other sites in China, had just been placed on the UNESCO world cultural heritage list. According to the July 4 edition of the *China Daily*, the UNESCO list was established in 1972 as part of the "Convention Concerning the Protection of the World's Cultural and Natural Heritage," whose purpose was to safeguard "unique natural and cultural properties" from the damage caused by global development. As one of the 140 parties to the convention, China hoped to preserve its "diversified landscape features and 5,000 years of civilization."

The Mountain Villa's new status as a global as well as national treasure seemed to be epitomized in part by the large crowds of domestic and foreign tourists, including large numbers of overseas Chinese, present in the city in mid-summer. All the streets were bustling and there were good-sized crowds in the parks and temples. Since my last visit, the restoration of the Putuozongcheng Temple and a few of the other outer temples had been completed and work had begun on the Xumifushou Temple. But restoration marked only part of the changes now evident. For one thing, there were many more Buddhist images present in all the temples, and large thangkas adorned the Pule Temple. There were also numerous signs of active religious worship at all the temples.

Perhaps the most interesting developments were in the Putuozongcheng Temple itself. In a side courtyard overseen by the triple-tiered galleries and parapets on the top of the structure's massive walls, a stage had been set up. The galleries themselves had tables along the railings with waiters selling snacks, beer, and soft drinks to Chinese and western tourists. On the stage, people dressed in costumes representing Tibetans, Mongols, and other minority groups, emerged in turn, dancing and singing "ethnic" (*minzu*) music. After each group had performed, they took up positions at the front end of the stage. When they were all done, the Qianlong emperor and his consort emerged from a middle doorway in the rear of the stage. The minority peoples paid musical homage to the emperor and empress, and the show concluded extolling the virtues of the unified, multi-ethnic motherland.

This theme resonated with similar sentiments to be found in Chinese and English information boards at the entranceways to this and other temples. For example, at the recently restored Puning Temple, a sign indicates that the "temple fully manifested the interchanges and harmonies of culture between the Han and Tibetan people and the unity of the multi-national country."

These displays of national unity and the multi-ethnic character of the Chinese nation-state may appear incongruous at a religious site that also witnesses daily Tibetan Buddhist religious ceremonies in the same temples. But it is not too surprising when one considers a subtle shift over the last several years in the messages present in guide and souvenir books on the Mountain Villa. Recall the 1988 guidebook discussed above. According to it, the Mountain Villa had not simply been built for "pleasure-seeking," but because of its political and military strategic importance. The Kangxi emperor, we are told, saw Chengde as a site "to keep the peace in this troubled location and provide the restless tribes north of the border with a view of the Qing government's power."[8] It was, in other words, not designed to proclaim multi-ethnic unity, but to dominate the peoples of Inner and Central Asia. This interpretation of Chengde is absent from the Chinese and English language texts of souvenir booklets produced from the late 1980s forward. These tend, instead, to emphasize the aesthetics of the site, while in their prefaces, they claim that the site symbolizes the unity of the Han, Manchu, Mongol, Tibetan, and Uyghur peoples.[9] The latter message is much like that to be found on the stage at the Putuozongcheng Temple and on information boards around the Mountain Villa's Buddhist temples.

Yet, if Chengde has now been incorporated into the state propaganda machinery that promotes tourism, development, and international recognition of China's historical greatness, other messages also circulate here. A tourist map, for example, recalls the pre-reform era. Its caption interprets Chengde as an example of the labors and creativity of the Chinese masses, a reference to another version of Chinese history that expropriated imperial palaces from China's feudal aristocracy and returned them to the people of the People's Republic.

Other kinds of messages are evident in various parts of the park. Chengde is also a place for people to have fun, to enjoy the scenery, and to breathe

the fresh mountain air. Tourists can literally walk through the deer herd in the Mountain Villa gardens, play at nomadism by staying in the yurt hotel located in the Wanshu yuan, dress up in court robes and be photographed on palace thrones, or enjoy local opera performed on the stage at Ruyi Island (where the Panchen Lama was entertained in 1780). They can also row a boat on one of the inner park's lakes, have their fortune told, and join local people on a hike along the wall that circles the inner park. In this sense, Chengde has become a place where Chinese and foreign tourists can enjoy leisure.

Worship has also taken on a variety of forms, some of which are reminiscent of earlier eras when state sponsored cults vied with popular groups over the meanings and significance of sacred sites.[10] In the temples themselves recently restored images of Tibetan Buddhist gods and their consorts, officially justified as art, are draped by pilgrims with offerings which redefine them as active deities. In a few unobtrusive and previously neglected corners of the Putuozongcheng, Xumifushou, and Pule Temples, minor gods have been repainted in colors that could not have met the aesthetic standards of any restoration bureau, and inscribed rocks piled around tall poles adorned with animal horns mark each pilgrim's tribute to local gods.[11] Ever-larger numbers of prayer flags flap in the breeze near paintings full of otherworldly iconography.

To put all this in another perspective, Chengde has never lost its political, ideological, religious, and artistic significance. The Kangxi emperor may have built the site for bald political reasons – as a means to awe Mongol and Turkic peoples – but by the reign of his grandson, the Qianlong emperor, Chengde had increasingly become important as a place for patronizing Tibetan Buddhism. Moreover, since the Qianlong court promoted, and Tibetan Buddhist clerics reinforced, the notion that the emperor himself was an incarnate bodhisattva (see Lopez, Benard, and Ragnubs, Chapters 3, 10, and 16), the kinds of Tibetan Buddhist ceremonies that flourished here at the end of his reign went well beyond merely patronizing Buddhism. Further layers of significance were added when the Xianfeng emperor died (of disease, dissipation, or lightning) at the Mountain Villa after fleeing the Anglo-French invasion of north China in 1860. Chengde did not regain its prominence as a religious and political center of Qing imperial power for the remainder of the dynasty. By the time Sven Hedin arrived, the ruins of the palaces, pavilions, and temples of the Mountain Villa mirrored the fate of the Manchu dynasty, as well as that of monarchy in twentieth-century China.

And yet, the Mountain Villa did not become a "pile of crumbling rubble," as Hedin predicted. Instead, it was salvaged under the Communist Party's program of preserving the past within the safe confines of the institution of the museum and the public recreational park. Today, as an artifact of China's past glory, with the added imprimatur of UNESCO, the Mountain Villa furnishes ample opportunities for nationalist, internationalist, multi-cultural messages, and for commercial schemes. Perhaps this is no more than to be expected where fortunate configurations of the earth interact with human inventiveness. For if there has been one constant throughout the last three centuries, it is that Chengde's distinctive convergence of mountains, rocks, streams, and hot springs that first attracted the Kangxi emperor's attention three centuries ago continues to provide abundant resources for human beings to weave rich tapestries of aesthetic, political, and cosmological imagery.

Notes

1 Hedin, *Chinese Lama Temple*, 8.
2 Hedin, *Chinese Lama Temple*, 9.
3 See Igarashi Makita, *Nekka koseki to Seizô bijutsu*, and Sekino Tadashi and Takeshima Takuichi, *Nekka (Jehol)*.
4 In 1950, Harvard sold it to the University of Indiana and it was moved to a warehouse near Cleveland, where it languished until the mid-1980s. There were efforts to return it to Chicago in the 1970s, but they failed (see the *Chicago Tribune*, January 28, 1979 and *Century of Progress* records at the Chicago Historical Institute). Around 1985 the Swedish architect Max Woeler acquired drawings of the temple and eventually tracked it down in Ohio. Through a foundation he established, Woeler purchased the temple and moved it to Stockholm, where it was to undergo restoration. I am grateful to Elling Eide and Håkan Wahlquist, Keeper of the Sven Hedin Foundation, for sharing with me this information on the fate of the Golden Pavilion. For additional details on the temple's fate after 1939, see Barbara Lipton, "The Chinese Lama Temple," 261–267.
  Editors' note: Since Hevia wrote this article, the cause of the Golden Pavilion was once again taken up by Joe Scarry, a promoter of US–China business relations based in Chicago, who has attempted to continue the legacy of fellow Chicagoan Victor Bendix (see his newsletter, *Chicago China Newslink*.)
5 Yang Tianzai *et al.*, eds, *Chengde*, 6.
6 In the remainder of this essay, I draw on this and additional visits made in 1993 and 1995. On the first and last visit, I was accompanied by my wife, Judith Farquhar, whose observations are combined with my own in what follows.
7 See Hu Tan, comp., *Theses on Tibetology in China*. Also see Wang Furen and Suo Wenqing, *Highlights of Tibetan History*.
8 Yang Tianzai *et al.*, *Chengde*, 6.
9 See Zhang Wenxiang and Bo Qingyuan, eds, *The Mountain Manor for Escaping Summer Heat*, and Bo Qingyuan, ed., *The Mountain Manor for Escaping Summer Heat*, both of which were available in hotel bookstores and at various shops around Chengde in 1991 and 1993. A more recent publication, Xu Bang *et al.*, eds, *Chengde: Chinese Landscape Storehouse*, sold through China Books and Periodicals.
10 For discussions of such competition, see the articles in Susan Naquin and Chünfang Yü, eds, *Pilgrims and Sacred Sites in China*.
11 On this form of worship in Tibet see R. A. Stein, *Tibetan Civilization*, 203–206.

Bibliography

Adams, Vincanne. "The Production of Self and Body in Sherpa-Tibetan Society." In *Anthropological Approaches to the Study of Ethnomedicin*, ed. Mark Nichter. Tucson, Ariz.: University of Arizona, 1993.

Amiot, P. Joseph. "Monument de la transmigration des tourgouths des bords de la mer caspienne, dans l'empire de la chine." In *Mémoires concernant l'histoire, les sciences, les arts, les moeurs, etc. des chinois, par les Missionaires de Pekin*, vol. 1, 401–427. Paris: n p., 1776.

Aris, Michael. *Bhutan: the Early History of a Himalayan Kingdom*. Warminster: Aris & Phillips, 1979.

Arlington, L. C. and William Lewisohn. *In Search of Old Peking*, 1935. Reprint, New York: Oxford University Press, 1987.

Atwell, William S. "Some Observations on the 'Seventeenth-Century Crisis' in China and Japan." *Journal of Asian Studies* 45, no. 2 (1986): 223–243.

Aziz, Barbara Nimri and Matthew Kapstein, eds *Soundings in Tibetan Civilization*. New Delhi: Manohar, 1985.

Backhouse, Edmund, Sir. *Annals and Memoirs of the Court of Peking*. London: William Heinemann, 1914.

Bai Xinliang. "Qianlong jiating mian mian guan" (A View of Qianlong's Household). In *Gugong milu* (Secret Records of the Imperial Palace), ed. Zhu Jianjin, 198–209. Shanghai: Shanghai Literary Publications, 1991.

Baori jigen. "Menggu wanggong biaozhuan zuan xiugou" (An Examination of the Compilation of the "Genealogical and Biographies of Mongolian Princes and Notables"). *Neimenggu daxue xuebao (Zhexue shehui kexue ban)* 3 (1987): 19–32.

Barfield, Thomas J. *The Perilous Frontier: Nomadic Empires and China*. Oxford and Cambridge, Mass.: Basil Blackwell, 1989.

Barkman, C. D. "The Return of the Torghuts from Russia to China." *Journal of Oriental Studies* 2 (1955): 89–115.

Bartholomew, Theresa Tse. "Sino-Tibetan Art of the Qianlong Period from the Asian Art Museum of San Francisco." *Orientations* 22, no. 6 (1991): 34–45.

Bartlett, Beatrice. *Monarchs and Ministers: The Grand Council in Mid-Ch'ing China, 1723–1820*. Berkeley and Los Angeles: University of California Press, 1991.

Bawden, C. R. *The Modern History of Mongolia*, 2nd revised edn. New York: Kegan Paul International, 1989.

Bell, John. *A Journey from St. Petersburg to Pekin 1719–22*. Ed. J. L. Stevenson, 1762. Reprint, New York: Barnes and Noble, 1965.

Berger, Patricia Ann. *Empire of Emptiness: Buddhist Art and Political Authority in Qing China*. Honolulu: University of Hawaii Press, 2003.

Berzin, Alexander. "Tibetan Astro Sciences." In *Chos Yang, the Voice of Tibetan Religion and Culture, the Year of Tibet Edition*, 181–192. Dharamsala, India: Council of Religious and Cultural Affairs for H. H. Dalai Lama, 1991.

Beurdeley, Cécile and Michel Beurdeley. *Giuseppe Castiglione: A Jesuit Painter at Court of the Chinese Emperors*. Trans. Michael Bullock. Rutland, Vt: Charles Tuttle Company, 1971.

Bishu shanzhuang he Waiba miao quan tu (General Map of Bishu shanzhuang and Waiba miao). Chengde: n.p., 1980.

Bishu shanzhuang yanjiuhui (Research Committee on the Mountain Villa to Escape the Heat), ed. *Bishu shanzhuang luncong* (Collected Essays on the Mountain Villa to Escape the Heat). Beijing: Zijincheng chubanshe, 1986.

Bo Qingyuan, ed. *The Mountain Manor for Escaping Summer Heat*. N.p.: Huaxia Publishing House, 1993.

Bol, Peter K. *"This Culture of Ours": Intellectual Transitions in T'ang and Sung China*. Stanford, Calif.: Stanford University Press, 1992.

Bredon, Juliet and Igor Mitrophanow. *The Moon Year*, 1927. Reprint, New York: Paragon, 1966.

Brook, Timothy. *Geographical Sources of Ming-Qing History*. Ann Arbor: Center for Chinese Studies, University of Michigan, 1988.

Bulag, Uradyn E. *The Mongols at China's Edge: History and the Politics of National Unity*. New York and Oxford: Rowman and Littlefield, 2002.

Cahill, James. *The Distant Mountains: Chinese Painting of the Late Ming Dynasty, 1520–1644*. New York: Weatherhill, 1982.

Cai Jiayi. "Shiba shiji zhongye Zhunga'er tong zhongyuan diqu de maoyi wanglai lueshu" (Commercial Relations between Zungharia and China Proper in the Middle of the Eighteenth Century). In *Qingshi luncong* (Articles on Qing History), ed. Zhongguo shehui kexueyuan lishi yanjiusuo, Qingshi yanjiushi (Chinese Academy of Social Sciences Historical Research Center, Qing History Division), vol. 4, 241–255. Beijing: Zhonghua shuju, 1982.

Cammann, Schuyler. "The Panchen Lama's Visit to China in 1780: an Episode in Anglo-Tibetan Relations." *The Far Eastern Quarterly* 9 (November 1949): 3–19.

Cao Xueqin and Gao E. *Honglou meng* (Dream of Red Mansions; Story of the Stone). Beijing: Renmin wenxue chubanshe, 1982.

Cao Xueqin and Gao E. *The Story of the Stone*. Trans. of *Honglou meng*. Trans. David Hawkes and John Minford. 5 vols, 1973–1982. Reprint, Harmondsworth: Penguin, 1986.

CDDCS. See Chengde diqu minyan fenhui.

Chan, Wing-tsit, trans. and comp. *A Source Book in Chinese Philosophy*. Princeton, NJ: Princeton University Press, 1963.

Chan, Wing-tsit. "The *Hsing-li ching-i* and the Ch'eng-Chu School of the Seventeenth Century." In *The Unfolding of Neo-Confucianism*, ed. W. T. de Bary. New York: Columbia University Press, 1975.

Chang, K. C., ed. *Food in Chinese Culture: Anthropological and Historical Perspectives*. New Haven: Yale University Press, 1977.

Chayet, Anne. "The Jehol Temples and their Tibetan Models." In *Soundings in Tibetan Civilization*, ed. Barbara Nimri Aziz and Matthew Kapstein. New Delhi: Manohar, 1985.

Chayet, Anne. *Les temples de Jehol et leurs modèles tibétains*. Series no. 19. Paris: Éditions Recherche sur les Civilisations, 1985.

Chayet, Anne. "Une description tibétaine du Yuanmingyuan." In *Le Yuanmingyuan: Jeux d'eau et palais européens du XVIIIe siècle à la cour de Chine*, ed. M. Pirazzoli-t'Serstevens. Paris: Éditions Recherche sur les Civilisations, 1987.

Chayet, Anne. "Remarques sur les représentations d'architecture dans la peinture tibétaine et chinoise." *Acta Orientalia Academiae Scientiarum Hungarica* Tome XLIII (2–3), (1989; publ. 1992): 205–216.

Chayet, Anne and Corneille Jest. "Le monastère de la Félicité Tranquille, fondation impériale en Mongolie." *Arts asiatiques* 66 (1991): 72–81.

Chen Jinling and Zheng Guangrong. "*Mashu tu*: Weihu duominzu guojia tongyidi lishihuajuan" (*Horsemanship*: an Historical Painting about Preserving the Unity of the Multi-national Nation). *Wenwu jikan* no. 2 (1980): 77–79.

Chen Yunlong, comp. *Zhongguo bianjiang congshu* (Collected Essays on the Chinese Borderlands), 2nd edn. Taipei: Wenhai chubanshe, 1966.

Chengde Bishu shanzhuang. Beijing: Wenwu chubanshe, 1980.

Chengde Bishu shanzhuang waiba maio quan jingtu (A Panorama of Mountain Resort and Eight Outer Temples in Chengde). Shijiazhuang: Hebei renmin chubanshe, 1993.

Chengde diqu minyan fenhui (Research Group on the Folk Tales of the Chengde Region), ed. *Chengde di chuanshuo* (Chengde Legends). Beijing: Zhongguo minjian wenyi chubanshe, 1984.

Chengde dixu wenwu guanlisuo, comp. *Mulan weichang* (The Mulan Hunting Ground). Beijing: Wenwu chubanshe, 1986.

Chengde Gazetteer (*CDFZ*). See Hai Zhong and Lin Congshang, eds *Chengde fuzhi*.

Chia Ning. "The Li-fan Yuan of the Early Qing Dynasty." Ph.D. diss., Johns Hopkins University, 1991.

Chia Ning. "The Lifan yuan and the Inner Asian Rituals in the Early Qing (1644–1795)." *Late Imperial China* 14, no. 1 (June 1993): 60–92.

Choix des lettres édifiantes, écrites des missions étrangères. 3rd edn. Paris: n.p., 1835.

Chou Ju-hsi and Claudia Brown. *The Elegant Brush: Chinese Painting Under the Qianlong Emperor, 1735–1795*. Phoenix, Ariz.: Phoenix Art Museum, 1985.

Cohen, Paul A. *Discovering History in China: American Historical Writing on the Recent Chinese Past*. New York: Columbia University Press, 1984.

Cranmer-Byng, J. L., ed. *An Embassy to China: Being the Journal Kept by Lord Macartney during his Embassy to the Emperor Ch'ien-lung, 1793–94*. London: Longmans, Green and Co., 1963.

Crossley, Pamela K. "An Introduction to the Qing Foundation Myth." *Late Imperial China* 6, no. 1 (December 1985): 3–24.

Crossley, Pamela K. "*Manzhou yuanliu kao* and the Formalization of the Manchu Heritage." *Journal of Asian Studies* 46, no. 4 (November 1987): 761–790.

Crossley, Pamela K. *Orphan Warriors: Three Manchu Generations and the end of the Qing World*. Princeton, NJ: Princeton University Press, 1990.

Crossley, Pamela K. "Thinking about Ethnicity in Early Modern China." *Late Imperial China* 11, no. 1 (June 1990): 1–31.

Crossley, Pamela K. "Review Article: the Rulerships of China." *American Historical Review* 97, no. 5 (1992): 1468–1483.

Crossley, Pamela Kyle. *The Manchus*. The Peoples of Asia, ser. ed. Morris Rossabi. Oxford and Cambridge, Mass.: Blackwell Publishers, 1997.

Crossley, Pamela K. *A Translucent Mirror: History and Identity in Qing Imperial Ideology*. Berkeley and Los Angeles: University of California Press, 1999.

Crossley, Pamela K. and Evelyn S. Rawski. "A Profile of the Manchu Language in Ch'ing History." *Harvard Journal of Asiatic Studies* 53, no. 1 (1993): 63–102.

Cultural Relics of Tibetan Buddhism Collected in the Qing Palace – see Palace Museum.

Cura, Nixi. "Manchu Imperial Tombs: Interchanges in Iconography and Belief." Paper delivered at the annual meeting of the Association for Asian Studies, March 2003.

Da Qing huidian (Assembled Canon of the Great Qing). Guangxu edn, 1899. Reprint.

Da Qing huidian tu (Illustrations for the Assembled Canon of the Great Qing). Guangxu edn, 1899. Reprint.

Da Qing lichao shilu (Veritable Records of the Qing Dynasty). 96 vols. Reprint, Taipei: Hualian, 1964.

Da Qing tongli (Comprehensive Rites of the Great Qing) (*DQTL*). Qianlong edn, 1756.

Da Qing yitong zhi (Comprehensive Gazetteer of the Great Qing). 1764 edn. Reprint, Shanghai, 1902.

D'Anville, Jean-Baptiste Bourguigon. *Nouvel atlas de la Chine, de la Tartarie et du Thibet, etc., la plupart (des cartes) levées sur les lieux par ordre de l'empereur Cang-hi, etc., soit par les PP Jésuites missionnaires à la Chine, soit par les Tartares du Tribunal des mathématiques et toutes revues par les mêmes Pères*. The Hague: H. Scheurleer, 1737.

De Quincey, Thomas. *Flight of a Tartar Tribe*, 1837. Reprint, edited by Milton Haight Turk. Boston, New York and Chicago: Houghton Mifflin Company, 1897. Originally published in July 1837 in *Blackwood's Edinburgh Magazine* as "The Revolt of the Tartars."

Dehergne, Joseph. *Répertoire des Jésuites de Chine de 1552 à 1800*. Paris: Letouzey Ané, 1973.

Di Cosmo, Nicola. "State Formation and Periodization in Inner Asian History." *Journal of World History* 10, no. 1 (1999): 1–40.

Di Cosmo, Nicola. *Ancient China and its Enemies: the Rise of Nomadic Power in East Asian History*. Cambridge: Cambridge University Press, 2002.

Diamond, Jared M. *Guns, Germs, and Steel: the Fates of Human Societies*. New York: W.W. Norton, 1997.

Dkon mchog 'jigs med dban po, 'Jam Dbyangs Bzhad pa II (Gonchok Jigme Wangpo). *The Collected Works of Dkon-mchog-'jigs-med-dban-po II, the Second 'Jam dbang bzad of Bla brangfa bkra sis shis 'khyil*. 1785–1786. Reproduced from prints from Bkra sis 'khyil blocks. In the Gadan Sungrab Minyam Gyunphel series, 24. New Delhi: Ngawang Gelek Demo, 1971.

Dpal-ldan-ye-'ses, Panchen Lama III. *The Collected Works (gsun 'bum) of the Third Panchen Lama of Tashilhunpo Blo-bzan-dpal-ldan-ye-'ses*. Reproduced from tracings of impressions of the Tashilhunpo xylographic blocks. New Delhi: Mongolian Lama Gurudeva, 1975–1978.

Du Halde, (Père) Jean-Baptiste. *Description géographique, historique, chronologique, politique et physique de l'Empire de la Chine*. 4 vols. Paris: Lemercier, 1735.

Du Halde, (Père) Jean-Baptiste. *A Description of the Empire of China and Chinese-Tartary, Together with the Kingdoms of Korea and Tibet*, 2 vols. London: Edward Cave, 1738–1741.

Dumont, Louis. *Homo Hierarchicus: the Caste System and its Implications*. Chicago: University of Chicago, 1966.

Ebrey, Patricia Buckley. "Introduction." In *Marriage and Inequality in Chinese Society*, ed. Rubie Watson and Patricia Buckley Ebrey. Berkeley and Los Angeles: University of California Press, 1991.

Eisenstadt, Shmuel Noah. *The Political Systems of Empires*. London and New York: Free Press of Glencoe, 1963.

Elliott, Mark C. "Resident Aliens: the Manchu Experience in China, 1644–1750." Ph.D. diss., University of California, Berkeley, 1993.

Elliott, Mark C. *The Manchu Way: the Eight Banners and Ethnic Identity in Late Imperial China*. Stanford, Calif.: Stanford University Press, 2001.

Elman, Benjamin A. and Alexander Woodside, eds *Education and Society in Late Imperial China, 1600–1900*. Berkeley and Los Angeles: University of California Press, 1994.

Fairbank, John K. ed. *Late Ch'ing, 1800–1991*. Vol. 10, *The Cambridge History of China*. Cambridge and New York: Cambridge University Press, 1978.

Fairbank, John K. and S. Y. Teng. *Ch'ing Administration: Three Studies*. Cambridge, Mass.: Harvard University Press, 1960.

Farb, Peter and George Armelagos. *Consuming Passions: the Anthropology of Eating*. Boston: Houghton Mifflin, 1980.

Farquhar, David. "Mongolian vs. Chinese Elements in the Early Manchu State." *Ch'ing-shih wen-t'i* 1, no. 6 (1971): 11–23.

Farquhar, David. "Emperor as Bodhisattva in the Governance of the Ch'ing Empire," *Harvard Journal of Asiatic Studies* 38, no. 1 (1978): 5–34.

Feng, Mingzhu. "Waiba miao de xingjian yu Qingchu de xibei bianfang" (Early Qing Defense in the Northwest and the Construction of the Outer Temples). *Shihuo yuekan* (Taipei) 11, nos. 11–12 (1982): 506–513.

Feuchtwang, Stephen. "School Temple and City God." In *The City in Late Imperial China*, ed. G. W. Skinner, 580–608. Stanford, Calif.: Stanford University Press, 1967.

Fletcher, Joseph. "China and Central Asia, 1368–1884." In *The Chinese World Order: Traditional China's Foreign Relations*, ed. John King Fairbank, 207–224. Cambridge, Mass.: Harvard University Press, 1968.

Fletcher, Joseph. "Ch'ing Inner Asia c. 1800." In *The Cambridge History of China* vol. 10 (*Late Ch'ing, 1800–1911, Part 1*), ed. John King Fairbank, 35–106. Cambridge and New York: Cambridge University Press, 1978.

Fletcher, Joseph. "The Heyday of the Ch'ing Order in Mongolia, Sinkiang and Tibet." In *The Cambridge History of China* vol. 10 (*Late Ch'ing, 1800–1911, Part 1*), ed. John King Fairbank, 351–408. Cambridge and New York: Cambridge University Press, 1978.

Fletcher, Joseph. "The Mongols: Ecological and Social Perspectives." *Harvard Journal of Asiatic Studies* 46, no. 1 (June 1986): 11–50.

Flynn, Dennis O. and Arturo Giraldez. "Born with a 'Silver Spoon': the Origin of World Trade." *Journal of World History* 6, no. 2 (Fall 1995): 201–222.

Forêt, Philippe C. "Making an Imperial Landscape in Chengde, Jehol: the Manchu Landscape Enterprise." Ph.D. diss., University of Chicago, 1992.

Forêt, Philippe C. "La formation du paysage impérial mandchou." *Géographie et Cultures* 6 (1993): 84–104. Paris: L'Harmattan.

Forêt, Philippe C. "Les concepts géomantiques des trois capitales Qing." In *Asies 2. Aménager l'espace*, 123–137. Paris: Presses de l'Université de Paris-Sorbonne, 1993.

Forêt, Philippe C. "The Manchu Landscape Enterprise: Political, Geomantic and Cosmological Readings of the Bishu shanzhuang Imperial Residence of Chengde." *Ecumene* 4 (1994).

Forêt, Philippe C. "The Intended Perception of the Imperial Gardens of Chengde in 1780." *Studies in the History of Gardens and Designed Landscapes* 19, nos. 3–4 (July–December 1999): 343–363.

Forêt, Philippe C. *Mapping Chengde: the Qing Landscape Enterprise.* Honolulu: University of Hawai'i Press, 2000.

Franke, Herbert and Denis W. Twitchett, eds *Alien Regimes and Border States, 907–1368.* Vol. 6, *The Cambridge History of China.* Cambridge: Cambridge University Press, 1994.

Franke, Otto. *Beschreibung des Jehol-Gebietes in der Provinz Chihli. Detail-Studien in Chinesischer Landes- und Volkskunde.* Leipzig: Dieterich'sche Verlagsbuchhandlung Theodor Weicher, 1902.

Franke, Otto and B. Laufer. *Epigraphische Denkmäler aus China 1. Theil, Lamaitische Kloster-Inschriften aus Peking, Jehol und Si-Ngan, mit Unterstützung der Hamburgischen Wissenschaftlichen Stiftung.* Berlin: D. Reimer, 1914.

Fuchs, Walter. "The Peking Map Collection." *Imago Mundi* (Leiden) 2 (1937): 21–22.

Fu-heng, *et al.* comp. *(Qinding) Xiyu tongwen zhi* (Imperially Commissioned Multilingual Gazetteer of the Western Regions), 1763. *Siku quanshu* edn, 1782. Reprint, Minzu guji congshu, 2 vols, ed. Wu Fengpei. Beijing: Zhongyang minzu xueyuan chubanshe, 1984.

Gao Wende, *et al.* eds *Zhongguo minzu shi renwu cidian* (Dictionary of Historical Biography of Chinese Nationalities). Beijing: Zhongguo shehui kexue yuan, 1990.

Geertz, Clifford. *Negara: The Theatre State in Nineteenth-Century Bali.* Princeton, NJ: Princeton University Press, 1980.

Gernant, Karen. "Giving Voice to the Folk: Perceptions of Qianlong in Stories from Chengde." Paper prepared for the NEH Summer Institute, "Reading the Manchu Summer Palace at Chengde: Art, Ritual, and Rulership in 18th Century China and Inner Asia," Ann Arbor, 1994.

Gernant, Karen. *Imagining Women: Fujian Folk Tales.* New York: Interlink Publishing Group, 1995.

Goldstein, Melvyn C. *A History of Modern Tibet, 1913–1951: the Demise of the Lamaist State.* With the help of Gelek Rimpoche. Berkeley: University of California Press, 1989.

Gongzhongdang Qianlongchao zouzhe (Secret Palace Memorials of the Qianlong Period). Taipei: Guoli gugong bowuyuan; Gugong wenxian bianji weiyuanhui, 1982.

Goodrich, L. Carrington. *The Literary Inquisition of Ch'ien-lung*, 2nd edn, 1935. New York: Paragon Reprint Corp., 1966.

Granet, Marcel. *La pensée chinoise*, 1934. Reprint, Paris: Albin Michel, 1968.

Grousset, René. *The Empire of the Steppes: A History of Central Asia*, 1939. Trans. Naomi Walford. New Brunswick, NJ: Rutgers University Press, 1970.

Grupper, Samuel. "Manchu Patronage and Tibetan Buddhism during the First Half of the Ch'ing Dynasty." *Journal of the Tibet Society* 4 (1984): 47–75.

Grupper, Samuel. "The Manchu Imperial Cult of the Early Ch'ing Dynasty." Ph.D. diss., University of Indiana, Bloomington, 1980.

Gugong bowuyuan, ed. *Qingdai dihou xiang* (Portraits of Qing Dynasty Emperors and Empresses), 4 vols. Beiping (Beijing): Gugong bowuyuan, 1931.

Gugong bowuyuan, ed. *Qingdai gongting huihua* (Court Painting of the Qing Dynasty). Beijing: Wenwu chubanshe, 1992.

Gugong bowuyuan, ed. *Qinggong cang chuan fojiao wenwu* (Cultural Relics of Tibetan Buddhism Collected in the Qing Palace). Beijing: Zhijincheng chubanshe, 1992.

Guo Chengkang and Cheng Chongde, eds *Qianlong huangdi quan zhuan* (Full Biography of the Qianlong Emperor). Beijing: Xueyuan chubanshe, 1994.

Guoli Gugong bowuyuan, ed. *Shinühua zhi mei* (Glimpses into the Hidden Quarters: Paintings of Women from the Middle Kingdom). Taipei: Guoli Gugong bowuyuan, 1988.

Guy, R. Kent. *The Emperor's Four Treasuries: Scholars and the State in the Late Ch'ien-lung Era.* Cambridge, Mass.: Council on East Asian Studies, Harvard University, 1987.

Guy, R. Kent. "Who were the Manchus? A Review Essay." *Journal of Asian Studies* 61, no. 1 (February 2002): 151–164.

Hai Zhong and Lin Congshang, eds *Chengde fuzhi* (Gazetteer of Chengde Prefecture), 1st edn, Beijing 1830. Re-compiled by Ting Jie and Li Shiyin, 1887. Also known under the title of earlier edition, *Qinding Rehe zhi* (1781) and as *Rehe tongzhi*. Zhongguo fangzhi congshu saibei difang no. 17. Taipei: Chengwen chubanshe, 1968.

Harrell, Stevan. *Cultural Encounters on China's Ethnic Frontiers.* Seattle: University of Washington Press, 1995.

Hearn, Maxwell K. "Qing Imperial Portraiture." In *Portraiture, International Symposium on Art Historical Studies 6,* 108–125. Kyoto: Taniguchi Foundation, 1987.

Hebei sheng wenwu guanli chu, Chengde diqu wenhua ju, Weichangxian wenguanhui, eds "Qingdai Mulan weichang wenwu diaocha" (Investigation of the Cultural Relics of the Qing Mulan Hunting Grounds). *Wenwu jikan* no. 2 (1980): 86–99.

Hedin, Sven. *Jehol, City of Emperors.* London: Kegan Paul, Trench, Trubner & Co., 1932; New York: E. P. Dutton, 1933.

Hedin, Sven. *The Chinese Lama Temple: Potala of Jehol.* Chicago: Lakeside Press, 1932.

Henmi Baei. *Chūgoku Lamakyô bijutsu taikan* (Survey of the Art of Chinese Lamaism). Tokyo: Tokyo bijutsu, 1975.

He-shen (Hešen), Qian Daxin *et al.,* eds *Qinding Rehe zhi* (Imperially Commissioned Gazetteer of Rehe), 1781 edn. Reprint, Taiwan: Wenhai chubanshe, 1966.

Hevia, James L. "A Multitude of Lords: Qing Court Ritual and the Macartney Embassy of 1793." *Late Imperial China* 10, no. 2 (1989): 72–105.

Hevia, James L. "Lamas, Emperors, and Rituals: Political Implications in Qing Imperial Ceremonies." *Journal of the International Association of Buddhist Studies* 16, no. 2 (winter 1993): 243–278.

Hevia, James L. "The Scandal of Inequality: Koutou as Signifier." *Positions: East Asian Cultures Critique* 3, no. 1 (1995): 97–118.

Hevia, James L. *Cherishing Men from Afar: Qing Guest Ritual and the Macartney Embassy of 1793.* Durham, NC: Duke University Press, 1995.

Hilton, James. *Lost Horizon.* London: Macmillan, 1933. Reprint, New York: Pocket Books, 1992.

Hiroshi Onishi. "Portraiture Patterned After Images of Famous Buddhist Personages." In *Portraiture, International Symposium on Art Historical Studies 6.* Kyoto: Taniguchi Foundation, 1987.

Ho Chuimei and Cheri A. Jones, eds *Life in the Imperial Court of Qing Dynasty China.* Proceedings of the Denver Museum of Natural History. Series 3, no. 15. 1998.

Ho Ping-ti. "The Significance of the Ch'ing Period in Chinese History," *Journal of Asian Studies* 26, no. 2 (1967): 189–195.

Ho, Ping-Ti. "In Defense of Sinicization: a Rebuttal of Evelyn Rawski's 'Reenvisioning the Qing.'" *Journal of Asian Studies* 57, no. 1 (February 1998): 123–155.

Hobsbawm, Eric and Terence Ranger, eds *The Invention of Tradition.* Cambridge and New York: Cambridge University Press, 1983.

Holmgren, Jennifer. "Imperial Marriage in the Native Chinese and Non-Han State, Han to Ming." In *Marriage and Inequality in Chinese Society*, ed. Rubie Watson and Patricia Buckley Ebrey, 58–96. Berkeley and Los Angeles: University of California Press, 1991.

Hostetler, Laura. *Qing Colonial Enterprise: Ethnography and Cartography in Early Modern China.* Chicago: University of Chicago Press, 2001.

Hou Ching-lang and Michèle Pirazzoli. "Les chasses d'automne de l'Empereur Qianlong à Mulan." *T'oung pao* 65, nos. 1–3 (1979): 13–50.

Hou Ching-lang. *Mulan tu.* Taipei, 1983.

Hou Renzhi, ed. *Beijing lishi dituji* (Historical Atlas of Beijing). Beijing: Beijing lishi dituji bianweihui, 1985.

Hu Tan, comp. *Theses on Tibetology in China.* Beijing: China Tibetology Publishing House, 1991.

Hu Wenkai. *Lidai funü juzuo kao.* Shanghai: Shangwu, 1957. Revised edn, Shanghai: Shanghai guji chubanshe, 1985.

Huang, Pei. *Autocracy at Work.* Bloomington, Ind.: Indiana University Press, 1974.

Huang, Ray. *1587: A Year of No Significance: The Ming Dynasty in Decline.* New Haven: Yale University Press, 1981.

Hucker, Charles. *A Dictionary of Official Titles in Imperial China.* Stanford, Calif.: Stanford University Press, 1985.

Hummel, Arthur W. *Eminent Chinese of the Ch'ing Period (1644–1912)*, 2 vols. Washington: US Government Printing Office, 1943–1944; Reprint, 2 vols in 1. Taipei: Ch'eng-wen, 1970.

Igarashi Makita. *Nekka koseki to Seizô bijutsu* (The Rehe Remains of Tibetan Buddhist Art). Tokyo: Kôyôashakan, 1942.

Ishihama Yumiko. "A Study of the Seals and Titles Conferred by the Dalai Lama." *Tibetan Studies* (Naritasan Shinshoji, Narita) (1992): 501–514.

Jagchid, Sechin. "Mongolian-Manchu Intermarriage in the Ch'ing Period." *Zentralasiatische Studien* 19 (1986): 68–87.

Jagchid, Sechin and Charles Bawden. "Notes on Hunting of Some Nomadic People of Central Asia." *Asiatische Forschungen* 26 (1968) ("Die Jagd bei den Altaischen Völkern").

Jagchid, Sechin and Paul Hyer. *Mongolia's Culture and Society.* Boulder, Col.: Westview Press, 1979.

Jagchid, Sechin and Van Jay Symons. *Peace, War, and Trade along the Great Wall: Nomadic-Chinese Interaction through Two Millennia.* Translation and abridgement of Jagchid, *Bei Ya youmu minzu yu zhongyuan nongye minzu jian de heping, zhanzheng, yu maoyi zhi guanxi.* Bloomington, Ind.: Indiana University Press, 1989.

Jiaqing chongxiu yitong zhi (Comprehensive Gazetteer of the Great Qing, Jiaqing recompiled edition). Reprint, Beijng: Zhonghua shuju, 1986.

Johnson, David. "Communication, Class and Consciousness in Late Imperial China." In *Popular Culture in Late Imperial China*, ed. D. Johnson, A. J. Nathan, and E. S. Rawski, 34–72. Berkeley and Los Angeles: University of California Press, 1985.

Johnson, David, Andrew J. Nathan, and Evelyn S. Rawski, eds *Popular Culture in Late Imperial China.* Berkeley and Los Angeles: University of California Press, 1985.

Juvaini, 'Ata-malik. *Genghis Khan, the History of the World Conqueror.* Trans. J. A. Boyle, Manchester: Manchester University Press, 1958.

Kahn, Harold L. "The Politics of Filiality: Justification for Imperial Action in Eighteenth-Century China." *Journal of Asian Studies* 26, no. 2 (1967): 197–203.

Kahn, Harold L. *Monarchy in the Emperor's Eyes: Image and Reality in the Ch'ien-lung Reign*. Cambridge, Mass.: Harvard University Press, 1971.

Kahn, Harold L. "A Matter of Taste: the Monumental and Exotic in the Qianlong Reign." In *The Elegant Brush: Chinese Painting Under the Qianlong Emperor, 1735–1795*, ed. Chou Ju-hsi and Claudia Brown, 288–302. Phoenix, Ariz.: Phoenix Art Museum, 1985.

Kämpfe, Hans Rainer. *Ñi-ma'i 'od-zer/Naran-u gerel. Die Biographie des 2. Pekinger lCan-skya Qutuqtu Rol-pa'i rdo-rje (1717–1786)*. Monumenta Tibetica Historica, Abteilung (Series) II, Band (vol.) 1. St Augustin: VGH Wissenschaftsverlag, 1976.

Kanda Nobuo, ed. *Manbun rōtō* (Old Manchu Annals). Tokyo: Tōyō Bunko, 1955–1963.

Kennedy, Paul M. *The Rise and Fall of the Great Powers: Economic Change and Military Conflict from 1500 to 2000*, 1st edn. New York: Random House, 1987.

Kessler, Lawrence D. *K'ang-hsi and the Consolidation of Ch'ing Rule, 1661–1684*. Chicago: University of Chicago Press, 1976.

Khazanov, Anatoly M. *Nomads and the Outside World*, 2nd edn. Trans. Julia Crookenden. Madison: University of Wisconsin Press, 1983.

Khodarkovsky, Michael. *Where Two Worlds Met: The Russian State and the Kalmyk Nomads, 1600–1771*. Ithaca, NY: Cornell University Press, 1992.

Kipnis, Andrew. "(Re)inventing *Li: koutou* and Subjectification in Rural Shandong." In *Body, Subject and Power in China*, ed. A. Zito and T. E. Barlow, 201–223. Chicago: University of Chicago Press, 1994.

Ku Cheng-mei. "A Review of Su Bai's 'The Remains of the Liang-zhou Stone-caves and the Liang-zhou Model.'" Paper presented at the Dunhuang Symposium, Dunhuang, 1987.

Kuhn, Philip A. *Soulstealers: the Chinese Sorcery Scare of 1768*. Cambridge, Mass.: Harvard University Press, 1990.

Larsen, Jeanne. *Manchu Palaces*. New York: Henry Holt and Co., 1996.

Lattimore, Owen. "The Geographical Factor in Mongol History." In *Studies in Frontier History: Collected Papers, 1928–1958*, 241–244. Oxford and New York: Oxford University Press, 1962.

Lattimore, Owen. *Inner Asian Frontiers of China*. New York: Oxford University Press, 1940. Reprint, Hong Kong: Oxford University Press, 1988.

Ledderose, Lothar and Herbert Buta, eds *Palastmuseum Peking: Schätze aus der Verbotenen Stadt*. Frankfurt am Main: Insel, 1985.

Lee, Robert H. G. *The Manchurian Frontier in Ch'ing History*. Cambridge, Mass.: Harvard University Press, 1970.

Legrand, Jacques. *L'administration dans la domination sino-mandchoue en Mongolie Qalq-a: Version Mongole du Lifan Yuan Zeli*. Mémoires de l'Institut des Hautes Etudes Chinoises. Paris: Collège de France, Presses Universitaires de Frances, 1976.

Lessing, Ferdinand D. *Yung-ho-kung: An Iconography of the Lamaist Cathedral in Peking with Notes on Lamaist Mythology and Cult*. Stockholm: Elanders Boktryckeri aktiebolag Göteborg, 1942. Reprint, Taipei: Huyoushe wenhua shiye, 1993.

Lettres édifiantes et curieuses écrites par des missionaires de la compagnie de Jésus collationnées sur les meilleures éditions et enrichies de nouvelles notes. Paris: Bethune, 1832.

Li Guoliang. "Qing chudi xi wu" (Military Training in the Early Qing Dynasty). *Gugong bowuyuan yuankan* no. 2 (1980): 3–8.

Li Guoliang. "Bishu shanzhuang yushan zatan" (Tidbits on Imperial Meals in the Bishu shanzhuang). *Gugong bowuyuan yuankan* no. 1 (1988): 83–85.

Li Ruzhen. *Flowers in the Mirror.* 1828. Trans. of *Jinghua yuan*, translated and edited by Lin Tai-yi. Berkeley: University of California Press, 1965.

Lipman, Jonathan N. *Familiar Strangers: a History of Muslims in Northwest China.* Seatle: University of Washington Press, 1997.

Lipton, Barbara. "The Chinese Lama Temple: the Golden Pavilion of Jehol." In *Treasures of Tibetan Art: Collections of the Jacques Marchais Museum of Tibetan Art*, ed. Barbara Lipton and Nima Dorjee Ragnubs, 261–267. New York and Oxford: Oxford University Press, 1996.

Liu Dunzhen. *Zhongguo gudai jianzhi shi.* (History of Ancient Chinese Architecture) Beijing?: Zhongguo jianzhu gongye chubanshe, 1984.

Liu Wu-chi and Irving Yucheng Lo, eds *Sunflower Splendor: Three Thousand Years of Chinese Poetry.* New York: Anchor Books, 1975.

Lopez, Donald S., Jr. *Prisoners of Shangri-La: Tibetan Buddhism and the West.* Chicago: University of Chicago Press, 1998.

Lu Yanbian and Li Wenshan, eds *Zijincheng dihou shenghuo, 1644–1911* (The Lives of Emperors and their Consorts in the Forbidden City). Beijing: Gugong bowuyuan, and China Travel Publishing, 1981.

Lu Yanzhen. "*Yu*: huangdi zuo de jiaozi" (Palanquins: The Sedan Chairs of the Emperor). *Forbidden City* 4 (1980): 9.

Lu Yupeng, ed. *Rehe minjian gushi jingxuan* (Anthology of Rehe Folk Tales), 2 vols. Beijing: Zhongguo minjian wenyi chubanshe, 1989.

Luo Yunzhi. *Qingdai Mulan weichang di tantao* (Research on the Qing Mulan weichang). Taiwan: Wenshizhe chubanshe, 1989.

Ma Dazheng and Ma Ruheng. *Piaoluo yiyu de minzu: 17 zhi 18 shiji de Tu-er-hu-te Menggu* (A Nationality Adrift in Foreign Lands: the Torghut Mongols in the 17th to 18th Centuries). Beijing: Zhongguo shehui kexue chubanshe, 1991.

Ma Dazheng, Huang Guozheng, and Su Fenglan, eds *Xinjiang xiangtuzhi gao* (Collection of Local Gazetteers of Xinjiang). Zhongguo bianjiang shidi ziliao congkan, Xinjiang juan (Chinese Border History and Geography Series, Xinjiang volume). Beijing: Quanguo tushuguan wenxian suowei fuzhi zhongxin, 1990.

Ma Hongxian, ed. *Bishu shanzhuang luncong.* See Bishu shanzhuang yanjiuhui.

Macartney, Lord George. See Cranmer-Byng, J. L.

Manbun rōtō. See Kanda Nobuo.

Mémoires concernant l'histoire, les sciences, les arts, les moeurs, etc. des Chinois, par les missionaires de Pékin, 15 vols. Paris: 1776.

Mencius. Trans. D. C. Lau. Harmondsworth: Penguin, 1970.

Meng Zhaoxin, *Kangxi Di* (The Kangxi Emperor). Changchun: Jilin wenshi chubanshe, 1993.

Mi-la-ras-pa (Milarepa). *The Hundred Thousand Songs of Milarepa: the Life-story and Teaching of the Greatest Poet-Saint ever to Appear in the History of Buddhism = Rje-btsun Mi-la-ras-pa'i Mgur 'bum b'zugs so.* Trans. and annot. Garma C. C. Chang. Boston: Shambhala, 1999.

Millward, James A. "Beyond the Pass: Commerce, Ethnicity and the Qing Empire in Xinjiang, 1759–1864." Ph.D. diss., Stanford University, 1993.

Millward, James A. "A Uyghur Muslim in Qianlong's Court: the Meanings of the Fragrant Concubine." *Journal of Asian Studies* 53, no. 2 (May 1994): 427–458.

Millward, James A. *Beyond the Pass: Economy, Ethnicity and Empire in Qing Xinjiang, 1759–1864.* Stanford, Calif.: Stanford University Press, 1998.

Millward, James A. "'Coming onto the Map': 'Western Regions' Geography and Cartographic Nomenclature in the Making of Chinese Empire in Xinjiang." *Late Imperial China* 20, no. 2 (December 1999): 61–98.

Mish, John L. "The Return of the Turgut: a Manchu Inscription from Jehol." *Journal of Asian History* (Wiesbaden) 4, no. 1 (1970): 80–82.

Mitamura Taisuke. "Shoki Manshū hakki no seiritsu katei" (The Establishment of the Eight Banners in the Early Manchu Period). In *Shincho zenshi no kenkyū*, 283–322. Kyoto: Tôyôshi kenkyūkai, 1965.

Miyawaki Junko. "The Qalqa Mongols and the Oyirad in the Seventeenth Century." *Journal of Asian History* 18, no. 2 (1984): 136–173.

Mote, Frederick. "The Intellectual Climate in Eighteenth-century China: Glimpses of Beijing, Suzhou and Yangzhou in the Qianlong Period." In *The Elegant Brush: Chinese Painting Under the Qianlong Emperor, 1735–1795*, ed. Chou Ju-hsi and Claudia Brown, 17–55. Phoenix, Ariz.: Phoenix Art Museum, 1985.

Mukherjee, Bharati. *The Holder of the World*. New York: Knopf, 1993.

Mulan weichang. See Chengde dixu wenwu guanlisuo.

Naquin, Susan and Evelyn S. Rawski. "Topics for Research in Ch'ing History." *Late Imperial China* 8, no. 1 (June 1987): 187–203.

Naquin, Susan and Evelyn S. Rawski. *Chinese Society in the Eighteenth Century*. New Haven: Yale University Press, 1987.

Naquin, Susan and Chün-fang Yü, eds *Pilgrims and Sacred Sites in China*. Berkeley and Los Angeles: University of California Press, 1992.

Nath, R. *History of Mughal Architecture*, 4 vols. New Delhi: Abhinav, 1982.

National Palace Museum and National Central Museum, Joint Board of Directors, eds *Signatures and Seals on Painting and Calligraphy*, vol. 3. Hong Kong: Arts and Literature Press, 1964.

Nivison, David S. "Ho-shen and His Accusers: Ideology and Political Behavior in the Eighteenth Century." In *Confucianism in Action*, ed. David S. Nivison and Arthur F. Wright, 208–243. Stanford, Calif.: Stanford University Press, 1959.

Oertling, Sewall J. "Ting Yun-p'eng: A Chinese Artist of the Late Ming Dynasty." Ph.D. diss., University of Michigan, 1980.

Okada Hidehiro. "Mongoru no bunretsu" (The Break-up of Mongolia). In *Kita Ajia shi* (The History of North Asia), ed. Mori Masao and Kanda Nobuo, 183–228. Sekai kakukoku shi, vol. 12. Tokyo: Yamagawa, 1981.

Okada Hidehiro. "Origins of the Dörben Oyirad." *Ural-Altaische Jahrbücher* (Neue Folge) 7 (1987): 181–211.

Okada Hidehiro. "Origin of the Čaqar Mongols." *Mongolian Studies* 14 (1991): 155–179.

Onishi Hiroshi. "Portraiture Patterned after Images of Famous Buddhist Personages." In *Portraiture, International Symposium on Art Historical Studies 6*. Kyoto: Taniguchi Foundation, l987.

Overmyer, Daniel. "Values in Chinese Sectarian Literature: Ming and Ch'ing Pao-chuan." In *Popular Culture in Late Imperial China*, ed. D. Johnson, A. J. Nathan, and E. S. Rawski. Berkeley and Los Angeles: University of California Press, 1985.

Palace Museum (Beijing), ed. *Cultural Relics of Tibetan Buddhism Collected in the Qing Palace/Qinggong cang chuan fojiao wenwu*. Beijing: Forbidden City Press, 1992.

Pedrini, Teodorico. *Concert Baroque à la Cité Interdite*. Musique des Lumieres. Auvidis compact disk, Astree E 8609. Paris, 1996.

Perdue, Peter C. *China Marches West: the Qing Conquest of Central Eurasia, 1600–1800*. Cambridge, Mass.: Harvard University Press, forthcoming.

Petech, Luciano. *China and Tibet in the Early XVIIIth Century: History of the Establishment of Chinese Protectorate in Tibet.* Leiden: E. J. Brill, 1972.

Peyrefitte, Alain. *The Immobile Empire.* Trans. J. Rothschild. New York: Knopf, 1992.

Pirazzoli, Michèle and Hou Ching-Lang. "Les chasses d'automne de l'empereur Qianlong à Mulan." *T'oung Pao* 65, nos. 1–3 (1979): 13–50.

Pirazzoli, Michèle and Hou Ching-lang. *Mulan tu.* Taipei: Guoli gugong bowuyuan, 1982.

Pirazzoli-t'Serstevens, Michèle. "A Pluridisciplinary Research on Castiglione and the Emperor Ch'ien-lung's European Palaces." *National Palace Museum Bulletin*, no. 4 (1989): 1–12 and no. 5 (1989): 1–16.

Pirazzoli-t'Serstevens, Michèle, ed. *Le Yuanmingyuan. Jeux d'eau et palais européens du XVIIIe siècle à la cour de Chine.* Paris: Éditions Recherches sur les Civilisations, 1987.

Price, S. R. F. *Rituals and Power: the Roman Imperial Cult in Asia Minor.* Cambridge: Cambridge University Press, 1984.

Qi Jingzhi. *Waiba miao beiwen zhuyi* (Annotated Translations of the Steles of the Outer Temples). Beijing: Zijincheng chubanshe, 1985.

Qianlong chao neifu chaoben Lifanyuan zeli (Regulations of the Li-fan Yuan, Qianlong reign Inner Court edition). 1756. Reprinted in *Qingdai Lifanyuan ziliao jilu* (Compilation of Regulations of the Li-fan Yuan during the Qing Dynasty), ed. Zhongguo shehui kexueyuan bianjiang shidi yanjiu zhongxin (Chinese Academy of Social Sciences, Frontier History and Geography Research Center), 1–168. Zhongguo bianjiang shidi ziliao congkan series. Beijing: Quanguo tushuguan wenxian weisuo fuzhi zhongxin, 1988.

Qijuzhu (Diaries of Activity and Repose). Microfilm reproduction. Beijing: Diyi lishi dang'an guan, n.d.

Qinding Da Qing Huidian tu (Illustrations for the Assembled Canon of the Great Qing). Guangxu edn, 1899.

Qinding Rehe zhi (QDRHZ). See He-shen.

Qing Gaozong yuzhih wen erji (Qianlong's Prose Writings, second collection). 1785. In *Qing Gaozong yuzhih shiwen chuanji* (Complete Collection of Qianlong's Prose and Poetry). Taipei: Guoli Gugong bowuyuan, 1976.

Qing Gaozong. *Midian zhulin, shiqu baoji sanbian* (Catalog of Paintings and Calligraphy in Palace Collections), 1744–1745, 1791, 1815–1817, 10 vols. Facsimile, Taipei: National Palace Museum, 1969.

Qingchao tongdian (Dictionary of the Qing Dynasty). Reprint, Taipei: Xinxing shuju, 1959.

Qingdai bianzheng tongkao (Encyclopedia of Border Affairs in the Ch'ing Dynasty). Reprint, Taipei: Bianjiang zhengjiao zhidu yenjiuhui, 1960.

Qingdai gongting shenghuo (Court Life in the Qing Dynasty). Taipei: Nantian shuju, 1986.

Qingdai huangjia lieyuan – Mulan weichang (The Qing Royal Hunting Ground – Mulan). Hong Kong: Yazhou chubanshe, 1990.

Qingshi gao (Draft History of the Qing). Ed. Zhao Erxun. Beijing: Peking Historical Association, 1928. Reprint, Zhonghua shuju, 1977, 1991.

QLSL. See *Da Qing lichao shilu.*

Rawski, Evelyn S. *Education and Popular Literacy in Ch'ing China.* Ann Arbor: University of Michigan Press, 1979.

Rawski, Evelyn S. "Economic and Social Foundations of Late Imperial China." In *Popular Culture in Late Imperial China*, ed. D. Johnson, A. J. Nathan, and E. S. Rawski, 3–33. Berkeley and Los Angeles: University of California Press, 1985.

Rawski, Evelyn S. "A Historian's Approach to Chinese Death Ritual." In *Death Ritual in Late Imperial and Modern China*, ed. James L. Watson and Evelyn S. Rawski, 20–34. Berkeley and Los Angeles: University of California Press, 1988.

Rawski, Evelyn S. "Ch'ing Imperial Marriage and Problems of Rulership." In *Marriage and Inequality in Chinese Society*, ed. Rubie Watson and Patricia Buckley Ebrey. Berkeley and Los Angeles: University of California Press, 1991.

Rawski, Evelyn S. "Re-envisioning the Qing: the Significance of the Qing Period in Chinese History." *Journal of Asian Studies* 55, no. 4 (1996): 829–850.

Rawski, Evelyn S. "The Creation of an Emperor in Eighteenth-Century China." In *Harmony and Counterpoint: Ritual Music in Chinese Context*, ed. Bell Yung, Evelyn S. Rawski and Rubie S. Watson, 150–174. Stanford, Calif.: Stanford University Press, 1996.

Rawski, Evelyn S. *The Last Emperors: a Social History of Qing Imperial Insittutions.* Berkeley: University of California Press, 1998.

Rehe Gazetteer (QDRHZ). See He-shen (Hešen), Qian Daxin *et al.*, eds *Qinding Rehe zhi.*

Rhoads, Edward J. M. *Manchus and Han: Ethnic Relations and Political Power in Late Qing and Early Republican China, 1861–1928.* Seattle: University of Washington Press, 2000.

Richards, John F. *The Mughal Empire. The New Cambridge History of India*, vol. I.5. Cambridge: Cambridge University Press, 1993.

Ridley, Charles P. "Theories of Education in the Ch'ing Period." *Late Imperial China* 3, no. 8 (December 1977): 34–49.

Ripa, Fr. Matteo. *Memoirs of Father Ripa During Thirteen Years' Residence at the Court of Peking in the Service of the Emperor of China.* Trans. Fortunato Prandi. London: John Murray, 1844.

Roerich, George N., ed. and trans. *The Blue Annals.* Calcutta: Royal Asiatic Society of Bengal, 1949–1953. Reprint, 2nd edn, Delhi: Motilal Banarsidass, 1976.

Rol-pa'i-rdo-rje, Lcan-skya II. *Grub chen Dril-bu lugs kyi 'Khor-lo-sdom-pa'i lus dkyil kyi dmar khrid 'zal 'ses bde chen gsal ba'i sgron me 'zes bya ba b'zugs so* (Practical Instruction for the Esoteric Visualization Practices Focussing on the kāyamandala of the Chakrasamvara Tantra as Transmitted by the Mahasiddha Ghantapada). Xylographic print from blocks carved in Gangtok, Sikkim in 1969. Sgan tog, Sikkim: s.n., 1972.

Rossabi, Morris. *China and Inner Asia from 1368 to the Present.* London: Thames and Hudson, 1975.

Rossabi, Morris, ed. *China Among Equals: The Middle Kingdom and its Neighbors, 10th–14th Centuries.* Berkeley: University of California Press, 1983.

Rossabi, Morris. *Khubilai Khan: His Life and Times.* Berkeley and Los Angeles: University of California Press, 1988.

Rowe, William T. "Women and the Family in Mid-Qing Social Thought: the Case of Chen Hongmou." *Late Imperial China* 13, no. 2 (December 1992): 1–41.

Ruegg, David Seyfort. "mChod-yon, yon-mchod and mchod-gnas/yon-gnas: the Historiography and Semantics of a Tibetan Religio-social and Religio-political Concept." In *Tibetan History and Language – Studies Dedicated to Uray Géza on His Seventieth Birthday*, ed. E. Steinkellner, 441–453. Vienna: Arbeitkreis für Tibetische und Buddhistische Studien, Universität Wien, 1991.

Ruegg, David Seyfort. *Ordre spirituel et ordre temporel dans la pensée bouddhique de l'Inde et du Tibet – Quatre conférences au Collège de France.* Publications de l'Institut de civilisation indienne, fascicule 64. Paris: Collège de France, Diffusion De Boccard, 1995.

Sanjdorj, M. *Manchu Chinese Colonial Rule in Northern Mongolia.* Trans. and annotated by Urgunge Onon. New York: St Martin's Press, 1980.

Sekino Tadashi. *Summer Palace and Lama Temples in Jehol.* Tokyo: Kokusai bunka shinkokai (The Society for Interntional Cultural Relations), 1935.

Sekino Tadashi and Takeshima Takuichi. *Nekka (Jehol: the Most Glorious and Monumental Relics in Manchoukou),* 4 vols. Tokyo: Tokyo Bunka Gakuin Tokyo Kenkyujo (Tokyo Institute, The Academy of Oriental Culture); Zauho Kankokai, 1934.

Sekino Tadashi and Takeshima Takuichi. *Nekka: Supplement.* Tokyo: Zauho Kankokai, 1937.

Shakabpa, Tsepon W. D. *Tibet: A Political History.* New York: Potala Publications, 1984.

Sima Qian. *Shiji* (Records of the Historian). Reprint, n.p.: Tongwen yingdian kan, 1903.

Sopa, Geshe Lhundup, Roger Jackson, John Newman, and Beth Simon. *The Wheel of Time: the Kalachakra in Context.* Ithaca, NY: Snow Lion Publications, 1985.

Spence, Jonathan. *Tsao Yin and the K'ang-hsi Emperor: Bondservant and Master.* New Haven: Yale University Press, 1966.

Spence, Jonathan A. *Emperor of China: Self-Portrait of K'ang-hsi.* New York: Knopf, 1974.

Spence, Jonathan. "Ch'ing." In *Food in Chinese Culture: Anthropological and Historical Perspectives,* ed. K. C. Chang. New Haven: Yale University Press, 1977.

Staunton, Sir George. *An Authentic Account of an Embassy from the King of Great Britain to the Emperor of China,* 2 vols and maps. London: W. Bulmer and Co. for G. Nicol, bookseller, 1797.

Stein, R. A. *Tibetan Civilization.* Stanford, Calif.: Stanford University Press, 1972.

Stein, R. A. *Le monde en petit. Jardins en miniature et habitations dans la pensée religieuse d'Extrême-Orient.* Paris: Idées et Recherches, Flammarion, 1987.

Stein, R. A. *The World in Miniature: Container Gardens and Dwellings in Far Eastern Religious Thought.* Trans. Phyllis Brooks. Foreword by Edward H. Schafer. Stanford, Calif.: Stanford University Press, 1990.

Steinhardt, N. S. "Liao: an Architecture in the Making." *Artibus Asiae* 54 (1994): 5–39.

Steinkellner, Ernst, ed. *Tibetan History and Language: Studies Dedicated to Uray Geza on His Seventieth Birthday.* Vienna: Arbeitskreis für Tibetische und Buddhistische Studien, Universität Wien, 1991.

Struve, Lynn. "The Hsu Brothers and Semiofficial Patronage of Scholars in the K'ang-hsi Period." *Harvard Journal of Asiatic Studies* 42 (1982): 231–266.

Struve, Lynn. *The Southern Ming, 1644–1662.* New Haven: Yale University Press, 1984.

Stuart, Jan and Evelyn Rawski. *Worshiping the Ancestors: Chinese Commemorative Portraits.* Washington, DC and Stanford, Calif.: Smithsonian Institution in association with Stanford University Press, 2001.

Su Zhecong. *Zhongguo lidai funü zuopin xuan* (Selected Works by Women of Successive Chinese Dynasties). Shanghai: Shanghai guji chubanshe, 1987.

Sun Piren and Pu Weiyi, eds *Qianlong shi xuan.* Shenyang: Chunfeng wenyi chuban she, 1987.

Sun Wenliang and Li Zhiting. *Tiancong Han, Chongde di* (The Biography of Qing Taizong Huang Taiji (Hong Taiji)). Changchun: Jilin renmin chubanshe, 1993.

Sun Wenliang, Zhang Jie, and Zheng Chuanshui. *Qianlong Di* (The Qianlong Emperor). Changchun: Jilin wenshi chebanshe, 1993.

Suo Yu-ming. "Study of the Portraits of the Ming Emperor T'ai-tsu." *National Palace Museum Quarterly* 7, no. 3 (spring 1973): 29–47.

Tada Fumio. *Geography of Jehol: Report of the First Scientific Expedition to Manchoukuo, under the Leadership of Shigeyasu Tokunaga, June–October 1933*, vol. 3. Tokyo, 1937.

Tan Qixiang, ed. *Zhongguo lishi dituji* (The Historical Atlas of China). Vol. 8: The Qing Dynasty Period. Beijing: Ditu chubanshe, 1987.

Tan Zhengbi. *Zhongguo nüxing de wenxue shenghuo* (The Literary Lives of Chinese Women). Shanghai: Guangming shuju, 1930.

Tang Bangzhi. *Qing huangshi sipu* (Guide to the Qing Imperial Family). Reprint, Taipei: Wenhai chubanshe, 1966.

Tang Junzheng. *Qingdai huang jia lie yuan: Mulan weichang* (The Imperial Hunting Ground of the Qing-Mulan). Hong Kong: Yazhuo chubanshe, 1990.

Taylor, Rodney L. *The Religious Dimensions of Confucianism.* Albany, NY: SUNY Press, 1990.

ter Molen, Joh. R., and E. Uitzinger, eds *De Verboden Stad: hofcultuur van de Chinese keizers (1644–1911)* (The Forbidden City: Court Culture of the Chinese Emperors). Rotterdam: Museum Boymans-van Beuningen; New York: Thames and Hudson, l990.

Terrill, Ross. *The New Chinese Empire: and What it Means for the United States.* New York: Basic Books, 2003.

Thiriez, Régine. "Les palais européens du Yuanmingyuan à travers la photographie, 1860–1940." *Arts asiatiques* 45 (1990): 90–96.

Thiriez, Régine. "Old Photography and the Yuanmingyuan." *Visual Resources* 1: 6/3 (1990): 203–218.

Thiriez, Régine. "Ernst Ohlmer, ein Amateur-Fotograf im alten Peking." *Hildesheimer Heimat-Kalender.* Hildesheim: Verlag Gebrüder Gerstenberg, 1991.

Thorp, Robert L. *Son of Heaven: Imperial Arts of China.* Seattle: Son of Heaven Press, l988.

Thu'u bKvan bLo bZang Chos kyi Nyi ma. *Collected Works of Thu'u bkvan Blo bzang Chos kyi Nyi ma.* Ed. Ngawang Gelek Demo. New Delhi, 1969.

Tianjin daxue jianzhuxi (Tianjin University Architecture Department), and Chengde shi wenwuju (Cultural Bureau of the City of Chengde), eds *Chengde gujianzhu* (Old Architecture of Chengde). Hong-Kong: Joint Publishing Company; Beijing: Zhongguo jianzhu gongye chubanshe, 1982.

Till, Barry. "The Eastern Mausoleums of the Qing Dynasty." *Orientations* 31, no. 2 (1982): 27–31.

Tillman, Hoyt C. *Confucian Discourse and Chu Hsi's Ascendancy.* Honolulu: University of Hawaii Press, 1992.

Torbert, Preston M. *The Ch'ing Imperial Household Department: A Study of Its Organization and Principal Functions 1662–1796.* Cambridge, Mass.: Harvard University Press, 1977.

Tsang Ka Bo (Zeng Jiabao). "Ji feng gong, shu wei ji: Qing Gaozong shi quan wugongdi tuxiang jilu" (Record of the Portraits of Ten Martial Heroes Commissioned by Gaozong of the Qing Dynasty). *Gugong wenwu yuekan* 93 (1990): 38–65.

Tsang Ka Bo (Zeng Jiabao). "Portraits of Meritorious Officials: Eight Examples from the First Set Commissioned by the Qianlong Emperor." *Arts Asiatiques* 47 (1992): 69–88.

Tuken. See Thu'u bKvan.

Turner, Samuel. *An Account of an Embassy to the Court of the Teshoo Lama in Tibet*. London: W. Bulmer and Co., 1800.

Valéry, Paul. "Préface aux Lettres Persanes." *Œuvres*. Vol. 1. Paris: NRF, Bibliothèque de la Pléiade, 1957.

Veit, Veronika. *Die vier Qane von Qalqa* (The Four Khans of the Khalkha), 2 vols. Wiesbaden: Otto Harrassowitz, 1990.

Veritable Records. See *Da Qing lichao shilu*.

Vinograd, Richard. *Boundaries of the Self: Chinese Portraits, 1600–1900*. Cambridge: Cambridge University Press, 1992.

Von Glahn, Richard. *Fountain of Fortune: Money and Monetary Policy in China, 1000–1700*. Berkeley: University of California Press, 1996.

Wada Sei. *Tōashi kenkyū: Mōko Hen* (Research on East Asia: Mongolia Section). Tokyo, 1959.

Wakeman, Frederic Jr. "High Qing, 1683–1839." In *Modern East Asia: Essays in Interpretation*, ed. James B. Crowley. New York: Harcourt, Brace & World, 1970.

Wakeman, Frederic. *The Great Enterprise: the Manchu Reconstruction of the Imperial Order in Seventeenth-Century China*. 2 vols. Berkeley and Los Angeles: University of California Press, 1985.

Waldron, Arthur. *The Great Wall of China: from History to Myth*. Cambridge and New York: Cambridge University Press, 1989.

Waley, Arthur, trans. *The Analects of Confucius*. London: George Allen & Unwin, 1938.

Waley-Cohen, Joanna. "Religion, War, and Empire-Building in Eighteenth-Century China." *The International History Review*, 20 no. 2 (June 1998): 336–352.

Wan Yi. "Qianlong shiqi di yuan you." *Gugong bowu yuan yuankan*, no. 2 (1984): 13–20.

Wan Yi, Wang Shuqing, and Lu Yanzhen, comp. *Qingdai gongting shenghuo* (Palace Life in the Qing Era). Hong Kong: Commercial Press, 1985. Reprint, Taipei: Nantian, 1986.

Wan Yi, Wang Shuqing, and Lu Yanzhen, comp. *Daily Life in the Forbidden City*. Trans. Rosemary Scott and Erica Shipley. New York: Viking, 1988.

Wang Furen and Suo Wenqing. *Highlights of Tibetan History*. Beijing: New World Press, 1984. Translation of *Zang zu shiyao* (Chengdu: Sichuan minzu chubanshe, 1981).

Wang Jiapeng. "Tuerhute donggui yu 'Wanfaguiyi tu'" (The Eastern Return of the Torghuts and the Painting in the Wanfaguiyi Hall). *Wenwu* 485, no. 10 (1996): 86–92.

Wang Laiyin. *Qing gucang zhaojie mi* (Revelations of the Secret Qing Palace Photographs). Shanxi: Shuhai chubanshe, 1992.

Wang Shuqing. "Qingdai gongzhu" (Princesses of the Qing Dynasty). *Gugong bowuyuan yuankan* no. 3 (1982): 31–38.

Wang Shuqing. "Qingdai gongzhong shanshi" (Provisioning the Palace under the Qing). *Gugong bowuyuan yuankan* no. 3 (1983): 57–64.

Wang Shuqing. "Qingdai houfei zhidu zhong de jige wenti" (Some Questions on the Institution of the Empresses and Imperial Concubines in the Qing Dynasty). *Gugong bowuyuan yuankan* no. 1 (1989): 38–46.

Wang Shuyun. *Qiandao beixun yudao he saiwai xinggong* (The Northern Routes and Traveling Palaces of the Qing Emperors). Beijing: Zhongguo huanjiang kexue chubanshe, 1989.

Wang Xiangyun. "Tibetan Buddhism at the Court of Qing: the Life and Work of lCang – skya Rol-p'ai-rdo-rje (1717–1786)." Ph.D. diss., Harvard University, 1995.

Wang Xiangyun. "The Qing Court's Tibet Connection: Lcang skya Rol pa'i rdo rje and the Qianlong Emperor." *Harvard Journal of Asiatic Studies* 60, no. 1 (2000): 125–163.

Watson, Rubie and Patricia Buckley Ebrey, eds *Marriage and Inequality in Chinese Society*. Berkeley and Los Angeles: University of California Press, 1991.

Wechsler, Howard J. *Offerings of Jade and Silk*. New Haven: Yale University Press, 1985.

Wei Yuan. *Shengwu ji* (Record of Sagely Militance). *Sibu beiyao* edn, 1842, vol. 90.5.

Weichang wenshi ziliao (Mulan Hunting Ground Literary and Historical Materials). Compiled by Weichangxian wenshi ziliao weiyuanhui, vols 2 and 4. Weichang county, Hebei province, 1990.

Weidner, Marsha. "Painting and Patronage at the Mongol Court of China 1260–1368." Ph.D. diss., University of California, Berkeley, 1982.

Weidner, Marsha. "Aspects of Painting and Patronage at the Mongol Court, 1260–1368." In *Artists and Patrons: Some Social and Economic Aspects of Chinese Painting*, ed. Chu-tsing Li, 37–59. Lawrence, Kan.: University of Washington Press, 1989.

Weidner, Marsha. "The Conventional Success of Ch'en Shu." In *Flowering in the Shadows: Women in the History of Chinese Painting*, ed. Marsha Weidner. Honolulu: University of Hawaii Press, 1990.

Weiwuer Zizhiqu Minzu Shiwu Weiyuanhui, ed. *Xinjiang minzu cidian* (Dictionary of Xinjiang Nationalities), Urumchi: Xinjiang renmin chubanshe, 1995.

Widmer, Ellen and Kang-I Sun Chang. *Writing Women in Late Imperial China*. Stanford, Calif.: Stanford University Press, 1997.

Williams, C. A. S. *Outlines of Chinese Symbolism and Art Motives: an Alphabetical Compendium of Antique Legends and Beliefs, as Reflected in the Manners and Customs of the Chinese*, 3rd revised edn. New York: Dover, 1976.

Wills, John, Jr. *Mountain of Fame: Portraits in Chinese History*. Princeton, NJ: Princeton University Press, 1994.

Wittfogel, Karl August. *Oriental Despotism; a Comparative Study of Total Power*. New Haven: Yale University Press, 1957.

Wittfogel, Karl August and Feng Chia-sheng. *History of Chinese Society: Liao, 905–1127*. Philadelphia, Pa.: American Philosophical Society, 1949.

Wolf, Margery. *Women and the Family in Rural Taiwan*. Stanford, Calif.: Stanford University Press, 1972.

Wu Hung. "Emperor's Masquerade – 'Costume Portraits' of Yongzheng and Qianlong." *Orientations* 26, no. 7 (July/August 1995): 25–41.

Wu Hung. "Beyond Stereotypes: the Twelve Beauties in Qing Court Art and the 'Dream of the Red Chamber.'" In *Writing Women in Late Imperial China*, ed. Ellen Widmer and Kang-I Sun Chang, 306–365. Stanford, Calif.: Stanford University Press, 1997.

Xiao Tian. *Chengde mingsheng* (Famous Sites of Chengde). Nei Menggu wenhua chuban, 1997.

Xiao Yishan. *Qingdai tongshi* (Comprehensive History of the Qing Dynasty), 5 vols. Beijing: Zhonghua shuju, 1986.

Xiaohengxiangshi zhuren (Yao Zhuxuan), ed. *Qingchao yeshi daguan* (Conspectus of Historical Romances of the Qing Dynasty), 1921. Reprint, Taipei: Zhonghua shuju, 1959.

Xinjiang Weiwuer Zizhiqu Minzu Shiwu Weiyuanhui (Xinjiang Uyghur Autonomous Region Nationalities Affairs Committee), ed. *Xinjiang minzu cidian* (Dictionary of Xinjiang Nationalities). Urumchi: Xinjiang renmin chubanshe, 1995.

Xu Bang, ed. *Chengde: Chinese Landscape Storehouse.* Beijing: Xinhua chubanshe, 1994.

Xu Ling (*c*.545). *Yutai xinyong* (New Songs from the Jade Terrace). Reprint, Beijing: Zhongguo shudian, 1986.

Xu Moxi. *Qinggong lishi yanyi* (Popular History of the Qing Court). Shanghai, 1924.

Xu Xiaotian. *Manqing shisanchao yanyi* (A Romance of the Thirteen Reigns of the Manchu Qing Dynasty). Foreword written 1926. Reprint, Hong Kong: Mingliang shuju, n.d.

Ya Hanzhang. *Ban-chan Er-de-ni zhuan* (Biography of the Panchen Erdeni). Xizang: Xizang renmin chubanshe, 1987.

Yanbei laoren (psued.). *Manqing shisanchao gongting mishu* (The Secret History of the Private Quarters during the Thirteen Reigns of the Manchu Qing Dynasty). Preface dated 1919. Reprint, Taipei: Wanxiang shudian, 1957.

Yang Boda. "Leng Mei ji qi *Bishushanzhuang tu*" (Leng Mei and his *Mountain Retreat to Escape the Heat*). Gugong bowuyuan yuankan no. 1 (1979): 51–61.

Yang Boda. "*Wanshu yuan ciyan tu* kaoxi" (An Analysis of *Ceremonial Banquet in the Garden of Ten Thousand Trees*). Gugong bowuyuan yuankan no. 4 (1982): 3–21.

Yang Boda. "Guanyu *Mashu tu* ticai di zai taolun" (Further Examination of the Subject Matter of the Painting *Horsemanship*). Wenwu no. 7 (1983): 64–67.

Yang Boda. "The Development of the Ch'ien-lung Painting Academy." In *Words and Images*, ed. Wen Fong and Alfreda Murck, 333–356. New York: Metropolitan Museum of Art, 1991.

Yang Tianzai. "Bishu shanzhuang de beike jiqi lishi jiazhi" (The Steles at the Mountain Villa to Escape the Heat and their Historical Significance). In Bishu shanzhuang yanjiuhui, 217–229. Beijing: Zijincheng chubanshe, 1986.

Yang Tianzai. *Bishu shanzhuang beiwen shiyi* (Annotated Explanations of the Steles at the Mountain Villa to Escape the Heat). Beijing: Zijincheng chubanshe, 1985.

Yang Tianzai. "Bishu Shanzhuang de Wanshu yuan ji qi lishi zuoyong" (The Garden of Ten Thousand Trees in Bishu shanzhuang and its Historical Functions). In Bishu shanzhuang yanjiuhui. Beijing: Zijincheng chubanshe, 1986.

Yang Tianzai, ed. *Chengde.* Beijing: Xinshijie chubanshe, 1988.

Ye Zhiru. "Cong maoyi aocha kan Qianlong qianqi dui Zhunga'er bu de minzu zhengce" (The Nationality Policy of the Early Qianlong Period Seen from the Tea-brewing Trade Trips). *Xinjiang daxue xuebao* no. 1 (1986): 62–71.

Yuan Hongqi. "Qianlong shiqi de gongting jieqing huodong" (Celebrating Holidays in the Court during the Qianlong Era). *Gugong bowuyuan yuankan* no. 3 (1991): 81–87, 27.

Yuan Senpo. "Mulan weichang" (The Mulan Hunting Grounds). *Wenwu jikan* no. 2 (1980): 100–107.

Yuan Senpo. *Kang Yong Qian jingyin yu kaifa Beijiang* (Management and Development of the Northern Frontier under Kangxi, Yongzheng and Qianlong). Beijing: Zhongguo shehui kexueyuan, 1991.

Zhang Dongsheng. "Qingdi dongxun yu gongting yinyue" (Qing Emperors' Eastern Tours and Court Music). In *Qingdai gongshi tanwei* (Investigating the Minutiae of Qing Dynasty Court History), ed. Qingdai gongshi yanjiuhui, 238–250. Beijing: Zijincheng chubanshe, 1991.

Zhang Mu. *Menggu youmu ji* (On the Nomads of Mongolia), 1867. Taipei: Shangwu yinshuguan, 1971.

Zhang Wenxiang and Bo Qingyuan, eds *The Mountain Manor for Escaping Summer Heat*. Beijing: People's Fine Arts Publishing House, *c*.1987.

Zhang Yuxin. *Qingdai si da huofuo* (Four Living Buddhas during the Qing Dynasty). Beijing: Zhongguo Renmin Daxue chubanshe, 1989.

Zhao Lian. *Xiaoting zalu* (Miscellaneous Records of Xiaoting). 1880 edn. Reprint, Beijing: Zhonghua shuju, 1980.

Zhao Yi. *Yanbao zaji* (Miscellaneous Notes of Yanbao). Reprint, Beijing and Shanghai: Youzheng shuju, 1920.

Zhao Yuntian. "Qingdai de 'beizhi efu' zhidu" (The Qing System of "Son-in-law Registration"). *Gugong bowuyuan yuankan* no. 4 (1984): 28–37.

Zhongguo renming da zidian (Chinese Biographical Dictionary). Taipei: Taiwan shang-wuyin chubanshe, 1977.

Zhongguo Shehui Kexueyuan Minzu Yanjiusuo Minzushi Yanjiushi (Nationalities History Research Office of the Nationalities Research Center of the Chinese Academy of Social Sciences) and Manchu Department of the Number One Historical Archives of China, eds *Manwen Tu-er-hu-te dang'an shibian* (Translated Manchu Documents on the Torghuts). Beijing: Minzu chubanshe, 1988.

Zhou Junfu. *Qingdai zhuanji congkan suoyin* (Index to the Compendium of Qing Biographies). Taipei: n.p., 1986.

Zhu Jiajin. "Castiglione's *Tieluo* Paintings." *Orientations* 3 (1988): 83 88.

Zhu Jiajin. *Gugong milu* (Secret Records of the Imperial Palace). Shanghai: Shanghai wenwu chubanshe, 1991.

Zhu Xi, comp. *Sishu jizhu* (Collected Commentaries on the Four Books). Ming dynasty edn. Changsha?: Ji fu, Ming Chenghua 16 nian (i.e. 1480).

Zhu Yanhua and Yang Linbo, comp. *Xiangfei de chuanshuo* (The Legend of Xiangfei and Other Tales). Shijiazhuang: Hebei shaonian ertong chubanshe, 1986.

Zito, Angela. "Silk and Skin: Significant Boundaries." In *Body, Subject and Power in China*, ed. Angela Zito and Tani E. Barlow, 103–130. Chicago: University of Chicago Press, 1994.

Zito, Angela. *Of Body and Brush, Grand Sacrifice as Text/Performance in Eighteenth Century China*. Chicago: University of Chicago Press, 1997.

Zito, Angela and Tani E. Barlow, eds *Body, Subject and Power in China*. Chicago: University of Chicago Press, 1994.

Index

188–97; relations with Mongols 144, 154; as sage 114–17, 144, 147; steles 146–61, 157, 185–6; tomb 132; Torghuts and 102, fig. 13, 159; traveling 55–64, 171; Zunghar campaigns 100
Qijuzhu (*Diaries of Imperial Activity and Repose*) 58
Qingchui feng *see* Bangchui feng
Qing dynasty: and China 16, 115; conquest of Inner Asia 100, 172–3; foreign relations 3; governance 17; ideology 9–11, 19, 117–19, 147–60; Inner Asia and 9, 12 n. 8, 18, 36, 40, 75–7, 81, 85, 89, 91–103, 143, 155, 157; map fig. 1; multiethnicity *see* multiethnicity and multilingualism; studies 3, 12 n. 8, 20 n. 1; Tibetan Buddhism and 45, 103; views of, 20 n. 1, 212; Zunghar wars 103
Qi-shi-yi 103
Qufu, 56, 62

Rehe 62–3, 112, 169; distance from Beijing 59; spelled Jehol 1; 50 n. 1, 173, 176, 205
Rehe Gazetteer see Rehe zhi
Rehe xinggong quantu figs 6, 7, 18
Rehe zhi (*Rehe Gazetteer*) 92, 146
Rgyal tshab dar ma rin chen 185, 185 n. 2
roads to Chengde 59–60, fig. 2, 169
Rolpai Dorje *see* Jang gya Khutukutu
Romance of Three Kingdoms 66
root teacher 124
Russia 4, 33, 91, 99
Ruyi island 5, 212

sagehood 115–16, 121 n. 42, 150–1
Sakya (Sa skya) sect 24, 25, 126, 134 n. 21, 135 n. 36
samsara 28, 128
Samvara (Chakrasamvara) 7, 39–40, 125, 126–7, 131
Samye (Bsam yas) 6, 38, 42, 44–5
Sanfan *see* Three Feudatories, Rebellion of
Sanskrit 132
shamanism 117

Shang dynasty 154
Shangao suichang dian 86
Shangdu, 71 100
shastras (*śāstras*) 23
Sheli ta fig. 9, 160
Shengjing (Mukden) 20, 35, 56; imperial tombs 82 n. 21
Shereng, 91, 102, 105 n. 23
Shigatse 186 n. 3
Shilu (*Veritable Records*) 58, 117–18
Shiva linga 7, 131, fig. 18, 188
Shu jing (Classic of History) 61
Shun 61, 154
Shunzhi emperor 48, 68, 134 n. 23, 157, 185, 186 n. 5, 192
Shuxiang si (Temple of the Statue of Manjushri) 8, 41, 46, 49, 161, 188
Siguelbarth (Ai Qimeng) 140–1, 183
Simian yunshan (Clouds and Mountains on Four Sides) 6, fig. 10
sinicization 3, 17
sinification *see* sinicization
smallpox 12 n. 24, 32, 75, 100, 102–3, 126, 128, 198
Sonam Gyatso (Bsod nams rgya mtsho) 26, 97
Song dynasty 113, 116, 154
Songtsen Gampo (Srong-btsan sgam-po) 40, 51 n. 15
Songzhu Temple 124, 127, 133 n. 9
sources, non-Chinese 10; French, 171–83; Manchu,104 n. 5, 167–9, 170 n. 1; Mongolian 124; Tibetan 88, 123–32
Southern Song dynasty 120 n. 32
Southern Tours 55–8, 62
Staunton, Sir George 10, 59–60, 64 n. 12
stele inscriptions 93, 104 n. 5, 146–61; listed 160, 161 n. 3, 185–6
steppe landscape *see* prairie landscape
Stoddard, Heather 12 n. 13
stupas (reliquaries) 28, 39, 48
Sumeru, Mount 38, 92, fig. 13, 186 n. 1
Sun Dianyang 132
supra-tribal policy 95–6
Su Shi 112–14
sutras (*sūtras*) 23